A Woman Doing Life

Notes from a Prison for Women

Second Edition

ERIN GEORGE

EDITED BY ROBERT JOHNSON
American University

and

ALISON B. MARTIN
National Institute of Justice

INTRODUCED BY ROBERT JOHNSON

AFTERWORD BY JOYCELYN POLLOCK
Texas State University–San Marcos

and

ALISON B. MARTIN
National Institute of Justice

New York   Oxford
OXFORD UNIVERSITY PRESS

Oxford University Press is a department of the University of Oxford.
It furthers the University's objective of excellence in research,
scholarship, and education by publishing worldwide.

Oxford   New York
Auckland   Cape Town   Dar es Salaam   Hong Kong   Karachi
Kuala Lumpur   Madrid   Melbourne   Mexico City   Nairobi
New Delhi   Shanghai   Taipei   Toronto

With offices in
Argentina   Austria   Brazil   Chile   Czech Republic   France   Greece
Guatemala   Hungary   Italy   Japan   Poland   Portugal   Singapore
South Korea   Switzerland   Thailand   Turkey   Ukraine   Vietnam

For titles covered by Section 112 of the US Higher Education Opportunity Act,
please visit www.oup.com/us/he for the latest information about pricing and
alternate formats.

Published by Oxford University Press
198 Madison Avenue, New York, New York 10016
http://www.oup.com

Oxford is a registered trademark of Oxford University Press

Library of Congress Cataloging-in-Publication Data
George, Erin.
A woman doing life : notes from a prison for women / Erin George ; edited by Robert Johnson, &
Alison B. Martin; introduced by Robert Johnson ; afterword by Joycelyn Pollock, & Alison
B. Martin.
    pages cm
  Revised edition of the author's A woman doing life published in 2010.
  Includes bibliographical references.
  ISBN 978-0-19-993588-8
  1. Women prisoners—Virginia—Case studies. 2. George, Erin. 3. Life imprisonment—Virginia—
Case studies. 4. Reformatories for women—Virginia—Case studies. 5. Fluvanna Correctional Center
for Women (Va.) I. Johnson, Robert, 1948- II. Martin, Alison B. III. Title.
  HV9475.V82F584 2014
  365'.43092—dc23
  [B]

                                                                              2014021683

For Jack, Fran, and Gio
This, and everything, is for you.

Cloistered

Bowed with the weight
of my manacles
I enter a house of penitence.

My hair carelessly shorn
and my possessions stripped,
I am a novice in a mendicant order.

My new uniform of raw burgundy
stains my skin
with false stigmata.

Morning headcount is my matins,
evening lockdown is my vespers,
and the hours in between
marked not by counted bells
but by dictates hurled
from clamorous loudspeakers.

I am the bride of no one now
but will abide here in my cell,
a stony niche
in a two-tiered columbarium
until I return to ashes.

Erin George

*Reprinted with permission from Origami Heart: Poems by a Woman Doing Life (2008, p. 3),
by Erin George. Washington, DC: BleakHouse Publishing.*

CONTENTS

PREFACE

After the publication in 2010 of the first edition of *A Woman Doing Life: Notes from a Prison for Women*, my editor, Robert Johnson, told me that he had received questions from readers asking why I didn't delve into the circumstances of the crime that brought me here. As a result, Rob asked me to address this in the second edition of the book.

Doing so forced me to consider why, exactly, I had written the book to begin with. Clearly not for fame or money (you won't see many textbooks listed alongside Stephen King or James Patterson on the bestseller lists), and not to endear myself to the prison administration that controls my fate—although I've been gratified to hear from many prison staffers who've read it that they considered it to be fair and accurate. Rather, *AWDL* was an attempt to provide a thoughtful description of the lives of women enduring the harshest punishment the state can dole out. My main concern was that I exclude any bias. I'm not on the anti-prison bandwagon, saying that all staff members are monsters and the system utterly corrupt; this is not the case. Nor am I promoting the idea that every inmate is a poor, misjudged soul cruelly abused.

My desire to present an unbiased examination of prison led me to conclude that *AWDL* should not serve as a vehicle to support my own cause, either. Anyone can probably learn the official version of my case with a few mouse clicks. I've even had people contact me directly when they decided the public version of the story needed to be balanced by mine; I'm grateful people have cared enough to ask.

A second reason for omitting these details is that I have found that women inside fight back in different ways. Most simply rebel. They "buck the system" and engage in the sort of life that revolves around skirting the rules and working their shot. A few extraordinarily brave inmates commit to protracted legal battles against the Department of Corrections, fighting the many abuses that do, unfortunately, exist. These women pay a price in ways both insignificant and profound, and I admire their willingness to risk what few privileges they have for the rest of us. I, however, am not a courtroom brawler, nor am I a natural rule-breaker. I like order. I understand the purpose behind many of the rules here, and thus more willingly obey them. But I, too, care passionately about creating a more productive, humane prison system. I've chosen to try and work within the system rather than challenge it, though. For example, I have lobbied for years to establish an English as a Second Language (ESL) program here, and finally not only does it seem that will become a reality, but I'll be lucky enough to be teaching it. I've submitted proposals and worked with staff to develop positive changes. My latest goal is to start a literary magazine for the many talented prison writers here. I was even selected to describe a lifer's perspective in a video prepared for state legislators and other inmates. And it was with the encouragement and guidance of Rob Johnson that I tried to constructively influence policy by reaching out to the decision-makers of the coming decades—you who have cared enough to read this book. I would not disrespect you or the women whose experiences I have shared by touting my own story as the focus. I have been blessed with opportunities to be heard and will not taint my message with self-promotion.

Finally, I also take this stance because continuing to fight an unwinnable battle would only further hurt those who care about James or me. I am resigned to being here. Now my efforts are directed toward making Fluvanna a healthier, more constructive place.

I understand why people wonder about my story. It's human nature to do so. But I hope my readers will understand why I've chosen to leave that for another time and different circumstances. My experience is no more important than that of the 1200 women with whom I live. I want all of us to be heard equally.

NEW TO THE SECOND EDITION

- New preface by Erin George.
- Edited chapter introductions, highlighting new material.
- New material in Chapters 2, 3, 5, 6, 8, and 9.
- New epilogue by Erin George.
- Afterword has been updated with new statistics and sections on medical practices in prison and the Prison Rape Elimination Act.
- Appendix C, "Cell Buddy," with an introduction by Erin George.

ACKNOWLEDGMENTS

There are many people who were essential to the creation of this book. Unfortunately, I can't acknowledge by actual name any of the inmates who have shared their stories with me. To do so would only draw attention to them—never a good thing in prison. However, I thank these strong and compassionate women for the gifts of their words and wisdom and humor. I am particularly grateful to "Nadia" and "Tianne," whose friendship is one of the few constants in this place.

I especially thank my roommate, Mary, for the years of challenges, laughter, tears, and growth that will, I know, sustain me long after you've gone home. Mary, you are that gem beyond price: a wonderful prison cellmate. Surprisingly, perhaps, there are also many staff members and officers who have treated me with extraordinary kindness. Since such decency is discouraged here, they also must remain anonymous.

My parents were invaluable in helping me create this book: typing endless pages of handwritten copy, offering insightful comments, and supporting me unstintingly. Mom and Dad, I thank God for you, for this and countless other reasons.

And finally, not enough can be said to document the contributions of Robert Johnson, not only to this book, but to my reconnection with the world beyond these walls. You are a wonderful person and cherished friend.

Erin George

My thanks also go to the reviewers who commented on this manuscript for Oxford University Press:

Ashley G. Blackburn, University of North Texas
Rebecca Bordt, DePauw University
Joyce D. Carmouche, Eastern Kentucky University
Krista Cline, Butler University
Kim Davies, Augusta State University
Juanita M. Firestone, University of Texas, San Antonio
Ken Haas, University of Delaware
Heather C. Melton, University of Utah
Robbin S. Ogle, University of Nebraska at Omaha
Hillary Potter, University of Colorado at Boulder
Christine R. Raasche, University of North Florida

INTRODUCTION

Robert Johnson

Erin George is facing a 603-year sentence for the murder of her husband, a crime she denies. George is a woman doing life—she is living in prison today and fully expects to die behind bars in the coming years. I have come to see Erin George as a friend and believe she is innocent, but her innocence—true or not, provable or not—is not relevant to this book. *A Woman Doing Life* is not a plea for justice in George's case, but rather an ethnography, a story told from inside the walls of a prison for women by a woman who is a sensitive observer and a gifted writer.

In *A Woman Doing Life*, Erin George tells her story and the stories of her sisters in confinement. This book is, to my knowledge, the first of its kind: a comprehensive ethnography of life in a women's prison written by a prisoner. We have many fine books by and about men in prison, including the widely used book *Life without Parole*, written by Victor Hassine (2011). This book might be thought of as a counterpart to Hassine's fine book, which George has read and found useful in organizing her thoughts. Like Hassine, George faces what amounts to a sentence of life without parole. Although she does not use the term in the book, I know from my regular communication with George that she sees her sentence as a case of death by incarceration (see Johnson & McGunigall-Smith, 2008). When entering Fluvanna Correctional Center for Women, George observed that she was entering her involuntary home "until death or a miracle occurred." For some lifers, death is a miracle-the miracle of release-but George does not think that way. Not yet, and hopefully not ever. Sadly, Victor Hassine recently took his own life after some 25 years of confinement, and we can only hope that he found release from his suffering (for revealing stories about suffering in prison, some written by Victor Hassine, see Johnson & Tabriz, 2009).

A Woman Doing Life gives us a vivid and vibrant account of the hidden world of the women's prison. George writes about living and making do, about finding friends and avoiding trouble, and about the continuing quest to secure little freedoms and redeeming relationships in the cloistered prison world. George also writes at length about grief—about the loss of freedom, and about the collateral casualties of prison sentences, the children and loved ones left behind. George examines these engaging and often sensitive topics as they relate to her life and to the lives of the women who share her confinement. For the reader who wants to know what it is like to live in a prison for women, who wants to explore the people, the setting, and the daily ebb and flow of life in a world both foreign and familiar, Erin George's book is required reading.

REFERENCES

Hassine, V. (2011). *Life without parole: Living and dying in prison today* (5th ed.). Robert Johnson & Sonia Tabriz (Eds.). New York: Oxford University Press.

Johnson, R., & McGunigall-Smith, S. (2008). Life without parole, America's other death penalty: Notes on life under sentence of death by incarceration. *The Prison Journal, 88*(2), 328–346.

Johnson, R., & Tabriz, S. (Eds.). (2009). *Lethal rejection: Stories on crime and punishment.* Durham, NC: Carolina Academic Press.

CHAPTER 1

Jail Time

E rin George's journey to Fluvanna Correctional Center for Women, a state prison near her home, followed an old country road in rural Virginia, one she'd traveled many times before as a young woman and, more recently, a young mother. She knew the terrain, but now that old road led to a new, impoverished life in captivity. George was utterly unprepared for life as a prisoner. As a first offender and a decidedly middle-class woman, Erin George was an unlikely felon. But George is an observant woman, sensitive to her own reactions and the reactions of others, and her observations prove telling.

Like so many women and men before her, George entered the jail in a state of depression (Cornelius, 2007). She felt hopeless and lost, surrounded by a ragtag assortment of women coming and going, by a sea of drugs, including sleeping meds, as sleep was hard to come by in the noisy jail. She also learned that there was a class of offender known as snitches, women who made a cottage industry of fabricating stories to share with the prosecution to help the state make its cases in exchange for a deal securing leniency in their own cases. George was burned by a snitch and, on the advice of her lawyer, checked herself into solitary confinement. Solitary is an especially hard time for a woman new to the world of confinement, but at least in solitary George was safe from damning rumors transformed by snitches into dubious cell-side confessions of guilt.

George learned early that jail life makes people hard and encourages exploitation of the weak. George found herself slipping into "the life"—the world of the cell block hustle, the world of the snitch, the world of the tough convict who takes what she wants, described so vividly by Barbara Owen (1998; see also Kruttschnitt & Gartner, 2005). But this was not her. The hard pose was a front, fueled by fear and a hunger to blend in. George realized that she was on the descent and that there might be no turning back. As she put it, "I loathed the stranger I was becoming." Later, in prison, she apologized to the woman she'd bullied in jail.

Part of living in captivity is living with other prisoners and dealing with one's keepers. There are difficult cellmates, some in terrible shape due to sickness

or addiction; others prove accommodating, even endearing. Likewise, the insti-
tution offers officers good and bad; some are heavy-handed, and others are em-
pathic and willing to listen. There are bullies or would-be bullies on every tier.
George makes her way and shares revealing anecdotes along the way. Note that
Erin George entering the threshold of a maximum-security prison for women,
the subject of the next chapter, is not the naive person she once was. Prison
awaits, and Erin George, the lifer—the woman with the 603-year sentence—is
more or less ready for the experience, and certainly more ready as a result of her
days in jail.—Robert Johnson

I had traveled this way dozens of times in the past. A quiet, narrow road that
meandered through the rural Virginia countryside, I had first used it when
I drove back and forth from Longwood, the small southern college that I had attended a decade earlier, then later with my own family when we would visit the
pick-your-own apple farm in the Shenandoah foothills. It was as familiar to me
as my own driveway: the Dairy Queen where we would stop for chocolate-dipped
cones on the way home, the cluster of tiny houses surrounded by a graveyard of
abandoned appliances and vehicles, the weather-grayed building that, incongruously, contained a historic but defunct carousel.

This, however, was going to be my last journey through these woods and
decaying towns. For a few moments at a time I had been able to forget my destina-
tion, but for no more than that. Then my reverie would be disturbed as we'd
bounce over another patch of broken, patchy asphalt on the poorly maintained
road, and the clatter of my leg chains on the bare metal floor of the jail transport
van would bring me back to the present.

This time I wasn't on my way to the terrifically greasy truck stop that my
college boyfriend had loved and insisted that we eat at on every trip to and from
Farmville, or that jewel of an orchard that looked over the blue serenity of a
Virginia valley. I was going to the Fluvanna Correctional Center for Women
(FCCW), my new home until death or a miracle occurred.

FCCW was 3 hours away from the Rappahannock Regional Jail (RRJ), where
I had been housed for the past year during my trial and wait for transfer to prison.
As I shivered, shackled and handcuffed in the unheated cage of the dusty white,
unmarked van, the trip was silent except for the radio softly playing songs that
I had never heard before and a few desultory comments from the officer who was
driving. She was a decent person, I knew from my interactions with her in the
jail, but the purpose of the journey muffled her usual friendliness. Like an officer
preparing for an inmate execution, to her I had probably been dehumanized,
a product to be processed and delivered. I understood why she needed to do
that, and sympathized. It could not be easy for her to be my conductor to the
underworld of a life sentence, to know where I was going to spend the rest of my
tomorrows. I, on the other hand, was glad to be leaving the chaos and violence of
the jail for the relative stability and comforting finality of prison.

ARREST

Those were terms that I had always used interchangeably before: prison and jail. My dooming naiveté concerning the legal system seems laughable to me now. When I first entered the labyrinth of arraignment, bond, hearings, and trial, I learned, although not quickly enough, how ignorant my family and I had been. This was not the American ideal of justice reigning triumphant and progressive rehabilitative policy in action that I, a middle-class suburban mom, had heard lauded in social studies class and at home. It was a sordid, uneven battle between defendant and prosecutor (who had the might of the police and courts firmly behind him). In a system as strictly inviolable as Christian predestination, the indicted had very little chance to escape the fate that the state had designated for them, no matter what they tried to do.

I think in a way this realization was harder on my father than on anyone else in the family. To me he had always seemed the most idealistic about what America represented. Dad was never blindly patriotic. He didn't parrot pro-American sound bites or sport bumper stickers on the back of his pickup. There was no American flag hoisted up in our front yard. My father always knew that our country was flawed and that terrible injustices occurred every day.

He had lived through the grim era of presidential assassination, the Vietnam War, race riots, and Watergate and still had managed to come through that dark time intact with the knowledge that there was something fundamentally good and decent in our country, some core of purity that could never be diminished.

My arrest and incarceration did what all the great tragedies of the 1960s and 1970s could not: they stole his innocence. Before then, the stories that would occasionally appear in newspapers about police brutality or corruption were flukes: unconscionable, but only aberrations in a fundamentally decent police force. To Dad, the claims of progressiveness made by the penal system were not merely a facade. He believed in the innate decency of our judicial system, until he saw it at work in our lives.

My arrest was nothing like you see on *Law & Order*. The police didn't break down my front door or chase me through an open window. It was all very civilized, actually. In early September, about 4 months after my husband James was killed, I came home from grocery shopping with my 3-year-old daughter, Giovanna, to see a group of detectives dressed in plain clothes standing in my driveway, watching me expectantly. I knew what they wanted; it had been clear for months that they were going to try and charge me in the murder of my husband.

As I drove up to the house, I assumed that they had finally managed to weave together a story plausible enough for the notoriously uncritical grand jury to indict. During disclosure, the process by which the prosecution is legally mandated to provide the defense counsel with all the evidence they have, I found out that the case was entirely circumstantial: there was no forensic evidence linking me to the shooting of my husband, no witnesses, and of course no confession.

My lawyer later told me that circumstantial cases are, in fact, much easier for prosecutors to win, despite what I thought I knew about reasonable doubt—a concept that I, like most people, had known solely through crime mysteries, especially police procedurals, and sensationalized national murder cases. I can see why that is, now. It is much harder to dispute conjecture and supposition than mere facts.

I did appreciate that they had brought a social worker to take care of my daughter until my family arrived to get her. The woman from the state was nervous, clearly uncomfortable to be at the arrest of a murder suspect. When I handed her my daughter with murmured thanks, she took her tentatively, face averted. I doubt that Gio even realized that something wrong was happening. I can't be sure, of course, why the police were so considerate when they arrested me. I know that it wasn't out of any sense of kindness to me. Maybe because Stafford is a small, southern county there was an innate, unconscious courtesy toward women. Or perhaps it was for the same reason that I was so calm: the presence of Gio. I hugged her goodbye, pressing my face against the hectic bloom of her cheek and explained that everything was going to be fine, that this was a very nice lady who would take care of her until Aunt Shannon came to get her. The police refrained from slamming me against the SUV and slapping me into handcuffs in front of her. I am grateful, at least, that they spared Gio from seeing that.

After my arrest, they took me to a holding cell at the jail, a sprawling, modern building located about 15 minutes from my house. I had never paid it much notice when I had driven past it before, as its bland, municipal design made it benignly ignorable. After the admittedly anemic obligatory perp walk—one lone photographer from the local paper loitered outside the sheriff's until I arrived, and that was the only time in my dozens of trips to the courthouse that I ever saw any of the press there—I was fingerprinted and stowed in a profanity-scrawled holding cell. The cold of the cinder-block walls and bench seeped though the cotton of my shirt as I struggled against the nausea caused by overwhelming stress and the stench of the unflushable metal toilet. I wasn't limited to one phone call. As far as they were concerned, I could make as many as I wanted from the sticky pay phone. What did they care? Who could I possibly call to help me?

I was finally able to reach my brother-in-law, Keith. I can't remember anything about our conversation except that my parents were in Arizona on holiday and that he would get in contact with them. And, of course, he and my sister would pick up my daughter Gio, as well as my other two children, Jack and Francesca.

After a brief midnight interview with the jail psychiatrist (to ensure that I didn't kill myself that night), my possessions were taken, I took a delousing shower, and I was put into a cell in the women's pod of the jail. I don't remember much about my first, brief stay in jail before I was bonded out. For the most part I simply cried, a constant blur of white noise buffering me from the clamor of the jail. Every aspect of jail was alien and frightening, designed to humiliate.

DEMORALIZED

My family's belief in the system sustained us during the early days after my arrest. At first, things seemed to work as they were supposed to, albeit with a bureaucratic sluggishness. A day after being processed I was arraigned in Stafford County Circuit Court. Appearing in front of Judge Ann Simpson, I was given the opportunity to have legal counsel assigned to me and was allowed a $100,000 bond.

I was lucky to get it. Virginia courts rarely give bond for first-degree murder. However, I was a respected member of the community with no criminal history charged under circumstantial evidence. I got a break. My parents scrambled to get me home to Jack, Franny, and Gio. When my family learned from the bondsman that an unmortgaged house had to be used to secure my bond, my Uncle Michael and Aunt Lynne offered theirs. Afterward, my mom told me that when he and Lynne offered up their home of two decades, Uncle Michael said that I was his, too. He reminded her that when I had been born, it was he who paid the hospital bill so that I could go home with my parents. He had partial ownership of his oldest niece, so how could he do any less for me now?

They staggered me with their loving generosity. Because of them, I had another 7 months at home with my children: one more Christmas morning, another set of birthdays, and hundreds of those wee, inconsequential moments that become sacred when you polish them in your mind through endless recollections.

One of the great blessings of this entire ordeal has been the way my family has endured and grown closer through it. A boisterous Irish clan, we were always rich in our mutual love. I remember that on every holiday we would laugh, eat, tease, argue politics, and reminisce together. We had dozens of traditions and family stories that were inherent to our gatherings.

Prior to my husband's death that May, we were all relatively whole. The deaths of my grandfather, Douglas, and my cousin Anthony (a laughing boy who played the drums) years earlier were the only major losses our family had suffered. The year of my arrest, though, was our *annus horribilis*. We endured a string of events that individually would have been enough to fracture a lesser group: the shooting of James and my arrest, then the subsequent, almost simultaneous, cancer diagnoses of my father and his two sisters, Eileen and Marianne.

ISOLATED

The judge rescinded my bond about a month before my trial. Because so many women had told the police that I had confessed to them before I initially bonded out, my lawyer requested that the jail house me under protective custody (PC). PC consisted of isolation in a tiny cell located at the back of the top tier of the women's pod. If I were lucky, I had 15 minutes out of my cell during the day to make phone calls. Because the rest of the pod had to be locked down when I was out of my cell, every phone call was accompanied by clamorous jeers, threats, and the vilest profanity imaginable.

"Fuckin' bitch, get back in your fuckin' cell!"
"I'm going to kick your ass when you get out of PC, you goddamn bitch."
"Quit crying on the damn phone—it's your own damn fault you're here."
"Bitch, nobody wants to talk to you. Shut the fuck up!"

It was quieter when they let me out of my cell every other night at midnight. That was my 30 minutes to shower. If an extraordinarily kind officer was on duty, she might let me sit in the rec [recreation] yard for another half an hour or so before I returned to my cell. The rec yard was small, about the size of half a basketball court, and surrounded by a two-story cinder-block wall. It was capped by a heavy metal grate and chicken wire, so I couldn't see the trees or grass, and not even a leaf could make its way to me.

I always ignored the officer who stood near me, smoking her cigarette and enjoying, I suppose, an unauthorized break. Like a child, I would hold both my hands to my face, blocking out the walls and the guard, seeing only the dim stars above, beyond the gate. My glasses off, the metal barrier smudged into nothingness against the darkness. During those rare sweet interludes, I never let myself worry about what might happen during my trial. I would remember. I thought of the camping trip that James and I had taken before we were married, and when he and I would sit with our baby, Jack, in the hammock on my parents' deck, watching the gloaming settle over the day. Most often, though, I remembered the previous spring, when my sister's family and mine lay in the predawn cold one night to watch a meteor shower. I had never seen one before, and sitting crosslegged on the cement of the rec yard, I could re-create the moment when I saw the first streak of light just over the cottonwoods in our yard. Warm from hot chocolate and the ragged quilts wrapped around us, we gaped at the Leonids as the countless meteors blazed through the darkness. Francesca's small hand grabbed mine as the first one appeared, and she didn't let go until dawn. There in the blankness of the rec yard, I still felt Franny's small, flanneled body next to mine and heard nothing but her reverent breathing.

My days in isolation were endless. I had no watch or clock, so I soon became disoriented, unsure even of the day or month. I had a few ragged paperback romance novels to read, but those were quickly finished. There was no pen or paper because when the officers collected commissary orders each week, I was always forgotten. (The commissary is our canteen or store.) When I heard the officers gathering up the order sheets, I would bang on the door, begging someone to remind the guards that I was there, but all that ever happened was a limp apology offered after the orders had been finalized and the false promise that I would be allowed to order my writing supplies, my toothpaste, and a T-shirt to wear next week. This went on for weeks until my lawyer's office called to complain.

Inmates brought me meals three times a day, but I was too depressed to eat. Of course, no one told the staff that I was refusing my meals. The only benefit my fellow inmates got for delivering my trays was that they could eat what was left over. The hungriest inmates were the ones who worked tray duty. Whenever I would refuse my tray, the trustee would whisper, "Aw, honey, you gotta eat something," then snatch away the bologna sandwich and three desiccated carrot sticks before I could change my mind.

When an officer finally noticed that I had lost 30 pounds, they began to monitor my eating. However, it was easy enough to get around that when the trustees conspired with me to get the extra food for themselves. It was only when they put me into general population that I began to emerge from my grief- and isolation-induced daze enough to realize that maybe life wasn't finished for me after all.

JAIL DAYS

I stayed in isolation until several weeks after my trial was completed. By then, PC was pointless—no snitch could benefit from the alleged confession of a now-convicted felon—so I moved downstairs into one of the general population cells. That night, I woke up as a ragged blonde staggered in. She collapsed wordlessly onto the top bunk, smelling unspeakably of vomit, sweat, and some other odor that I couldn't identify. Later, I learned that it was the reek that junkies give off when they are detoxing.

I never knew her name—I was moved into another cell before she had roused from whatever stupor she was in. I was glad they moved me, though; a few days later the blonde was found to have a pharmacopeia of illicit drugs stashed on her person. Or rather, *in* her person. No wonder she had managed to sleep for a good 3 days straight.

There was a lot of contraband—unauthorized stuff—smuggled into the jail because the searches were so cursory. At least mine was, and you couldn't find a more serious charge than murder in a jail like ours. When I was arrested, they briefly frisked me, then left me alone. Eventually I was put in a tiny room that contained a curtainless shower and a window to the inmate property room. "Inmate, come get your supplies," the property officer said as she hoisted up the metal gate on the property window. After shoving a tan jumpsuit, plastic shower shoes, a small bottle of delousing shampoo, and a much-laundered towel through the window, she slammed the window shut.

The shower was nothing like mine at home. Instead of having controls for adjusting the temperature and turning the water on and off, there was only a small metal button embedded into a mildew-blackened wall. When I pressed it, the stream dribbled on for about 40 seconds, then petered out. The temperature just skirted the edge of unbearable—so cold that when I finished, I stood shivering, unable to dress myself for several minutes after I had attempted to dry off with the sodden, dishcloth-sized towel.

I banged on the property window to notify the officer that I was finished, and when she reopened the window, handed over my personal items. I kept nothing: no panties, no T-shirt . . . I couldn't even keep my bra. After I passed my clothes through the window, the guard gave me another jumpsuit, shoddy sneakers that Velcroed closed, and a small plastic bag of personals: hotel-sized shampoo, toothpaste, and a 2-inch-long toothbrush that lost half its bristles after one use. I was reduced to brushing my teeth with my finger before I was able to buy a proper toothbrush at commissary.

"Wait here for the C.O. to get you where you belong," the property officer said as the window thudded shut again. Because there were no chairs, I stood on the wet concrete floor. After 10 minutes of inspecting my scant new possessions, I noticed that the shoes and jumpsuit were from Bob Barker Industries. To distract myself, I pictured the avuncular game show host running a business empire no *Price Is Right* fan could ever imagine. I envisioned him providing jails and prisons all over the country with uniforms and supplies. Of course, I doubt it's *that* Bob Barker who sells correctional facilities materials, but it was a strange detail, Daliesque enough to engage me until the officer came to take me to the pod.

JAIL DAZE: AWASH IN A SEA OF DRUGS

Drugs were all over the jail. In fact, a few women subsidized their entire stay with revenue from the stash they brought in with them. One of the more entrepreneurial was Pia, a regular at RRJ. (All inmate and staff names used in this book are pseudonyms.) During my 9 months there, she came in at least three times for various charges: kiting checks, shoplifting, and prostitution. A week after her first arrival, I noticed that there was always a lot of activity at her cell door—women coming and going with the furtively casual look of the practiced rule breaker. I recognized the look, and as avid for gossip as any other inmate, I started to pay closer attention.

Although Pia never stood in line at the commissary window each Wednesday like the rest of us, she hosted lavish feasts for her friends and sycophants each night. Tables were heaped with Snickers bars, Mars bars, M&M's, popcorn, pretzels, potato chips, Coca-Cola . . . every delight offered by commissary appeared. She was as popular for the excesses of her entertainments as she was for her apparently endless supply of pills. Sporting the most expensive Reeboks from the commissary, Pia often made the comment (loudly, to provoke maximum envy among the more impoverished), "Damn, I only wish they sold TVs or something—There ain't enough shit I can buy for myself up in here." The rumor in the unit was that one of the guards was her cousin and that he kept her in pills, but I never saw any of that myself.

Most inmates carried for themselves. The hottest items were the drugs that let you sleep until your time was up. I often wished that I had enough nerve to use them myself. Because the officers couldn't be bothered to determine the difference between depression and intoxication, I would have been left undisturbed as I slept them off. It would have made my stay easier, and really, what more could they do to punish me? Put me back in isolation? Add more time to my 603-year sentence? Only my compulsive fear of authority and my innate distrust of a chemical solution restrained me.

Another popular contraband item was cigarettes. My jail was smoke-free, so cigarettes were in demand, either smuggled in or bummed from an officer in exchange for a quick grope in the housekeeping closet. Feening for nicotine, the women who managed to procure cigarettes were reckless enough to smoke anywhere and at any time. Their cells, the rec yard . . . one woman lit up while she was in the middle of a conversation with a guard. Because they didn't have access to lighters (unless they smuggled those in as well), women learned how to jerry-rig electrical fixtures in their rooms to get a spark.

One inmate even brought a cell phone into the pod. She kept the secret for a week (a major accomplishment in lockup) but was caught when her boyfriend called her in the middle of the night. Why she hadn't set it to vibrate I don't know, but the unit officer heard it ringing and crept along the rows of cells until he tracked down the source. That was one of the few times that someone got in trouble without a snitch being involved.

SNITCHES AND BITCHES: LESSONS IN LIVING

The popular image of a jailhouse snitch is not an unjustified stereotype. Snitching is pervasive and indiscriminate. A woman will snitch out an enemy, her cellmate, or even a friend for no discernable reason other than that the victim has something that the snitch does not. There are no benefits for snitching while you're in jail other than the satisfaction of seeing someone made more miserable than you (unless the Commonwealth Attorney needs one to bolster a shaky prosecution). I always found the whole idea of tattling to be distasteful, but I did once accidentally snitch on a massive woman in my pod named Clarice.

Suffering from severe joint pain, I went to medical to ask for a hot water bottle. I had seen Clarice with one, and it seemed reasonable that I be allowed one as well. "Sorry, Ms. George, we don't have those here," said the nurse on duty.

Being new to the system, I unthinkingly broke one of the great unwritten rules of prison survival: I mentioned another inmate by name. "Well, Clarice J. has one," I said. "Can't I get one, too?"

The nurse looked puzzled. "She does? Well, let me call over and get it back." Picking up the phone, she spoke to the officer in the unit. When she had finished talking, she told me to go back to my pod and get the water bottle from Clarice, who apparently wasn't authorized to have it. Every medical item had to be issued from the jail nurse or doctor. I once had to pay a $10.00 co-pay to medical when I needed Band-Aids for an infection in my foot. When I told the nurse that I would need more than the two she had given me, which were already becoming saturated with blood and pus, she said that if I needed more, I would have to put in another sick call to come back to medical again. And, of course, pony up another $10.00 co-payment. I was a little nervous about taking Clarice's hot water bottle, because she was notorious for her foul temper and willingness to use her fists. But I reassured myself that she would act OK if a guard were there.

When I got to the unit, the dayroom was unusually empty and Clarice's cell door was locked shut. I felt as if I were in one of those old western movies: a silent, dusty street with frightened townsfolk hidden behind doors, maybe a tumbleweed or two skirting by. As I walked in, I saw the hot water bottle lying flaccidly on the officer's desk. Clarice had managed to slash it several times. I can't say what weapon she used to do it with—it could have been her fangs for all I know. Thankfully, she never delivered her message more personally, but I learned my lesson anyway. Since then, I've never mentioned an inmate's name to a staff member or officer.

Everyone knows who the snitches are in jail. The most notorious when I was at RRJ was named Deena. Someone pointed her out to me within a half an hour of hitting the dayroom.

"Look out for that one," a chatty woman said as she settled herself next to me at one of the long cafeteria-style tables. She didn't bother to introduce herself, just plunged into the conversation. "Don't tell her nothing you don't want the police to know. She's a goddamn snitch." She went on to tell me that Deena was in for child molestation and neglect and that her husband was also locked up. It didn't take me long to realize that everyone in jail knew everybody else's business, or some version of her business.

Deena had the double stigma of being a child abuser and snitch. Each would have been enough to condemn her in the strict caste system of life behind bars, so as it stood, she was doomed. She seemed determined to earn her bad reputation.

Whenever I saw her, I would find her skulking around the unit like a scourged animal, sidling up behind people as they opened their mail or talked on the telephone, blatantly dipping [eavesdropping] for information to share with the guards.

Most of the women alternated between verbally abusing and ostracizing Deena, although they never physically harmed her. I'd like to say that I never participated in the abuse, that I set the benchmark for rectitude in the moral abyss that was the jail. I wish I could, but the truth is that the more I became enmeshed in the alternative reality that is life incarcerated, the more I found myself acting in ways that would have been unthinkable at home. So I spewed foul epithets at her along with the others, both behind her back and to her face. As I absorbed the details about Deena's case from other inmates, I grew more outraged. How dare this woman hurt her children? I would cut off my right arm to be at home with mine, and this monster didn't seem to give a damn about hers. I didn't care when it came out in court that she had been abused sexually and psychologically since infancy. I seemed to have lost the compassion that had been an integral part of me.

It shames me to think of how I acted. My loss of empathy was temporary, a brief foray into lunacy during the months after my conviction, but nonetheless reprehensible. At first it stemmed from my outrage at my own conviction, the soul-killing loss of my children and former life, coupled with a desire to conform to my new world. I thought that I needed to prove that I was not too educated, too mainstream, and too timid to be one of them. Frightened of being victimized myself, I sought the tenuous safety of the mob. I can understand those feelings, as unworthy as they are. Inexplicable to me, though, is the corrupt pleasure that the abuse began to give me. I began to seek Deena out so I could vilify her. It was wonderfully empowering to see someone more terrified than I was, especially someone terrified of *me*. A potential victim myself, I embraced the profane, violent jail culture to use as a shield.

There was a grim satisfaction to it at first. I used the words that I heard constantly around me, aping the fractured syntax and pervasive profanity. Speaking the patois of the streets exhilarated me, made me feel safer. Standing out, after all, would put me at more risk. I constantly looked for ways to blend in.

The only times I reverted to my persona of educated suburban mom were when my parents visited. Then I might joke about jail having "a deleterious effect on my grammar," but I never let slip how much I had spiraled into the sordidness of my new habitat. It seemed surreal, portraying the person my parents knew.

After my experience with Deena, I began to bully a few other women as well. I would lend inmates food from commissary and harass them if they didn't repay quickly enough. I didn't want the potato chips or coffee back. I never needed to be physically violent to destroy someone; I could gut them with my words alone. If that didn't work, I would send someone more imposing to hassle them. Usually it was a former cellmate of mine, Martina.

"Hey Martina, you want a bag of coffee?"

"Yeah, sure," she'd answer. "Who's got it?" Martina knew the drill. She'd been my enforcer before.

"Gina. That bitch has owed me for 2 weeks. She keeps saying that her husband is sending her money, but I haven't seen shit. You get it, you get to keep it." Martina didn't say another word, just lumbered off to Gina's cell as I watched from the safety of my own doorway.

I couldn't hear what they were saying, but I saw that Gina was getting more and more agitated as Martina loomed over her. Finally, Gina pivoted and stomped into her room, emerging a few minutes later with a bag of coffee. I found out later that she had been forced to borrow it from her own roommate, a lender more ruthless than I. At least I didn't charge two for one. Those are the brutally usurious loans where an inmate has to return two of whatever she borrows, a major hardship in a place where a woman must depend on the often skimpy generosity of her family for whatever she has.

One of my victims finally reported me to the guards. Officer Cisneros called me to the officer's front desk. "George, have you been menacing Callahan about some coffee that she owes you? She says that you've been at her door giving her a hard time."

"No I haven't," I answered, technically truthful. I had, in fact, sent one of my lackeys to shake her down. "Check the tapes if you don't believe me," I said, referring to the omnipresent security camera.

Officer Cisneros seemed to lose interest. He knew I was lying. This was the same scam he saw every day. "Well, make sure that you don't," he said, gesturing me away. Callahan's complaint had now been investigated and he could file the paperwork. As usual with inmate complaints, the officer was too lazy to find out the truth.

My exchange with Officer Cisneros was a minor one in the scope of jailhouse infractions. Women in the jail were constantly getting into trouble for both minor and major offenses. I remember when a cellmate of mine was put into seg [segregation] merely because she had been bitching to me about a particular officer while we were locked in our cell. Kitty didn't realize it, but the officer had been dipping, in inmate slang, through the intercom. Thank God I hadn't had the chance to respond to her before they yanked her out of the room. I don't even know what charge was given, but she ended up spending 3 weeks in isolation for her complaints. I had heard from the other inmates that the officers listened in on private conversations in this way but never really believed it. I assumed that the C.O.s surely had something better to do, and I had scoffed at the women who kept sanitary pads stuck over their intercoms to muffle their conversations. I certainly paid more attention to any advice more seasoned inmates could give me after that.

I was lucky, though, when it came to my own misconduct. If Cisneros had actively pursued it, I would have done a hell of a lot more time in seg-like solitary confinement than Kitty. And seg meant no commissary, so most women who ended up there for any significant period of time staggered out at the end of their confinement dazed and half-starved.

Although there were no formal repercussions for my behavior, finally being called up on my actions by an officer had some pretty startling results for me. Raised to obey the rules and respect authority, I had always been the kind of person who returned the money when I had been given too much change and used my turn signal even if it was 2:00 in the morning on a deserted street. My profoundly kind, inherently decent parents had made every effort to instill in me the necessity of order in a chaotic world, and they had always, in word and action, demonstrated the absolute requirement that we, as human beings who shared the same world, must interact with each other with graciousness, respect, and consideration.

It seems like such a small thing now, a lackadaisical reprimand that the officer had probably forgotten before I had made it back to my cell. But talking to him made me realize that if I went on like this, I would never be able to go back to who I had been before my sentencing. If I continued, the next time I would probably get seg time. Then even more seg time. When I eventually moved on to prison, there would be harsher punishments and stricter officers. And inevitably there would be someone I would harass who wouldn't just roll over like everyone else had. I would eventually miscalculate and would end up getting beaten.

As frightening as that future seemed, though, it wasn't those images that forced me to change my behaviors. They were horrifying enough to make me realize that the situation was becoming untenable, but my main motivation for change was the realization that I loathed the stranger I was becoming. I had to make a choice: Would I continue to evolve into a predator that satisfied the darker parts of my personality, or could I remain, even amid the fears and angers of imprisonment, the compassionate human being I and my family knew? It was not as obvious a choice as it might seem. The allure of intimidation will always be attractive to anyone behind bars. Through it, I could have my share of the limited power available to an inmate. In the end, though, I chose to remain the same person I had been before. It's not always an easy choice to stick to. There is a ready supply of voluntary victims in prison, those women who seem to display their need to be abused in flashing neon, and during my darkest times here, when my longing for home and family is almost overpowering, I feel the momentary, sneaking desire to demean someone into feeling worse than I do, anticipating the mingled sweetness and bile of corrupt dominance in my mouth. Through my own behaviors, I can now understand the cycle of enmeshed needs that feed both the abuser and the abused, and I feel more genuine empathy for both than I ever did from my safe, judgmental suburban life. If the situation is drastic enough, anyone, no matter how "properly raised" or "good," can fall into either of those roles. I was just lucky enough to be able to pull myself out again before it was too late.

I've always been too ashamed to tell my parents about this period in my life. I know they wouldn't condemn me for it, but it still sickens me that I was capable of such cruelty, no matter for how brief a period. In a fundamental way, I was like Deena, who expended her rage and hurt on people less powerful than herself.

I saw Deena in the library at FCCW recently. As I approached her, she tried to avoid me by scuttling behind the shelves of paperback romances but stopped when I called her name. Without preamble, I said, "Look, I'm sorry for everything that happened back at RRJ."

She didn't make eye contact. Muttering, "Don't worry about it," she turned away. I know that inmates still treat her the way they did in the jail. "I'm sorry" is probably not something that she has heard very often in her life on either side of the walls. It's not some magical cure—we're never going to be friends, or probably even speak again. Nevertheless, I was glad that at last I had found it in me to apologize to her and that I somewhat managed to take responsibility for my abuse. Atonement is sometimes more for the sinner than the sinned against.

FINDING A NICHE

For the most part, jail society accepted me. With my murder conviction, I was a big shot among the crack heads, prostitutes, and shoplifters. New inmates who hadn't read the newspaper coverage of my case sometimes tried to guess what I was in for. Bad check, maybe credit card fraud. Never anything violent. I began to take a perverse delight in telling them what my sentence was. After my brief trial as head of a jail intimidation syndicate, I decided that I would do my best not to be pulled out of my character by prison. A sense of humor, not violence, was going to be my refuge.

Inmates were, for the most part, civil. There was never a strong feeling of solidarity among us (there was too much flux in the population for that), but excluding the sporadic outbursts of violence, we existed together. Just by being there, I was one of them. Where I would rank in the hierarchy, however, was up to me. I'd have to carve out my own niche.

On my first day out of isolation, a tattooed, unkempt woman approached me. "Do you want to play spades?" she asked.

Trying to appear as inoffensive as possible, I allowed that I didn't know how to play spades or any other card game. But I thanked her for the invitation.

"Not play spades!" she said, "Why, girl, you can't be in jail and not know how to play spades!" She hustled me to a table where two equally disheveled ladies sat, and not wanting to appear snobbish, I sat down.

"You're my partner," said Melinda, my new friend. Melinda introduced the two other players, and we began to play. She was patient, a natural teacher, as she explained the scoring and strategy. Soon I was proficient and began to play every day, all day. At first I went from table to table as a random spades partner was needed, but eventually I found three people with whom I got along well, and our little group would play marathon games until lockdown.

That's how most people would spend their time. Card games like spades, tonk, five thousand, hearts, and killer—there were hundreds of games I had never heard of. The jail rules didn't allow gambling, but of course it was always part of the game. The usual currency was M&M's.

Conversation was minimal while we played, but I did learn the fine art of talking "smack" during these games. Talking smack is an oratorical art form, a delicate balance of bravado and insult that just skirts the edge of unforgivable offense. These exchanges are often deftly nuanced and offer glimpses into the psyche of each player. Like testosterone-flooded jocks, we garnished every sentence with profanity when the game was in full smack mode. This definitely was not your momma's bridge game.

Because spades is a game played in pairs, there is the piquant joy of smug exchanges added to one's repertoire of smack talking. You can only be truly obnoxious when you are allied with a partner in pissing off the other two. Most games follow the same pattern. You begin each game with the unwavering, loudly asserted belief that you and your partner are going to get a Boston. (A Boston in spades is when you win every book played. What that has to do with Massachusetts I still don't know.) It doesn't matter how dismal your hand actually is—reality has nothing to do with smack.

"Whaddaya think partner, should we bid eight?" a player might ask after the cards are dealt.

"I don't know—I've got at least three myself, maybe even four, depending on the cards," her partner might say. "Can we go a dime?" A dime is the highest bid that can be made.

"Why not? I ain't scared." The words have a ritualistic quality, the grammar never changing, and the word *scared* is always pronounced "skeered." You can be from Appalachia, New York, or California, but the inflection stays the same. It's probably no coincidence that it rhymes with "sneered."

If you carry it off well, the other team caves. "Shit. We'll take a save." A save is four books, the lowest that can be bid. It is reserved for only the lamest hands. The implicit insult is that you are too weak of a player to squeeze out even one book above the minimum.

But in the best games, where the teams have been playing together for months or even years, you can read your partner as well as the cards in your hand. A glance conveys volumes, and throwing down a queen the first time a suit is played will tell your partner how she should play the rest of her hand.

"Who dealt this shit?" someone invariably asks after each deal. Blame is then assigned.

"I dealt it, but your partner cut it, so it's her fault that you have such a fucked-up hand."

"Don't worry, I'm never gonna cut on your damn deal again," protests the maligned deck cutter.

As the game progresses, what little is said becomes increasingly pointed. It is against the rules to "table talk," which means to give any verbal indication, however veiled, about the content of your hand. Instead, we focus on trying to intimidate the other team.

Complete attention must be given at all times. Any lapse in an opponent's concentration will be noted and commented on immediately. "Hah! Your partner stole your book! Well, isn't that a shame." Oozing mock sympathy, you and your partner discuss the perfidy of the player who failed to pay proper attention to what had already been played. And God forbid that a team bids incorrectly more than a few times. If you say you are going to get five books, you bloody well better get only five books. Players who consistently get more books than they bid are labeled disparagingly as "underbidding bitches," and penalizing scoring modifications will be instated.

The most important thing to remember when you talk smack is that you should only do it with partners you know relatively well. More than one card game had been abruptly stopped because of an ill-received insult. It's not unusual to hear someone at a card table say, "Damn, it's a good thing you have another 600 years in here . . . maybe by then you'll know how to bid your hand!" Definitely not the sort of thing one can say unless there is a bond between an insulter and insultee.

Scrabble was even more popular in the unit than cards. People would reserve the single battered Scrabble board days in advance. As I gained a reputation as a bookworm and nerd, I became the official referee for the Scrabble games because we didn't have a dictionary. Inmates take their Scrabble very seriously. Challenges over spelling almost reached the point of bloodshed several times.

"Bitch, *dinero* is a foreign word. It comes from fucking Mexico!" Almost all the women in the jail call each other "bitch." It is either an insult or term of approbation, depending on who says it.

"No it's not. How would I know some foreign word? I speak American, don't I?"

"Shit. You never know what the hell you're saying."

After several more minutes of bickering, one or both players would come to my cell door to plead their case. It didn't matter if I were sleeping or writing letters. I made several key judgments while using the toilet.

"I have a quick question," someone would say, craning to see me on the stainless steel commode through the cell door's narrow window. Eventually I wouldn't even bother to try and cover myself. Any sense of modesty is useless in the jail.

I stayed out in the dayroom as much as possible. Not only did the socializing make the time go faster, it also offered an escape from the unpleasant roommates that appear with distressing regularity in the turbulent population of the jail.

BAD COMPANY

My worst roommate in the jail was Gloria. One afternoon I was reading on my bunk when I heard the unmistakable sound of my roommate masturbating. Loudly. Now, in jail, even the most gauche of us tried to maintain the illusion of privacy whenever possible. This wasn't the first time I had to share a room with someone who enjoyed this particular hobby to help pass the time and ease tension, but normally she would do it at night, when the chances were high that I might be asleep. If I weren't, I'd pretend to be.

Not Gloria, though. It was her habit to masturbate vigorously several times a day. There was no pattern to it: they were like Kamikaze attacks. Even more disturbing, she would intersperse her groans with invocations and praises to Jesus Christ. The first time she did this, I lay on my bunk too stunned to move or speak until she finished. I praised Jesus myself when she was released 2 weeks later.

My roommate Kelli was, sadly, all too typical of the women that were incarcerated in the jail. Kelli was in on her fourth or fifth prostitution charge. Her medical issues were profound: she was detoxing from her heroin habit and she had AIDS. Housing assigned her the top bunk, but because there were no ladders to climb, she had to step on my bed to get to hers. Kelli was in bad shape. I had never seen anyone coming off serious drugs before, and I couldn't believe how horrific the whole process was. Because the guards yelled at her when she tried to lie on the floor next to the toilet in our cell, she had to haul herself off the top bunk whenever she needed to vomit or use the bathroom. Weeping sores from infected injection sites covered her legs, and I would often come in to find my blanket and sheets delicately sprayed with her blood.

When her detoxing was at its worst, I tried to get an officer to help her, but they refused to put her in medical, examine her themselves, or even bring her fresh clothes. I tried to argue with them through the room's intercom.

"She at least needs a new uniform and blankets," I said. Kelli had the severe diarrhea that comes when anyone comes off heroin, and both of her uniforms were foul tangles I had tossed onto the floor by the locked door. Wrapped in a sheet and shivering on her bed, Kelli was in a stupor. She barely roused when I tried to speak to her, but at least for the moment she appeared to be resting.

The intercom distorted the voice of the answering officer enough that I couldn't tell who was replying. "Property is closed. We'll get her a new uniform in the morning."

"Can she at least take a shower? She's covered in this crap!"

"Showers are not permitted after the dayroom has closed." The guard sounded as if he were speaking through a length of aluminum pipe. I knew that this was a lie from my own midnight showers, but debating the issue would be fruitless. "She can clean up in the morning. We'll give you a trash bag to put her dirty uniforms in."

I fell asleep as I waited for them to pop my door to give me the trash bag. After a few days, Kelli was well enough to come out into the dayroom herself, and things returned to what passes for normal in jail.

GOOD C.O.s

Not all of the officers who worked in the jail were as callous as the one who answered my intercom call that night. Although the procedures in the jail seemed intended to dehumanize, the guards did their job professionally enough. Because many of them had friends or relatives incarcerated at RRJ, most were as kind to us as they could be without breaking any rules. At least they were to me. Maybe they felt sorry for me.

It took several weeks after my incarceration for me to emerge from my fugue of despair long enough to realize that the guards were not members of some Gestapo unit maintaining our subhuman flesh until it could be disposed of. The brief flashes of consideration that I experienced from them made a real difference to my time in jail.

I remember when I was preparing to be transported to the courthouse for the first time. Officer Shaw, the guard who called me to come out of my cell, said, "OK, George, get yourself together to go to court. Pack up your stuff and bring it out with you. Oh," she added as an afterthought, "and be sure to wear all your socks, too." I thought she was screwing with me, the newbie, so I ignored her suggestion. *Huge* mistake. By the end of the day, my ankles were circled with bruises and chafed raw from the heavy leg irons I had to wear when I was in court. When I saw her the next day I was still limping, so I had to tell Officer Shaw that I hadn't done as she had suggested.

"You goddamn inmates," she said, "You don't ever listen to anything anyone tells you. You think I was talking just for my own health? I'm just going to start minding my own goddamn business and see how well you do then. No wonder most of you are in here, you're too goddamn stupid to be out there on your own."

For some reason, her comment made me laugh until I was weak. It was, I think, my first real laughter in that awful place. Not that what she said was tremendously witty. Just the tone, like a crotchety old woman sniping about her disrespectful grandchildren, tickled me. In my family, laughter had always been our strongest tool for survival, but lately I hadn't been able to muster up that much joy. Officer Shaw inadvertently helped to bring it back to me.

A TEST

At first, things were pretty interesting at RRJ. Rather than focus on my sentence, I learned all I could about the people around me. There were new inmates to gossip about, and a few of the regulars could always be counted on to liven things up.

Felicia was one of these. "Hey Erin, can I borrow a pack of noodles?" she asked me one evening after chow. I had never spoken to her much, but I already knew that she was one of those people who were so unstable, it's a good idea to do what you can to stay on their good side.

"Sure, no problem," I answered. As I handed it to her, she smiled sweetly and said that she would hook me up next commissary day. About 10 minutes after that, Felicia walked up to her roommate, who was watching *Oprah* on the day-room television, and slugged her. The roommate crumpled, dazed, as 15 guards swarmed into the unit, screaming at us to "Get down, get down, get your asses on the floor by your cells NOW!"

Felicia stood calmly as they handcuffed her. "She snores too loud," she was explaining to the officer as they passed me. I, of course, never did get my Ramen noodles back. I was willing to eat the loss, though.

Whenever any trouble broke out, we were all supposed to do the same thing: move directly to our cell door and sit silently beside it on the floor until they popped us back into our cells. Under no circumstances were we to involve ourselves in the fracas. Of course, when a fight did occur, most of the women circled around it, cheering on both participants. This not only provided a healthy dose of adrenaline for everybody but also helped hide what was going on from the guards and the cameras. Most of the injuries occurred behind that concealing wall of tan jumpsuits. Because few people sought medical treatment after a fight, no one was ever charged (unless someone was hurt so badly that she couldn't conceal her wounds).

Some of the fights were famous. Months after it happened, we still talked about the time one very pregnant inmate cold-cocked another equally pregnant woman with her dinner tray because, she said, "that bitch stole my extra milk." Most fights were petty squabbles that never reached the physical stage.

I didn't get involved in too many altercations. The majority of the troubles I had were minor, like coping with roommates who stole or bickering over what to watch on TV. The most popular program was the *Maury Povich Show*, especially when he offered any paternity tests. "Baby Daddy Day" always drew a big crowd, and no one ever dared to suggest that we watch anything else during his time slot. These squabbles over TV were the natural result of spending months with the same group of emotionally broken women 24/7. I found jail to be like a huge sorting bin, where everyone, regardless of physical or mental state, is dumped to wait until the state decides what to do with her. Most are sick, drunk, detoxing, mentally ill, or some combination thereof. A check kiter can get anyone as a cell-mate: a shoplifter, a murderer, an embezzler, or a schizophrenic prostitute.

Little was done by the jail for the women who were severely impaired, although some of the other inmates would do their best to keep them out of too much trouble. The oddest pairings sprang from this, like when Chicago, a butch more infamous for her fists than her empathy, gently consoled June as she sat weeping, soaked in her own urine and begging for her husband. Chicago "adopted" June, stopping her from hurting herself too badly and defending her from the less compassionate inmates. When June would try to wash her towels in the vile communal toilet, Chicago would tenderly lead her back to her cell, taking the fouled linen from her. June appeared to be suffering from Alzheimer's. At least her swings between paranoia and confusion seemed to indicate that. No one knew for sure because she was never seen by medical or the jail psychiatrist, a compassionate but overwhelmed man. No one ever came to visit June, although she frequently said her daughter was coming to get her out that very afternoon and that all the people who had been stealing from her should get ready, because she was rich and her lawyer was going to sue them all. I don't know what finally happened to June; she was still there when I was shipped.

There was only one time that I had a major problem with another inmate. That woman, aptly named Mal, loathed me from the day that I arrived, and eventually provoked me into an uncharacteristically aggressive stance.

My beef with Mal lasted for several months. I still don't know what it was that got it started. Certainly nothing I did. It was just one of those visceral animosities that flourish behind bars, where so much rage is unmanageable and uncontainable. She hated me, and I, soon enough, hated her right back.

My interaction with Mal started with passive-aggressive comments, and then, when that didn't get any response from me, moved on to more blatantly intimidating behavior: brushing against me when she walked by, shoving me as I stood in line for chow, and even making overt threats to do me bodily harm. I managed to ignore her. But instead of leaving me for easier prey as I had hoped, my detachment seemed to piss her off more. Everything was resolved between us, however, in one afternoon.

That day, Mal was locked in her cell on the upper tier while I was out in the dayroom getting a sick call form from the unit officer. As we talked, Mal stood at her cell door and began to scream at me, pounding on the door. I tried to ignore her until she yelled, "Hey, bitch, you deserve a life sentence. I hope they never let your sorry ass out!"

I snapped. One thing you should never do in prison is throw someone's time up in her face. Only the most volatile inmates used sentencing as an insult, knowing that it demands immediate, violent response. Well, it got one. "You fucking bitch, you're doing a life on the installment plan!" I retorted, "Why don't you get your ass down here. I'm not afraid of some pissy little bitch like you."

Mal was a bully. I had seen her slapping her girlfriend, Tweety, down in the showers, but Tweety seemed to like it. Not me, though. I knew that if I let this go, Mal would dog me until I left the jail. So I bluffed, hoping that would be enough to save face. Anyway, she was locked up in her cell, so I was safe enough.

Until the idiot officer I'd been talking to popped her door open. I had noticed in the past that when two inmates were beefing, a guard might "accidentally" pop one of them out so that a fight would ensue. Certain officers were prone to doing this, so when there was a long-standing feud going on, the participants would wait until that particular shift was on to start things up. I hadn't been thinking about that, though, when I started mouthing back to Mal. Even if I had, I had to do what I did. Weakness of any kind is utterly exploitable in jail.

Mal came barreling down the stairs, looking more like a small, stocky man than a woman. She had cropped her hair so that whenever she fought, it couldn't be grabbed. Women in the jail didn't fight like any man: They very rarely used fists. Instead, they bit, slapped, gouged, spit, kicked, and yanked. That's if they didn't just sneak up behind you and wallop you with a blunt instrument, dropping you where you stood.

Mal didn't bother to sneak. She erupted with profanity-laced threats as she steamed toward me, and through some divine intercession, I managed not to flinch. In my memory, I even kept a menacing look on my face as she stood inches from me.

"Who the fuck do you think you are, saying shit to me, you white bitch? Don't you know who you're talking to? I'll beat your ass for you."

"Get out of my goddamn grill," I answered her. "I know exactly who you are, I know that you ain't worth shit to me so do whatever the fuck you think you need to do. I'm not afraid of you, you nasty bitch." By then, I had been down long enough to pick up the vocabulary of confrontation.

The officer who had followed our exchange without saying anything finally strolled over to the two of us.

"I don't feel like hassling with either of you, so cut that shit out before I put both of you in seg," he said. "Y'all need to get over it." Stepping back, he looked at us, bored.

Our mouths snapped shut, as if a switch had been hit. Mal liked to fight and she was good at it, so it was not any fear of me that shut her up. She had correctly sized me up as someone she could take in about a minute and a half. And she had never seemed to care much about what the officers did, either. So I can't explain why, but like a tornado that suddenly dissolves into a Texas sky after leaving a mile-long swath of devastation, her animosity toward me was gone.

Mal and I got along well after that, and I found that most of the small harassments that I had been experiencing from others stopped as well. Even the officers seemed to treat me differently, occasionally joking about the jail bureaucracy or debating last night's Redskins game. Some of them even began calling me by my first name. I had, apparently, passed my initiation.

PRISON LOOMS

Life at the jail grew more difficult as I waited to be shipped to Fluvanna, sometimes called Flu-flu for short. I was eager to get to Fluvanna, where I could begin the process of starting my new life. Also, being at the jail was becoming intolerable. RRJ had gotten so overcrowded that in cells designed for one inmate, they would house three: two in bunks and a third on the floor. The woman assigned to the floor slept in a "boat"—a heavy plastic frame that took up every inch of the available floor space. I couldn't even use the toilet in the cell without having to put my feet on someone's mattress.

There were more than 100 women crammed in a unit designed for 50. Tension ran high and fights broke out several times a day. To better keep us under control, the jail staff put us on quarterly rotation. Under quarterly rotation, one half of the bottom tier would be let out for 2 hours at a time, then the other half. Next the same process was followed with the top tier. At most I would have 4 hours a day out of the cell, but usually it was 2. Even that limited time was often curtailed because of maintenance going on in the pod. All of us were irritable, including the officers who had to deal with our constant bitching about the schedule. I was one of the worst when it came to that.

When the quarterly rotation system began, I had a medical profile, a doctor's certification, that meant I should be placed in the handicapped cell in the front of the unit, one of the few cells that had a view of the clock hanging above the sally port. Because none of us had watches, I ended up being the one who kept track of the schedule for my half of the tier. As they began to let us out less and less, I started to log exactly when each tier was unlocked. After a few days, I submitted a formal grievance, including a copy of the documented hours, asking that we be allowed the appropriate amount of time out of our cells. They never did reply to my grievance, but I was moved to the very last cell in the wing a few hours after I complained. There was, of course, no way for me to see the clock from there.

When the night officers came on, I told the guard that I had a medical profile for the handicapped cell (which I did), so she moved me back. I stayed there until the day shift came back on duty. By 8:30 a.m., I was back in that distant cell. When I formally complained, I was told that medical profiles could be overridden for security reasons. I guess it was a threat to their security that I knew what time it was.

That cell at the distant end of the tier, in Siberia, was where I spent the remainder of my time at RRJ. Mal, who was also waiting to be shipped (she had been convicted of assaulting a police officer after she had tried to run him over with her car), lived in the cell above mine, and she got into the habit of checking each morning to see if I had finally packed out. At 6:00 a.m. I would hear her voice, drifting from the vent like a fog, saying "George. George! You down there, George?"

"Yeah, I'm still here," I'd answer.

"Shit. Well, maybe tomorrow we'll both go, right?"

"I guess so," I'd answer without much hope. I had been at RRJ for so long, it felt like I would never leave.

"Stay tough," was all she would say. "Stay tough."

One morning in January, 5 months after my sentencing, the officer woke me at 4:00 a.m.

"Ms. George," I heard over the intercom as I shook off sleep. "Ms. George."

My head cleared immediately. I knew I didn't have any more court appearances scheduled, and if there had been a death in my family they would have at least come to my door in person. There was only one reason, then, why they would be calling for me at this hour. At last I was shipping out.

"All right, Ms. George. Pack up your property."

I could hear Mal through the vent whooping in excitement. "At least you're finally getting the hell out of this dump!" she said.

"Hey, thanks," I said. "I hope that you'll be next."

"Whatever," she said. She laughed ruefully. "I know I'll get there eventually. Just be cool, OK?"

"Yeah, as cool as a nerd like me can be, I guess."

Mal laughed again. "See you around." That was about as personal as goodbyes in jail got. I said goodbye to my sleepy roommate, leaving her some of the bags of potato chips I knew I couldn't fit in the one cardboard box I was allowed to take. She also tried to get me to leave my Walkman, saying I wouldn't be allowed to have it at Fluvanna anyway, but I ignored her. I was a lot less easy to scam than when I first got to Rappahannock Regional Jail.

Stumbling from the heavy leg shackles I had to wear, I at last stepped up into the grimy prison van that was going to transport me to a maximum security prison. The inmate journeying through the ice-bright Virginia countryside that winter day was very different from the terrified and broken woman who had come to RRJ more than a year earlier. As we traveled through those beloved towns and trees of my home state, I only hoped that, tempered by the violence and deprivation of the jail, I had managed to find the balance between the self-preservation that was vital for my own safety and the empathy necessary to keep myself human behind prison walls.

REFERENCES

Cornelius, G. (2007). *The American jail: Cornerstone of modern corrections.* Upper Saddle River, NJ: Prentice Hall.

Kruttschnitt, C., & Gartner, R. (2005). *Marking time in the Golden State: Women's imprisonment in California.* New York: Cambridge University Press.

Owen, B. (1998). *In the mix: Struggles and survival in a women's prison.* Albany: State University of New York Press.

CHAPTER 2

Prison Time

George is eager to depart the jail but understandably harbors some anxieties about prison life. She imagines prison as a place with things to do, in contrast to jail, where empty time is the norm. But she also envisions the prison as a tough place, the sort of place depicted in movies, a Big House replete with brutal guards and rapacious inmates (Ferguson, 2014; Johnson, 2002). George is amazed to see Fluvanna Correctional Center for Women, which looks more like an "office park" than a penitentiary and fits nicely into the lovely surrounding countryside (Pollock, 2004).[1] George's reception is remarkably cordial.

George is new to prison but has learned from her jail time; she knows about living in confinement and now must adapt to the particulars of long-term confinement, which is different from jail, of course, but similar in many ways (Irwin, 2009; Johnson, 2002; Toch, 1992a). She knows enough from her jail experience to be suspicious, to steer clear of conversations she doesn't start, to avoid being touched, and to say "no" to requests for sex or goods. At the same time, George has the sense and savvy to turn a woman down in a way that allows the person to save face. "Maybe," she says, "Just give it a rest." Later, George gives her would-be victimizer a token gift. George has a deft touch with others, and it serves her well.

As she settles into her new home, however, the reality and enormity of her term—effectively, a death sentence—begins to sink in (see Johnson & McGunigall-Smith, 2008). George simply isn't ready for this, if anyone can be ready for such a thing. To survive in the jail, George had adopted a strategy of psychological denial. The focus was on her case and getting through each day in jail, not on the disastrous sentence she faced on conviction. Even the harsh sentence—a cruel 603 years—was met, initially, with denial. The focus of her life in jail after conviction and before transfer became getting to prison and settling into a routine in that new world. Once George got to prison, however, she had reached a dead end: she isn't going anywhere. Ever.

Understandably, she is bereft, at one point depressed and preoccupied with suicide, a disturbingly common problem among new arrivals to prison (Liebling, 1999; Toch, 1992b). Called in to talk to the personnel in the mental health area, her fear of being put in isolation—the standard mental health response to crisis in prison, and a setting she knew and feared from her jail experience—moves her to say she is alright, that she is fine, that she can make it on her own. And by saying she is well, she resolves to pretend, to fake it. By faking it, she begins to make it. She meets other women and begins to forge a life behind bars.

And thus her prison adjustment—adapting to high-security housing, to mail calls that don't include her name (a problem that, perhaps inevitably, grows worse over time), to cellmates good and bad, to loneliness as a way of life made more stark by pervasive and invasive cameras in virtually every nook and cranny of the prison—starts with a lifesaving lie that leads to her acceptance of her fate as a lifer. For George, the irony is delicious, because as far as she is concerned, her prison sentence is based on a lie, the lie of her guilt. —Robert Johnson

As thrilled as I was to leave RRJ, I was also, naturally enough, more than a little nervous about coming to prison. My idea of what a maximum security prison would be like was molded by everything I had seen on TV and at the movies: *The Shawshank Redemption*, HBO's *Oz*, those dreadful Lifetime movies set in women's facilities in California or Texas. I expected imposing walls of rough-hewn stone, barbed wire, a graveled recreation yard, and the glint of reflected sun on the rifles in the guard towers. Its inhabitants, I assumed, would be all the characters that are so familiar from those same grittily "realistic" TV shows: corrupt and brutal guards; mindlessly violent inmates; and a venal, implacable prison warden. I had prepared myself for a seething maelstrom of abuse, rage, and indifference that I was sure would greet me.

So I was surprised when the jail van turned into what looked to me more like an office park than a prison. There was a set of chain-link fences topped with barbed wire, of course, but the buildings were all low, painted a pleasant cream color with dark green trim. Surrounded by rural Virginia countryside, FCCW did not appear at all out of place in its setting. As we entered the gate, I noticed that a few horses were peacefully cropping at the lush grass across from the quiet street. At the sight of them, much of my anxiety drained away. This was a place, I hoped, that my children could visit without being terrified. I hadn't seen them at all during my tenure at the jail—my whole family agreed that an unintelligible conversation with them through the greasy Plexiglas in the hectic jail visitation room would have been utterly bewildering to them, so we were waiting until I got to Fluvanna to see Jack, Fran, and Gio.

As we pulled up to the officer's station between the inner and outer gates, the officer was busy inspecting an outgoing trash truck. We waited as the C.O. took a pointed metal rod and pierced each bag of trash, then viewed the underside of the truck with a long-handled mirror. When she was finished, she checked the undercarriage of the transport van as well, then waved us through to the intake building.

After the restrictions of the jail and my own preconceived notions of prison, I was shocked to see smiling inmates, each one dressed in a lime green T-shirt emblazoned with the words *DOC Inmate Work Force*, cleaning floors and moving boxes of property. They chatted easily with the officers, more like amiable co-workers than inmates and guards. The van driver handed the intake officer, Ms. Devlin, my paperwork and plunked my flimsy carton of possessions onto the floor, then left, wishing me good luck. As the driver exited, the intake officer turned to me, smiling pleasantly.

"You're Erin George? Welcome to Fluvanna. Malikah Gordon says hello," she said.

I stared at her. Malikah was a buddy of mine from the jail who had shipped to FCCW 3 or 4 months earlier, and Officer Devlin casually dropping her name, passing on a message even, was not at all what I expected. I didn't know how to handle this—being treated so well before I had to prove myself. Maybe this was going to be easier than I thought. I answered, "Uh, thanks," but didn't know what else to say. I certainly couldn't ask her to say "Hi" for me the next time she saw Malikah! I decided that my best bet was to keep my mouth shut until I knew how I should act with the C.O.s here.

Officer Devlin pulled my box of property onto a long table and began sorting through it. I didn't have much. The three books that the jail allowed my parents to buy for me, a couple of gray T-shirts, socks, and panties. I had two sweatsuits (one dark gray, one light gray) mailed to me by a friend when I was at the jail to be held in my property until I was shipped, but I was only allowed to keep the light gray one—dark gray items were not permitted. As for jewelry, I was told I could keep my necklace and wedding ring if they weren't too expensive.

"Let's see," said Officer Devlin, "you have one gold-colored wedding band, plain." She stood there with her clipboard poised. "What is the cost of that item?"

"Um, I'm not sure. It belonged to my husband's grandmother, and I know it's real gold. . . ." I ventured a guess: "Three hundred dollars?"

"All items must cost no more than 50 dollars. Ms. George, how much does your wedding ring cost?"

I still didn't get it. As I looked at her blankly, she gentled her tone and said, "Honey it's gotta cost 50 dollars or less. So tell me, how much did it cost?"

The fog lifted. "Well, it cost 50 dollars," I said.

"Good." She logged the cost down on the inventory sheet. "And this silver-colored cross necklace?"

"That was 50 dollars, too," I answered. The necklace had been given to me after my arrest by my godmother, Sandy. It was one of the two things that I still had with me from before my conviction, that and my wedding ring.

Officer Devlin spent most of her time browsing through the commissary I had brought with me. The inmate workers hovered nearby as she verbally listed my possessions, down to the brand of the shampoo I had and my Nivea skin cream.

"Hmm, they're sure gonna want to be *your* friend," she said as she pulled out my six containers of onion dip and small box of Club crackers. Most of what

I brought was not sold by the prison commissary, and new food items were popular with the inmates, who in most cases had been ordering the same snacks for years.

When she was finished, only a sad little heap of possessions was left. Everything else was either shipped home or trashed.

After being deloused, showered, and given three sets of the loose, baby blue scrubs that earn all unclassified inmates the nickname "Smurf," I was escorted to my unit: one of the infamous intake wings of Building One. Intake is notorious for being clamorous, unrestrained, chaotic—"off the hook" in prison parlance. Filled with inmates fresh from jail, it is a volatile mix of predator and prey.

The worst are the sexual manipulators. Like waves breaking on the shore, women regularly pair up for furtive sexual encounters, then just as quickly detach and move on to someone else. If sex isn't a vulnerability, another tack is strong-arming a newbie into coughing up some commissary. The abusers in prison are expert in sussing out any weakness, relentlessly probing until you waver. I have never seen one of the predators be physically violent: psychological profiling is their area of expertise. It's easy enough to avoid them. All you need is enough self-esteem to say "No," and they'll usually let you alone. Unfortunately, most of the women who make it to Fluvanna are too broken to offer any real resistance. Predators can find too many women willing to be victimized to waste time on someone who won't succumb quickly.

When I showed up in 1-D, I immediately made it clear that I wasn't interested in sex, so one woman decided to try for my commissary. Despite her innocuous nickname, Boo Boo had a terrifying appearance: A long knife scar hooked down one cheek, dragging the corner of her right eye with it, and her beefy arms and neck were covered with clumsy prison tattoos. Sidling up to me my first night in intake, she tried to smile ingratiatingly. I was a little afraid of being approached by someone who appeared to be the stereotypical menacing convict, but my time at RRJ made me determined not to show anything but cool detachment.

"What's your name?" she asked.

I'd spent too much time in jail not to be suspicious. "I'm George," I said, and turned toward my room. I wasn't interested in any conversation that I didn't initiate myself.

"Hold up a second," Boo Boo said, trying to grab my arm. I slipped from her before she could make contact. Unsolicited touching is a dicey thing on the inside. A healthy sense of paranoia can only serve you well in here.

"George . . . that's a funny name for a woman." She got to her point. "Look, I just wanted to ask you to get me some stuff off of commissary," she said. "I'll hook you up next week. My money's going to be here by then."

"No."

She looked shocked, then tried again. "Shit, c'mon now. You don't want to be no tightass bitch, do you? You're gonna need some friends in here. I'll pay you back two for one."

"No," I repeated. "I never lend commissary, and I won't buy anything else for people either, so don't bother asking."

Several women watched our exchange, most surreptitiously, but a few blatantly dipping, slang here for eavesdropping. Boo Boo tried to save face. "Damn, you're tight," she said. "Can I just have a couple of lollipops then?" By now she seemed more sad than menacing. I decided to cut her a break.

"Maybe," I said. "Just give it a rest, OK?"

"Thanks," she said.

Three days later, when I got my first commissary, I gave her two lollipops from the six-pack of Tootsie Roll Pops I had bought. I figured that was enough to salve her ego but not enough to encourage her to ask again.

"Appreciate it," she said as I handed them over.

"All right, but that's it. Got it?"

"Yeah, yeah," she said. "Whatever." Boo Boo had already moved on to the most recent batch of new inmates. Chances were high that she would find someone a little more accommodating there. I might have given up two lollipops, but I wasn't going to be anyone's sucker.

Because intake was so unruly, the officers were especially tough on us. Our cells were inspected daily, and every time the wing got too loud, the officer in the bubble (the main control area of the building) would lock us all down in our rooms. Every C.O. had his or her own area that he or she liked to police. One might be bitching at us to clean the dayroom, another hollering at us to "tighten up that line" as we waited to get chow. It was like being in boot camp, but without all of the good times.

Every few days an officer would come around and do a mallet check. The first time it happened, I thought I was going to have a stroke. I was dead asleep in my bunk at 10:00 p.m. when I woke to see an officer looming over me, a small rubber mallet in his hand.

"Hammer time," he said, grinning. He knew exactly how much he had frightened me. "Don't move."

He leaned over me and hit the 5-inch-wide window with two solid whacks. "Just gotta be secure," he said, and strolled out of my room. Eventually my heart stopped thudding enough that I was able to go back to sleep.

After a week in intake, I found myself so depressed I could barely function. I was weeping constantly, only leaving my cell to occasionally shower or make another of my expensive, hysterical phone calls to Mom and Dad. I had been in denial at the jail; I rarely thought about my sentence and its repercussions while I was there. I had focused solely on moving to the next stage of confinement. But now that I was at FCCW, I realized that this was probably it for me. I had to deal with the fact that I was never going home and all of the attendant grief that went along with my time. The anxiety of being surrounded by potentially violent strangers, separation from my parents, the knowledge that I would die behind bars—I was coping with all of these things at once.

Most devastating was dealing with the loss of my children. Their absence from my life left me bereft. Their living arrangements, I learned, had finally been

decided. My sister and my husband's brother, who shared legal custody of them equally, had decided that the kids would go to live in England, where my husband was from. Fran and Gio would be with my mother-in-law and Jack with his uncle. They would only be in America during summer holidays.

I can see the wisdom of this decision now. My sister, Shannon, has three children of her own, and doubling her family size would have been overwhelming for her both financially and emotionally. Plus, the benefits of England's better educational system are undeniable. In a way, I also think that it was very healing to have the kids in a new environment to try to distance them from their double loss of a mother and father. It was certainly the best choice to make, but at the time I went a little crazy when I heard that the kids would be moving an ocean away. All I could ask myself was if I would ever be able to see them again.

My parents were trapped in the middle, and I didn't make it any easier on them. Each of my phone calls was a nightmare of vitriol, accusations, and incoherent weeping. They've never said anything about it, but I'm sure that every time they answered the telephone and heard that bland robotic voice saying, "This is a phone call from a correctional facility. Will you accept a collect call from . . . Erin George?" they must have shuddered, bracing themselves for another onslaught of abuse. Thank God they kept taking my calls. If I had been on their end, I can't say that I would have.

Because I knew that I couldn't drive them away, I blamed my folks for everything: Why didn't they take the kids themselves (no matter that my Dad had recently had to undergo treatment for cancer and that both of them still worked full-time jobs)? Why didn't they stop Shannon from taking my children away from me? Because I was terrified that I would never see my children again if I lashed out at Shannon, Mom and Dad caught the bulk of my rage. Despite my irrational behavior, my parents did all they could do for me, accepting my phone calls, listening, and reassuring me that they loved me, that this really was the right thing to do. They forgave the unforgivable things I said and met my irrationality with reason and reassurance.

I was afraid to call Shannon. We had spoken a few times on the telephone since I had heard about the kids, but each call was agonizing. I didn't want to say or do anything to make the situation worse. In my warped mindset, I had decided that Shannon was doing this to punish me for some reason and that if I didn't say exactly what she wanted, she would completely cut me off from my children. In retrospect, I'm grateful to my sister for her strength during this ugly time and her steadfast commitment to doing what was the absolute best for Jack, Franny, and Gio. It could not have been easy for her to send away three small children whom she loved very much and who in her mother's heart she must have wanted to care for and heal. Nor did she want to cause more pain, however necessary, to her already broken sister. It's never easy to be the strong one. Where I could selfishly lose myself to my grief, Shannon had to keep it together. She never thought of herself: my family and her family had to be protected.

That's easy for me to recognize now. But in the frenzy of my grief, the only solution I could imagine when I contemplated the loss of my children and freedom was death. Wouldn't everyone be better off if I weren't around to be a constant drain on their finances and emotions?

I fantasized about elaborate plans to kill myself. As an intelligent, creative woman, I knew that I would be able to pull it off without being caught. How hard could it be? There had been at least one man who had hanged himself while I was at the jail, and I had made sure to get the particulars of how he had accomplished that as soon as I heard about his successful suicide. I suppose that subconsciously even then I was planning on trying something like this.

Oh, I was clever. My mind was engaged in crafting my suicide down to the smallest detail. If I cut my wrists, I could do it in the large, handicapped shower stall, but if a leg poked out from under the stall door during my death throes (I was more than a little melodramatic during this stage of adapting to prison) or, more likely, an impatient inmate demanded to use the shower herself, I could be discovered and, God forbid, saved. Starving myself seemed too time-consuming, and, as had happened at the jail, they might notice my drop in weight. I certainly didn't want to be force-fed. I didn't know anybody well enough to get pills from them (and wouldn't know what the best pills were anyway). Hanging or smothering myself with a plastic garbage bag might work, but the officers in intake checked the cells too often for me to be sure that I would have time to finish.

No, the best bet seemed to be cutting my wrists. We were allowed to buy safety razors from commissary, and I would easily be able to use the blade. To prevent any incriminating, spreading bloodstains, I planned on stealing an extra blanket to soak up the excess and to line my bunk with torn garbage bags to prevent dripping. With my back turned to the wall, the officer would never realize what I had done. I even went so far as to write a note saying that I had done this myself and that neither my roommate nor any other inmate was involved in my suicide. Even in my selfishness, I didn't want to jam anybody else up.

I'm still not sure why I didn't go through with it. Grief like that cannot be sustained, though, so when the sergeant pulled me into her office to determine if I needed to go to mental health, I forced myself to regroup. Debbie, a woman who had been processed on the same day as I was, noticed my nonstop crying and finally reported me to the staff as a "risk to self." Sergeant Childes and some random counselor I had never seen before steered me to the ratty sofa in the Sergeant's office and asked a few desultory questions about my mood, appetite, and family situation. All I knew about mental health was what I had seen in the jail, and there was no way I would survive being put in a freezing strip cell with no mattress or sheets and no clothes but a paper gown, which was the state's usual response to someone in an emotional crisis. I knew the kinds of answers they wanted to hear, so I reeled off some bland responses and got out of there as quickly as possible. Feeling as if my head were filled with ground glass, I started going to a few meals and stopped crying so obviously on the telephone. By pretending to cope, I began to heal a little.

CLASSIFIED

A few months after my arrival, the Department of Corrections (DOC) gave me a security level 3, one of the highest levels assigned to women inmates (unlike men, who can go as high as 5 or 6). My security level determined to which prison I would be assigned. These levels are based on a numerical rating system where certain factors, such as your crime, your sentence, your previous record, your age, or your educational level, are worth a predetermined number of points. The higher your total number of points, the higher your security level. College graduates, for example, score lower in the education category than those who have never completed high school, so those few points can be the difference between being sent to a lower-security prison or staying at Fluvanna. When I first got here, I was told that I have to stay here for at least 15 years. After that, if I have been an exemplary inmate and managed to lower my security level somewhat through good behavior, I might be eligible to be shipped elsewhere. I hear from other, more seasoned, lifers that this doesn't happen too often, though. I've also been informed that the minimum time at Fluvanna is now 20 years, not 15.

There are several women's facilities in Virginia, but Fluvanna is the only female maximum security prison as well as the only place that offers comprehensive medical treatment to women. If you are scary, dangerous, or chronically ill, this is where you will end up. Women who are assigned a lower security level will be shipped to another facility, like Goochland or Pocahontas, but those of us who are going to be staying at FCCW are given new blue jeans and chambray shirts and released into general population.

I was assigned to Building Three when I finally left intake. It was a little calmer there, and the officers were significantly less overbearing. No more nocturnal mallet checks, at least. And by then I had settled into the grinding routine of the prison, even finding comfort in its consistency.

Every day, I learned, was basically the same. There are three meals a day: breakfast served anywhere between 3:30 a.m. and 5:00 a.m. (depending on where your building stands in the rotation to be sent to chow), lunch between 12:00 p.m. and 1:30 p.m., and dinner between 3:30 p.m. and 5:00 p.m. Standing count is held at least four times a day: 6:00 a.m., 11:00 a.m., 5:45 p.m., and 9:30 p.m. Until count has cleared, inmates remain locked in their cells. If you have a job or go to school, you leave your wing at about 7:45 a.m. for mass movement, then return to your cell en masse by 11:00 a.m. count. The same process is repeated during the afternoons—going to work directly from the chow hall after lunch and returning to the wing when 3:00 mass movement is called.

This is the schedule every weekday. It's a depressing thought, though, that until the day I shake off this mortal coil I will have to get up at 6:00 a.m. and stand for count four times a day. One of the subtlest torments of prison life is the chronic lack of sleep. Even if you are able to block out the constant nocturnal clamor, you get less than 5 hours of uninterrupted sleep a night if you need to go to morning pill line (held at 2:45 a.m.), followed by breakfast an hour and a half later, then 6:00 a.m. count. And that 5 hours of sleep estimate only applies if you are blessed with the ability to instantly fall asleep once 9:30 p.m. count is over. Most of us lie in our freezing metal bunks until exhaustion finally overtakes us and our minds can rest.

The only real bright spot of the day is at mail call, when you keep your fingers crossed and hope to get a real letter, not just some junk mail or, very frustrating, a meaningless reply to an IMS (the request forms that inmates have to send out every time they need to get in contact with a staff member). All complaints, requests, and comments need to first be sent out as an IMS before any official action on them can take place. Unfortunately, 90% of the time an IMS goes out, it never returns. And if you do get a response, it usually has nothing to do with the original request. More often than not, the response is that you have written the wrong person. Of course, they frequently fail to tell you just who the right person is, so the cycle continues.

It's too easy to become institutionalized in here—enslaved by the routine that governs our every move. I know that I have. I am dependent on the schedules and regulations to keep myself calm and, surprisingly, to make myself feel in control. Any break in the routine truly upsets me, be it shakedown, late mass movement, or unplanned recount. It's even hard for me to enjoy the rare pleasant disruptions in the routine, like the 2 days a year when the Kairos ladies are allowed to bring a dozen homemade cookies to each inmate. When things are disrupted, I'm always nervous that I am doing something the wrong way, missing some important activity that I need to be a part of, or, worst of all, that something really bad is about to happen and I am powerless to prevent it.

MAIL CALL

I tend to dread weekends, mostly because there is no mail call. Even when I don't get mail myself (which happens far more often the longer I am down), I enjoy seeing the photos that the other women get and hearing about their families who have, through our time together, become like my own. I have heard so much about Naomi's crazy sister Susan, Mina's son who is flunking out of 11th grade, and Penny's new grandbaby, it's as if they're extended family now.

It's an especially wonderful day if I hear from home myself. My parents write to me often, sending me anything that they think will catch my interest: newspaper articles, song lyrics, old family pictures, and photocopies of the *Washington Post*'s Sunday crossword. The crosswords that Mom sends have special significance for me. I remember when I was growing up, Mom and Dad always competed to see who would finish first. Dad's copy would be clipped to his clear blue plastic clipboard, reserved for that use, and Mom's to her pink one, and throughout the day they would pick them up between their weekend tasks to fill in a few more squares. No cheating was allowed, and both would gleefully gloat over their progress. "Did you get 42 down yet? It's a real toughie," my mom might say. Dad was typically less verbal, but his body language was clear whenever he figured out a particularly puzzling clue. There seemed to be bonus points for figuring out what the theme of the puzzle was each week. My folks take care to send me each week's puzzle, and I am absurdly grateful to be included in the family ritual that, in so many ways, captures the loving, competitive spirit that we all share.

I used to particularly treasure the cards and letters that I would receive from Jack, Francesca, and Gio, but it has been a long time since I've heard from them. Teenagers now, they are busy and popular, and all three live too far away to have a real relationship with.

I had managed to accumulate several manila envelopes stuffed with their artwork and carefully printed messages. My daughters had sent me sweet, innocent drawings of cats and butterflies. A common subject for their artwork was, heartbreakingly, portraits of us together. Franny, my tender, quietly intelligent middle child, would send me birthday cards in which she and I are portrayed side by side holding hands. We would be wearing fantastically extravagant ballgowns, she just a smaller replica of me, down to the waist-length, curly hair that I never sported in real life. We were often framed by a giant, embellished heart.

Gio is fey and exuberant, and I laughed over her drawings of grumpy sheep and artistically cropped giraffes (her favorite animal when she was young). But I noticed that her drawings of the two of us were more in Francesca's traditional style, and I always wondered if that was because her memories of me were so limited that she had to adopt her older sister's.

Jack, now 18, is well launched into adulthood, but I still can't put a stamp on a letter without remembering teaching him that an upside-down stamp on an envelope means I love you, I miss you, you dwell in my heart always. That is something I never do anymore.

I held on to their letters for a long time but rarely looked at them. Why invite heartache? It was with great ambivalence that, a year ago, I packed them all up and mailed them home to my parents to keep for me in the unlikely event that I ever make it out of Fluvanna. Mom and Dad have a large carton of things, all that is left of my former life, stuffed in a closet somewhere in their new home, a place that I have never visited. Maybe someday I'll be able to read them again.

BEFORE

Few words in a lifer's vocabulary evoke more longing and nostalgia than the word "before." You don't hear it very often in our conversations. The use of it signals the poignant intimacies in which we rarely can indulge. The simple phrase, "I remember before, when I could . . ." opens myriad doors, behind which a million bittersweet memories still linger. When we talk about our lives before our incarceration, these echoes from the past can, even for the most seemingly innocuous memories, snarl together to make a throat-closing mix of emotions: regret, grief, despair, and, faintly shimmering amidst the sorrows, long-absent joy.

I have found that "before" is a time that I can't afford to think of too often. In my own long, dim hallways of memory are the doors to my children, James, Mom and Dad, my whole laughter-loving clan. There, behind that one is Jack at his first birthday party, with his monotoothed grin and chubby hand clutching a moist wad of squashed hamburger bun, his blue and white striped outfit spattered with watermelon juice. The next holds the sound of Gio and Fran playing Barbies busily in the backyard, their laughter twining together to make a chord of pure pleasure that pulls my soul. But I have to keep those doors closed. Remembrance can be paralyzing.

Lifers have three basic choices as to how they will live their lives in prison. A rare few choose denial. These live every day the same way: quarreling with their girlfriends, bending the institutional rules, scamming everyone they can. During my time here I've learned that the catalyst for change and emotional growth is acknowledgment that the way things are going right now is simply too painful to continue. But a few lifers won't admit that the choices they have made are not the best. It's always someone else's fault that they are here: that bitch that lived next door turned her in, or her asshole husband was the one who did it—she just took the charges to protect him. But it's all good. She can handle everything that comes her way all by herself. The women like this will be the same until the state gives their body to whoever is left to care. Usually, though, it's only the short-timers who cruise through their short bids in this way.

Some lifers briefly choose the second option, bitterness, but the energy required to sustain a mindset like that is just too exhausting: They either end up hurting themselves or they finally realize that the only way to keep going is to take the third, most difficult, choice, which is acceptance.

Acceptance is the path that I follow. This is true for most of my friends, almost all of whom are lifers (it's too painful to get attached to someone who will only be here for another year, 3 years, or even 10 years). We accept where we are and that if we're going to have any kind of substantive life here, we will have to cobble it together ourselves from the few opportunities the DOC allows us. No one else is going to do it for us.

Before I was locked up, I imagined that the women serving harsh sentences like mine would fall into one of two categories: angry and violent or simply broken by their time. Neither of these sounded sustainable to me. But when I began to meet other people at Fluvanna who also had a life sentence, I was actually quite surprised. For the most part, lifers are the women in prison who are most dedicated to improving themselves academically and emotionally. The achievements of these women are inspiring. Some read voraciously. A few paint or draw on an astounding level. We master carpentry, printing, and cosmetology, even though we will probably never have the opportunity to put those skills to use in the free world. Sadie and Celia are learning to transcribe books into Braille for schoolchildren. (It is tediously painstaking work, but both were tremendously moved by the idea of being able to actively contribute to children in the outside world.) Naomi, a close friend of mine in the wing, is state- and nationally certified in computer-aided drafting (CAD), which enables her to draw professional architectural blueprints and mechanical drawings. She and another, equally well-trained inmate (also serving a life sentence, naturally) now teach the complex CAD software to other women incarcerated here. Naomi and Lily ended up teaching me CAD as well, and I became a CAD tutor until the class was inexplicably closed. Naomi, Lily, and I became the only three female inmates in Virginia to earn a national certification in both mechanical and architectural drafting.

The contributions of the women here can be subtler, as well. Someone who has suffered the loss of a parent or child will find dozens of cards under her door, all expressing sympathy from those who have also endured the death of a family member while inside. Because many lifers are completely isolated from anyone on the outside, they must depend solely on their meager state pay to survive. These women might find anonymous gifts of food and personals sitting on their desks after a commissary day. The gifts are precious: a bottle of real shampoo for Janine, who can only afford to wash her hair with the cheap bar soap that the state gives out once a week; for Alicia, handmade stationary emblazoned with adorable cartoon puppies and kittens to send to her preschool-age children.

I've crafted my own life in prison. I work 30 hours a week as a library aide cataloging books, tracking donations, and performing other clerical tasks. Books have become my great joy here, and I'm grateful that FCCW has the largest prison library in Virginia. I have had some of my poetry published and am teaching myself Spanish through books that I have been able to buy. I've learned to play the handbells and belong to a small handbell choir that gives regular concerts at our church services. I live in the Honor Wing. I even hope someday to achieve my Bachelor of Arts degree.

Like many of the lifers here, I've managed to find the decent staff members and opportunities to help me create some semblance of a fulfilling life. It's certainly nothing like I had at home, but, in a way, it is more satisfying. After the abundance of my life before, I am now more aware of my every blessing in prison. I can help students achieve lifelong goals and make music that fills everyone who hears it with pleasure. I could have done any of those things before (there's that word again), but now I savor every bit of it. As saccharine as it sounds, the greatest lesson that I have learned here is gratitude.

Every so often the rumor goes around that the state is building a "supermax" prison for women. Like the Red Onion Correctional Facility that houses highly violent, dangerous male inmates, the story goes out that the state legislature has finally allocated funds for a similar women's prison that the inmates call "Pink Onion." Life in such places is unbelievably psychologically damaging. With no jobs available, no educational opportunities, no more contact visits, and being locked down 23 hours out of each 24, a prison like that is a nightmare compared to FCCW.

One of my great fears is that they will, finally, build a prison like that, and that I will be sent there merely because of my sentence. My great institutional record and work history are pretty meaningless when stacked up against my 603 years. That is what happened when they opened Red Onion, from what I hear.

The state needed to fill the beds, so every male inmate serving a long sentence was sent there, no matter how flawless his behavior had been while he was locked up. My understanding is that this practice ended only after the men filed a lawsuit against the DOC.

When I heard that rumor for the first time (before I learned how improbable most inmate rumors can be), I spoke with one of the counselors about it. Mr. Beck was a decent man who, despite working for the DOC for years, had managed to remember that we are human beings. He has always been honest with me, so I trusted him to tell me the truth about a supermax prison for women.

"Don't worry, Ms. George," he said to me when I approached him about it on the boulevard, the main walkway connecting the prison buildings [this and other specialized terms are defined in a prison glossary found in Appendix A—Ed.]. "I haven't heard anything about that. Anyway, long-termers are the most stable ones in the mixture here. You work most of the jobs and keep most of the programs running. I don't think that they would send you all anywhere else."

I try to remember what Mr. Beck told me each time the Pink Onion rumor makes the rounds again, but the thought utterly terrifies me. It's a helpless, dreadful feeling to know that everything I've worked so hard for here, all of the little blessings that make life bearable, can be yanked away just because a bed needs to be filled somewhere.

My experiences with Mr. Beck had a tragic ending. Years after I met him, rumor went around that he was quitting the facility. I saw him across the yard the day before he was scheduled to leave and, defying all rules, rushed up to him.

"Mr. Beck, you have made such a big impact on my life here. I can never tell you how grateful I am for all that you've done for me. Thank you for being a voice of sanity and compassion in this crazy place."

The yard was crowded with other inmates and officers, but Mr. Beck flashed me a huge grin and grabbed me into a giant hug. I was stunned into motionlessness for a moment—a staff member is hugging me! Like I'm actually human! He could get fired! All that flashed through my mind, but then I melted into it. It wasn't sordid or sexual; it was a profoundly human connection and is one of the greatest blessings of my time here.

"God bless you, Mr. Beck," I said. "You are a wonderful person. Thank you." He just gave me a cheery wave and strolled down the boulevard toward the staff chow hall.

The next day, inmate.com reported that he had changed his mind and wasn't leaving after all, that he was actually pressured to stay because the need for decent counselors was so dire. I was thrilled that he was staying and couldn't wait to see him again to tell him that.

I didn't run into him for at least a week, though, and before I did, Dizzy came up to me in the dayroom, ashen and shaken. I could tell something terrible had happened.

"Oh my god, what is the matter? Are you OK?" I grabbed her arm and led her to a chair. She sat down shakily and drew a deep breath.

"Oh, shit, Erin, haven't you heard? Mr. Beck is dead!"

"Dead? How? What happened?" I couldn't fathom what she was saying. How could that vibrant, amazing, loving man be dead?

"It was terrible. It turns out that he'd been having some trouble at home with his ex-wife, I guess, and was staying with Mr. Valezquez. Jesus, he shot himself in Mr. Valezquez's garage! Another counselor went to the house to see where Mr. Beck was, I guess, because he hadn't come to work, and she found him. Suicide . . . I can't believe it." She and I began to weep and we held each other tightly.

We still talk about Mr. Beck often. He's been elevated to legend around here, and a legend of the rarest kind: a prison staff member who did his job effectively, compassionately, intelligently. I wish that more people around here, inmate and staff, took him as a role model.

HOUSING

"I have a theory on how they should put people in rooms," Donna announced one afternoon as we waited to be called for chow. Donna, a sarcastic, keenly intelligent young woman who was doing time for knocking over a couple of Dairy Freezes, had an opinion on everything, from the pervasive homosexuality of the Roman elite during Augustan times to Dick Cheney's profanity on the congressional floor. (Donna was especially vehement on the issue of Cheney's profanity, as she had once been given a $100 fine for profanity in public. Outraged, she wrote several letters to various authorities trying to get the vice president charged as well.) But this time, Donna was on to something. "Put the people who don't take showers in the same room together. If someone steals, put 'em in with another thief. If they're crazy, the same thing. If they like to fight, close the door after them and see who ends up walking out of there alive."

A bad cellmate in prison (as in jail) can be one of the most stressful aspects of inmate life. The housing gods are capricious, at best. Their official story is that placement is random, but certain people seem to have extraordinary bad luck when it comes to their cellmates. For the most part, I've been fortunate.

My first prison roommate in intake was a self-described "ghetto princess." Elisha was just a kid, but one facing a life sentence. I could see that in her mind, she was playing the starring role in a film: Billy Bob Thornton would turn up as the racist prison guard, maybe Queen Latifah as the nurturing old-timer. And here was Elisha, the cynical gang member, keeping it real amid all of the prison bullshit. They weren't going to make her do any of that useless crap that they made other people do. She didn't need any GED or classes. She was fine as she was, she had a sexy girlfriend on the street that sent her money every week and another in here that she could fight and reconcile with passionately and daily. Now, 10 years later, she seems to have changed not at all. I don't see her around much. She spends most of her time in seg. We got along well when we were housed together, though. I would give her the Milky Way bars and onion dip I had brought from the jail, which eased our relationship considerably.

When Elisha moved into general population, K'drea took her place. K'drea was older, serving a year on her third parole violation. She would talk endlessly about her daughter, whom she hadn't seen in more than 4 years, but whom she hoped to take custody of when she got out this time and kept clean. Because I was a nonsmoker, she would huddle by the crack under the cell door, trying to blow smoke from her cigarettes into the dayroom. She and I also lived together amicably, and this time no bribery was necessary. Our worst moment was when I awakened at 2:00 a.m. to find her squatting over a plastic cup, urinating. I rolled over and went back to sleep. Really, what else could I do? Things might have gotten worse if we were going to be housed together for any length of time, but in intake roommates come and go quickly: you are there for a month or so, then rapidly move into general population (GP).

After moving into GP myself, I had a series of semi-psychotic roommates. One of them, Shandra, would scream at me if I tried to open my storage bins while she was sleeping. And because she seemed to sleep 20 hours out of 24 (and those 4 hours when she was awake were between 12:00 a.m. and 4:00 a.m.), I was yelled at a lot. The C.O.s only had to mediate a few times, though. Mostly, she would wind down after 5 or 10 minutes, and then we'd go back to ignoring each other.

Four months later, someone on the top tier needed a downstairs bunk for medical reasons, so she and I were told to swap beds. I moved in with Delilah. Delilah and I had always gotten along well in the dayroom. We had played Scrabble together and chatted while we waited for rec or mass movement. All that changed in the room, however. Any pretense of affability was gone; instead, I found that everything I did was a violation of her personal space. Now, I am a decent roommate by prison standards. I take a shower every day, I don't steal, I don't try to cadge commissary, I'm quiet, and I never touch any of my roommate's stuff. Really, you can't ask for more than that in here. But my mere presence was an affront to her—I could understand now why her old roommate had been so eager to get her bottom bunk medical profile and move out. But I'll bet that she wasn't too pleased with her new roommate, either.

Delilah was a master of the passive-aggressive. She never said anything directly to me. Instead, the muttered comments from the top bunk were barely audible. When I asked if she were speaking to me, she'd say no, she was praying and could I please let her worship in peace. She amped up her attacks quickly after I moved in. Fingernail clippings would appear in my water cup. My radio was accidentally brushed off my desk. Appointment slips or mail that was slipped under the door by an officer while I was asleep would disappear before they reached me. Delilah was the only roommate that I've ever actively feared. She possessed a volatile combination of religious mania and sociopathy that is only exacerbated by close confinement. Luckily, roommates are moved around a lot in GP wings. I have had several roommate changes since Delilah.

There has been a cavalcade of roommates in my prison life: most indifferent, a few truly terrible, and one absolutely outstanding. Mary was that wonderful roommate. We shared a tiny room for 5 years, and in that time she became closer to me than my own sister.

Our relationship began when I rejoined the dog program several years after leaving it initially. I had left for two reasons: one was that there was a lot of scrutiny and pressure as a dog handler—every officer marked everything you did, and every inmate did as well (which caused a lot of jealousy issues because, among the other benefits of being a dog handler, we were able to take long walks outside with our dogs on gorgeous, sunny days while the rest of the wing had to suffer with rec being canceled for the third weekend in a row), and either group could cause you a lot of grief if they had a grudge against you, the dog program, or both; and second was that the women in the program were extremely dysfunctional. The whole group was rife with backbiting, gossip, and *Survivor*-style alliances that came and went with brief but destructive regularity. But Chris had assured me that all of that stuff was no longer tolerated and that it was all rainbows and butterflies. So it was that I allowed myself to be suckered back in. I can't regret it, though, because it allowed me to become friends with Mary.

She was new to the dog program herself, and I was slotted to be her new roommate/handling partner as soon as the move could be arranged. I was dimly aware of her, a petite, pretty woman in her forties. I liked her comforting face, so I was hopeful that we would get along well as roommates. She mostly kept to herself, certainly didn't spend much time hanging out in the dayroom, and I had pegged her as rather shy. But the evening that we found out that we were going to be partners, she came skipping up to me in the dayroom, wearing a deceptively sweet smile.

"Hi, Erin. I'm so excited that we are going to be roommates!" She burbled.

"Me, too," I said. "I hope that they move us soon."

"Oh, I do too. We're going to get along great. I like for my room to be a sanctuary, a happy place, and I hope that you're comfortable there."

I allowed as how I enjoyed the same thing, and we chatted for a few moments more.

Then she said, "I am writing to my mom and dad about you, and I have a question. I heard that you are really good at English and spelling, do you mind helping me?"

"Sure," I answered.

If it were possible, she looked even more angelic. "Great!" she enthused. "Can you tell me if the word 'shithead' is hyphenated or not?"

I stared at her, stunned, as she blinked up at me with big doe eyes. It was then that I saw the glimmer of mischief in her eyes and realized, "Oh, yeah, I'm gonna love this girl. She actually has a sense of humor!" Mary threw her head back and laughed uproariously and crumpled up the sheet of paper that she had been brandishing.

We hadn't been together for long when we reached the first challenge of our friendship. I had told Mary prior to my moving in that I was not much of a talker in the room. If I want to socialize, I go out in the dayroom. "That's all right," she said, and I thought the matter was settled. Apparently not.

After about 2 weeks of cohabitating in what I thought was peaceful amity, her head suddenly swung down from the top bunk. "I can't stand it anymore! You never talk! What *is* that?"

I was confused. I had thought that we were getting along great. "Well, I told you that I'm not much of a talker," I said.

"I know, but you never talk!" The pitch of her voice rose as she gave vent to the feelings that had clearly been percolating for quite a while. "My ex-husband used to do that to me, just shut me out for days at a time and I hate that!"

Before that, we had not really talked about our personal lives. I knew about her daughter, and she about my three children, but we hadn't discussed much beyond that. This was the first time we had delved into deeper stuff. Truth be told, even though I had been down for over 5 years by then, it was the first time I had had a conversation like that with any of my roommates. Intimacy has never come easily to me in prison, and I can still, after 13 years, count on one hand the number of people I feel genuinely close to inside.

"God, I'm so sorry," I said. I had never realized that a silence I was so comfortable with could be toxic for someone else. "I didn't have any idea about that. I'll try to be more aware of what I'm doing, but please be patient with me. I've been this way for a long time."

We did begin talking more, but in some ways it was one of my greatest struggles in prison because I had reached the point in my life where I had promised myself that I was going to be more frank in my interactions. By inclination and habit, I am a circuitous talker. I could hover around a subject for 15 minutes before finally landing when a simple "yes" or "no" was all that was necessary. "Baffle 'em with bullshit," I remember my dad once saying, and that was a motto I could embrace. Glib and loquacious, I have the stereotypical gift of Irish blarney. Spin was my métier; a dream job for me would have been press secretary to the president of the United States (as long as he was a Democratic president, of course).

So candor and directness were new things for me. I'd managed to duck that resolution thus far by avoiding any conversation that could lead to confrontation, but obviously this was no longer an option. It helped, I think, that Mary seemed as committed as I to cleaving to open communication. It gave us permission to throw down the worst aspects of ourselves (and hoo boy were there lots of those between the two of us) and thrash them out. In reality, it was one extended experiment in maximizing interpersonal relations. Forget all those stupid groups that they force (in my case) inmates to participate in. (Even the word, *group*, creates within me a Pavlovian shudder of revulsion, since in a prison setting "group" as an unarticulated noun refers to a bunch of inmates yammering on for as long as you let them about the cruel tricks that life has played on them. I don't deny the therapeutic value of such activities, but I don't want to be there to see it, just like I wouldn't want to be in the operating room to see brain surgery. It may be necessary and beneficial, but I don't want to have any part of it.)

So Mary and I began a friendship that is, years later and separated by walls and miles, still a powerful force in our lives. We laugh now over some of the stuff that happened. I conveniently can't recall the many things that I used to do to get on her nerves, but some situations remain vivid. I'll never forget the time that I was sitting in the dayroom with Nadia one Saturday morning. I noticed that Mary was passing our table somewhat furtively but didn't give it much thought beyond that. It wasn't until I got back to our cell at the 5 minutes to count announcement that I realized what had happened.

Mary was in the top bunk, a book held up in front of her face as she resolutely "read" it. And there, spread across the floor, was a flood of water and, I fear, other stuff as well. The toilet had overflowed! "What the hell?!" I said. Mary peeped at me from over the top of her book. She was obviously frightened. I don't recall if she responded, but I added, "I don't care that you didn't clean this crap up, but you could have at least told me early enough that I could have cleaned it up myself before count. Now we are stuck in here for an hour with this mess!"

"I'm sorry, Erin," she said. "I accidentally dropped a sanitary pad down the toilet, but I'd hoped that it had just flushed away. And then I was afraid to tell you."

That stopped my irritation. I knew that her husband was a complete ass who had emotionally abused her in many ways, including verbal abuse whenever she, in his opinion, "crossed the line." Mary was operating under a strong self-preservation instinct, as many women have learned to do. My job—no, my opportunity—was to help her realize that she could be, at times, less than perfect without being beaten down in some way.

I spent a lot of time thinking about Mary. She was the first person in my whole life that I had gotten to know so intimately. And since neither she nor I were at all interested in any kind of romance with another woman, we could focus on our friendship without that particular distraction. I was learning to love Mary like the sister she came to be to me, in a Christ-based relationship sprinkled with the psychologically healthy habits that she and I were attempting to internalize. It wasn't always easy, though.

Once she was so angry at me that, apparently, she was bitching about me to someone at the lunch table. Of course a passel of other people heard her, and some helpful soul felt compelled to share that with me. I confronted her about it in the room.

"Did you say something about me at lunch today?"

I could see by her eyes that she was desperately tempted to deny it. It would have been so easy to lie. Then, to my vast admiration, she visibly steeled herself and said, "Yes, I did." No apologies, no excuses. Just honesty. I was still too pissed to acknowledge in that moment just how huge that was for her to do, but I didn't forget it, either. Still, some boundaries needed to be set.

"Mary, you cannot talk about me to other people. If you have a problem, let me know. We can discuss it. But I won't live with someone who does that to me."

Mary slowly climbed the ladder to her to bunk, and I heard her begin to weep, quietly at first, but slowly growing in volume. I, resolute, ignored her, just as loudly flipping the pages of the book I was in reality too upset to read. After about an hour, I heard her sniff, and her voice came wafting down from above, "I can't believe that you didn't try to comfort me."

I was snippier than I should have been when I said. "Well, that would have defeated the purpose of what I said, wouldn't it have?"

Our final conflict was over something that I can't even remember now. I think that it had to do with our dog, but am not sure. What is important is the ending of that conversation.

I was fed up. I believed that Mary was determined to push me away, as she had every other person in her life she had gotten close to. She'd been hurt so badly, trust wasn't safe for her. Rather than be abandoned again, she was going to do the abandoning herself. Hell no, I thought to myself. She's too important a friend to lose.

"Mary," I said, "You need to know that I have considered going to the counselor and asking to be moved into another dog handler's room. But you know what? I'm not going to. No matter what happens, you are stuck with me until they send you home. I'm committing to you. I am not going anywhere."

Mary gasped a little, then began to cry. We ended up talking for hours, the first of many such talks. It was no rare thing for the officer to come by the room at 2:00 a.m. count and peer in to find me sitting on the toilet (the only way I could see her face without sitting on the cell floor), engrossed in discussion. Everything cracked open after that: our most shameful secrets spilled out. We would cry together, laugh together, strategize, and gossip. She told me that no one had ever done that before, completely committed to her. I don't know why not—she was and is an amazing person. As for me, no one had ever known me so completely yet still loved me. It was a revelation to me, what a friendship based on faith and honesty could be. We never had a disagreement again, as I can recall.

The bulk of my memories of Mary are wonderful. For example, she's funny. Seriously, the girl should have been on *Saturday Night Live*, her gift for improv is that outstanding. There's Mary, standing in the sally port dancing like Beyonce, crooning "If you like it than you should have put a ring on it. . . ." Or holding the entire MILK group rapt as she told the story of how she was, in a former life, a small dog that was run over by a carriage at the palace of Versailles. Her storytelling skills were so great that we completely bought her story (even I, who doesn't believe in reincarnation, completely believed that *she* believed it), and didn't realize that it was a practical joke until she had subtly moved up to me and abruptly barked loudly at me and pretended to chomp my neck. OK, it sounds lame in the retelling, but I almost fell off of my chair when she did it, she startled me so badly, and the rest of the women laughed. The girl can command a room, I'm telling you. If that wasn't enough, she is also smarter than she will admit to, deeply thoughtful, and about as kind as a person can be.

Mary and I were roommates until she was shipped to another facility. I cried, she cried . . . neither of us wanted her to go, although we realized that this was just the next step in her going home, which was slated to occur in less than a year. It was so odd for me, not having her there. Even now, years later, something will come on TV or I will read an article about her "husband," Mark Wahlberg (this is Mary: she had pulled a full-page photo of Mark Wahlberg from some magazine and scrawled on the bottom: "To my beloved Mary, with much love, your affectionate Mark. XOXOXO." Then she propped it on her desk. God knows what the police thought, but it sure tickled me), and I will begin to swing my head upward to get her attention, then remember that she was home.

Because we were not allowed to write to each other while she was at Goochland Prison, we arranged a plan. I would send her mom letters, which Martha would read to Mary over the telephone (thus not breaking the rule against "three-waying" letters to other prisoners), and Mary would respond by writing my mom, who would return the favor by reading them to me on the phone. Because of MILK (Mothers Inside Loving Kids), Mary had met my parents and both my girls once. I knew her family much better because they lived closer to Fluvanna and thus were able to come to every visit. Since I seldom had a visit myself, I spent most of the day hanging out with Martha and Larry while Mary concentrated on her daughter, A. (A., like her mother, is one of the sweetest people I have ever met. She recently sent me a letter because, I guess, Mary had told her about my separation from Jack, Fran, and Gio and how painful that was. A. wrote to tell me that I was a wonderful person and that someday she was sure that my kids would want to get back in contact with me. Also, that she loved me herself. I don't know if what she predicted will happen, but I do know that I will keep that letter forever.) Her family graciously adopted me into theirs.

Mary's time at Goochland was terrible. She later told me that she couldn't seem to stop crying sometimes and that she was almost too depressed to function. There were all the pressures of preparing to return to real life (and it is a lot of pressure if you are determined not to repeat the mistakes that brought you here), being stuck working for someone who treated her like crap (her co-workers nicknamed her "Cinderella" because the staff supervisor seemed to dislike her so intensely), and, worst of all, her father died just before she was scheduled to go home.

But despite that, my indomitable Mary could not be completely squelched. She had me and my mother in stitches describing her obnoxious roommate who insisted on looming over her every time she watched her TV. Mary fixed her, though. She took to only watching conservative Christian programming. Ha! The roommate quickly found other things to do. Her sense of humor got her through that, I believe.

Mary is home now. It took her over 10 months to find a job (fortunately, she was able to move in with her mother, who is having a lot of medical issues since

Mary's father died, so Mary is the caretaker of her mother as well), and she has ended up working at a fast food restaurant that is owned by a high school friend. She takes pride in her work, though, and has been there for a couple of years now. Despite her good looks, she doesn't date much, since she refuses to go out with a man who doesn't share her Christian values as well as accept her past. Another reason I am proud of her: she doesn't hide the fact that she was in prison. Instead, she uses her experiences to talk to church groups and others. She has also remained lean since going home, and her bond with her daughter couldn't be tighter. We remain very close. Although she is not allowed to visit me—ex-cons can't come to FCCW unless they are related to the inmate—we talk on the phone weekly. She also takes care of me generously, buying me precious books sometimes, purchasing the ACS food package that friends are allowed to send us twice a year . . . when I called her last week to tell her about the JP4 players that they were supposed to be letting us get, her immediate response was, "You need one of those. You need to be one of the first with one of those, actually! Give me the details."

As great as that is, the best thing, though, is that she is deeply active in my life. No birthday, Christmas, or other occasion passes without a card from her (and usually her mother as well). She remembers what it is like inside, which is why I know that she will always remember me. Having shared my fears about what my life will be like when my mom and dad are gone, she has told me many times that she will be my "person," the one who calls the prison when I'm not getting medical attention and looks up vital information on the Internet. Not one of the dozens of people who have sworn to write me has ever followed through except for Mary. The small step in faith that I took in committing to her? She has already repaid that 100-fold. Say what you will about prisoners, their perceived lack of empathy, their brutality, their baseness, whatever. You may find that here, I don't deny it, but there are also many decent and kind people incarcerated as well. And even a few genuinely great ones. Mary is one of the latter.

Terrible cellmates are not as much of a problem if you have developed a good relationship with a sergeant or a lieutenant. Housing issues are usually resolved through their intercession. They might arrange for an unpleasant roommate to be removed, or even move out a decent one so that a favorite inmate can be housed with somebody of her choice, a friend or girlfriend. Barring a physical assault, the intercession of an official is usually the only way you can get rid of a roommate. Pandering to the police has never worked for me, though. I am unwilling to project the mixture of sycophancy and inappropriateness necessary to cultivate relationships like these. For my own self-respect, I prefer to be friendly but distant with officers.

Some of the housing horror stories are legendary. We retell them in tones of mingled awe and disbelief. There was tiny Rachel, who was so severely beaten once during count time by her 240-pound roommate that she had to spend 2 weeks in the infirmary. It took 5 minutes of screams and frantic intercom pushes from the surrounding cells for officers to respond.

Then there was Lorna, an unmedicated paranoid schizophrenic who was housed with a series of blameless elderly ladies, all of whom (according to Lorna) were dedicated to destroying her property, stealing from her, and urinating in her shampoo when she left the room. When Lorna was finally removed, the entire wing heaved a collective sigh of relief. Not even the officers had been able to ignore it when she was popped out of her room one night and smeared used sanitary pads over the walls of the bathroom.

Most of our anecdotes are more humorous than violent. My good friend Nadia often talks about the time that she walked into her cell in Goochland and found her roommate having sex on her bed. To Nadia's astonishment, the roommate didn't see what the problem was. She genuinely didn't know what more she could have done to be considerate. After all, she did put a sheet down on Nadia's bunk before she and her girlfriend used it.

Selfishly, it is always hard for me when a decent roommate goes home, or to seg, or is shipped to another facility. Not because she is someone I can trust not to slather herself in my Calgon Tropical Seas body lotion whenever I leave the room or because, even more important, she showers. Instead, any inclination I might have to miss her is consumed by the fearful anticipation of who is going to be sliding her boxes into my cell that night to take her place.

UNDER THE CAMERA

A few years ago, a new monitoring system was installed at the prison. Now there are cameras in the chow hall, the kitchen, the educational buildings, and on the yard. "State of the art," the inmates whispered. "Jesus, they can zoom in close enough to actually read your lips or catch you passing a kite. And it can see you in the dark, too, like its infrared or something!"

Officers were delighted with their new toy, flipping from camera one's view of the boulevard to camera two (library), three (DCE hallway), or four (gymnasium) with dizzying rapidity at the C.O. monitoring stations. Inmates would watch them as they demonstrated what the system could do, all the while oohing and aahing.

I just found the whole thing depressing. To me, here were more places where I couldn't even pretend to have a little privacy, those small oases away from the scrutinizing, video-recording eye of the camera lens. There aren't very many of them left: the bathroom stalls, our cells, and the bathrooms. When I first got here, the area at the back of each wing that is just beyond camera range was a regular hot zone of illicit activity at times, but they got rid of the camera's blind spot there as well.

I don't know why it bothers me so much. Obviously, I realize that there can be very little privacy in prison for security reasons. I know that I and my few belongings can be searched at any time, that all of my incoming mail is read, and that every phone call I make is recorded. And it is not as if I was doing anything wrong, really, that requires secrecy. I don't pass contraband or sneak around where I'm not supposed to go. I certainly don't have a girlfriend, so I don't need to find places where we can have sex. I guess I just liked the idea that I was trusted, if only a tiny bit and in a few places, not to break the rules.

The constant presence of the camera is one of the most emotionally difficult aspects of prison. For me, the pressure of knowing that I am constantly being observed, my every action judged (or misjudged), is incredibly taxing psychologically. Prison is a place where almost anything can be a violation of the rules if the officer writing the charge couches it in the correct terms, and I have seen enough bullshit charges served to know that I am always vulnerable. Hug a friend whose daughter had died? That can be deemed a 209 (the numeric code for sexual contact between inmates). Stand too close to another inmate, who then goes out and complains about you to the officer she is buddy-buddy with? That might be threatening or behaving in an intimidating manner. God forbid you touch her on the arm—then it's simple assault. And like the sword of Damocles hovering overhead, the camera is there, ready to bolster any charge, however specious. I find the camera to be a demeaning reminder that, as "state property," I have no privacy left, no matter how innocent my actions. Who can bear constant observation and not be reduced to quivering paranoia?

The camera's tapes never seem to be much use in exonerating an inmate from charges, though, or very helpful when there is a complaint from an inmate about a theft or other violation of her rights. A radio disappears from a table in the middle of the dayroom, but it is just too much bother to review the tape and see who stole it, or the tape will be too "unclear" to see the culprit. But rest easy, America, the officers can read our lips when we are sitting in the chow hall complaining about yet another scanty, poorly prepared meal.

Despite the seeming omnipresence of the cameras and guards, the women here have found several ways of evading observation. Every one of us knows exactly what area each camera covers and where any blind spots are. For example, a few of the wing's cell doors used to be out of camera range, so those were the best cells in which to hook up with your girlfriend or just hang out and talk (standing at each other's door is, shocker, yet another charge).

In the rear of the wing, back by the washers and dryers, was another great place to take care of business before all of the new cameras were installed. It was like a Moroccan bazaar back there when a shakedown was about to happen, and it's still the best place to be whenever you need to pass anything larger than a kite. Of course, you have to be pretty smooth when you make the transfer or you will attract the attention of the officer in the bubble who can see back there. My few early attempts to carry out such illicit acts were so lame that I've given up any pretense of prison suaveness. Although I like to think otherwise, it might be fear of my own ineptitude more than any reverence for the regulations that keeps me from getting into trouble sometimes.

The most pathetic contraband switch I was ever a part of was when I tried to give a former roommate, Twin, a bag of commissary. (All twins in prison seemed to be nicknamed "Twin." It is probably the least imaginative of the prison monikers.) Of course it is against the rules to give anybody anything in here, but she was broke and asked if I would hook her up with some sodas and chips. I'd lived with her long enough to know that she never got any money at all from home, and because she only made $0.23 an hour working 30 hours a week as a housekeeper in the wing, all of her money went to buy her personals—deodorant, shampoo, toothpaste, and soap can take quite a bit out of your paycheck if you only make $7 a week. Plus, she never gave me any scam about how she would "pay me back when her money got here." She and I both knew that it was a gift, and I respected that she didn't go from room to room in the wing constantly mooching food. I was the only person that she came to, and she only did so when she was really hungry.

So I loaded up a commissary bag with a few bags of BBQ potato chips, noodles, some oatmeal, and two six-packs of root beer. Not very much by outside standards, about $10 worth, but it would make a big difference on the days when the prison chow was so foul that not even a starving inmate could stomach it.

I sidled up behind Twin as she sat in the dayroom doing some homework for her GED class. "Hey, come over to my door when the police aren't looking," I said casually. "I've got some stuff for you."

Her face lit up. "Hey, thanks," she said. "We're cool, right? I really appreciate this."

"Don't worry about it," I answered. "I got it like that, so the least I can do is share a little, right?" I went back to my cell door to wait for the bubble officer to be distracted enough that Twin felt safe to come to my door. She walked up and, taking the bright orange commissary bag, started back to her own cell, her path casually swooping to the back of the wing, out of camera. I was just turning back into my cell when I heard a tremendous clanging. In the relative quiet of the dayroom, it sounded like 20 bowling balls thundering down the metal chute.

It was the root beer. Twin had managed to drop the commissary bag, and now she was frantically scrambling around on the floor trying to gather up the rolling cans. One had burst, and the sweet, sticky soda was foaming out like a geyser. Trying to look uninvolved, I glanced at the bubble and saw the officer standing up to get a better look at the ruckus. The few people that had been sitting in the dayroom looked on, frankly amused at Twin's plight. Neither they nor I made any move to help her. It's not that she was disliked, but she was clearly on her own. Any help from me or anyone else would involve us in a potential hassle with the C.O.s. And Twin didn't expect any help. Why should anyone go down with her?

The officer in the bubble watched Twin pick up the soaked commissary and blot the mess with piles of sodden paper towels, then he sat back down at the control panel. Either he was too lazy to fill out any paperwork for a charge or he was simply cutting her a break, but she emerged sticky but unticketed from the mishap.

The camera is the most powerful psychological weapon available to the DOC. It does exactly what the state intends for it to do, not only recording our every move but also never letting us forget for even a moment where and what we are. I can, with a great deal of effort, ignore the uniforms and unhealthy prison pallor of my friends. I can sit and laugh, play cards, or watch a recent release on the DVD player with them. I sometimes try to pretend that we are just a normal group of people hanging out together, but I will never be successful at visualizing this small fantasy of normality because that damn camera never, ever goes away. No matter how hard I try to ignore it, its presence is burned into my brain. My babysitter, judge, and stalker: forgetting it for even one moment might free me enough to do something I would have done before prison, like hug a friend or share a pack of noodles with someone who is hungry, all illegal acts if captured by the unrelenting eye of the camera.

NOTE

1. As a general rule, modern prisons are tame-looking establishments. This is especially true for women's prisons.

REFERENCES

Ferguson, R. A. (2014). *Inferno: An anatomy of American punishment*. Cambridge, MA: Harvard University Press.

Irwin, J. (2009). *Lifers: Seeking redemption in prison*. New York: Routledge.

Johnson, R. (2002). *Hard time: Understanding and reforming the prison* (3rd ed.). Belmont, CA: Wadsworth.

Johnson, R., & McGunigall-Smith, S. (2008). Life without parole, America's other death penalty: Notes on life under sentence of death by incarceration. *The Prison Journal, 88*(2), 328–346.

Liebling, A. (1999). Prison suicide and prisoner coping. In M. Tonry & J. Petersilia (Eds.), *Prisons, crime and justice: An annual review of research* (pp. 283–360). Chicago: University of Chicago Press.

Pollock, J. (2004). *Prisons and prison life: Costs and consequences*. New York: Oxford University Press.

Toch, H. (1992a). *Living in prison: The ecology of survival*. Washington, DC: American Psychological Association.

Toch, H. (1992b). *Mosaics of despair: Human breakdowns in prison*. Washington, DC: American Psychological Association.

CHAPTER 3

Love in a Cold Climate

Troubled relationships are the norm in prison. Abusive homes and destructive domestic relationships are transplanted to the prison and sometimes play themselves out in the cell, the domestic world of the prison, and sometimes a microcosm of all that is wrong in the lives of women in prison (Johnson, 2009; Pollock, 2002, 2009). A short story on this delicate but vital subject, entitled "Cell Buddy," is included in Appendix C, with introductory remarks by George.

Sex is common, even easy to find behind bars. There is the "boo," short for booty call. The boo is the "girl on the side," a sexual plaything rather than a candidate for a lasting relationship. Lifers, we learn, scrupulously avoid entanglements with boos. "Most of these women share the sexless, gently bickering bonding of the long-married." (The long-married might dispute this characterization, but George's point is well taken.) Most prisoners are short-termers, and many of them form couples in search of sex—emotional comfort, too, but definitely sex. Other inmates will "10-4" for these women—serve as lookouts—but even so, couples often are caught, largely because a jilted lover or some other disgruntled person turns them in.

Prisons for women are notable for the surrogate families that are spawned there, where women hope to replace lost family ties or, even more often, to create the family ties they never had (Owen, 1998; Pollock, 2002). Prison families can be dysfunctional, with inmates variously behaving as squabbling kids, promiscuous teens, and irritable parents. Following this line of analysis, there is child sexual abuse in prison—with some inmates and, as the stereotype goes, many officers taking advantage of the vulnerable, emotionally immature women. Yet the problem of sexual abuse in women's prisons, serious as it is (see McNaughton, 2007; Struckman-Johnson & Struckman-Johnson, 2002, 2006), is in some ways not as bad as outsiders think. Many women find genuine comfort in their relations with one another. Some liaisons with staff, George believes, are consensual, even though they technically count as rape since consent in this context is a legal oxymoron. In others ways, sexual abuse in prison is as bad as one might imagine, if not worse: one major, a *large and powerful man and a formidable figure of authority, exploited women freely until his reign of abuse ended with his own incarceration for rape.*

People will argue about whether sex in prison can ever be consensual, even among inmates, but from the prisoner's point of view, consensual sex, especially among inmates, is a distinct and desirable possibility, sometimes resulting in ersatz prison marriages (see the romance of Dusty and Babygirl in this chapter). To deny the possibility of bona fide sexual relationships in prison is to deny what little autonomy the prisoners feel they have.

Erin George's advice for prison love life, whether that love life is played out by mail (as in prison pen pals) or in person (with a boo or stable partner; more rarely with a staff member) comes down to this: it is safer and wiser to commit to your showerhead, a "straight shooter" you can count on and that is not against the regulations. Hassine (2011) makes a similar point for men, although the details of method differ, with form (of relief) following (organic) function. —Robert Johnson

A screech of pure rage woke me up one morning. It was 5:00 a.m., and the wing had just returned from the breakfast chow that I choose to try and sleep through every weekday. Startled into a wary half-wakefulness, I tried to identify the source of the sound. No, it wasn't my alarm clock, and my roommate hadn't turned on the TV too loud again. Then I heard, "If you don't stop meeting that bitch at breakfast both of us are gonna end up in seg and her ass will be in the infirmary!"

Dammit. Pam and Angel were at it again. Pam and Angel had been an item since Pam realized that Angel had too much commissary to eat by herself and not enough self-esteem to realize or care that she was being played. Theirs was a passionate relationship, with the stormy desire attendant to most prison romances. This time Pam had apparently hooked up with yet another of her former boos in the chow hall, and some friend of Angel hadn't wasted any time running back to let Angel know about Pam's indiscretions.

Angel was one of the "cute little girls," a petite brunette who typically carried herself as if she were a wee bit better than everyone else. She wasn't exactly pretty—too-lavish makeup failing to disguise the evidence of a hard life kept her from that. But she could be appealing enough with her face scrubbed into a semblance of vulnerability. Any traces of softness were gone, though, as she thrust her rage-twisted face a few inches from Pam's impassive expression.

"Why do you keep chasing after that bitch?" she demanded, arms flailing dramatically as they stood by the bathrooms on the top tier. Pam let Angel rage on without interruption. Pam was a "boy," one of the prison studs that makes no secret of her sexual orientation. Many boys aren't just "gay for the stay" like most of the cute little girls. They had been lesbians on the street, and nothing has changed for them in here. You can identify a stud immediately. Most of them have buzz cuts or short, tightly braided plaits. Although they wear the same uniforms as the rest of us, boys manage to give them their own distinctive look. The elastic-banded pants droop low, in some cases barely clearing the knees. Under them are at least three more layers of clothes—sweatpants, long johns, and the thin blue athletic shorts we are allowed to wear during rec time. Boys wear their uniform shirts about five sizes too large over sweatshirts and a long john top, even on the most miserable and humid Virginia summer days. Many of them look eerily masculine, sometimes even down to having obvious facial hair (there is actually a regulation on the books that female inmates have to have clean-shaven faces), and there is always one inmate that everyone whispers is a "morpha-dite" (the prison corruption of the word *hermaphrodite*).

Pam had a long, repetitious history at FCCW. She had been moved out of every building at least once for getting the 209s and the "unauthorized area" charges that accompany most sexual activity, so wherever she was housed now, odds were good that she could find at least one former girlfriend to restart a relationship with. Angel was just the latest in a long string of women, although during the calmer times she liked to say that what she and Pam had was real, that none of those other bitches meant anything to Pam but a way to get cigarettes and get off.

When Angel finally seemed to be running out of steam, Pam started talking to her earnestly, a look of studied innocence on her face. I couldn't hear what she was saying, but the wheedling tone was obvious. I imagine that she was giving her the same excuses that they all give when they are screwing around on their girlfriends—that her ex came up to her in the chow line, she wasn't looking for that bitch at all. Or she might be using the "blame it on the best friend" scam, that whoever had told Angel that fucked-up lie was just another earth-disturber who was jealous of the good thing that Angel and she shared.

It didn't take long before Angel was nodding her head in agreement with whatever it was that Pam was saying. The quarrel finished, I put in my earplugs and tried to get a bit more sleep before morning count.

Girlfriends are the source of the majority of the drama and tickets here. If it doesn't spring from the boo fights, then the ingenious machinations of star-crossed (or C.O.-crossed) lovers to be together are a sure way to get charges or seg time. After all, it's risky work, bulldagging. Bulldagging refers to any ploy you use to be with your baby. It ranges from walking really slowly on the boulevard in the hopes that your sweetie can manage to be outside at the same time (this is called delaying and hindering, and it's a charge) to the extreme of swiping a worker's green uniform so you can sneak into the building where your girlfriend works (that might include theft, entering an unauthorized area, or lying to an officer or a staff member, all of which are, of course, charges as well). The variations on this theme are endless and inevitably discovered by the officers. Usually there is a disgruntled former girlfriend to help the police look in the right direction.

These bulldagging schemes rarely work, and the payoff, if any, is limited, but it's hard to keep a sex-starved, highly motivated inmate down. Bulldaggers will pay the $5 co-pay to medical for a phony illness in the hopes that they will be given sick call appointments at the same time and maybe get to spend half an hour together in the stuffy, overcrowded waiting room. They will volunteer to clean trash cans in the yard on the off chance that their boo might come out for a walking rec. And FedEx would make a fortune if they could deliver all the notes and messages that get passed in here. Kites, prison slang for the notes that we are not supposed to write to each other, are everywhere: stuffed in library books, stashed in potted plants, and of course hand-delivered by accomplices who live in the same wing as the intended recipient. All this subterfuge, all of these complex schemes, and so much effort is put into play just to connect with a boo.

Ah, the boo. The boo is the most maligned, gossiped-about, ridiculed figure in the pantheon of prison characters. Boo, which is short for the street term "booty call," is the casual girlfriend, the cheap feel in the sally port, the temporary object of someone's affections (although most boos don't realize the impermanence of their positions). Boos bounce from stud to stud in their search for true love. They're usually not really gay—they just equate self-worth with being attached to someone, anyone, and the more jealous and controlling the better. But no one in a serious relationship uses the term boo. You might refer to a girlfriend, or even call your significant other your wife, but never (except perhaps in jest) will she be your boo.

There are some relationships that do last, but those are usually found among the long-termers, and they are typically based on something a little more substantial than the foundations of the majority of the prison romances. Unlike those couplings that are based solely on dysfunction and greed, many women serving long sentences come together more from a desire to have a connection with a partner, a significant other with whom they can share the pains and the rare joys that can be found in here. Couples like this are relatively stable, and most of them have managed to be housed in the same unit or room together through the assistance of sympathetic staff members. This is not so they can have sex conveniently—most of these women share the sexless, gently bickering bonding of the long-married. More important is the knowledge that they will be coming home to the same trusted person each day after work, someone who has shared their losses and triumphs and, like survivors of the same war, has seen the same slow erosion of privileges and changes in the staff and policy that they have. They know all the same people and stories, which is a great comfort for someone who has in all likelihood lost contact with spouse and family.

Prison relationships are typically of short duration, but sometimes a couple chooses to make a firm commitment. Dusty and Babygirl were two who decided to do this. After a year together (which is like 10 years on the outside), they sent out invitations to their wedding. Even though Babygirl had a man on the street that came to visit her every weekend and Dusty was married with four kids, they invited all their people on the wing to witness their vows.

"Babygirl, I love you. We are going to be together forever, even when we get home. Nobody else means nothing compared to you," Dusty said in front of the assembled dayroom (including a few mildly interested officers). "You are going to be my true wife."

Babygirl smiled up at Dusty. "Baby, I love you. There's nobody here who comes close to you. I'll be with you forever." They exchanged rings that Dusty had bought from an inmate who had gone home a few weeks earlier, and as they hugged, the inmates around them laughed and cheered, showering the couple with confetti made from newspaper and stolen construction paper. One enterprising kitchen worker had even stolen a bag of dried white rice.

Afterward was the highlight of any prison gathering: the food. Fats, Collie, and Gina made a wedding dinner, including nachos, pasta salad, potato chips, and a chocolate cake made out of Swiss rolls. Everyone had contributed to the feast, which was served festively from garbage bags and potato chip packages. There was even a pile of creatively wrapped presents for the newlyweds.

Sadly, these relationships are about as successful as their counterparts on the street. Typically, these experiments in monogamy, though, end with both participants in segregation rather than divorce court.

For most of the couples, though, the primary goal is sex: how to get it and how to hide it from the officers. Girlfriends aren't often housed in the same cell, because even the most clueless C.O.s figure out who they are pretty quickly, so their pressing need is to find a way to be alone together. Plans range from subtle to outrageous.

Because so many relationships in here are based more on proximity than any genuine connection, new relationships form quickly when staff breaks up a couple by moving one of the women to another building or wing. These women seem unable to be partnerless for more than a few days, but the chances are good that they can immediately find a new soul mate that lives in the same wing. This makes hooking up with someone somewhat easier. When both parties live in the same unit, the usual way to have some time alone together is to find someone in the dayroom to 10-4 for you. The 10-4 is the lookout who will holler something innocuous when an officer comes into the wing to do cell checks while you and your boo are in your room (this happens most often while the roommate is out at work or class, blissfully unaware of what goes on in her absence).

"Hey Teenie, can you bring me your *TV Guide* to look at when you get a chance?" someone might yell as a veiled warning when the C.O. pops open the wing door. Then the lookout will engage the officer in conversation or distract him with a complaint, providing an effective diversion while the girlfriend makes her escape. A few officers are pretty cool about girlfriends. They're the ones who will make an excessive amount of noise at the desk before their rounds when they suspect two favored inmates are having sex. Shoot, sometimes the officers even like to watch. Girls can get away with a lot if they have an officer covering up for them. If the price is a third-party voyeur, well, so be it.

Sometimes women try doing it in the showers and the handicapped bathrooms (there's a lot more room to maneuver in there, and the entrance is partially obstructed from the wing camera by the overhanging top tier), but they are inevitably caught. They're usually snitched out by someone in the wing. It's a humiliating experience for those who are discovered *in flagrante delicto*, although the rest of us find it highly entertaining.

"Ms. Carver," the officer standing outside the shower will intone, "will you please exit the shower?" A shamefaced inmate hastily tying up her robe slinks out, snapping the shower curtain closed tightly. Maybe if she comes out quickly enough, they won't look inside of the stall. No dice, though. The busybody in room 101 intercommed the bubble as soon as Carver's girlfriend had joined her, so the police knew exactly what was going on. The C.O. has to go through the motions of asking, though. "Were you alone in there?"

No matter how busted they are, all of them try to bluff their way out of it at first, either feebly (knowing that the 209 is inevitable) or with a show of great outrage. "I don't know why the hell you police always mess with me. Shit. I was just taking a shower. Ain't no other bitches in here. How stupid do you think I am? This is just harassment."

By now, the inmate has worked herself up into a righteous fervor. She has almost convinced herself that she was indeed alone in there, and this is just another of the myriad injustices that have been fabricated against her. The C.O. calmly listens to her diatribe, then raps on the metal shower stall. "C'mon out," he says.

And out comes the boo. She has had a bit more time to pull herself together, so she is fully dressed. There's nothing really that either of them can say at that point, so both are trotted off to the sergeant's office. After a brief flurry of gossipy whispers, the wing settles down again, but the whole story will be spread around the compound by lunchtime the next day. This is the kind of anecdote that can be enjoyed for years, with no embellishment necessary.

Some women barely bother to try and hide what they are doing. A few months ago in the structured living unit, for example, several girls were busted because they were all clustered around two girls who were actually having sex there in the dayroom, trying to block them from the officer's view. That's pretty rare, though. Most inmates are willing to take a few risks to get it on with their girlfriend, but not usually to that extreme.

PRISON RAPE ELIMINATION ACT

We're number two! We're number two! Number two in what, you may ask. Well, I'm glad that you did. Are we second in the nation in, oh, I don't know, the awarding of GED degrees? Nope. No way. How about one step from the top in successful anti-recidivism programs? No, not that either. Not even close. But we have earned one distinction: FCCW is nationally renowned (within the extremely limited circles that pay attention to such statistics) for having the second-highest rate of substantiated allegations of sexual misconduct in the United States. This is not just prison rumor. We are so famous, in fact, for these inappropriate hijinks that our former warden, Wendy Hobbs (her real name), was called on to testify before the federal Justice Department's Review Panel on Prison Rape. Obviously I wasn't there, but I hear that she gave what I shall diplomatically term a politically adroit representation of the situation at our prison. 'Nuff said on that.

We ground-scuttling prisoners had our own introduction to the fabulous world of the Justice Department's attempt at prison reform regarding (in our case) inappropriate attention—or lack of attention, as the case may be—to convict lady parts. As they like to do, they began by rousing us from our hard metal bunks at 5:00 in the morning. "You're going to see a video!" a counselor informed us. Bleary-eyed and semi-somnambulant, everyone staggered into the dayroom.

"Where are the donuts and bagels?" I joked as I pulled up a chair to an already crowded table. My sally was met with the amount of warmth that you might expect at that ungodly hour, so I proceeded to shut up. But that's OK; the counselor had his own elaborate joke that he was about to present, one even less funny than mine.

"This morning we are here to talk about the PREA program," he said. Huh? What the hell was PREA? Dear god, what new horror was this? Mr. Cornwell droned on, "Blah blah federal law blah blah blah President Bush blah your safety blah blab blab free confidential hot line blah blah any questions?"

We stared at each other blankly. One woman raised her hand tentatively. "What exactly is PREA?" she asked.

The counselor sighed and said, "Look, we got a video. Just watch that and then we can see if it answers your questions." After 15 minutes of fumbling with wires and VHS tape players, he got the darn thing working. I have mercifully blanked out the specific contents of the video, but by the end I had the dim idea that this was some new federal program intended to save us from the sexual predations of not only other inmates, but staff as well.

"Any questions?" the counselor asked us again, looking at his watch. It was getting close to count time, which is one of their favorite tricks: scheduling meetings right before we have to be locked back into our cells so they don't have to face lots of pesky questions from the lower beings.

Apparently Logan had been paying closer attention than I had, and her hand shot up into the air. Logan is very forthright, intelligent, and articulate. She is also as relentless as a pitbull when it comes to sniffing out and attacking instances of unfairness or illegality regarding inmates. She has the oratory skills of a lawyer and the morals of a Mafia hitman (at least in regard to issues like this), and if we ever elected a formal inmate spokeswoman, she'd have my vote in a heartbeat.

"So let me get this straight," she said. "If we are being in any way harassed sexually, your fabulous plan is to lock us up in segregation?"

The counselor winced and tried to gloss it over. It was obvious that that particular aspect of PREA (which I eventually learned stood for Prison Rape Elimination Act) was one that he wished she hadn't noticed. Mr. Cornwell lacked the political acumen of Warden Hobbs, but he did his best to set that topic a'spinnin'.

"Well now, that's for your own safety, of course. It's not segregation, it's protective custody." Oh, that makes a big difference. All right, then. "We don't want anyone to ever feel threatened at this facility," he added piously. As one, 45 women gave a snort of derision.

"So" said Logan, drilling down relentlessly, "if I am the victim of sexual harassment, attack, or other related misbehaviors, I am the one who is punished?"

Poor, poor Cornwell. He fell right into that giant hole that she'd deftly dug. Didn't even see it coming. "It's not a punishment," he insisted. "You are in no way punished for protecting yourself."

Logan sneered and bared her fangs for the kill. "Not punished? How in the world can you suggest that I wouldn't be punished? Say some officer gropes me in the sally port. I do what you say you want me to do and report it to another officer. And then what happens'? I am whisked out of my cell and plunked into seg *for my own protection.* I cannot go to work from seg, so I will lose my already pathetic paycheck for as long as it takes to get the investigation sorted out. How long are these investigations, anyway? Weeks? Months?" She doesn't pause for him to answer. That's probably a mercy on her part, because there is clearly no way he can respond without looking like a complete administration stooge. "I also lose my bed, and if I have a decent roommate for once, let me assure you, that is quite a punishment. I've been in the Honor Wing for two years. Would I lose that all because of some C.O. with twitchy hands? And being shackled like a dog on a leash whenever they deign to allow me to shower? Yeah, that's a real incentive to tell. Not to mention the other things that I would lose: contact visits with my family, classes, church. . . . And worst of all, I would be a snitch. You can't tell me that every inmate and staff member on this compound wouldn't know that I was the one who ratted out nice Mr. So-and-so who is such a good guy, and I become either some pathetic inmate who has an axe to grind and is targeting him for no good reason or I am a mental health case who misconstrued his wonderful niceness and twisted it into something else. Yeah," she finished up, openly scoffing, "I would come out of that one completely unscathed."

Mr. Cornwell looked stunned. "Um, we have time for one more question. Anybody?" Other than a few quiet cheers of, "Go Logan!" and "You rock, girl," there were no takers. Obviously no one in their right mind would be taking avuncular President Bush up on his offer of protection.

After that, for the most part PREA drifted from our awareness. Things carried on as they always had: inmates had sex with other inmates, C.O.s made off-color remarks to each other and the prisoners, and we continued to hear rumors about far worse shenanigans occurring in utility closets and staff bathrooms. Actually, the only accomplishment of PREA was the posting of what was, in my mind, the most magnificent memo ever in the history of the Fluvanna Correctional Center for Women.

I had ambled over to the bulletin board as I do on occasion to see what latest piece of stultifying prose has made its way there. I was delighted, nay, thrilled, to see the following memo (this is a paraphrase because the original memo is long gone and I lacked the foresight to hand copy it. Damn it.):

> The PREA hotline has been established for use by inmates in order to comply with the regulations set forth in the Prison Rape Elimination Act. This hotline is only to be used when actual incidents of sexual harassment and other misconduct have occurred. This hotline is NOT to be used to report rotten food in the chow hall, lack of access to the bathroom, or failure of the building staff to respond to the buzzer in the control area. Failure to use the PREA hotline for its intended purpose may result in a charge.

The memo blathered on a bit more in that vein, but the jist of it was that while pesky inmates were calling it up to bitch about everything from petty annoyances to major concerns, the administration didn't want to hear about anything unless a hoo-haw, pee-pee, or ta-ta (or any combination of these) was involved. It simply delighted me to imagine a convict huddled over the mouthpiece of the phone, muttering to an anonymous answering machine in downtown Richmond that they had been served rotten strawberries in the chow hall again and why couldn't we get edible food here? I don't know why it tickled me so much. I guess it was because it was just so stupid, this inane, insane memo. It really wasn't funny. I know that. People here are so desperate to get some help, they would even reach out to a robot that in no way would address their issues just to go on the record. Plus, it was further confirmation that the DOC does not give a damn about anything unless they are forced to, either by federal law or public outrage (which is pretty thin on the ground when it comes to the confined).

One balmy afternoon we all returned to the housing unit at mass movement only to discover absolutely enormous, bright blue signs posted over each telephone. These frickin' things were huge—like 4 feet by 1 foot, with one over each of the 5 telephones—and in massive letters they had the phone number for the PREA hotline printed, urging us to use the number if necessary. Someone, somewhere downtown, was getting pretty antsy about the situation here and he laid out the cash for these monstrosities. And again I laughed, because I knew exactly why they were freaking out.

"Sheesh, look at those things," I said to my roommate of the time, Mary. "Well, I guess you know why they've put those things up, don't you?"

"No, why?"

I was shocked that she hadn't heard the latest, most (to make a small pun) major gossip to hit FCCW in probably ever. I gave a long, drawn-out "*Well!*" (We had been roommates for several years by then, and this syllable with that emphasis had become our shorthand for "I know some really good dirt, so sit down and brace yourself.") "You didn't hear about Major Gee? Hoo, boy, he's in some deep shit. You know Kiki, the one who used to work in the kitchen, who just got home, right? Well, I heard that she turned up on his doorstep to let him know that she was pregnant! And since she's only been home a minute, it's not like it happened on the street. Apparently he wasn't as welcoming as she hoped he would be—must like his women only when they are in prison uniforms—so she turned him in for messing around with her. That's what they're saying, at least."

Mary gasped. "No way! Seriously?"

I took far too much pleasure in saying, "Oh yes indeed. Not only that, I hear that she's not the only one who he fooled around with. Word is that one of his kicks was to call someone to his office and have her, well, service him under his desk. Rumor of course, as to the details, but it's the truth that he's going to be on the news tonight. They're actually pressing charges against him, can you believe it?"

Mary shook her head. "And this guy is in charge of security. Awesome."

I'm betting that the assumption by much of the public is that the inmates who have sex with any officer are just a bunch of whores anyway. What more can you expect from a convict? Major Gee was probably seduced. Thirty times. It could happen to anyone, right?

Major Gee did indeed have charges filed against him. Not only that, he ended up being sentenced to multiple years in prison. I hope he received the same careful, quality attention that the women under his charge did.

After this scandal, the warden in charge at the time, Ms. B. J. Wheeler, left unceremoniously and rapidly, and other staff members were scrutinized. Her replacement, the aforementioned Wendy Hobbs, was brought in as a reformer, someone who "really understood the issues facing women in corrections and she is a good Christian to boot!" Hmm. She stayed about a year before moving up the ladder to a more influential position in the DOC system. Things did change a little bit, but not as much as one would have hoped, as future events would demonstrate.

For example, it came to light after subsequent Justice Department investigations that women were still being held in cells without access to a toilet and being charged and held in segregation if they were unable to stop from soiling themselves. This was especially hard on the older ladies, or the ones who had medical conditions, but anyone was vulnerable. It even happened to me once, to my great shame. All I can say is thank God that my roommate was being outcounted at her job that evening, otherwise it would have been almost unbearable.

We had been locked down for several hours due to pill line and count, and I was in distress. EXTREME distress. One of the delectable prison meals had not gone down well, and I found that I had an excruciating case of diarrhea. By 7:00 p.m. (we had been locked down around 4:30 p.m.) I couldn't take it any more, and my pleas to the control area went unanswered. I fortunately had a bag of pretzels, the entire contents of which I dumped on my desk, and I then proceeded to squat over the empty pretzel bag, praying that I wouldn't overflow or miss. I managed to hit the target (barely), but then had to sit there for another half hour clutching the full, warm, fetid bag of liquid feces, unable to put it down for fear that it would spill.

As soon as count cleared, I slammed my door wide open to air out the room before my cellie returned and rushed to the toilet with my humiliating package. This happened recently, long after Warden Hobbs had departed for the lusher pastures of a higher administrative calling, so I can say with certainty that things still have not improved significantly.

Since the ignoble departure of Major Gee, we have had other majors. The best was a woman who had been in corrections for years and managed to balance sensible discipline with compassion. She didn't stay long, though, because, tragically, her son was murdered and, from what I hear, she was unable to return to work at a place like Fluvanna. Of course we all understood that, but everyone was grieved by her situation, not only for the selfish reason that she was a great major who made life here actually bearable but also because she was a truly good person. She has since been replaced. Since said replacement is still here, it behooves me not to make any sort of comment about her. I will say that she is inordinately fond of making sure that we always walk in straight lines. This is a really, really important concern. Vital. As far as I can tell, that appears to be the main priority of her agenda.

We have also had other sex scandals since Major Gee. You would think that officers would learn, but apparently not. One recent incident involved a cocky jerk of a C.O. who is also going to court for his inappropriate conduct regarding female inmates. Since this fella had been infamous for years for his behavior in this area, it surprised me that they actually bothered to finally take action. It only goes to show that you can get away with a lot before you make a big enough mess that they can no longer ignore it or cover it up.

And just to show that men aren't the sole victimizers in this world, a few months ago, C.O. Ricardo, a lesbian officer, was walked off the grounds because of her relationship with an inmate. This one is particularly sordid, not just because this C.O. gave up her career for a woman that is serving over 30 years with no possibility of parole and thus can never have a real relationship with her, but it turned out that the whole thing was brought to the attention of the administration because the lesbian officer's girlfriend (another C.O. at Fluvanna, Ms. Swisher) got jealous of Ms. Ricardo's tête-à-têtes with Malina, so she (Ms. Swisher) found Malina's girlfriend from the street on Facebook and clued her into what was going down (ahem). Oooh, juicy! So C.O. Ricardo was walked off the grounds and Malina spent a stint in seg "under investigation." No institutional charges were ever filed against Malina, and I guess since Ricardo didn't manage to perform a miracle and knock up her inmate paramour, she is free from the fear of being criminally charged.

The administration almost seems more accommodating to those inmates who find their lovin' with male staff members rather than their fellow incarcerated individuals. I suppose at least that is more natural to the wholesome people who are our moral betters. And they made that bias quite clear.

For a long time, the prison ran what we all called the "locker room," a housing unit stuffed with every stud on the compound. Ha! The inmates got the better of the staff in that case, though. Like the sexually versatile earthworm, many of them promptly switched from stud to femme and paired off with one of their new housemates. Curses! Foiled again.

This was an especially bad deal for those women who were genuine lesbians and carried themselves in that way. It didn't matter if they were actually involved in destructive relationships, just the appearance of masculinity was enough to send you over there.

Thus, despite the better angels in Washington, the environment here remains one in which sexually inappropriate behaviors are tacitly condoned, if not blatantly supported by the efforts of staff to cover up said transgressions. There is an atmosphere of hopelessness at Fluvanna right now, that plunge into despair that is only made more painful in contrast to those brief interludes where things actually appear to be improving. We all know that such positive moments are temporary, that we will inevitably spiral into worse and worse situations where you begin to wonder why you even bother to try and behave properly. Most of us get punished for the behaviors of others, while someone's own destructive actions are largely ignored until that is no longer possible.

Even in the Honor Wing things have come to such a point that it is almost like living in GP. Most of us live in the Honor Wing because we are older, tired, and just want a little peace at the end of the day. There are no privileges associated with the wing to speak of, just blessed calm. Calm, that is, until Tessie and Tina's relationship blew up.

Tessie and Tina had lived in the Honor Wing together for several years when true love suddenly bloomed. True love, or Tina realized that Tessie got a boatload of cash from home each month and was willing to feed her insatiable appetite daily. Either way, they were suddenly "a thing." At first, they were merely an annoyance to the rest of us. They would spend their time either touching each other in a decidedly creepy way (relatively rare behavior in our housing unit, although the norm elsewhere) or arguing. They would hog the microwave for an hour at a time while a line of impatient inmates who only wanted 2 minutes to heat up a bag of microwave popcorn stretched out behind them. They bogarted a table all weekend long so others were forced to pull chairs together and socialize around the trashcans. Plus, they were downright nasty about it. Rude? Check. Irritating? Check.

One evening, however, the dayroom was relatively calm. Suddenly, there was a scream and a thud from Tina's room. Every head swiveled to the top tier, and a second, smaller thud, was heard. Ann and Katie were at the microwave, and they had a clear view of the noisy whatever that was obviously happening in Tina's cell. Logan and Teeny gingerly walked to Tina's room, peered in, and hurried back to their respective rooms. The rest of us openly stared. After about 5 minutes, Tessie shuffled out of Tina's room and returned to her own. As soon as her door shut. I collared Ann.

"Jesus, what happened?"

Ann laughed. "It was crazy. After that giant thud nothing happened. You couldn't see Tessie or Tina. Then a moment later I saw Tessie come flying across the room and hit the wall high up, then sort of slide down to the floor. The next thing I knew, Tina had her in a headlock and was beating the crap out of her."

I must admit that it was kind of satisfying to hear that Tessie was on the receiving end of the violence for once. Tessie was usually the abuser in her pairing with Tina, plus every other relationship she'd been in. Shoot, she was in here for killing her man on the street. Dizzy told me that she used to be housed next to Tessie when she lived with her old girlfriend, Puff, a teeny little thing who must have liked getting smacked around because she sure liked being with Tessie. I figured that Tina must have finally snapped. And unlike Puff, she was no little thing. She was a big, healthy girl like Tessie, all bulked up on Ramen noodles and chow hall bread, and could match her pound for pound.

Ann is somewhat of a *rara avis* at Fluvanna: white, middle class, well educated. I wondered, therefore, at her sanguine reaction to the violence she had witnessed. "You don't look like that bothered you at all," I commented.

Ann shrugged. "I lived so long in population where that kind of thing happens all of the time, I guess I got used to seeing it. It's just what happens around here."

"Doesn't it bother you that you have gotten used to violence like that? That prison has changed you so much?" I asked her.

Ann looked unconcerned. "No, I plan on forgetting all about this place as soon as I go home next year. Good riddance to all of them!"

I guess that about twenty IMSs dropped immediately, because the next afternoon first Tina, then Tessie, was called to the unit manager's office for a good long while. The police must have looked at the cameras, because Logan and Teeny were also called out, although they were only out there for a minute or two. I'm guessing that they said they didn't see anything, which is what I certainly would have done in that situation. As much as I wished Tessie and Tina out of the wing, I sure wouldn't have tried to play a role in making that happen. They didn't need to hear anything from Logan and Teeny anyway, since it was all on tape.

But as great as cameras are, Tina was smart enough to do her business in a blind spot in her cell, so all the authorities could give them tickets for was an unauthorized area charge for Tessie (it wasn't her room, and therefore verboten) and an abetting charge for Tina. So here was the situation. Everyone knew that they were in a physically abusive relationship. The powers that be had certainly gotten an earful on that. And what was their proactive response to a sexually harmful situation? Although the building manager could have moved them out of the wing and separated them immediately, the prison let them stay together for another week and a half, giving either of them more than enough opportunity to do some real damage if that had been the intent. Luckily it wasn't—they were still as sickly enmeshed as they had been before, eating together, bickering, and caressing each other just as they had been prior to the dust-up.

Probably the saddest thing about this whole incident is that after the fight went down, the focus immediately shifted from "What the hell is wrong with someone who will beat up someone they supposedly love and why do I need to live with that crap?" to "Who told?" Nothing much more was said about the brutality of the fight, the sordidness of the situation. Instead, while Tessie and Tina were still out in the office, Clary was almost in tears because one of Tina's friends had accused her of being the one who snitched. Yes, that's the issue that needed to be addressed. As usual, personal responsibility falls away, and instead it's all about the blame game. This is the same mindset where someone says, with all sincerity, "Yeah, I'm back in prison because my damn parole officer pee tested me and I had a dirty urine result." Sure, it's the P.O.'s fault. Or your mother's. Or the government's. Or frickin' men from Mars, for all I know. So I can't entirely blame the administration for perpetuating this environment. We inmates share the blame as well.

It is thus that despite PREA, despite Wendy Hobbs's avowals to the contrary, despite the thick coating of whitewash that the prison administration flings so liberally about the joint, Fluvanna is the once and future cesspool. Gives society a reason to be hopeful, doesn't it?

There are, of course, a few officers whom all the prisoners know to be skeezy little perverts. C.O. Valezquez was one of these. He was fond of peering over the bathroom stall doors when a female inmate was using the toilet. He did this once to Ginella, a hulking, good-natured woman doing a year on a meth charge. Now, Ginella was a sweetie, but she definitely fell into the "boy" category and was not the most obvious choice for a peeping Tom, but Valezquez didn't discriminate by race or appearance. After Ginella's initial squawk of outraged indignation, there was a few seconds of silence while, I presume, Ginella yanked up her baggy uniform pants. The leering officer continued to stand at the stall door, I guess enjoying her discomfort. Ginella didn't take this passively. She slammed the metal door open, nearly taking Valezquez out in the process. The 8 or so inmates in the dayroom watched in stunned fascination as Ginella berated the sheepishly smiling officer. He tried to tell her that it was an accident, that he "forgot" that he didn't have to check bathroom stalls during cell checks, but she wasn't buying it. She ended up filing a grievance against him, but the only apparent result of that was his eventual transfer to another position; he became a counselor, which gives him relatively unlimited private interactions with inmates. He can call for a particular woman to come to his office whenever he likes or seek her out in her housing unit without any questions.

Then there's the officer who doesn't work here anymore, but who visits his inmate girlfriend with clockwork frequency. They are obviously, passionately affectionate at his arrivals and departures, but fortunately for the rest of us in the visitation room, physical contact is not allowed during the visits themselves. I don't think that it is a coincidence that this couple always seems to be seated directly in front of the officers' station during his visits. I would guess that the C.O.s are as creeped out by his unseemly behavior as I am.

There are always rumors going around about this or that officer having an inappropriate relationship with an inmate, but like most inmate rumors concerning the personal lives of officers, I try to give the C.O. the benefit of the doubt. Officers might joke around with inmates, but for the most part they are careful not to cross the line into sexual comments. If, for example, an officer sees you nude or partially nude in your cell while he (or she—female officers are potential objects of sexual harassment complaints as well) makes rounds, you will immediately be called out to the sergeant's office, told that the officer inadvertently observed you in that condition, and informed that an incident report would be filed. It's always very professional and courteous. I've never heard of anyone being raped or forced into a sexual act. If anything happens here, it is most definitely consensual.

Another sexually charged area for the women here is the world of prison pen pals. This, however, is more of a business than a sexual release for the women involved. There are, apparently, dozens of Web sites devoted to profiles of lonely female inmates looking for love letters, what one might call epistolary companionship. Inmates can fill out a questionnaire about their interests and send that, along with a photo (not always of themselves) to be posted on these sites. Lonely guys find a picture of what they believe to be an attractive young inmate, and the letters begin pouring in.

Inmates might have several pen pals, and the skilled ones can have each of these pathetic guys sending them money every week or month after just a few letters. Some women even convince themselves that they sort of mean all of the protestations of love and desire that they have to include in their letters to get the cash, but most are sneeringly dismissive when they talk about their "sugar daddies." They string the poor guy along until he, at this point desperately in love, addicted to the sexual excesses each letter describes, and in many cases ready to marry the girl when she gets out, demands to meet the inmate in person. The kinder ones will let the guys show up and buy them snacks from the visitation vending machines before they cut them off, but often the pen pals will drive hours to get here only to be told when they arrive that the inmates are refusing their visit.

Inmates can be victims, too, although the costs they suffer are emotional, not financial. Lots of women here have been rejected by their man on the street, divorced, or simply cut off from the husbands or boyfriends who swore to wait for them until they got out. Or an inmate's man might be in prison as well for the same crime that brought her to FCCW. "Co-defendant" and "boyfriend" are frequently synonyms inside. Either way, these women are utterly vulnerable, miserable in the loneliness that is the perpetual punishment of those confined. Because they aren't interested in a lesbian relationship, they begin writing to a friend's cousin or some other guy who saw their arrest photo and felt compelled to make contact.

These women commit completely to the men they write. Genuinely, deeply in love, they wait avidly at each mail call to hear from him. A day that a letter from him doesn't arrive is a blighted expanse of endless despair. Each letter that arrives is a confirmation that this is the eternal passion that will rule their lives forever. Fortunes are spent on stamps and stationery because they write to their men every day, pushing for more and more commitment. The obvious result of this pressure is that the guy stops writing. After all, why should a man put up with so much drama from someone he can't even sleep with? The inevitable trickling off of letters means profound depression for the women for a while, but soon enough they get some other guy's address and the cycle begins again.

Lots of women write to a prisoner at a men's facility that they "met" through another woman here. This is a tricky business that requires a trusted friend on the outside to serve as a conduit for all of the cards and letters. Because it is against the rules to write to someone at another correctional facility or jail without special permission from the warden (which is only given when the man is a relative or husband), women have to "three-way" any letters that they want to send their prisoner boyfriends. An inmate might send the letters for her guy enclosed in a letter to her mom, who will in turn send it on to the men's prison. The recipient does the same with his replies. Because all of our mail is read by staff before we get it, each correspondent has to be careful not to refer to anything too "prison-ish." Many women get found out because their boyfriends bitch about commissary or C.O.s in their notes to them or, even more obvious, send in a photo of themselves posing in what is obviously a prison yard. Another sure way to get caught is to confide in anyone that you are three-waying mail. The safest assumption to make is that no one can keep a secret in prison.

Most of the lifers I know eschew any romance at all. It's just too much effort in a situation where it sometimes requires all of your energy to slap on a smile and not harm yourself in some way. It's easier to develop a relationship with one of the showerheads that are affectionately called "straight shooters" for their powerful, tightly focused spray. No drama, no angst, just the mindless release of stress, and best of all, *that* is something that's not against the rules!

REFERENCES

Hassine, V. (2011). *Life without parole: Living in prison today* (5th ed.). Edited by Robert Johnson & Sonia Tabriz. New York: Oxford University Press.

Johnson, R. (2009). Cell buddy. In R. Johnson & S. Tabriz (Eds.), *Lethal rejection: Stories on crime and punishment* (pp. 122–130). Durham, NC: Carolina Academic Press.

McNaughton, C. (2007). Just another death. In W. Lamb (Ed.), *I'll fly away: Further testimonies from the women of York Prison* (pp. 182–188). New York: Harper Perennial.

Owen, B. (1998). *In the mix: Struggles and survival in a women's prison.* Albany: State University of New York Press.

Pollock, J. (2002). *Women, prison & crime.* Belmont, CA: Wadsworth.

Pollock, J. (2009). Prison lullabies. In R. Johnson & S. Tabriz (Eds.), *Lethal rejection: Stories on crime and punishment* (pp. 131–142). Durham, NC: Carolina Academic Press.

Struckman-Johnson, C., & Struckman-Johnson, D. (2002). Sexual coercion reported by women in three midwestern prisons. *The Journal of Sex Research, 39*(3), 217–227.

Struckman-Johnson, C., & Struckman-Johnson, D. (2006). A comparison of sexual coercion experiences reported by men and women in prison. *Journal of Interpersonal Violence, 21*(12), 1591–1615.

CHAPTER 4

Violence behind Bars:
Women, *Mano a Mano*

L ethal violence is comparatively rare in men's prisons and virtually unknown in prisons or jails for women (Mumola, 2005). But some of the violence in women's prisons is carefully orchestrated and quite serious (Owen, 1998), and some women's prisons have high rates of assault (Wolfe, Blitz, Shi, Siegal, & Bachman, 2007). Recall that in Chapter 1, George discussed several serious assaults that took place in jail while she was waiting to be shipped to prison.

A prison incident involving Cherry and Maya, two women at Fluvanna, is described by George in this chapter as a case of serious violence. These two women grease up their faces in preparation for the fight so that any punches they receive won't land well. Cherry borrows rings to wear so that the punches she throws will cut the victim's face. Together, Cherry and Maya ambush and "double-bank" Kendra (attack from front and behind). The cause at issue: trouble in love. The assailants thought their victim, Kendra, had ratted out their romance. Kendra is badly hurt, scarred permanently; the assailants face criminal charges. George stresses that double-banking someone is "uncool" because it violates rules of engagement that call for fair play. But ultimately there is no fair play in the violence of women, just as there is none in men's prisons. "In reality," we learn from George, "anything goes," although weapons are rare and shanks "are almost never seen in here."

Riots are as rare as shanks, but just as the occasional shank emerges and enters prison lore, so does the rare riot become part of a prison's oral history (see Law, 2009). As George recounts Fluvanna's one real riot, some 10 years ago, trouble starts with tension between the "fed girls" (from federal prisons) and the "staties" (from Virginia state prisons). The object of tension: a girl, or, more accurately, a boo. The main riot takes place in the chow hall. It's a bloody fight marked by "total chaos" but there are no fatalities. The riot draws on quintessential prison themes, sparked by relationships gone bad fueling bad blood brought to a boil against a backdrop of bad food. —Robert Johnson

The fight wasn't a spur-of-the-moment thing like so many of the altercations here. It wasn't over a perceived slight between girlfriends. No, Cherry and Maya had been planning it for days. They finally put their plan into action the evening that they knew would be their last in the same wing. The staff was moving Maya into a different wing (albeit in the same building) in an effort to break up the couple. Their victim was Kendra, Maya's roommate, whom Cherry and Maya thought had been responsible for snitching them out to the officers.

Everyone in the wing knew that something was up that day. Cherry and Maya had both smeared their faces heavily with the hair grease that is sold on commissary, a sure sign that a fight was in the offing. If you grease your face, punches are more likely to slide right off rather than to connect solidly. And although shanks are almost never seen in here, weapons aren't completely unknown, so Cherry had spent the day borrowing rings from her friends so that when she hit Kendra, she would do maximum damage to her face. This wasn't going to be a few bitch slaps and scratches. Blood, and lots of it, was going to flow.

In the rules of prison altercations, it is definitely not cool to double-bank someone, which is what occurs when several inmates gang up on a solitary victim. It's a sign of cowardice to resort to that. Be woman enough to fight *mano a mano* or keep your fists to yourself. It's reassuring for those of us trapped in here to think that even in a prison fight there is some standard of morally acceptable actions, but, in reality, anything goes.

Almost everyone on the compound knew when the fight went down because all officers except those actually working the building control panels suddenly sprinted (or attempted to sprint—FCCW is not exactly a bastion for the physically fit) across the yard to Building Five. That happens every time a fight of any real severity occurs—the call for assistance goes out over the radio and then dozens of C.O.s stream out of each building.

Those of us who live in Building Eight, which also houses the segregation and structured living wings, have an unprecedented amount of dirt on just who is brought into seg and in what condition they arrive. Cherry came into the building first, flanked by at least 9 officers carrying her shackled and handcuffed body. She was still struggling and spewing profanity as they lifted her through the sally port into the isolated segregation wings. Three minutes later Maya followed, also shackled and cuffed but not resisting. Defiantly silent, she stalked into the sally port, ignoring the C.O. jostling her through the door.

There was no sign of Kendra, even though it is normal for all participants of a fight to be locked up in "Under Investigation" status, even when they are victims of an ambush. The call for medical assistance that went out a moment later explained why; she had been beaten so badly that she had to be taken directly to the infirmary. Maya and Cherry emerged largely unscathed from the altercation; all of their preparation for the fight had paid off. Kendra had lost a great deal of blood and suffered violent blows to her head and stomach. Her face was shredded from Cherry's improvised brass knuckles—she will always be scarred from the assault.

Although there were a lot of rumors later about how exactly it had happened, the witnesses agree about the main points. One of the most tragic aspects of the whole event was that Maya and Cherry had at least 5 uninterrupted minutes to pummel Kendra before an officer assigned to another building happened to come in to deliver some paperwork and saw what was going down in the wing. For some reason the bubble officer, who has an unrestricted view of the dayroom, somehow didn't notice the assault that was happening on her watch.

Cherry and Maya are both probably going to get street charges, which means that they will be tried in court for criminal charges in addition to the sentences they are already serving. This will be in addition to the extremely long time that they will both probably spend in seg, then in the Structured Living Unit (SLU), which is a transitional wing for inmates who have served time in segregation or received multiple tickets that alone did not necessitate seg time.

Since moving to the Honor Wing, I've seen a few verbal altercations and no physical fights. But every few days a few bedraggled women, in various stages of undress, stagger past our wing on their way to segregation, flanked by a coterie of grim-faced officers. In class, I hear about the beat-downs that are occurring with distressing regularity in the other wings: beat-downs, boo fights, and blanket parties (where a sleeping inmate is covered with a blanket, then pounded by assailants unknown). And, of course, no one tells, lest she be the next honoree. The fights are getting out of control as the rules become more rigid and inmates are increasingly isolated in their wings. There is no outlet for aggression—little recreation or exercise, just a smoldering group of women who, almost to a man, suffer from poor impulse control, inadequate decision-making skills, and a general lack of empathy. The wise ones go to their cells and stay there, emerging only for showers, commissary, bathroom, and work. There's always potential conflict brewing in the day room. It is best to avoid it altogether, because proximity might be cause enough to become embroiled in a fight.

Trips to seg are usually over the same petty BS: Street is two-timing her boo; Bee stole her roommate's Avon lotion; Lisa stole ink from the print shop; Davita stole a pair of jeans from property. There are a few interesting ways to land time in seg. Cub is there right now because she refused to cut her hair and shave her facial hair. Buffy spent two weeks back there because she put on so much weight after moving to the Honor Wing, an officer accused her of beefing herself up for an escape attempt. The seg workers gave us constant updates on how she was doing. "It's just fat, not muscle!" Buffy would protest to any staff member who walked past her isolation cell. "The Honor Wing has a microwave oven and I cook a lot!"

A few of the more candid officers admitted their puzzlement over the allegations. "Buffy's not going anywhere unless she could take her girlfriend Peri with her," said Officer Poston. "And if they locked up every inmate who larded up here, all the general population wings would be empty." Eventually they let Buffy out with no charges, and to this day she is slightly baffled as to why she was even back there to begin with. Did some troublemaking inmate drop an IMS on her? Was an officer having a bad day? God only knows, and He sure isn't telling.

My friend Dizzy, who has been at Fluvanna since it opened, often tells stories about the riot that went down in one of the two separate but adjacent chow halls on the compound. When the riot happened, Fluvanna housed about 200 women from the federal system in addition to the Virginia DOC inmates who make up the majority of the inmates here. The two groups never got along well because the fed girls, legally entitled to better treatment than "staties" (state prisoners), were perceived as lording their federal status over the Virginia prisoners. What sparked this conflict, though, was, of course, a boo. Apparently a federal prisoner was messing around with the girlfriend of a state girl. Some of Dizzy's anecdotes describe events that must have been frightening at the time, but with her natural gifts as a raconteur, Dizzy captures the black comedy of the situation.

"Oh God, it was a crazy day," she says, laughing:

Dinnertime, I was coming out of A side dining hall when I saw a lot of commotion going on in B side—people running to B side. I saw that the Assistant Warden was outside, and she was one of the people who ran to look as well. She went up to the right-hand door of the chow hall and ran in. A few seconds later she was pushed out of the left-hand door of B side, where she proceeded to wave her arms frantically over her head screaming "Save yourselves!" It sounds comical now, but the situation was a lot worse than we realized at first. A lot of the officers panicked, you could tell by the sounds over the radio and hear it in their voices, see it on their faces, but they stayed firm when the fighting was going on. Some of the more gung-ho ones really seemed to enjoy it.

During the fight, a girl slid through the dirty dish window to get to an inmate in the chow hall. Needless to say, administration made the dish windows really small after that. Inmates were using locks in a sock, the coin boxes from the washing machines, anything they could get their hands on. They had come in prepared for a fight. The women who cleaned up the dining room afterwards said it was a frigging nightmare. Blood, food, everything everywhere.

Well, about that time officers came running in from everywhere. I was frozen outside the chow hall as they streamed past me. Afraid to move, I was like a deer in the headlights. Inmates were running from A side to B side to watch or get in on the fighting themselves. It was total chaos. You could hear the officer screaming over the radio for help. Me and my friend took off to go over to medical because we needed to get our meds on the pill line like we do every evening. We still didn't realize how bad it was at that time, and when we finally got over there, the building officers kept telling us "go in, go in," so we went into medical for our pills (which we never ended up getting).

After we got inside, inmates started coming in from the fight with their t-shirts ripped, faces all bloody. They had managed to get out of the chow hall before the officers had grabbed the rioters, and by that time any inmate on the yard had been told to just go into any nearby building. These women ended up in the medical building because that was the one they were closest to when they got away from the riot. They were all trying to act cool, tucking in their shirts, rearranging their uniforms so that the holes were hidden, wiping the blood off their faces.

After 5 or 10 minutes, some of the big hats [high-ranking officers] came in and lined us up against the wall, and we had to stand there for about 20 minutes. Then they locked all of us up in the mental health acute wing, which was empty at the time. Thirty of us were in there for about an hour and a half, most of us sitting on the tile floors. It was freezing cold over there, and there were not enough chairs for the inmates. When they finally let us all go, they sent us out separately by buildings. An officer walked us down through medical—you could see women sitting in the waiting room all beaten up, clumps of hair pulled out of their heads, black eyes, scratches, one girl had a broken arm—they wouldn't let us speak to anyone, just hurried us past to Building One. The thing I remember most when I got outside was the dead silence out on the compound. It was eerie. You know something was not right because there is always noise out there. It was so quiet you could hear a pin drop.

When I got outside, I kept thinking "Whoa, this is not good, some serious shit's going on right here." When they got us back to our building, we all had to lock down in our cells. I can't remember how long we were locked in our cells, maybe about a week until they had shaken everyone down, going through every sheet of paper, everything we owned.

We were released on modified lock, where we could come out into the dayroom, but not leave the wing, even for meals or medical. If we needed to get out, we had to be escorted by an officer. But we didn't get far because there was a new officer in the bubble and she let an inmate out of B wing, who walked right into C wing, all the security doors popped open for her by the bubble officer. The girl then proceeded to get into a fight with a girl from C wing. An old officer we called Grandpa broke it up. He's an officer that was arrested after the riot for molesting his grandchildren. But when he was here he was like the grandfather type to us, and I remember thinking at the time he was breaking up the fight, "Go, grandpa!"

The fight was all stemming back to the riot. It was Virginia Beach girls against the Feds and it was over, you know, girlfriends. The fed girls had never gotten what time in Fluvanna was like. I remember when they first got here they wanted to know where the salad bar was! I was like "Welcome to the real world. There is no salad bar in prison!" They expected a lot. They expected jobs making minimum wage like I guess they get in fed prisons, but we only made 23 cents an hour. They hated the lack of movement and freedom. I used to have to do orientation with these people when they got here. Try talking to a bunch of people who hate your guts.

Dizzy adopts the cheery tones of an airline attendant: "Welcome to Fluvanna! I hope your stay here is marvelous. It was marvelous all right," Dizzy continues sarcastically.

That was one way to get out of here, I guess. For the life of me I can't figure out why they didn't renew their lease. Everybody seemed to have such a good time. Seriously, though, some of the fed girls were real nice, but most acted too entitled. They were criminals just like the rest of us. Just because you did your shit across state lines doesn't mean you're any better than me.

There were little mini fights all over the compound the first time they let us out, so we were locked back down again in our cells for ten days. Staff told us that we might never come out again. You got a 5-minute shower every 2 or 3 days—they timed it. One girl washed her hair in the sink when she went to brush her teeth and they wrote her a ticket. There was no hot water for coffee because they took out our hot water pot since it could be used as a weapon. Everything became a weapon at that point: the coin boxes on the washing machines, anything metal, they even pulled out the trash cans from the wing.

When they finally let us out, a lot of things had changed. When we got the trash cans back so we could empty out our ash trays, they were tethered to the wall. The temperature of the water in the hot pots was turned down to barely tepid, the hot comb was screwed down, cabinets in the wing were attached to the floor. Everything was locked up, like the iron, hair dryer, even games. Lock-down was now 9:15 instead of the 11:00 p.m. lockdown we'd had before.

When we were allowed to go to chow out of the wing, we had to line up single file and be escorted by officers. There were attack dogs all over the yard. That was weird. You would be walking and them damn dogs looked like they wanted to have you for dinner. Each building ate separately, they wouldn't mix any of us together. We didn't have rec, especially population rec, where all the buildings walked together. Officers went with us to and from work when we were finally allowed to go back and the dogs escorted us everywhere. It was a couple of weeks before we were allowed to go back to our jobs.

When we were locked down, the officers and staff had to do all the work. First couple of days you could look out the window and see that the trash was just mounding out in the yard, so the officers got a flatbed truck and piled it up. The teachers and counselors cooked for us and the officers had to clean wings, which was usually done by the inmates. About all the C.O.s would do was take a dust mop and sweep and maybe empty the trash. It was a mess. The bathrooms were foul.

They didn't have enough room in seg for all of the inmates involved, there were at least 30 or 40 of them. The state inmates went to seg and the federal inmates were put into the acute [the mental health unit] because that was the only place they had to hold them. Eventually, all of the federal inmates were let go. I don't know why, maybe because the state didn't have jurisdiction over federal inmates, but I really am not sure.

For some of the state inmates, the ones really heavily involved, they were shipped out of state. One girl went to Connecticut I think, one girl went to Kentucky. A girl I had been down with for a long time was just gone. I never saw her again.

I really don't know, being locked up like that, I began to wonder if I would ever get out again. Would I starve to death because I have no money from the outside? I depended on my job for everything I needed. I was one of the lucky ones though because I worked in the academic building. The ones who worked in VCE (where the vocational classes like electrical and wood shop were located) would be around tools, so they weren't allowed to go back until much later. Things were never the same here after that, and the bad thing about it is that most of those assholes that caused it have gone home while we're still here, suffering the consequences, no doubt about it.

We were pissed that we were being punished for their stupid shit because everything changed after that—the amount of freedom we had, we were watched more closely, the attitude of the staff really changed towards us. The powers that be kept telling us that it would be a long time before we ever saw the people in seg but, funny thing, while they were in seg they were getting rec, but we weren't. And then when they let a bunch of them out, they started having walking rec again, but not us.

That's when there were no more smoke breaks or coffee in the classrooms at DCE [Department of Correctional Education]. All that changed thanks to some bitches fighting over a fucking girl. Never a dull moment at Fluvanna!

It still pisses me off. This place was really laid back when we first got here. The officers treated us with respect, we didn't have to lock our doors at night. Wasn't no lifers involved in this mess, I guaran-damn-tee you that. For every single stupid rule we have here, inmates have caused it. Some short-timer has done something stupid. The powers that be didn't come up with all of these rules without reason.

Dizzy shakes her head philosophically. "You have to find the humor in it, though. You would go crazy if you didn't. You have to find humor in everything here. I couldn't do my time otherwise."

REFERENCES

Law, V. (2009). *Resistance behind bars: The struggles of incarcerated women*. Oakland, CA:PM Press.

Mumola, C. J. (2005). *Suicide and homicide in state prisons and local jails* (Special Rep. NCJ 210036). Washington, DC: Bureau of Justice Statistics.

Owen, B. (1998). *In the mix: Struggle and survival in a women's prison*. Albany: State University of New York Press.

Wolfe, N., Blitz, C. L., Shi, J., Siegal, J., & Bachman, R. (2007). Physical violence inside prisons: Rates of victimization. *Criminal Justice and Behavior, 34*(5), 588–599.

CHAPTER 5

Shakedowns, Fakedowns, and Solitary Confinement

I nmates are exquisitely attuned to the ebb and flow of searches major and minor, *a reflection of what George terms a "swarm mentality," like that of bees that instinctively communicate danger. Major searches can turn a woman's world upside-down, but even minor or cursory searches, called "fakedowns," have impact. The idea of a fakedown is intriguing. Announced in advance, fakedowns allow the women to clean out contraband; the women barter and trade to keep valued possessions within the rules. The social transactions have a curious precision and also a sensible balance. One can't help but think that these transactions work for staff and inmate alike in maintaining a stable social order (see Rierden, 1997; Toch, 1992a).*

By contrast, shakedowns can be brutal. Women are locked in their cells for days on end, without showers, waiting for intrusive searches, which for many women may be painful reminders of the sexual abuse they suffered in the free world, often as children (Bloom, Owen, & Covington, 2003; Kruttschnitt & Gartner, 2005; Parsons, 2007; Pollock, 2002). For rape victims, as George points out, these searches are a kind of replay of the crime, done over and over again as their sentences unfold.

George is accustomed to body searches; they are like a handshake to her, with the notable exception of when she is menstruating. One has to assume that some depersonalization has set in and allowed her to function during these searches in a kind of numb, neutral (if not neutered) state (see Johnson & Chernoff, 2002). Waiting in a closed cell for days on end, dirty and unkempt, only to have one's "cavities" searched—the very notion of a cavity search is dehumanizing—and then to have one's possessions, including one's intimate possessions, pawed through by officers, is the paradigm of degradation in the civilized world. Some officers can do these searches tactfully, and some inmates, notably the lifers, respond with practiced poses, but the whole sordid business is a painful reminder of the price we exact from inmates and pay as a society when we make prisons the centerpieces of our punishment policy. (For a vivid description of crudely done strip searches undertaken with utter disregard for the dignity of the women, see Parsons, 2007.)

Erin George is a lifer, and like most lifers she is scrupulous about obeying the rules. She has too much to lose. The world she has built for herself in prison is modest by free world terms, but it is all she has and she wants to keep it (see, generally, Cunningham & Sorensen, 2006; Johnson & Dobrzanska, 2005). Still, most inmates, George tells us, break the rules now and again. Most rule violations are minor, and the result is a loss of privileges, privileges short-term inmates seem willing to forgo. More serious violations land a woman in segregation, a setting described as "dark and clamorous," with few amenities and little freedom of movement. The segregation prisoner is held in a prison within a prison. If misbehavior continues (or is perceived by staff to continue), the woman can be put on a restricted "diet loaf," a gooey, starchy concoction that is a punishment in itself. A woman can also land in segregation for the administrative convenience of officials or for no reasons that are apparent to the women in the prison population, a complaint echoed in men's prisons as well (see Dobrzanska, 2009; Hassine, 2009, 2011).

Segregation, sometimes called solitary confinement, is vividly described as a setting of deprivation and loss (there is an extensive body of research supporting George's observations and assertions; see Guenther, 2013; Kupers, 2008). Suicidal women are regularly placed in segregation to restrain them, but the stress of isolation often feeds their despair (see Toch, 1992b). Uncertainty about why one is locked down and for how long can add considerably to the prisoner's misery, as seen in the case of Tianne, discussed in this chapter. One prisoner who lives around the clock in a modified version of segregation is Virginia's only condemned woman, who awaits execution by lethal injection. As grim as this fate is, and George does not minimize it, the case can be made that the "death by incarceration" suffered by the woman facing life without the possibility of parole is as bad or worse (Corley, 2008; Hartman, 2013; Johnson & McGunigall-Smith, 2008). These women, George among them, face the loss of their health and self-esteem as they decline in their later years, only to die alone behind bars, a lonely death and one likely accompanied by physical pain. —Robert Johnson

There are all kinds of women incarcerated at Fluvanna. As a maximum-security facility that offers medical treatment, there are offenders here of all classification and security levels. But I've found that whatever our background, race, or education level, we all seem to share some sort of swarm intelligence. Like swallows or army ants, we simultaneously absorb information (usually baseless rumors of policy changes or scurrilous gossip), then respond as one. Although most of what we hear turns out to be ludicrously inaccurate, sometimes there is uncanny precision. One area where the inmate grapevine is especially accurate is when it comes to shakedowns. Although they are supposed to be a surprise, we usually know they are coming at least a day in advance, thanks to our information underground. Still, the threat of a shakedown is always there, waiting to shatter any fragile illusion we have of privacy and place.

The purpose of a shakedown is not only to make sure that you don't have any contraband (that vague, delightful term that encompasses anything that an officer might deem dangerous, inappropriate, or questionable), but also to ensure that you don't have too much of any permitted item. There's a limit to everything an inmate has, either expressly stated, such as the six T-shirts we are allowed, or falling under the more nebulous category of "reasonable amount allowed."

Officers will hassle you if you have too much of something. But in a place where even the most mundane possessions are precious and hard-earned, we are loath to discard them. One way around this is when you have a roommate who is under the limit for everything. For a small bribe of a pack of noodles or candy bar, she will hold your extra shampoo bottles or panties and claim them as her own until after a search. Those who have been around for a while have an entrenched network of friends who can stash their extra possessions. They might have personals scattered all over the compound, waiting for the next shakedown.

There are several different kinds of shakedowns of varying degrees of intrusiveness. The least disruptive is what inmates call a "fakedown." During a fakedown, the bubble officer will make an announcement over the intercom right before 7:00 a.m. count, telling us to get rid of all of our contraband. So out we stagger as soon as count clears, bringing excess blankets, old magazines, extra toilet paper rolls, empty cracker boxes, and illicit love letters. Women gather at the back of the wing, out of camera range, and broker hasty bargains: "I only have four makeups, so I can hold some of yours if you hold on to my extra craft item." Surreptitious exchanges are deftly made. David Copperfield would be dazzled by the sleight of hand and misdirection that these semi-somnambulant inmates can perform in this high-pressure situation. After the 10 minutes or so during which all this dumping and dealing takes place, the C.O. locks us all down in our cells for 5 minutes, then releases us to go to class or work.

If it's a good day, that's where it stops. Lately, though, there have been fewer fakedowns and more full-fledged searches. Now bear in mind, very rarely is anything found in an inmate's room that is truly dangerous. I remember hearing a story that might be apocryphal (but *should* be true) that administration gave the officers a memo describing what they should be looking for when searching inmate cells. At the top of the list were excess craft items (by which they mean crocheted stuffed animals, blankets, or shower bags—imagine the damage we could do with those!) and too many makeup items. Bringing up the rear were shanks and makeshift weapons. In fact, during the 13 years that I have been locked up, I have never *seen* a shank–although I hear that a padlock inside a sock is a quick and effective weapon if I should ever need it. This is a highly useful tip, I suppose, but not one I ever hope to employ.

When it comes to shakedowns, you know that you're in for it when you don't have the chance to pitch all of your contraband. Instead, the cell door remains locked, even when the count has cleared. There are no announcements over the intercom, and the wing is silent—none of the usual calling from cell to cell.

Instead, we're all listening for the distinctive clang of the main wing door opening and plastic chairs being dragged to the first cells. That means the shakedown has begun.

It can take days for the officers to show up after the initial lockdown. Until then, we sit in our cells, let out in small groups for long enough to get one of the meal trays the staff has prepared and brought to the wing. There is no talking as we stumble down the stairs to the dayroom, ungainly from inactivity. We cannot take showers. If you live in a wet cell (one that has a toilet and a sink), you aren't even allowed out to use the common bathrooms.

As we wait, we get ready for the search. Inmates seem to fall into two categories. Most leave their possessions where they would normally keep them: bulky uniforms stuffed into one of the gray plastic storage bins, papers heaped on the gunmetal desk. I, however, prepare as if for a military inspection. I group property together by type: books in one place, shampoo and lotions in another, clothing folded on my bunk. Although in reality this is probably a symptom of the obsessive-compulsive disorder that has come to afflict me since my incarceration, I justify my precision by saying that if I make it easier for the officers, they might go a little easier on me when it comes to tossing my cell. Those of the messier inclination disagree, saying that if the C.O.s can't tell immediately how much you have of something, they'll probably be too lazy to try and figure it out. After many opportunities to test my hypothesis, I've come to the conclusion that what I do has zero impact on how badly my cell is trashed. Like everything else here, it all depends on the whims of the officer.

The C.O.s, when they do arrive, are there in vast numbers. Suddenly, there will be dozens of them milling around in the dayroom, joking with each other and with some of the inmates. Many of us have been going through this together for years. Only the trainees look nervous, snapping on their latex gloves as if they were girding for battle. This is a serious business, they seem to be saying, and the rest of us would do well to understand and defer to the gravity of the situation.

You know that your room is about to be searched when the two beige plastic chairs are plunked down in front of your locked door. After one last room scan as the bubble officer unlocks your door, you step aside as two female officers enter. They're the unlucky ones, because it's their job to strip search each inmate. Inspecting 45 naked women who haven't been able to shower for days must be no stroll through the botanical gardens.

I'm used to being body searched by now, shedding my uniform and underwear, and then squatting down while I cough to make sure that I've hidden nothing in my vagina or anus. Lifting my breasts, opening my mouth for inspection like a mare for sale, balancing clumsily on alternating feet to show my soles: I do this as casually as shaking hands. The only time I feel self-conscious is when I am menstruating. I still find it difficult to remove my tampon in front of someone else. I can't imagine that will ever come easily to me. Frankly, I'm just grateful that the body searches are not even more thorough.

A rather delicate etiquette of the body search evolves between most officers and lifers. We know what to do, the choreography of jetés and pirouettes necessary to expose ourselves for inspection. We comply docilely, either in silence or with glib chatter designed, oddly enough, to put the inspecting officer at ease.

On their part, most C.O.s seem to do what they can to make the process as painless as possible. They hang towels over the door so that none of the male officers can catch a glimpse of us. Like a new arrival in a seraglio, our bodies are both callously explored and rigorously concealed. While we splay ourselves, they look discreetly away, as if they are alone and bored in the small cell. C.O.s rarely make eye contact: The officer might find her new manicure of profound interest or study the label of a lotion bottle as if it held the answers to life's great questions.

I found that I quickly became inured to the humiliation of this process. I could understand the purpose of the search and create a mental distance between myself and the pasty, overweight woman squatting gracelessly on the grainy tile. Although neither the officers nor I wanted to be there for this institutionalized debasement, we all had roles to play, and better done quickly than not.

I'm one of the fortunate ones in that respect. Many incarcerated women have suffered profoundly damaging sexual abuse, so for them these violations are all-too-vivid echoes of the past. Every body search is a reenactment of the rape they suffered at 14, or their father's nocturnal visits. And they must endure it again and again. The officers know this, and most of them do what they can to be professional and as quick as possible. But what can they do to offer succor? C.O.s have their restrictions, as do we. They can't hug an inmate as she shakes in trauma, or even reach out a hand in comfort. Technically, they can't even call her by her first name. If they obey the rules, we can never breach the distance between us.

After the guards search us, my roommate and I are handcuffed and hustled into the plastic chairs to wait for two more officers to tackle searching the cell itself. I always hope to get a good officer to do my shakedown. I don't mean good in the traditional sense of the word. A "good" officer in prison is one who:

1. Likes you as a person. Getting an officer like this is like buying the right instant-win ticket at the Fast-Mart: not as great as winning the PowerBall lottery, but still good enough to make the day bearable.
2. Is lazy. These guys will hang out in your cell for 5 minutes looking at your photo album and asking questions about who are in the pictures, discuss with you who won the Lakers game last night, then leave without opening up anything.
3. Simply doesn't care anymore. This can be tricky, though. Catch them in a cranky mood and you're toast.

If good officers walk by while I'm waiting for my room search, I try to engage them in conversation so that they will spontaneously begin searching my cell on their own. I become bright and chatty, hoping to distract them from their task.

It's not because I have any contraband: I have far too much to lose to risk getting a ticket for something stupid, like sugar packets from the chow hall or an extra pair of uniform pants. I just don't want my room too ravaged in the searching process.

There are a few officers who, when you see them approaching, you pray not to get. Lieutenant Cole is one of those. A swaggering misogynist who endlessly hassles us in the yard, he strutted into my cell once without even cursory acknowledgment of my presence. Typically, even the dourest officer can manage a slight nod of the head in my direction, but not him. He used to be decent enough until he made some rank and, I guess, developed ambition. He's one of the ones determined to prove that he's a hard-ass.

"Where'd you get this?" he said, snapping up from my desk shelf as if he had found a semi-automatic weapon. What he held in his hand was a blue ink pen.

"From commissary," I replied. "They used to sell them."

"If they don't sell them anymore then it's contraband." The pen disappears into the bulging black plastic garbage bag he has been toting from cell to cell.

"Why do you need so much notebook paper?" he asks me next. I have two unopened packs of notebook paper and a few lonely sheets left of a third.

Speechless, I can only shrug my shoulders. A pack of paper follows the pen into his abyss of lost contraband. I don't bother bringing up the fact that we are, in fact, permitted to buy two packs of paper at a time from commissary. I'd rather eat the loss of the $2.00 and get a new pack next time I can. Arguing will keep him in my room that much longer.

After dumping the contents of all my boxes on my bunk and fingering my panties and bras, he seems satisfied and leaves without another word. Gratefully, my roommate and I return to the cell and the door locks behind us.

Just as dreaded, but less deliberately malignant, are the officer trainees. As thorough and destructive as Lieutentant Cole, the indignities they inflict seem to come more from a desire not to miss anything that might get them in trouble. With them, it's not personal. Unfortunately, they have the habit of checking in with their supervising officer (usually one of the officers that you hope will never step foot in your wing, much less your room) before making any decision as to whether something is all right or not. Inevitably, the supervisor in question deems the item in question contraband.

The worst shakedowns are the ones that are directed at a specific inmate. These come when someone has snitched to the sergeant or lieutenant (by anonymous IMS) or fabricated a story out of revenge or boredom. These officers have an agenda: They know exactly what they are looking for. Shakedowns like this almost never happen during the day. Instead, the ominous sound of officers moving plastic chairs in an otherwise empty dayroom awakens you at midnight. I'm as classically conditioned as any of Pavlov's dogs: The sight of an officer wearing latex gloves is enough to make me feel queasy. The clatter of chairs in a locked-down wing sends me, and every other inmate, to the narrow windows of our cell doors to see who the target is.

"Who is it?" we mouth to each other. Women in prison become expert in reading lips and charades: any means of communicating that allows one to silently converse. When we learn the name, we know what has happened. There's no privacy in here. If you've been beefing with your girlfriend, or managed to piss off the wing's gossips, we all know about it, and thus identify the source of the shakedown.

Unlike the relatively cursory general shakedowns, directed searches can take up to an hour. They read every letter and dump each bottle of shampoo. They even pull photos from albums to make sure that there is nothing hidden behind them. Instead of letting you dump marginal contraband as they normally do, the officers will charge you with every infraction, however minor. If the officers have received extraordinary precise information, though, the search won't take more than a few minutes. They will come in and go directly to the pair of shoes where you've hidden the necklace that you had smuggled in during visitation. These searches normally result in charges. Even if they don't find what they were looking for, they will always find something if they look hard enough.

THE PRISON'S PRISON

Most inmates break the rules sometimes, although often it's for something petty: borrowing commissary, bringing a pack of mayonnaise to the chow hall (to make the food more palatable), or smuggling sugar packets back to the wing from your breakfast tray. I don't judge anyone who does stuff like that. I know just how hard it is to make life bearable here, but I work pretty hard at not getting into trouble. My friends know that I am not the person to ask if they want a kite delivered or some commissary snuck into the wing, and people who do ask are told point-blank that I do not break the rules for anyone, especially someone who really could care less if I end up in trouble over her mess.

It's not that I'm particularly ass-kissy around the officers, although some people probably assume that's why I don't involve myself in that stuff. There are several reasons why I avoid breaking the rules. An important one is that I like having a good reputation. Most staff members and officers know that if I am someplace, it's because that is where I am supposed to be. If I have something, it is because I'm supposed to have it. For the most part they treat me with either respect or indifference (the ones who treat me badly would do so no matter how I acted). Inmates are hassled considerably less often when they aren't trouble-makers. Most important, I don't want to be ashamed of how I conduct myself in here. I promised myself during that awful time in jail that I would always try to be as decent and honorable in here as I can be.

Another reason I keep my nose clean is that I'm just too tired to put in the emotional effort necessary to successfully violate the regulations. It's too much work to have a girlfriend smuggle cigarettes or hide contraband. It reassures me to know that the officers can shake my room down at any time and I will probably be OK.

Not that I'm perfect, of course, but anything ticketable a shakedown might uncover in my property is definitely an accident or ignorance. There are so many rules about what you can and can't have, rules that seem to change constantly without inmates even being informed of it, that if they tried hard enough, I'm sure they could get me on something. I think I'm in pretty good shape, though. I've only had one brush with the police over contraband property. That came with Sergeant Hollis.

Sergeant Hollis is a decent guy. A tall, burly black man whose face is always serene, even in moments of crisis, he's one of those rare officers who is the same to every inmate every day (some officers seem to change up from minute to minute). He would joke with us about who was supposed to bring the potato chips when we were watching a football game on the dayroom television. We would tell him that he was supposed to bring the keg, so where was his contribution? But he believed in following the rules. One thing, though, about Sergeant Hollis that made him stand out from many officers (some of whom are virtually crippled intellectually by the prison bureaucracy) was his ability to temper his adherence to the rules with common sense. For example, we were having a birthday for Sylvia one afternoon, and each of us was wearing a party hat that Gloria had made. Sergeant Hollis came in for rounds and asked what was going on. When we explained that it was Sylvia's birthday, he said that we could wear the hats for the duration of the party but that we had to get rid of them immediately afterward. Technically we could have been considered to have been altering our appearance, a 100 series charge (100 series charges are the major ones; minor offenses are 200 series charges). That was cool. As soon as the party was over, we all filed up to the glass front of the wing so that he could see each of us deposit the hats in the garbage can. A man who always gives respect, he always received the same from most of us.

He and I had our own interaction over contraband, though. I came home from my job in the print shop one afternoon to be met by Sergeant Hollis as soon as I entered the wing. "Ms. George, does this look familiar?" He pulled from his pocket an orange three-plug adapter. Clearly engraved on it was my name and inmate ID number. They had inspected my cell while my roommate and I were out of the unit.

I knew what this was all about. There had been random rumors for months that the orange adapters that commissary had sold for years were now contraband and many women had thrown theirs away just to be on the safe side. Not me. I wasn't getting rid of mine until I saw a memo telling me to get rid of it or an officer told me that it was contraband.

"Yes, Sarge," I said. "That's my adapter." I was a little nervous. I didn't think that I was in trouble because I didn't officially know that these were forbidden, but anything goes in here.

"Ms. George, I'm afraid that I'm going to have to write you a ticket for this contraband." He watched my face to see my reaction. I'm sure that he could see the indignation there. This was an item I had purchased legitimately, that I had never been formally told I could not have, and that, most important, allowed me and my roommate to use the same electrical outlet so that we could both watch television in our bunks (if I gave up my adapter, then my TV would have to be plugged in across the room so that the cord drooped over my roommate's desk and so that it was almost too far away for me to make anything out on the tiny 5-inch screen). Quite frankly, I loved my orange adapter. It was one of my most precious possessions, allowing me the luxury of watching TV comfortably *and* having my fan on at the same time!

I tried to keep my cool, but my anger was obvious. "Well, then I'll need to ask for an Inmate Advisor before I sign any ticket," I said. Inmate Advisors were prisoners trained in all of the rules and regulations of FCCW, and they could advocate for you if you received charges. Any inmate receiving a ticket was allowed to ask for an Inmate Advisor. "I've never seen any memo telling me that I can't have it any more, and I wasn't going to throw it away just because some inmates said that they were now contraband. I try to get along in here, but I'm not going to let myself get taken advantage of either!" My hands were on my hips and my chin jutted out as I squawked my outrage. I could see some of my friends watching, openly shocked at my display. I was the one who always kept her mouth shut, who smiled and nodded when the injustices were at their worst. And here I was going ballistic over a plug adapter!

Sergeant Hollis laughed. "Simmer down, Ms. George. You can just throw it away in my office. I'm not going to give you a ticket."

His laughter did not placate me. Still fuming, I stomped out of the wing and ostentatiously clanged my beloved adapter into his metal trash can. I still think about it sometimes when my cell is about 95 degrees and I have to choose between broiling or television. I see it, lying there in the battered trash can on a bed of crumpled papers and candy wrappers. When I get to Heaven, one of my main wishes is that there be plenty of electrical outlets! The only good thing was that, with the loss of my adapter, I lost my last property that could even marginally be considered contraband. It's nice not to have to worry any more, at least.

I've only received one ticket during my years behind bars, that for being in an unauthorized area. At the time the housing unit I lived in had telephones on both the upper and lower tiers. Because all of the lower-tier phones were broken, I was given permission one day to use an upper-tier phone. I didn't give the incident any more thought until several months later when I was served my unauthorized area (U.A.) ticket by C.O. Halpern, a particularly unpleasant officer who clearly found inmates to be several steps lower on the evolutionary scale than she was. Someone who worked in the investigator's office had done a computer search and identified everyone who lived on the bottom tier but used an upstairs phone, issuing a flurry of tickets all over the compound. In my wing alone, several other women received the same charge.

But I had never gotten into any trouble before, and I had no idea what to do. Because of that, I didn't realize that there was an appeal process, or that I was entitled to an Inmate Advisor. I found out later that the officer serving the tickets is supposed to explain the process to you, somewhat like Mirandizing a suspect, but Halpern did nothing but hand me the paperwork with barely concealed glee.

I don't think she was prepared for it when I burst into tears. U.A. charges are, after all, pretty minor in the list of inmate offenses and I was being offered an informal resolution—there would be no repercussions for me and the charge supposedly would be removed from my record after 2 years. I was so angry, though. All I could do as I scrawled my name on the paper acknowledging that I understood the charges and that I was accepting the penalty offer was weep angry tears and say again and again, "This is just not right. You know that this is not right."

Afterward, I was angry with myself that I had let someone like C.O. Halpern see my emotions, then even more outraged when I learned a few weeks later that everyone else who had gotten the tickets had appealed them and the charges had been dropped. My own ignorance and passivity (it hadn't even occurred to me to question it—I assumed that inmates had no process for appealing a charge) blemished my otherwise pristine prison record. I learned a valuable lesson. I'm never going to go down without a protest again.

More seasoned malefactors are intimately familiar with the rules and loopholes of the Divisional Operations Procedures (DOP) and Internal Operating Procedures (IOP), the two sets of regulations that mandate our every move. The DOP is a broader set of regulations created by the Department of Corrections that is applied to all DOC inmate facilities in Virginia. Our IOP is specific to FCCW. It is tailored to fit the needs of a specific facility rather than the more general DOP. Both are bulky, richly detailed documents that are barely comprehensible to many inmates. I've adopted the general philosophy that unless I'm 100% certain that something is permitted, I assume that it is forbidden. A small group of inmates, however, takes an opposite view: if it is not expressly forbidden, then go ahead and give it a try!

A couple are pretty good at it. Ticket after ticket is dismissed because of improperly filled-out paperwork or some other minor irregularity. Or the inmate is a snitch, so her infractions aren't even ticketed. She might even get hauled into the sergeant's office week after week, but it's the people around her that seem to spend an awful lot of time in segregation. The majority of the habitual rulebreakers aren't as lucky.

It is this relatively small percentage of prisoners, usually short-timers or lifers who are fairly new to prison, that ends up filling up most of the segregation cells. They go from seg to SLU, spend a few weeks or months in GP, then are right back in seg again on similar charges. There must be some sort of psychological payoff for this cycle of behavior, but I haven't been able to figure out what it is. Self-sabotage? Bravado? Uncontrollable rage? Just plain "I don't give a damn"? The motives are probably complex, but the results are simple: cold and bitter isolation.

Most infractions are resolved without the inmate having to go to seg. Punishments are basically deprivations of privilege, like loss of telephone, commissary, or visitation. An inmate is often placed on cell restriction, which means that she will not be allowed out of her cell for any reason other than meals, medical appointments, and showers. This particular punishment is a pain to the restricted inmate's roommate as well, because her door is now locked at all times. Whenever she wants to go in or out of her cell, she has to call up to the bubble officer to pop her door open, which tends to annoy the bubble officer. And as you can imagine, an annoyed officer is not someone you want working your wing.

Almost a guarantee of seg time, in many cases lots of it, are the serious charges like fighting, theft, drugs, or failing a "piss test," which can result from either testing positive for drugs or being unable to urinate within a brief allotted time. If I know that I am being called on a piss test, I drink mad amounts of water before I go over to Building Nine, which is where the investigator's office is. I am usually called right after I have gone to the bathroom. I'm just glad that I don't have the same crippling shame issues about urinating in front of another person that the women here who have been raped and abused have to endure. I've known women who have gone to segregation because they are simply unable to urinate in the presence of an officer, although their bladders are so uncomfortably full they can barely hold it in.

There are two segregation wings at Fluvanna, both dark and clamorous with the constant yells of women isolated within. I have only been back there a few times to bring in cleaning supplies or deliver library books, so I have never been inside one of the cells, thank God. The amenities are few. The wing's "dayroom" is a bare cubbyhole that contains a table, a few chairs, and a box of battered discarded books for the women to read. Segregated prisoners are allowed 3 hours of rec a week. You can sit in the tiny, windowless dayroom or, if you have outdoor rec, be placed in one of the enclosed miniature rec yards, one inmate per cage. It looks like a series of outdoor dog runs, and it is the only opportunity the inmates have to talk quietly to one another, hear the latest gossip, or discuss what was on the day's lunch tray.

An inmate is allowed almost nothing inside her cells: a security pen (a 2½-inch-long, flexible pen that cannot be disassembled and made into a weapon), paper, stamps, envelopes, and a radio. She can't have any personal books. Even her clothes are restricted. Although the cells are terribly cold, the inmates in seg aren't allowed to have the thermal long johns that the rest of the population is permitted to wear to stave off the icy temperatures. Neither are they allowed their sweatshirts or sweatpants. Instead they have to wear the thin blue uniforms of unclassified inmates. They sleep in a prison nightgown, which looks like an oversized navy blue T-shirt.

They can't buy any commissary except for stamps, stationery, and batteries for their radios. None of the Ramen noodles, tuna fish, chips, and candy bars that are desperately craved by perpetually underfed inmates are allowed. And as poorly fed as we living in GP are in the chow hall, at least we can snag unwanted food from our cohorts if we are starving. The women in seg get nothing but the scanty prison tray that always has smaller portions than those mandated by the DOC prisoner menu. For example, one of the seg workers told me that breakfast in seg yesterday was a scoop of farina, a half cup of boiled potatoes, and two slices of bread, with no margarine or jelly.

If an inmate flushes her food down the toilet to clog it or otherwise abuses the "privilege" of a regular meal, she might be served the diet loaf, a foul combination of potatoes, flour, low-grade meat, oatmeal, and God knows what else, melded together into one vile mass of the inmate's minimal daily nutritional requirements. We might joke about the "segregation diet," but in reality the women emerge from seg time significantly thinner than when they went in. The inmates are supposedly monitored to make sure that they aren't becoming too emaciated, but I don't know how emaciated is "too emaciated." You can tell someone who has done a long stint in seg immediately by her pallid complexion and half-starved frame.

Like rec, showers in seg are allowed three times a week: Monday, Wednesday, and Friday. The shower is especially depressing, a dank niche that has bars instead of a curtain, and the women have just a few minutes to bathe. Unlike the rest of us, inmates in seg can't buy the shampoos, soaps, deodorants, and other personal items necessary to maintain proper hygiene. They are instead given small bottles of cheap shampoo, the tiny toothbrushes that (like the one I was initially given at the jail) shed their bristles immediately, and harsh soap that leaves the skin as desiccated as an autumn leaf.

I've heard that there are four cells in seg that are reserved for women on suicide watch. Women deemed at high risk for this are housed in one of these cells, where they are strapped down to the bed at all times. They are not given the blue uniforms that other seg inmates wear. Instead, they wear a heavy fabric sleeveless smock, little comfort in the perpetual cinder-block–trapped chill of the cell. Officers walk by the cell every 15 minutes, noting on the clipboard outside the cell door that they have done their required rounds. Inmates are released from suicide watch after they have been examined by one of the mental health professionals on staff.

All of the inmates confined to segregation, however, are at risk of dangerous mental health issues because of the exacerbating effect of extreme isolation and deprivation, and officers aren't always as assiduous about caretaking duties as they should be. More than one woman has managed to hurt herself while confined in segregation. An inmate seg worker who lived in my wing a few years ago would sometimes tell me about her job, always swearing me to silence. Knowing that I am a writer, she told me that once she went home she hoped I would "tell anybody who'll listen about what goes on back there. Most everybody else around here is afraid of saying anything. Maybe you'll do something if the right person hears about it."

The stories that Lena told horrified me—I was appalled that such cruel carelessness existed in the place where I would have to spend the rest of my life, even if it was hidden behind forbidding metal doors. I remember one afternoon after pill call when Lena emerged from her cell looking wan and unkempt. As she was a fastidious Hispanic woman in her late 30s, I was shocked by her tousled hair and lack of makeup. I hadn't seen her all day, and worried that she was ill. I approached her as she sat alone at one of the dayroom tables, her head cradled in her arms.

"Lena, what's going on? Are you OK?" I asked. She lifted her head wearily, looking even worse up close.

"I'm alright," she answered. "They called me to work at 3:00 a.m., so I didn't get much sleep last night." Inmate workers were always on call, and I knew that they might be summoned at any hour to prepare a cell in seg for a new arrival. I assumed that was what had happened. Unfortunately I was wrong. What Lena had been through was devastating to her, an unfair and barbaric demand that, as an inmate, she was forced to comply with.

"You knew that Lauren was back in seg, right?" I didn't, but I wasn't surprised to hear it. Lauren spent most of her time there because she was prone to threatening suicide and cutting herself. Her arms and legs were striated with layers of razor blade and knife scars, some dating back to her early adolescence. It was almost painful to have a conversation with her the few times we would meet on the yard. She would be so obviously, falsely cheerful, standing alone outside the chow hall, chattering on about nothing as her fingers nervously wandered over the familiar terrain of her ridged forearms, the battle-scarred landscape of a war that she was clearly losing.

"She tried to kill herself last night and I had to clean it up. It took forever to get it all up, Erin, and it was the bloodiest mess I've ever seen in my life." She pressed her cheek wearily into her hand.

I was shocked that Lena had been told to do this. It was well known on the compound that inmates were not supposed to clean up any spilled bodily fluids. Officers who have had special training in using spill kits and other precautionary measures are the only ones authorized to handle situations like that. Theoretically, this rule is in effect to protect inmates from potential infection. It's a sad reality that many of the women in here are infected with something contagious: hepatitis, HIV, full-blown AIDS, as well as myriad lesser afflictions. But like most of the rules here, application of this directive was mandated more by convenience than consistency.

At my expression of surprise she shook her head. "Girl, I don't tell you half the stuff that goes on back there. They tell us that we're not allowed to talk about it, that if we do we'll lose our jobs and not be able to work anywhere else. I need that money too much to say anything—I live on state pay. My momma can't afford to send me anything; she's barely able to make it herself." Lena suddenly paused, then added, "But I'm a damn sight luckier than that poor child."

I didn't really want to hear the details, but I could see that she needed someone to listen. "Do you want to talk about it?" I asked.

I've never seen anything like it, and I've seen some bad shit on the street (Lena said). My brother got shot once right outside our house, but that was nothing compared to what Lauren did to herself. I didn't see her, she'd been taken to the infirmary by the time they called me. I just saw the mess she left behind. The worst thing is that they sent me into the cell and didn't prepare me at all for what was in there.

You know that I'm used to being called up in the middle of the night, that's no big deal. But I knew that something bad had gone down because the first thing they had me do was put on booties, gloves . . . all this stuff that I never have to wear just to clean up a cell. And when I asked them what was going on, they would just keep saying "Hurry up, hurry up." I was scared to death. Was there a body or something in there that I would have to drag out by myself? I knew that people had to wear this when they cleaned up really dangerous messes.

When the C.O. popped the cell door I almost puked. I was half asleep, and I felt like I was in a horror movie or something. There was blood everywhere: smeared on the wall, in the toilet, even in the girl's shoes. After I was done, one of the officers told me that Lauren had smuggled in a razor blade she had hidden inside her Bible, but to me it looked more like someone had cut somebody up with an axe. The blood was so thick, and it had congealed so much that I thought it was balls of bloody tissue on the floor. I didn't realize what it was until I got down on my hands and knees to scoop it into garbage bags.

I was outraged. "You shouldn't have to do jobs like that! You should grieve it." I was ready to spring into action, write an IMS, fetch grievance forms, call the *New York Times*. This was a terrible injustice!

Lena touched my arm. "Erin, I told you that they said they'll fire me if I tell anyone or complain. And I don't got it like that so I can't afford not to work. You know what they do to you in here if you tell. I don't have a choice." She looked away, then added in an amazed voice, "You know what? They had that damned cell filled again within 10 minutes."

Fluvanna doesn't have a "hole" like you see in the movies, but the deprivation and isolation of segregation is, I think, punishment enough. I don't think that the inmates are usually physically abused (other than the poor diet, lack of exercise, and neglect), and I have heard few rumors about actual beatings, but even the briefest stay in seg is a scarring experience. In extreme cases, women spend years back there, usually forgotten by the rest of us who have the opportunity to take part in the daily activities of the prison.

As a rule, most of what goes on in segregation stays hidden from the inmates in general population, but we get brief glimpses of the sad stories of these women imprisoned within prison: the calls for medical assistance to the segregation wings that are made over the prison intercom system, a stooped and pale woman who shuffles shackled to a medical appointment, the troop of riot gear–clad officers pouring though the sally port to quell yet another inmate who has lost it while in segregation.

Many inmates are reluctant to discuss what life in segregation is really like. Some variation of "I don't want to bring it on myself" was the usual response when I asked inmates for an insider's view of isolation. Those who don't want to look superstitious will give a vague response, like, "I just slept a lot." There might be some truth to this fear. Three days after a friend of mine offered to discuss her stays in seg with me, she was hauled off to isolation for 10 days. Eventually she was released without a charge, but after that she regretfully declined to discuss the subject with me.

ONE WOMAN'S EXPERIENCE IN SEGREGATION

One woman was willing to describe her times in segregation to me. Tianne has been down for 22 years and had been in and out of seg several times. She is a lovely, intelligent person who looks very much as she did when she was first locked up, except perhaps a bit grayer. I commented on her youthfulness one afternoon as she was showing me her photo album. Tianne laughed. "Lots of people say that. I'm what they call 'pickled by prison.'" Although prison time is hard time for lifers—poor diet, inferior medical care, lack of restful sleep, and an abundance of grief age most of us far more rapidly than would be normal outside—a rare few lifers seem untouched by the years. Tianne was one of these.

One afternoon we sat together in the dayroom and talked about her time in prison:

> I've been sent to seg four or five times since I was locked up. The first three times were for conspiracy to commit escape. I've never actually gotten a ticket behind any of my stays in seg, but someone with a sentence like mine (four consecutive life sentences) is easy prey for cruel and stupid people.
>
> The first time I was 22 years old and had been at Goochland prison for all of a year. At the time I was locked up, all lifers were housed at Goochland—FCCW hadn't been built yet. It all started when a rather rotund, beefy woman was trying to jack me out of my canteen. The first time she asked me for a bag of noodles I gave it to her, but the second time I was really irritated and said that I didn't have any, so she harassed the shit out of me.
>
> Finally, I guess she got pissed that a scrawny little white girl wasn't bending to her will, so she told the police I was planning to escape. Prison policy says that they have to investigate a charge like that, even if it comes from an inmate, so if you want to make trouble for someone, accusing her of planning to escape will screw things up for her. So, because of that big bitch I spent 16 months in isolation under investigation before they finally let me go without a charge.
>
> This wasn't as hard as it sounds because I was so new to the system and didn't know any different. I had money on my books, so I bought plenty of coffee and cigarettes. I was OK. The investigator was really fair and good to me. It wasn't as hard as later lock-ups because I didn't have much to lose: no friends, no job.
>
> Flash forward five years. I never found out what sparked my next time in seg. Me and a friend were both locked up for conspiracy to escape. We stayed there for 30 days. I think this was all behind somebody pissed off at us, probably over cigarettes.
>
> When they cut me loose, I had a conversation with the shrink. I really fucked myself big-time by talking to her, but I was angry about the 30 days in seg. I guess I looked it, because she asked, "Why are you being such an ass? What's your problem?"

So I said, "I got three options the way I see it: I can shut the fuck up and do my time, I can shut the fuck up and kill myself, or I can shut the fuck up and leave." My point was that of the three, I was going to shut the fuck up and do my time. I knew I was being an ass, so I was going to chill out and get over myself. But she stopped listening at "shut the fuck up and leave," so I went back to seg, this time on Administrative Hold. They didn't know what to do with me.

It was Friday, October 31, about five years later that I went to seg for a third time on another conspiracy to commit escape charge. We were still allowed to wear our street clothes then, so I had on my Arizona blue jeans, a black tank top, and my Pumas. I had a pack of Marlboro Reds in my back pocket. It was the end of the day, so I went into my room, climbed up onto my bunk, and unhooked the smoke detector to get to my stash of pills. I had percoset (pain pills), real Motrin (not that useless prison crap), and Tylenol. I've always had lots of pain in my hands—I had juvenile arthritis—so the Motrin and the Tylenol were for that. The percoset was for my migraines.

Medical would never help me, so the nurses would slip me pills for the pain. I climbed up to get them because I was hurting really bad. I had a plastic bag full of over thirty pills, and really needed a Motrin. After I got one, I checked my back pocket for my stogies, grabbed my lighter, and left the room to go to the back porch of the housing unit. Where we lived then was an old, dilapidated building, and the porch is where we liked to go out and smoke. Notice that I neglect to say that I put the pills back before leaving my room. I left them lying on my bunk.

When I was standing in the doorway smoking, Captain A., an unbelievably nice, fatherly guy, came out and leaned next to me. I knew I was in trouble, I had a sixth sense.

He told me to come with him into the office, and I knew that meant he was going to cuff me, so I said, "I don't want to go to your office."

Captain A. said, "Please?" so I went in and got handcuffed. As he walked me to seg, past all of the women in pill line, I could hear the ripple of conversation. It was like the Doppler Effect. When I asked why he was locking me up, he said that it came from down the hill to arrest me, and that he didn't know why. He promised me that he would find out, and I believed him.

Sitting in the search room, I started to panic because I'd been told for years that when they finally executed Ben, my husband and co-defendant, they would put me in seg. So I'm sitting there thinking, "Oh fuck, this is it." That scared me because I didn't want to be isolated and alone when it happened. I sat alone in the search room from 5:30 to 11:30 thinking this. I had only brought two cigarettes, and needless to say they were gone by 5:35.

At 11:30, C.O. Oakes came in. She was great, a realist. She treated us really well. She served me PHD [prehearing detention] papers for possession with intent to distribute. I've never been happier in my life. I jumped up and down and hugged her. Oakes was completely floored by my reaction. She stepped out for a while, then came back in a little later with a Pepsi and a pack of Newports. She left a second time and came back with a baby blue blanket. I realized that these were all from my friend, Tori, who was already in seg. Tori had seen me brought in and knew that I'd be cold and upset, so she'd given the soda, cigarettes, and blanket to Ms. Oakes when she'd done her rounds. I immediately popped the Pepsi, offered Ms. Oakes a cigarette, and sat smoking with her. I told her what I'd been afraid of so she would understand why I'd been so happy.

After we finished smoking, she dropped another bomb: I was also on Administrative Hold for conspiracy to commit escape again. I didn't care. Ben was alive. C.O. Oakes told me that a letter had been received at Atmore [the Department of Corrections headquarters in Richmond] about me.

The Monday after I was locked up I got a handwritten letter from a former prison counselor I'd had a romantic relationship with. He had quit his job at Goochland so that he could legally visit me, but a week before the letter about my planned "escape" showed up downtown, we'd had a huge argument. In the letter he sent me he threatened to bring me down. He also insinuated threats against my sister, saying he knew where she worked. After I read the letter, I turned it in to the officer.

I spoke to the building sergeant after I got the letter because I wanted to get my visitor list flagged [at that time inmates had to submit names of potential visitors to the prison administration to get permission for them to come]. I was afraid that he would try to come and see me. The sergeant told me that the prison didn't do that. I went up the chain of command about my fears, but everyone was blasé about it.

So I was locked up because of an anonymous typed letter. When I saw the investigator, she said that the letter was typed and unsigned, but that the dumb ass had put his return address on the envelope. She knew all about our relationship. I asked to see a magistrate for a restraining order so that this guy would have to leave me alone, but a C.O. told me that the magistrate said no one gave a damn because I was just a prisoner.

I was chilling in seg when the institutional investigator assured me that everything would be fine. Through the next couple of weeks I kept getting continuances on the drug charge. It got to the point where whenever I knew that they were doing hearings on tickets I would beg to go downstairs to get sentenced. I wanted to serve out my punishment while I was stuck in Administrative Hold anyway. I was going to plead guilty—Ben was alive, what did I care about a shitty little drug charge? I have four consecutive life sentences. Fuck you! It was so petty in the grand scheme of my life.

Periodically, I was pulled from my cell to chat with the investigator so it would look like she was actually investigating me.

One night a C.O. came to my door to tell me I had mail. They had been screening all of my letters in case any of them were threatening. While she handed me my mail, I started to beg her about a hearing. I'd had five continuances by then, which was way beyond legal. "Oh, that charge has been dismissed," she said.

I was pissed. "What?" I asked.

"The charge has been dismissed."

"Why?"

But she told me that I didn't need to know why. I couldn't believe it. They'd threatened me with street time over this! I needed to know why the charge was dropped, but all she would tell me is that the reporting officer had dropped the ticket.

By this time I had at least learned how the drug charge had come down. It turned out that when the officer had gone into my room to pack up my shit for the Administrative Hold, she found my stash. To this day I have no idea why the charges were dropped. It had to have been God. As the C.O. was leaving, I said, "Can I have my pills back?" The only answer I got was her slamming shut my door. Two weeks later I was released after 7 months on Administrative Hold.

I have only been to seg once since they moved us to Fluvanna. They never gave me a specific reason for it, but I spent 10 days in isolation without being questioned, signing any papers, or even being told what the charges were.

About 2 months before I got locked up, I had left my job in the Tailor Shop. When I worked there, I had fixed one of their saws. As a joke, I had submitted a bill to the supervisor. The supervisor, also joking, created a fake "check" for payment. It had my name on it and one of the male supervisor's name on it. The supervisor laminated it and stuck it up on the wall. I hadn't given it a thought since leaving my job there. I'd forgotten all about it—the whole thing had happened 5 months ago.

I remember really clearly what was going on when it all went down. We all knew that the Tailor Shop was being tossed big-time. Since I hadn't worked there in months I was surprised when Sergeant Beale approached me and asked me if there was anything I wanted to tell him. He pulled me out of my job in maintenance, but seemed surprised that I wasn't in the Tailor Shop anymore.

I didn't know what the fuck he was talking about. So we did the whole little dance thing for 2 or 3 minutes.

"You sure you don't have something to tell me?"

"Yes."

"Positive?"

"Yes."

I got the message that there was something specific he wanted me to tell him, but I was truly clueless. Then Beale asked me if there was anything in the Tailor Shop with my name on it. I still didn't know what he was fishing for, but got embarrassed by the question because there was a ton of shit with my name on it in the Tailor Shop. [Putting your name on almost anything can be deemed altering state property, a charge.] I listed all the stuff I could remember: 2 cups, 4 aprons, several pillows for my chair, and my tool bag—all stuff I'd left behind when I quit.

The whole time we were talking I was looming over this guy. I was about a foot taller than him, and I was just standing there with my hands on my hips. I could see that I still hadn't given him what he wanted, and all I could say was, "You aren't happy with that?" That was a lot!

Finally he asked, "You don't have anything with your name and a supervisor's name?" That's when I remembered the check. So I told Beale about the fake bill and the story behind it. Up to this point he'd been rather pleasant, he hadn't gotten all shitty. I told him that I remembered it because I'd saved them $900 when I fixed that saw, and I was proud because I wanted to be a mechanic someday.

The atmosphere changed in a second, it got all cold. It wasn't anything he said, it just turned on a dime. Then the sergeant sent me back to my room. That kind of shocked me. I thought he was just asking me about it, but when he sent me to my room I felt like a scolded child. I asked if I were in trouble, and he said, "Maybe." He was leaning against the wall, his arms crossed, with this "I rule the world" manly-man face.

I asked again if I were in trouble. He said, "You might be."

"But it was just a joke!" I said.

"Well, this is a joke that may get you sent to seg," Beale said. "Go back to your room." This happened about 10:00 in the morning on a Wednesday. I went back to my cell and explained to my roommate, Marie, what was happening. She was very encouraging. I started to feel a little bit better. We began hearing bits of pieces of what was going on in the Tailor Shop, that three waves of C.O.s had been in there looking for a missing tool [all tools must be accounted for before any inmate leaves her workplace].

By mid-evening I was calming down enough to relax. I'd been locked up before for shit I hadn't done, so I was still a little nervous. The funny thing was that I had just told Marie the last week that I seem to go to seg every 5 years, and that this was almost 5 years since my last trip. That night they called me to Building Nine [where security and administrative offices are]. My stomach dropped. I thought I was going to leave a trail of pee behind me the whole way.

I got ready to be locked up. I told my roommate where my contraband was hidden, gave her my new lotions from Garden of Fragrance, and asked her to give my good hairbrush to my friend Dana. It's odd what we think about in those moments, packing up, assuming that you're going to seg. I was concerned about my contraband, and for some reason it was imperative that Dana get my brush. Those were the important things in my panic. I'm surprised now by my clarity in remembering this-it all happened four years ago.

It seemed like an endless walk to Building Nine, but each time I turned around to look at my housing unit, I saw Marie's bright orange knit cap waving in the window, silently supporting me.

It turned out that the reason that I'd been called was to sign for some legal mail [which has to be opened by an officer in front of the inmate. The inmate has to sign a log confirming that they did receive their legal correspondence], but I couldn't quite believe that was why I was there. As I got to the lobby, an officer said, "Please sign the book."

"What for?" I asked.

She said, "Tianne, you've got some legal mail."

I walked up to the desk feeling like I was walking through syrup. I was still afraid that this was a trick so that they could take me to seg. Since I'd never been in trouble at Fluvanna, I didn't know how things worked. What I'd seen happen before was the TPS (Treatment Program Supervisor) having his guys swoop in literally in the middle of the night like they were the KGB. They did it this way so that there wouldn't be friends around to cause drama and so the detainee wouldn't be as likely to show out in front of an audience. So it seemed perfectly logical to me that they'd call me for pretend legal mail to avoid complications.

So, I got to the desk and signed the book. Damned if she didn't actually hand me some legal mail!

When I started back to my building, I still felt like they were going to come get me. I was waiting for the bullet. As I went into the yard I was jumping up and down a little, and I saw the orange hat fluttering in the window. I slept alright that night, I'd been telling myself that the whole thing was absurd and that my boss would save me. The next morning it was business as usual. I got dressed, had a cup of coffee, and waited for my supervisor to show up. When he got there at 8:00, he told me that I couldn't come to work. He hadn't been told why, though.

Of course I instantly had that knife-in-the-gut feeling. I don't remember much, but my guts were a mess. I spent the whole morning in the bathroom after hearing that. When I came out of the stall, I saw Sergeant Beale coming out of my cell saying, "Where is she?" I knew immediately that this was it—that I was going to seg. He told me to pack up my shit. This was a little weird because normally C.O.s come in and pack up a person's property when she is going to seg. They like finding contraband so they can stick more charges on the person going to seg. As I was packing, the sergeant went straight to my uniforms. He took my greens [inmate worker uniforms], my safety glasses, my boots, everything related to my job, and threw all of it into a big trash bag. He almost seemed victorious. My roommate and I packed up the rest of my property. Beale kept rushing us because it was almost time for count and he wanted to get me to seg before that.

When everything was packed up, my roommate hugged me—all the while with Beale shouting at her to stop it. He didn't cuff me, which is not how it's usually done here, so I was still confused as to what exactly was going on. Was I going to seg, or just going to be questioned?

As he escorted me through the dayroom everyone was staring at me. I felt humiliated. I also was angry. My friend Mandy yelled, "We love you girl!" But all I could do was throw up one of my hands. I couldn't even raise my head. I understand that if my behavior dictates that kind of punishment, but I hadn't done anything wrong. Even getting arrested for murder was different because there was some guilt in that. But I hadn't made the check they were locking me up for, if that was even the reason.

When we got to the sally port, Beale handcuffed me. The whole time I'm asking him why I was being locked up. He wouldn't speak or make eye contact, not even turning his head in my direction. I just kept rephrasing the question.

As we walked, Beale had a gentle hold on my left elbow, and another officer, Sergeant Timmons, held my right. I kept asking them what was happening, and finally Sgt. Beale muttered an answer. Without thinking, I stooped low so that my ear would be level with his mouth. All I was trying to do was hear him better. I only realized how embarrassing this was for him when Timmons started smirking and I felt Beale tighten his grip painfully on my elbow. That was it for any attempt at conversation.

After they dropped me off at Building Eight, they threw me into a cell and slammed the door. It was odd; they didn't take my jewelry or hair clip or search me to see what I might be carrying. At some point I was given a seg bag that held sheets and toilet paper. The inmate who delivered was my friend, Kaylee. She wasn't allowed to speak to me, so she settled for making goofy faces at me, trying to get me to smile and reassuring me that she loved me.

Later that day the officer brought me the property I was allowed to have. I spent the next 9 days manic, swinging between strength—"I can do this, I'm fine"—and the other extreme: despair and hopelessness. I'd also just gotten my first parole turndown and a 3-year deferral, so my brain was my own worst enemy. I sat back there and beat the shit out of myself mentally. I rehashed my crime, ways I could have prevented the murders, Ben's execution. I listed all the ways I had destroyed my life, my family, and how I had hurt my mother. . . . I punished the shit out of myself. It was like utter self-loathing. I hadn't let myself feel that way for a long time.

They didn't pay me much attention because I was quiet. No one cared that I didn't eat (I ended up losing ten pounds), they would just stroll past my cell during their rounds, only stopping to note on a clipboard hanging outside my cell that I appeared to still be alive. The first week I asked every officer who came by why I was back there, but no one seemed to know. A C.O. I was friendly with told me that no one seemed to know anything about it. The real pisser was that the building sergeant, the institutional investigator, and the watch commander were all on vacation or had quit, and apparently they were the only people who had any answers.

I went to an ICC hearing [a hearing where charges against an inmate are reviewed and punishment given] and was told I would have to wait until all those people came back. Essentially, I had to stay in seg for another month without even being able to find out the reason why.

A friend of mine, Beth, happened to get locked up too, and they put her in a cell next to mine. We would lay on the floor in front of our doors and holler through the air vents to talk with each other. That's the way we communicated in seg. If you wanted to talk to someone not next to you, you would yell your loudest and hope that they could hear you. Seg gets pretty noisy sometimes.

Nine days later Beth yelled to me that they were doing ICCs again and that the Assistant Warden was running it. I told her that it didn't matter, that I needed to see the institutional investigator, but she said, "You never know." Sure enough, they pulled me to ICC a few minutes later. I thought maybe I'd found out something, but I didn't expect to get out. I just wanted to know why I was there.

When I got to the hearing, the Assistant Warden was smiling at me like a shark. I was sitting in front of her in a dingy, dark room, handcuffed. As I sat there quietly, she leaned over the table towards me and said, "What are you doing in my building?"

I spewed out words to her for at least 7 or 8 minutes—I was telling government secrets, man! When I finished, I had the audacity to say, "Do you know what I'm talking about?" She hadn't moved the whole time I was talking. It was like she was switched off.

Finally, she leaned back and said, "Oh, yes." My heart fell out of the bottom of my pants leg because she did not have a good vibe when she answered. I knew that I was never going to see daylight again. Satan herself (the Treatment Program Supervisor) was in there, too. The Assistant Warden and the TPS literally went head to head to confer. All I could hear were hisses as they whispered. It was very rude.

The TPS turned her computer screen to the Assistant Warden to show her I-don't-know-what. The Assistant Warden said, "Oops!" and looked at me again with that dead grin shark face. By this point I'm bouncing in my chair in handcuffs, and she says "Oops"? What oops? What does that mean? She had the power to let me out and all she was saying was "Oops?"

The Assistant Warden leaned towards me again and said, "I wasn't supposed to meet with you today." I deflated like a balloon and felt my stomach fall out through my other pants leg. Bitch! I'm jacked up in this cheap plastic arm chair—and in handcuffs for God's sake, with not even enough room for my elbows.

I said "What does that mean?" She said something like my ICC hearing was scheduled for 5 weeks later. All I could think to say was, "Oh."

Then she said, "Sign this paper."

I awkwardly took the pen into my cuffed hand, but before I signed I asked, "What am I signing?"

"You're going RGP."

"What's that?"

"Release to General Population."

I don't remember exactly how I responded, but it was something asinine like, "Well, what if you need me for something else?"

"Oh, I know where to find you," all the while with that same shark smile. Then she said, "Get out of my building." The next night I was moved.

While I was still in seg, my boss came to see me. I asked if he were mad at me, and he said no. I told him that they were letting me out. When I asked if could have my job back, he said, "You never lost it."

Once I was back in GP, my work supervisor got me new greens and boots from property. He even brought me a new pair of safety glasses that he'd had engraved with my name and ID number. He was so angry that Sergeant Beale had thrown away all of my stuff. I still have those glasses—I'm taking them home with me.

I ended up moving into Building Five—a new housing unit with a new roommate. When I got to my new cell, I opened up my [property storage] trunks and saw that Marie had stuffed all her commissary in my trunk without my seeing her. It was full of food: snack mix, M&M's, soda, tuna . . . it was like she'd been to the grocery store. I sat on the floor and cried, I was so touched. I knew we were friends, but I didn't realize how much it was reciprocated until I opened that trunk.

Tianne's visits to segregation on bogus charges and false assertions are not anomalies. Many women do their time there without a solid charge behind it. Bitsie was once locked up in "under investigation" status. After a week, she was told it was because the institutional investigator had seen that she'd gained weight and thought she was "bulking up" in order to escape. At that, Bitsie told them, "Hell, no—I just got a new girlfriend who feeds me good!" She was released almost immediately.

DEATH ROW

I was never fortunate enough to meet Teresa Lewis, although I certainly heard enough stories about her and even glimpsed her smiling face a couple of times. Unlike the "hardened cons" found on television's more lurid shows, we are, actually, a far more sentimental and gooey bunch than you might imagine (excluding

CHAPTER 5 • Shakedowns, Fakedowns, and Solitary Confinement   95

a certain segment of the prison population that pretty much hits the mark of the hard-assed, foul-mouthed bellicosity of fiction's more colorful incarcerated characters. Think "Prison Break" with breasts).

However, we do tend to exhibit a generalized feeling of "ya get what ya get" toward most of our fellow sisters in bondage. For example, I like Sadie well enough, but I am also fully aware that she was deeply and deliberately involved in the cold-blooded murder of several people and thus am not outraged at her incarceration. I try not to judge—and am largely successful, except when I learn that someone is inside for brutality toward a child (which is why I'd prefer *not* to know why someone whose company I enjoy is locked up). But even the most miserable, hateful prisoners demonstrate compassion on occasion, and Teresa was someone towards whom almost everyone at Fluvanna, including staff, felt such an emotion.

Teresa's story was well known on the grounds. She was convicted and sentenced to be executed because, according to the Commonwealth of Virginia, she had masterminded the murder of her husband, ensnaring two men into a conspiracy to kill him for insurance money. On the surface, simple enough. The facts are a little murkier though.

There are two variables that make her execution particularly abhorrent. I need to make one thing clear, however: much of what I know about her case and execution was heard second- or third-hand because I didn't have much access to newspaper reports about her appeals and execution. Most of what I learned I had to base on statements from inmate segregation workers and sympathetic staff members.

The first variable was known and misrepresented even prior to her trial. Teresa Lewis was, by the accounts of everyone who really knew her, barely capable of going to the grocery store unescorted, much less planning and executing a sophisticated murder plot. Although her IQ was tested as being officially a few bare points into the lowest range acceptable for state-sanctioned murder, my understanding is that both anecdotal evidence and other tests not admitted to the court showed her to be below that arbitrary level. In any case, the poor woman was clearly *not* the Napoleon of crime that the state painted her to be.

The second issue was even more tragic, if that was possible. As everyone knows, the appeals process for someone facing the death penalty can stretch out for years, and such was the case for Teresa. Her two co-defendants, the men that actually committed the murder, had not received a death sentence; they were sentenced to life in prison without the opportunity for parole. Well, during Teresa's long, long stay in the closest thing that Virginia has as a death row for women, one of the segregation wings of FCCW, one of her co-defendants was diagnosed as being terminally ill. Before he died, he sent a letter to the governor of Virginia, telling him that he and the other man had actually been the ones to plan the crime. They had deliberately chosen Teresa's husband because of Teresa's tractability and proceeded to manipulate her every step of the way. He, in fact, took responsibility for much of what occurred.

This letter had no impact on our fine, Christian governor (you know, the kind of fellow who has grand political hopes for high executive office. It was with much glee that I learned a few years later of a scandal incriminating him and his family members in the inappropriate transfer of substantial "gifts." It is my profound desire that any chance he had for advancement has been thoroughly and permanently scuttled.) What is one shattered life, after all, when you need to cater to a ravening horde of conservative nutjobs in order to promote yourself? Soft on crime, me? Hell no! If nothing else, Ms. Lewis may have committed adultery. For that alone she should have been taken outside the village and stoned. She's fortunate she got to spend several long, lonely years in Spartan segregation before she got what was coming to her.

And a long, lonely stretch it was. Fluvanna's segregation wing is not pleasant. Dimly lit and clamorous, a week there is uncomfortable. I can barely imagine years there, and I am used to the depredations of confinement.

In its own way, the prison did what it could to make her time as bearable as possible. Unlike other seg inhabitants, Teresa was allowed to buy commissary. I would imagine that C.O.s looked the other way when seg workers exchanged a few words with her. But there really wasn't that much they could do for her.

As the time for her execution drew near, Teresa became a major presence on the compound, unseen as she may have been. At the time, the honor unit was still housed in Building Eight with the segregation unit, and one morning, as we all sat in the dayroom waiting to go to work, an announcement was made that there would be no inmate movement that morning.

"Good lord, what now?" I groaned. I hated losing a morning's pay (all $1.35 of it) for some typical prison bull.

Logan said, "Oh, don't you know? Teresa's going to cosmo today!"

"What? That's great!" I said. I hadn't ever seen Teresa, but if she was going to go to cosmo to get her hair done, I'd be able to give her a wave as she passed our wing. "I think that it's pretty cool that they're letting her do that," I said. The next thing I knew, this sweet-faced lady, escorted by two officers, came out of the seg unit. Everyone in the wing started cheering, waving frantically, and hollering things like, "We love you, Teresa!" The two officers with her just grinned at us, and Teresa looked thrilled.

"That poor woman," I said to Mary, who was sipping from a cup of instant coffee. "I wonder what it's like back there for her." Mary, my long-time roommate, was a segregation worker. There was really no perk to that job, unlike other prison employment. (For example, kitchen workers get to sneak extra food; yard workers spend a lot of their time sunning themselves; intake workers identify who is coming in here with the best hair clips and other goodies and thus lay the groundwork for the long game of getting their hands on said swag. The best part of my library job was being able to get my hands on new books as soon as they were cataloged.) Being a segregation worker is just misery and toil. And Mary's gentle heart had always been drawn to Teresa, wanting to make her time better. Mary didn't talk about it much because it was so painful, but that morning she opened up.

"You should see her, Erin. Did you know that she sings all of the time? She is about the most pleasant person I have ever met. Always smiling. She never lets her situation get to her. In fact, I hear her comforting the other women in the adjoining isolation cells a lot. She gets in trouble sometimes because she tries to pass Hershey Bars to the ladies who are locked up with her."

"How do the C.O.s treat her?"

"They're as nice as they're allowed to be, I guess. They try to look the other way when they can, but there really isn't much that they can do for her. They are real gentle with her, though.

Mary isn't the only person who described the warmth and joy of Teresa's spirit. As her death date drew closer, she began spending more and more time with the prison chaplain, a dear friend of mine. When the chaplain and I had pastoral sessions, we found ourselves talking more about Teresa and the chaplain's struggle not to get too emotionally involved in the impending execution rather than the issues that ostensibly brought me to her office.

The chaplain ended up leaving the institution prior to her execution, for which I largely blame her attempts to help Teresa. She was so outraged by the fact that this poor woman was being essentially murdered that she could no longer cope with the administration. After quitting, she in essence became a full-time advocate for Teresa, struggling in any way she could to bring attention to the injustice occurring and pleading with anyone who would listen for help. I was stunned when, during mail call, I leafed through an issue of *Newsweek* only to find an opinion column writing by our former chaplain about Teresa's case. As painful as it was for the chaplain, she fought to support Teresa to the end—she even had to battle the prison administration to be allowed to be present when Teresa was executed, as Teresa had asked.

We in the Honor Wing tried to get permission to visit with Teresa back in seg, to play cards with her or just to talk, but our proposals were ignored. Teresa's daughter was doing time here as well, and would have been allowed to see her mom if she had been so inclined, I believe, but she didn't show much of an interest in spending time with Teresa. The prison did do one remarkably humane thing before Teresa died, though. It turned out that Teresa loved dogs and had always wanted to be able to pet one of the rescues from the pen pals program. Clearly, that was utterly against the rules, but one afternoon Logan plunked down beside me. She had just walked her dog out to the intake area (the front part of building eight) and come back without her.

"Where's Callie?" I asked.

"This is the coolest thing," she said. "Ms. Silverman [the Building Eight unit manager] arranged for Teresa to have a play visit with Callie. Teresa is going to go to Ms. Silverman's office and get to love all over Callie as much as she likes."

"I can't believe that they're letting her do that."

Logan grinned, "Ms. Silverman doesn't give a damn, she is 3 months from retiring from this pit. Plus, she's a decent person. Why wouldn't she do it?"

Teresa got a little less than an hour with Callie, a frisky mutt from the Charlottesville SPCA, but came out of the intake area grinning as if she had just won a reprieve from the governor as she made her way back through the multiple locked doors to segregation.

That was the last time most of us saw Teresa. A short time later she was moved out of the prison in the middle of the night to be transferred to the death house in North Carolina, where the execution would take place (since Virginia doesn't commit enough executions to warrant its own death house, I suppose). There were the usual last minute appeals and protests, but they were fruitless. Teresa died at the hands of the state, the first woman in almost a century to have been executed. A brief interview that I saw on the local news right before she died was, not surprisingly, proof that her spirit was unbowed. It even featured a clip of her singing.

The aftermath of her death lingered for quite a while, especially among the staff who had done time with her in segregation and the lifers. One officer had to actually take time off because she was so upset at Teresa's death. And there were women doing time with me who had had first-hand experience with the death penalty already when their own co-defendants had been executed. They were the most affected by the execution. I spent the most time talking about it with Tianne, whose husband had been sent to the death chamber over a decade before.

Actually, "talking" would be the wrong word for it, because she was reluctant to articulate most of her feelings. Mostly we sat at a table in the dayroom, drinking coffee and being silent together. Sadie's co-defendant had been executed as well, but she, the ultimate queen of melodrama, was far more vocal about her feelings. Large tears were wept, long soliloquies delivered with emotive vim. It was "devastating" to her that Teresa had been executed. Oh, the humanity! (Hmm, imagine how poor Teresa and her family felt about it.)

Although I never faced the prospect of execution (except, probably, in the fervid fantasies of my prosecutor who would have loved to use my inert body to slick his way into state office), obviously Teresa's death left me groping with issues that I had heretofore been largely successful in ignoring.

I think that I can admit that I cried in my room that night, but it is harder to confess that those tears were self-pitying ones. I hated what happened to Teresa, but I was terrified by the thought of dying (or even living) here alone. My parents would be dead long before the time I kicked it, unless I was supremely fortunate, and I already had lost any substantive contact with my sister or children as time had passed and they had understandably moved on. The only person that I could rely on to be around for me was Mary, who had sworn that she would never abandon me.

Damn, I hate that phrase, "moved on," but I don't know how else to say it. Moved on they had, and I was stuck where I had been for 10 years and would be for decades more to come, a pathetic, ever-shrinking little blip in the rearview mirror, too weary and diminished to even wave anymore. And, damn it even more, I hated that in an effort to be "healthy," I had to accept this loss cheerfully. I wanted to rail at them, or send begging letters saying "I still love you and want you in my life! Why have you left me?" Instead I have to sigh and smile and say, "That's OK. I understand. You do what is healthy and right for you."

I'm torn. I do want that, for my children to be healthy and happy. That is more important to me than anything else. And I do understand. But that selfish part of me insists on whispering to me every Christmas, birthday, and Mother's

Day that passes with yet another absence of cards or affection, making me ask myself, "Is there a situation where I could let a family member, no matter what they have done or why they are imprisoned, fall off the face of the earth? Would I just let go of someone who loves me, no matter how painful it is for me to acknowledge their situation?" I like to think that I would not.

I'm not the only one to walk away from mail call empty-handed time and again. And I have seen too many women languish in here for years, only to have their families "rediscover" them in the year or so before they are finally due to come home. Suddenly her name is called more frequently at mail call, money shows up in her account, visitors start showing up. Where were these people 13 years ago? Now that it's easy to think about her, they are all rainbows and butterflies, fonts of familial attention. Do they think we don't notice?

The night after Teresa died I stared at the metal bunk above my head in the half-darkness and cried my pathetic cry as I envied her more than a little. She, after all, had finally made it out. If you had offered me the chance to swap places with her at that moment, I would probably have taken you up on it. Maybe I even would today.

Karen, an outspoken, intelligent woman and fellow lifer, has said that we should be offered the opportunity to choose to be executed humanely instead of suffering a sad decline behind bars. I think that a surprising number of inmates would take advantage of that option. Tragically, I also believe that there would be several people who hold legislative power in Virginia who cannot openly espouse their desire for the wholesale slaughter of anyone convicted of first-degree murder or a comparable crime but must be satisfied with entombing us forever within Fluvanna's walls.

A lot of people wonder why I am so scrupulous about obeying the rules. After all, they reason, I don't have any real chance for parole, I'm serving a life sentence, I can't even get any good time. Good time is time that is credited by the state for good behavior, which often allows inmates to leave earlier than their sentence might otherwise permit. The loss of good time is a very real threat to those short-timers to whom it applies, but obviously not to me. Why not buck, do whatever I want? What do I have to lose?

I normally don't bother to explain myself to them, but I have often explored my own motivations. Why do I bother to behave well? Following the rules here is not the norm, and I have gotten a lot of flak from other inmates for my "goody-goody" behavior. I'm more likely to be regarded by them as a brown-noser than a role model. I like to think that my good reputation helps me a little, but I am also morbidly aware that when it comes down to it, I will always be considered by most staff here to be just an inmate, in the long run untrustworthy and dishonorable.

But I do have my reasons. I have too much time to do to spend it worrying about getting a charge and losing what is important to me over a girl or some stolen commissary. There are things of value even in prison, and what I treasure are my contact visits with my family, my job, living in the Honor Wing, and my reputation. Any and all of those can be taken from me if I get in trouble, and it would take a long time to earn them back again. It all comes down to how I want to do my time. Time is easier if you stay under the radar and keep it together, and as the women who have been doing a long time often say, I'd much rather do my time than have my time do me.

REFERENCES

Bloom, B., Owen, B. & Covington, S. (2003). *Gender-responsive strategies: Research, practice, and guiding principles for women offenders.* Washington, DC: National Institute of Corrections.

Corley, J. (2008). Life in four parts: A memoir. In S. Nagelsen (Ed.), *Exiled voices: Portals of discovery-Stories, poems, and drama by imprisoned writers* (pp. 41–60). Henniker, NH: New England College Press.

Cunningham, M. D., & Sorensen, J. (2006). Nothing to lose? A comparative examination of prison misconduct rates among life-without-parole and other long-term high-security inmates. *Criminal Justice and Behavior, 33*(6), 683–705.

Dobrzanska, A. (2009). Dances with dragons: Memories of the hole. In R. Johnson & S. Tabriz (Eds.), *Lethal rejection: Stories on crime and punishment* (pp. 91–95). Durham, NC: Carolina Academic Press.

Guenther, L. (2013). *Solitary confinement: Social death and its afterlives.* Minneapolis: University of Minnesota Press.

Hassine, V. (2009). The hole. In R. Johnson & S. Tabriz (Eds.), *Lethal rejection: Stories on crime and punishment* (pp. 96–105). Durham, NC: Carolina Academic Press.

Hassine, V. (2011). *Life without parole: Living and dying in prison today* (5th ed.). Robert Johnson & Sonia Tabriz (Eds.). New York: Oxford University Press.

Hartman, K. (Ed.). (2013). *Too cruel, not unusual enough.* Lancaster, CA: The Other Death Penalty Project.

Johnson, R., and Chernoff, N. (2002). "Opening a vein": Inmate poetry and the prison experience. *The Prison Journal, 82*(2), 141–167.

Johnson, R., & Dobrzanska, A. (Nov-Dec 2005). Mature coping among life-sentenced inmates: An exploratory study of adjustment dynamics. *Corrections Compendium, 30*(6), 8–9, 36–39.

Johnson, R., & McGunigall-Smith, S. (2008). Life without parole, America's other death penalty: Notes on life under sentence of death by incarceration. *The Prison Journal, 88*(2), 328–346.

Kruttschnitt, C., & Gartner, R. (2005). *Marking time in the Golden State: Women's imprisonment in California.* New York: Cambridge University Press.

Kupers, T. A. (2008). What to do with the survivors? Coping with the long-term effects of isolated confinement. *Criminal Justice and Behavior, 35*(8), 1005–1016.

Parsons, B. (2007). Reawakening through nature: A prison reflection. In W. Lamb (Ed.), *I'll fly away: Further testimonies from the women of York Prison* (pp. 215–240). New York: Harper Perennial.

Pollock, J. (2002). *Women, prison & crime.* Belmont, CA: Wadsworth.

Rierden, A. (1997). *The farm: Life inside a women's prison.* Amherst: University of Massachusetts Press.

Toch, H. (1992a). *Living in prison: The ecology of survival.* Washington, DC: American Psychological Association.

Toch, H. (1992b). *Mosaics of despair: Human breakdowns in prison.* Washington, DC: American Psychological Association.

CHAPTER 6

Quality of Life (Loosely Defined)

Prison accommodations are pretty much what you'd expect. The food is bland and starchy, measured in small portions and served in unappealing ways. Meager servings might come as a surprise to persons in the free world, who sometimes think of prisons as a species of country club (see Johnson, 2004, 2007), but prisons were never comfortable. In these days of cost-cutting, prisons are becoming less hospitable by the day, sometimes serving food that is inedible by free world standards. George reports an incident in which officers came to the aid of inmates served moldy food. The incident is at once troubling and reassuring—troubling because the food service workers were willing to serve up inedible food, and to do so repeatedly; reassuring because the officers went out of their way to make sure the women got something decent to eat.

The best food served in prison, we learn, is the food made by inmates for their own consumption. On the Honors Unit, inmates like George have microwaves and ambitious imaginations, and on any given day can be found deploying supplies from the commissary (a prison store for inmates) to make appetizing food for consumption in the cells. The women on the regular cellblocks have fewer tools, and the tools they possess come with some risk—burns, exploding food packages, and charred servings—but they, too, work to make a meal of the meager food at their disposal. The details of these adventures in convict cuisine are testimony to the impetus toward innovation in prison, where the goal is to forge a life behind bars that goes beyond the narrow regimen of punishment and includes homemade approximations of basic creature comforts (see Appendix B, Erin George's prison cookbook).

Women in prison pay top dollar for essentials, which include food as well as phone calls, commissary purchases, and television. Prisons have become an industry, and some aspects of this industry are quite profitable, including those services like phone calls and television that link offenders to loved ones, especially children, and to the larger culture (see Bernstein, 2005; Jewkes, 2002; Johnson, 2008; Nagelsen, 2008). In prison, calls often must be made collect, which is surely a

burden on many families. Televisions must be purchased from the prison commis-
sary. At commissary prices, which are much higher than those in the free world,
this is a financial strain as well. (Commissary prices reflect free world economics
applied to prisoners paid prison wages, a mere pennies an hour, for those who can
find work.) Whether they like it or not, many women become financial burdens on
their families, which often foot the bills for calls, televisions, snacks, and the like.

The commissary charges punitive prices, but simply placing an order is a big
event. As with fakedowns (see Chapter 5), where women barter adeptly to make the
most of what is available to them, women work together to make the most of the
commissary ordering system and thereby improve the quality of their daily lives.
Arbitrary rules limit commissary purchases and reach deeply into other aspects of
prison life, notably the decoration of one's cell. The ostensible reason for many of
these restrictions is security, but many of the prohibitions seem gratuitous. Perhaps
these restrictions are entirely a matter of bureaucracy, with its passion for stan-
dardization, reaching new heights with the advent of CORIS, a computer-based
management system now in place to bring order, or a reasonably facsimile, to the
daily lives of the prison's inhabitants.

With her light touch, George introduces us to the "institutional safety officer,"
who would seem to be a case of bureaucracy run amok. That officer keeps track of
the "Chemical Safety Data" for everything that comes into the prison. A laudable
idea, to keep the prisoners safe from toxic imports, but the practical result is that
highly valued Christmas packages are denied to the women. After all, the contents
of each package are different, and no one can say for sure exactly what chemicals
lurk within those various and sundry gifts. —Robert Johnson

Here is what I had for dinner last night: potato soup sprinkled with croutons, chicken salad and peanut tortilla rolls, and for desert, a rich chocolate cake with fudgy icing. No, it wasn't in the chow hall. On the menu for FCCW that evening was an unbreaded square of fish about the size of a deck of playing cards, unpeeled semiraw carrots, a third of a cup of steamed rice, and about 12 long-past-their-prime grapes. So no surprise that a couple of my friends and I decided to eat dinner on the wing.

We have become fair to extraordinary cooks using only what is available on commissary. Because we live in the Honor Wing, we at least have access to a microwave, so our culinary options are much wider than that of most other inmates here. Every other woman in Fluvanna has to do all of her cooking using just hot water from the hot pots that are in each wing. That's if she cooks legally. There are other, nonlegal methods of cooking. More daring chefs use the wing's clothes iron, swaddling the bag of food in a towel or T-shirt so that the police think they are only ironing clothes. You have to be careful using that method though. I've seen bags of chili explode because uneven ironing creates too much steam.

A 6-foot-diameter blast zone splattered with tomato sauce and beans is somewhat difficult to hide from the C.O.s or the wing snitches. Safer are the flat irons we are allowed to buy for our hair because they can be used in the privacy of our rooms. They are easily adapted to heating the bags of chili and Mexican beef we can get from commissary and are also handy for toasting bagels and making melted cheese and tortilla quesadillas. Blow dryers are used to cook the swoles and burritos that are prison staples. Each of those dishes is a combination of crushed Ramen noodles, crushed cheese curls, mayonnaise, beef sticks or tuna fish, and chopped pickle.

There may be minor variations to the recipes, but the basic process for making them is the same: shove all the ingredients into an empty potato chip bag and add enough hot water to make a glutinous mass. Roll the bag out thinly and let sit. Heating it up cooks the meal more thoroughly, though, thus making it worth the risk of blow-drying your culinary creation to steamy deliciousness.

Laura used the microwave to make the soup and cake, both dishes that she is renowned for. She's like the MacGyver of the kitchen, using the most improbable ingredients to work wonders. I am convinced, for example, that her potato soup literally saved my life once. I had caught one of the tenacious viruses that frequently sweep though the compound leaving a swathe of retching, sneezing, shivering inmates in its path. Refusing to spend $5.00 on a medical visit that I knew would garner me nothing more than vague promises that I will be called to see a provider "soon," I lay in my bed waiting for death to take me. It couldn't be too soon, as far as I was concerned. When I heard a knock at my cell door, I hoped that it would be a figure robed in black and brandishing a scythe. Instead it was Laura, her sweet, grandmotherly face smiling at me through the narrow window.

I croaked out a feeble, "You can open the door . . ." and listlessly tried to hide the clusters of cheap prison toilet paper that littered my bunk. Laura swung the door open, and in her hand was not an instrument of death, but a richly redolent elixir of life. I hadn't been able to drag myself out to the chow hall for 3 days and had been unable to stomach commissary food for the same period, so Laura had taken it upon herself to see that I didn't starve to death.

There, in one of the small plastic bowls we are allowed to buy from commissary, was her potato soup. The best part was the croutons, soaked by the tasty soup into the perfect comfort food, halfway between dumplings and toast. Just the smell of it revived me a little, and after my first tentative spoonful, I knew this was something I could actually eat.

After I recovered, I asked her how she made it. The recipe was surprisingly simple: a few bags of sour cream and onion potato chips, soaked for several hours in warm water; crushed cheese curls; evaporated milk and thinned down onion dip; croutons made of bagels seasoned with the flavoring packets from the Ramen noodles that are a commissary staple. The results, though, were heavenly! All of her ingredients are bought from commissary—I can't even imagine what she could do if she actually had access to real ingredients and a kitchen.

Her chocolate cake is equally amazing. She makes it from crushed Oreo cookies flavored with melted cherry Jolly Ranchers hard candies to cut the bitterness. The deeply chocolaty frosting had a rich coffee undertone that perfectly offset the melted Hershey bars she uses for topping. Because food is about the only comfort we are allowed to enjoy in here, I'm grateful that I don't need to rely on the paltry provisions that the chow hall offers.

The Fluvanna chow hall is the site of too many inedible or meager meals. Inmates who came here when Fluvanna opened over a decade ago like to describe the mouthwatering delicacies that used to be available here, the large portions and wide variety of food they had in the beginning. There was a legendary inmate cook, Rachel, who would make garlic bread for the spaghetti, cinnamon rolls for brunch, and three kinds of desserts at Thanksgiving. I can't even imagine such a thing anymore. Long-termers still lament that she was sent to serve the rest of her time in Utah.

By the time I got to FCCW, the meal situation had begun to devolve and had, I sincerely pray, reached its nadir. I find it hard to believe that it could get worse. During my year working in the kitchen, I learned far more about how the food service system works here than I really wanted to know. The Food Services Director is an amiable, chatty man who speaks grandiosely of his glorious inmate meals, citing decent portions creatively cooked and attractively served. He freely offers lots of tantalizing images of what his kitchen can produce, but we haven't seen many of them come to fruition. More significant to me are the awards that are proudly displayed outside his office. They proclaim that Fluvanna Correctional Center for Women had managed several years running to feed its inmates more cheaply than any other DOC facility in Virginia. This is accomplished by using donated food items (always of the lowest quality or beyond their expiration date—businesses don't give away food that they can sell), using dubious bargains found on the Internet and from suppliers, and serving portion sizes that are smaller than mandated by the DOC.

By policy, all meals and serving sizes are determined by the DOC dietician. In theory, they contain the recommended daily allowance of vitamins and minerals that adult humans require to avoid scurvy and beriberi and other ravages of malnutrition, but I have my doubts. The staples of the prison meal are the foods that fill you up but don't substantially enhance your nutritional intake: watery, unpeeled boiled potatoes; gummy spaghetti noodles; rice; and the omnipresent bread. Lately they have begun serving us stale poppy seed bagels, torture to the majority of women here because of the dentures most of them wear. I guess that the Food Services Director got a bargain on them, which is usually the case when we see a new food appear repeatedly within a short period.

Whoever the DOC dietician is, he or she is particularly enamored of the unidentifiable meat known as the "patty": meatloaf patty, pork patty, chicken patty, or sausage patty. Sometimes they try to camouflage it by giving it a deceptive moniker like Salisbury steak, or the infamous Cajun burger, a relatively new addition to the DOC menu that is probably so named because it washed up on the shores of New Orleans after Hurricane Katrina. They're still patties, though, and particularly loathsome, whatever they are called. Patties are, I'd guess, manufactured solely for use in institutional settings like ours—prisons, juvie facilities, orphanages, and insane asylums.

Vegetables are scarce and frequently range from merely aged to the obviously moldy. The same goes for the fruit. The kitchen's idea of an appropriate serving of fruit is extremely flexible. Once in the chow hall my friend Sadie was handed her tray. She started to take it, sighing as she saw that among the other delicacies it contained was a serving of disgusting strawberries. These strawberries were so black and molded that Sadie's roommate Belinda, who despite having long resigned herself to the inedible, bucked on Sadie's behalf. Belinda was the quiet one of the pair, actually, a good foil to Sadie's passionate outspokenness. She usually kept her opinions to herself, at least in the public view. I knew that she must be beyond livid to act out like this.

"These strawberries are disgusting! We can't eat these," said Belinda, shoving Sadie's tray back through the serving window. "I need a new tray."

The sullen, anonymous inmate on the serving line (all we could see were her hands through the narrow slot under the metal window shield) heaved the tray back through. "You have to eat it," she said.

"Aw, hell no," said Belinda, by this time outraged. She hailed the officer who stood nearby, not noticing the ruckus at the serving window. "Excuse me, ma'am, could you please look at these strawberries? I can't eat these."

The officer ambled over and scoped out Sadie's tray. C.O.s are used to inmates bitching about the food here, but this was undeniably beyond acceptance, even for us. She took the tray from Belinda and put it back through the slot herself, "Please give this inmate another serving," she requested.

The server, I guess thinking that the officer was just another inmate, said something rude. Out came the embattled tray.

Sergeant Ashton, who had been standing at the opposite end of the chow hall, wandered over, drawn by the rising noise of disgruntled inmates. Ashton is better known for his semi-inappropriate interactions with the more comely inmates than any activism on our behalf, so I was astounded when he took one look at the strawberries and flung the tray back into the serving line again. "Find these women something they can eat. I wouldn't even feed a dog this shit."

His basso profundo could never be misconstrued as an inmate's, so the woman in the serving line adopted a more conciliatory tone with him. "Sir, they're all like that."

"Get the kitchen manager," he ordered. There is supposed to be a kitchen manager stationed at each serving line to guarantee that the portions are correct, but because the kitchen is understaffed, these managers are frequently called away to perform other duties. After a few moments, a manager came to the window.

"Inmates can't eat this," said Sergeant Ashton.

The kitchen manager protested that he couldn't just change the menu, that the moldy strawberries were all that were available. Ashton grew visibly outraged. "You had better find something. I ain't no snitch but I am going to write this up myself if you try and serve these women this."

After a few minutes a new tray appeared, this time with half a lemon replacing the moldy strawberries. Ashton put that tray back through the window as well. "This is not an acceptable substitute. Find something else."

Those of us in line were silent, watching in stunned fascination as we observed the rarity of an officer visibly and loudly speaking on our behalf. When officers do things to help you out, it is usually on the down low and directed solely toward one favored prisoner. I had never seen an officer advocate for inmates as a group.

Minutes later, a third tray appeared. This one had a small piece of cake in the dessert slot. Ashton glanced at it and motioned for Sadie to take it. She did so silently, moving quickly to the dining table. Cake is a rarity here, so it was a double victory for us—the vanquishing of the moldy strawberries and the pleasant surprise of cake. Sometimes life can be sweet, even in the chow hall.

LET THE PROFITS ROLL IN

"Dammit!" I said, slamming the phone back into the cradle in frustration. This was the second time in a week that a phone call home had been terminated because the faulty computer monitoring system had incorrectly decided that my parents were forwarding my phone call to an unauthorized number.

I spun around and vented to the sympathetic woman standing behind me waiting to use the phone herself. "It really pisses me off when they say that I'm three-waying and I'm not. Phone calls are expensive enough without having to pay twice."

Deborah nodded in agreement. "It always seems to happen when you're calling someplace out of state, doesn't it? Or talking to someone that you haven't been able to talk to in years? It's a good way to squeeze more money out of our families, I guess. Damn MCI. Are you going to call them back?"

I shook my head in disgust as I vacated the chair. I hadn't been three-waying my call but that didn't matter. My parents were out the money it cost to accept my outrageously expensive phone call. I could have called back and incurred an additional connection charge, but anything I had to say would hold until my next weekly phone call.

For most lifers, visits are a rare or nonexistent joy, so we rely on our phone calls home to stay connected with our loved ones. The problem is that these phone calls are so expensive that in many cases families have to regretfully limit these vital contacts because they simply can't afford to pay the phone bills. It is not unheard of for one 20-minute call to cost as much as $13.00, quite a luxury for families who have to struggle to put food on the table each day.

The phone system at Fluvanna is regulated by a computer monitoring system that tapes each phone call so it can be reviewed later by security. This same system is the one that can arbitrarily decide that some rule is being violated and abruptly end the call with a terse message that a violation has occurred. Usually this is not the case. My Luddite parents have no truck with technology. They never even had a cell phone until a year ago, much less employed technology to forward calls to someone else.

To phone someone, you must enter their telephone number into the system so that they can be automatically contacted by MCI (the company responsible for our phone issues) to say that they will accept calls from a prisoner. It usually takes 2 or 3 days for a number to be made available to us. We are allowed to have 15 phone numbers on our list of permitted phone numbers.

The cost of phone calls is one of the greatest financial hardships to inmates and their families. We all had a brief glimmer of hope when the rumor made the rounds that the state legislature had decided that calling cards would finally be made available to inmates. I knew that on the street there were calling cards that allow people to pay as little as 10 cents a minute anywhere in the United States, so it had been a constant source of outrage that my mom and dad had to pay outrageous sums for the almost obsolete collect phone calls that were my only option.

Like most hopes here, this one turned out to be baseless. Yes, the state had passed legislation to that effect, but it did not apply to prisoners in maximum security prisons, only those in lower levels of security. Never mind that it has been shown that increased contact with family improves the behavior of inmates and chances for rehabilitation, and that for some children it is the only way that they can stay in contact with an absent mother. More important is the lucrative contract that MCI has with the state and the cozy financial relationship they share.

Phone calls are not the only way inmates are ripped off. Commissary is another vital revenue source to outside interests. We are systematically exploited on every level, from the Ramen noodles that we pay 30 cents a package for (but can be had 10 for a dollar at Sam's Club) to the fabulous 7-inch Access brand television that they sell us for $210. I've had 3 of these in a year. The first 2 I bought died in a puff of acrid chemical smoke within months of receiving them. I'm keeping my fingers crossed that my current model will last a little longer. When you make 23 cents an hour and save for 2 years to buy a television set, it is a little dispiriting to have it explode the first time you turn it on.

After my second television committed spectacular suicide during the climactic scene of 24's season finale (timing is everything in prison), I sent it to the vendor to be replaced. I didn't hear from them for 3 months, so I asked my mom to track it down. It took her a few weeks, but she was eventually able to speak to a human being who told her two things:

1. That my television had been sent to the wrong address, but rather than letting me know that, the vendor stuck it on a shelf in a warehouse somewhere and forgot about it.
2. The model of television that Keefe Commissary sold (Keefe has the contract to provide all of our commissary, including food, personals, clothing, and electronics) is not actually intended for the daily use that inmates demand, but instead was created to be used in vehicles and watched for brief periods.

I wasn't surprised by either of her findings. I estimate that the retail price of that TV is probably about $140.00, if that. I've certainly seen much larger name brand televisions at Wal-Mart for less than we pay. The model we have has the battery port stripped out (so we can't use the metal inside as a weapon) and required earphones—there are no speakers.

We have begged commissary to provide name brand items to us, but to no avail. So we live with radios that don't receive any radio stations unless you contort yourself into odd pretzel shapes in the dayroom and outdated food, all yours for the low, low price of 20% (or 40% or 60%) above suggested retail price!

Every now and then the state tries to get support for the idea that inmates pay a certain amount each day for their "room and board." That scheme has been used at several jails, I know, but prisons are a substantially different environment from the short-term incarceration of the jail. Even a dollar a day would be a hardship for women who can earn no more than $13.50 a week on state pay, and that is assuming that they work the maximum hours allowed (which rarely happens due to shakedowns, state holidays, prison-mandated staff training, or any other conceivable reason).

Inmates would be so deep in the red that they would be unable to buy anything they needed, such as deodorant, shampoo, or toothpaste, unless they received large sums of money from home to cover the costs of their daily "rent." The truth is that an overwhelming majority of inmates get almost no financial support from the outside. And if women are stripped of everything but the barest basics for minimal survival, they will be reduced to no more than animals. Every attempt at rehabilitation will be useless faced with the bestial want of the utterly impoverished. The sad fact is that prisoners cost the public an enormous amount of money, money that looks like it is wasted from our view in the cells. Prison is, above all, a profitable business venture for some people. Those people are not the general public or the prisoners, both of which groups are shortchanged, and the human cost is negligible compared to the state's bottom line.

SUNDRY PLEASURES

"Will the following inmates report to property for package pickup: Lomax, Pendleton, Milton, Lowe, Pettit, Pleasance, George, Flowers, Alavera, Gowen, and Heidler." The bubble officer's announcement managed to sneak through the clamor of the dayroom, and I snapped my head up. Whoa, did they say George? My Beauty Boutique order must be in! Around me other women were scrambling to their rooms to get copies of their yellow PPR forms and the orange mesh commissary bags that we use to carry our possessions around. Everyone wants to be at the beginning of the line in property, to be the first person to walk into the dayroom with their bag stuffed with flashy new goodies like decent shampoo or CDs.

I was excited because this was my first commissary order since my arrival at Fluvanna and I had ordered some makeup and a curling brush for my hair. At the jail we hadn't been allowed any cosmetics, so some of the women had improvised their own, using cinnamon candy to make rouge and lipstick and colored pencil shavings in petroleum jelly for eye shadow. This look smacked too much of a circus tent for my taste, so I had done without for over a year. Now I was delighted at the prospect of actually looking feminine again.

I was the last person to get to property, so I waited impatiently for my turn, surreptitiously eying the swag my fellow inmates had received. We were only allowed to make one outside vendor order each month (this rule has changed—now we can order once every 3 months), and I was already compiling a mental list of what I wanted to buy next. Because I was fresh from the jail, I didn't have much property yet, so I needed to get myself set up for my new life. It was like buying for your first apartment, only one that is 7 × 12 feet with no amenities beyond some metal furniture. Because everything I owned had to be able to fit in the two black plastic boxes we are issued to store our possessions, I was limited in even the permissible items I could get, but some things were a must: panties, socks, T-shirts, bras, and a pair of pajamas.

After my initial splurge, I got down to the necessities and made an order to JCPenney for all of the clothing items I needed. It's great when you can get most of what you need at one store. To consolidate orders inmates will often "hitch a ride" on each other's orders. Say that Janine is going to Walkenhorst (a vendor that sells all sorts of cosmetics, shampoos, and conditioners) and Mandy is going to Music by Mail to get some CDs. They might get together and have Janine buy the two bottles of shampoo that Mandy needs, and Mandy will hook Janine up with the Daughtry CD that she's been waiting to order.

I didn't know anyone well enough to try that little ploy, so I did all of my ordering for myself. My PPR request for my JCPenney order was processed and a money order duly drawn from my inmate account and sent out, and about 6 weeks later I was called again to pick up my stuff. It was right on time, too—I had been forced to use prison-issued underwear, which, not shockingly, is of extremely low quality. After the first washing the panties' elastic waist had fallen off, and after only a week's wear all of the tissue-thin socks had holes in the heels and toes.

I was quicker on the uptake this time, so I managed to be one of the first in line when the inmates were called. Our building's packages were crowded on the metal sorting shelves in the property room, and the one with my name on it was satisfyingly enormous. There were two property officers who took turns distributing packages: C.O. Bering, who was pretty easygoing, and C.O. Vane, who was notorious for making up "rules" about what you could and could not have on the fly. At least C.O. Vane didn't play favorites. She was difficult with every inmate, not just ones she disliked. As luck would have it, Vane was on duty that morning.

Tearing open the brown package that contained my order, she began comparing what I had received with the yellow PPR form. "Six gray T-shirts . . . you don't have to turn in any old ones because you don't have any listed on your inventory. Six pairs of panties, all unpatterned. Those are OK. Three blue underwire bras. You know you can't order black bras, right?" I nodded my understanding.

Apparently we weren't allowed to buy black bras because that was the color of female officers' bras. I have to take that on faith, because I've never independently confirmed it. "Good. One pair of light blue pajamas. Six pairs of socks—hold on, you can't have these."

Dammit! So close! These were just white socks. I didn't see anything objectionable about them. "Um, why can't I have them? I really need some new socks. Mine are full of holes."

"Sorry, but they're too fluffy."

I stared at her, dumbfounded, as the women in line behind me began to murmur in disgust. They had seen this happen dozens of times, but this was my first experience with C.O. Vane. "I'm sorry, did you say 'too fluffy'?"

"Yes. You need to have regular socks. These are too fluffy."

"Girl, you can have her hold on to those socks and get the major to approve them. Don't let her pull this shit with you," an inmate behind me whispered as Vane turned away from the desk. I just shook my head in disbelief. I didn't have the energy to argue.

"Do you want to donate these to charity or send them back for a refund?" asked the officer.

"Send them back, I guess. Do I have to pay for the postage on that?"

"Yes, your account will be debited. Fill out these forms," she said.

"Ma'am, could you please tell me what kind of socks I'm allowed to buy?" I asked.

"Plain, white athletic socks."

"OK, well, thank you." I took my sockless armful of clothes back to the wing, still puzzling out how a pair of socks can be "too fluffy."

The next month I had to use up my precious vendor order at JCPenney yet again. This time, I was only ordering socks, but my prison socks were like cobwebs by this point, and for some reason I had been left off the list for new ones 3 months in a row. When I was called to property again the next month, I strolled in confident that I had ordered the right thing.

My package this time was distressingly small. C.O. Vane ripped it open, glanced at the appropriately unfluffy pile it contained, and announced, "Sorry, you can't have these."

"Can't have them?" I managed to squeak out. "Why can't I have these? There not too fluffy, are they?"

She ignored or missed completely my sarcasm. "No, but they're not athletic socks. All socks have to be plain, white athletic socks."

"What are you talking about?" I was visibly angry by now. "It says right there on the label that these are softball socks. The last time I checked softball was a sport, which is played by athletes, so doesn't that make these athletic socks?"

"Sorry," she repeated tonelessly. "You can only buy regular athletic socks. Do you want to donate these or send them back?"

"Well, I'm not paying postage again to send back more socks. You can donate them. I'm sure that there are some homeless softball players out there that need socks." I scrawled my signature on the donation form.

Although eventually I managed to find the perfect socks to satisfy Officer Vane's rigid standards, we had several other frustrating interactions. She wouldn't let me have my plastic pump bottle of hand lotion, saying that those kinds of bottles weren't permitted (even though pump bottles were, in fact, sold by commissary), and she tried to prevent me from getting the Land's End sweatpants I had ordered because they didn't look like regular sweatpants (they were gray and had a pull tie at the waist, so I'm not sure what the distinction there was). I had been down for a while when she tried that one, so I was confident enough to dispute it with her supervisor. I was allowed to keep my sweatpants. Eventually, she was transferred out of the property department, and there was a string of decent property officers.

One of the most popular was Officer Robicheaux. Man, he was great. He'd probably give you a handgun if you somehow had a yellow PPR form saying you were allowed to have it. I bet he would've even let me have my dangerously fluffy socks! Needless to say, Robicheaux's tenure in property was brief. The property officer we have now is excellent. She doesn't get too angry when you collar her on the boulevard to ask if your stuff is in yet and goes out of her way to make sure that packages are distributed as soon as possible. Best of all, she doesn't fabricate arbitrary rules about what you can and cannot have.

Once I started to accumulate some personal property, my little cell began to look a bit homier. Of course we weren't allowed to put anything on the walls or metal desks. I've seen enough prison movies to understand why posters on the wall can't be permitted, but how could a greeting card taped to the metal frame of my bunk be a security risk? Because I was on the bottom bunk, I didn't have a shelf (the foot-long metal shelf was used by the inmate on the top bunk to put her 5-inch TV on), but I bought a few hardback books that I kept on the desk. I also bought a forest green towel to hide the graffiti and nicks on the desk's gray metal surface (now though, we are no longer allowed to cover the surface of our desks). I couldn't tape up any of the cards that my children sent me, but I had three of them on my desk all of the time—one each from Jack, Francesca, and Gio.

We all do what we can to bring some warmth into our lives, both literally and figuratively. Each inmate is permitted one craft item. Now we are only allowed to have a craft item measuring 8" × 8" × 2" (Yeah! I'm gonna make me a pot holder!), but when I first got to FCCW we were still allowed to have a small crocheted afghan on our beds. Cinder block might have many fine qualities when it comes to durability and resistance to tunneling, but its insulating properties are negligible, so our rooms get cold. They are actually bitterly cold, especially for the poor souls in the Siberia of the top bunk, which is directly in the path of the arctic blast of air streaming through the ventilation system. It is a charge, of course, to cover these vents in any way. Because we're only supplied with two thin blankets, on the worst nights we put on several layers of clothes, including a state-issued orange watch cap and the cheap woolen gloves you could purchase from commissary, and burrowed under both state blankets, a crocheted blanket, and, if you had one, your bathrobe. (End rooms have two walls that are exposed to the outside, and because they are particularly cold, their inhabitants get three blankets, which are still not enough.)

We all had to send our afghans home when the rules changed, but that's OK. In return we now have a new kind of blanket. Unfortunately, though, it is even smaller and thinner than the ones we originally had. They remind me of those little lap blankets that you are given on airplanes, only slightly larger. They are a lovely shade of turquoise blue, which actually does compensate a bit for their deficiencies in warmth. We are so starved for color here—almost everything is white or gray—that we have become like magpies, hoarding anything bright and colorful that comes into our possession. Gina got a pretty bottle of fancy hand lotion in one of the chaplain's Christmas packages 3 years ago, and she now pours the cheap commissary lotion into it when it gets empty. The product is still basically useless, but the floral bottle looks very nice sitting on her desk.

Gina had better hold on to that bottle: the institutional safety officer informed the chaplain this year that she will no longer be allowed to distribute the annual Christmas packages. The reason? The institution won't be able to have requisite Material Safety Data Sheets—a mandatory list of all the ingredients and any safety requirements for items like soaps and cleaning agents. In the past, churches from the community had donated to each inmate a plastic bag that contained a bottle of shampoo, 2 bars of soap, lotion, toothpaste, toothbrush, and a bottle of conditioner or hair grease, in addition to 20 or so cards for various occasions. Chaplain's packages were always much anticipated. For the many people who can't afford vendor orders, it was the only way they could get name brand shampoo and soap. Sometimes the people donating would purchase Dollar General store brand, but occasionally you would get lucky—Aussie shampoo! Toothpaste in a pump! My first year I was given a bar of Yardley of London lavender soap. I still have it, the box somewhat battered, but still smelling just like the small lavender plant that had grown by the driveway of my house. When I'm feeling especially melancholy, I take in deep draughts of fragrance, close my eyes, and wish I were home again.

TECHNOLOGY AT ITS FINEST

Fluvanna Correctional Center for Women is contemplating engaging the twenty-first century. Slowly. Reluctantly. Like a Victorian bathing beauty with a case of the vapors, it is dipping one teeny, little toe tip into the vast ocean of the digital age. It began a few years ago with the unveiling of CORIS. CORIS is a computer system that, in theory, tracks every aspect of an inmate's existence: classes, disciplinary infractions, housing assignments, annual requirements, appointments . . . everything. The past, present, and future encapsulated in one glorious, pulsating array of 1s and 0s. Sounds great, doesn't it? Efficient, intelligent, helpful. But there is one variable that no algorithm can encompass: the unconquerable incompetence of the human factor. To wit:

> "Ms. George, you are not on the master pass list for the library. You need to go back to your building."

I look imploringly at the impassive officer's face. My big doe eyes have no effect, so I move on to my smooth oratorical skills, made more emphatic by the fact that it is pouring down rain at the moment, and I don't fancy another long trek back to my building swathed only in my cheap plastic rain poncho, which has torn apart at every seam and which I have had to clumsily repair with a stapler. *Project Runway* it ain't. "But Ms. Toler, I work at the library." Noting her lack of response, I helpfully add, "I've worked there for 3 years now." Seeing that she is not budging, I reluctantly bundle myself back up into my tattered shreds of cheap plastic and mutter under my breath, "Which you know because you have worked in this building for as long as I have."

"Get back to your building, George," she says, clearly bored.

Dizzy looks at me sympathetically. She, lucky girl, is on the pass list, so she'll be able to get to work today. "I'll let Ms. Artis know that you tried to come in. She can try to call for you."

Ms. Toler breaks in. "If you aren't on the master pass list, you aren't getting in. Now get back to your building before I give you an unauthorized area charge."

After a less-than-refreshing swim back to my housing unit I am just shaking the worst of the rainwater off of my poncho when the bubble officer comes over the intercom. "Ms. George, you are needed at the library."

Dammit! A *third* trip out in that wretched rain? "Ms. Toler told me I wasn't on the list."

"I guess she found your name. She says to get to work."

Resigned, I pull my soaked socks back onto my feet and prepare to head back to the academic building. When I finally arrive, Ms. Toler doesn't make eye contact or otherwise acknowledge my presence other than to take my rain-spattered ID badge and slip it into the correct slot. To make up for this breach of manners, however, for the rest of the day she is louder and even more surly to me than usual every time she sees me.

Master pass list screwups are not a rare occurrence here at Club Fluvanna. I have witnessed more times than I can count some poor sap that desperately needs to get somewhere—a college class that they have paid hundreds of dollars for, a cosmo appointment prior to a special visit, a job interview—only to be told that they are not on the list. Often, the inmate really *isn't* on the master pass list because the staff member who was in charge of adding the appointment to CORIS dropped the ball. Even more frustrating is when a helpful staffer does some investigation as to why the appointment is not recorded and she discovers that some superhelpful soul has decided to "clean up" the inmate's file. And thus, along with the appointments for classes that no longer exist, work assignments and other vital information are also deleted.

Even when you are on the master pass list, it is so poorly organized that the officer who must check it can't find the class that you are supposed to be going to, much less any specific individual. And since all movement hinges on being on that list, at mass movement it is like the VIP list to the trendiest club in Manhattan; there is always a gaggle of eager girls clustered around the gatekeeper to all egress, a harried officer bitching about the chaotic jumble of names that sprawls over several pages as he frantically flips back and forth, gripping his yellow highlighter like a lifeline. Officers that have been down with us the longest skip this whole process and simply write the names of all the offenders on a separate sheet of paper, going back to properly fill out the pass list after women have moved on to their appropriate destinations.

The nabobs of the penal system have also recognized the financially exploitative possibilities of technology. Rather than constructive uses, such as transforming the paper-bound bureaucracy that would send an environmentalist into apoplexy into a streamlined, paperless system, they are instead focusing on strip mining even more money from inmates and their families under the guise of "progress." This insidious trend is embodied by a nefarious, murky octopus of a company known as J-Pay. I don't know which state senator's brother-in-law owns J-Pay, but they are well on their way to monopolizing every aspect of inmate life (I suspect that they are a subsidiary of the equally robber baron-esque Keefe Company, which has a stranglehold on the lucrative commissary franchise of the DOC). I have to doff my hat to the criminal genius that thought up this scheme. There are big bucks to be had here, if you are willing to ruthlessly squeeze out every possible cent from families desperate to keep in contact with their loved ones and provide what little material comfort they can afford.

J-Pay began its reign innocuously enough. A few years ago, as I loitered in the small lobby area of the commissary building waiting to receive my overpriced Ramen noodles and potato chips, I noticed a new sign (helpfully written in both English and Spanish—don't want to miss a potential victim, er, I mean customer). It was large enough that even I, with my vision destroyed from poor nutrition and the almost complete absence of natural light from my existence, could make it out. The sign was heralding the arrival of a wonderful new service that would make my life easier—J-Pay, my access to quick money. Rather than relying on your folks to send you money via snail mail and ever-reliable money orders, you can have the money deposited DIRECTLY INTO YOUR ACCOUNT (emphasis mine), and thus more easily buy, buy, buy even more of the great products that Keefe makes available to the discerning convict. I nudged the girl standing next to me.

"What the hell is that? I've used direct deposit before, but I don't think I would trust my parents' bank account info to anybody that does business here."

She glanced at it and shrugged. "Hell if I know. Just another way to rip us off, I guess." By that evening, the housing units, bubble area, chow hall, and academic areas were emblazoned with the J-Pay posters. Shoot, for all I know, they were hanging in segregation as well. We had photocopied J-Pay information sheets helpfully slipped under our doors during the darkest hours of the night. The same sheets were stuffed into bewildered visitors' hands that weekend. Clearly, a major marketing initiative was afoot.

Now, most people have the idea that convicts are, for the most part, pretty dumb. We may have the sly craftiness of the criminal, they think, but otherwise we are incapable of concerning ourselves with the nuances of solid financial management. But even a passel of dumb prisoners knew enough to stay away from J-Pay (and the barely mentioned colossal surcharge for each transaction). As a result, J-Pay didn't receive much traction until a memo came out informing us that, as of September 2013, all financial transactions must be in the form of a cashier's check sent directly to the inmate or be made via the J-Pay system. My dad and I had initially discussed J-Pay when it first strutted into my world and decided that money orders were working just fine for us, thank you. But now I had to call and tell him about the new changes in the system.

"Well, J-Pay is taking over the world," I announced to him as soon as he picked up the phone.

"Who? What?" He thought for a moment, "Do you mean those jokers with the direct deposit stuff?"

"Yep. Get this: you aren't allowed to send me money orders any more. Instead, you have to send me a cashier's check now or go through J-Pay if you want to send me any money."

My father is, by any measure, a fairly sophisticated guy. He's exchanged money during his travels to foreign lands, served in our nation's military, graduated from the University of Maryland, negotiated home purchases, and managed a mortgage. In short, he is not some sub-rock dwelling schmo. Still, he said, "A cashier's check? I don't think I've ever gotten a cashier's check. Wouldn't know where to get one actually, because we do all of our banking online and don't have a physical bank to go to. J-Pay it is, I guess."

"Here's the deal. You can direct deposit money into my account, but don't do that, because they charge you a huge service charge. When Thurbs got $175 put into her account, J-Pay took out $16. But if you send the money order along with a deposit slip, you can download from their Web site to this address in Florida, and they will put the money into my account. I'm sorry that this is such a pain in the ass. They don't make it easy, do they?"

"I don't think making our lives easier is their main objective, no," responded Dad dryly.

Dad and Mom have been forced to endure many of my tirades about the substandard and exploitative treatment of my fellow inmates, and though I try to restrain myself, this time I wasn't able to. I was, quite frankly, pissed at this new system that unfairly hampers women of a lower socioeconomic class by setting up difficult hurdles for their families to leap just to provide a little comfort to their incarcerated loved one. As usual, most of the victims of institutionalized injustice are the poor.

"Do you want to know what really ticks me off?" I didn't actually *hear* my father sigh at yet another patented Erin oration, but I can imagine. Not that he and Mom don't completely agree with me. It's just that I can get, well, a tad strident at times. "I'm fortunate in that I have someone who not only is willing to send me money—for which I am profoundly grateful—but that someone is able to navigate the Internet, understand online financial stuff. What about the woman whose family doesn't have a computer? I know that there are still a *few* of them out there, and the odds are that they know someone in a place like Fluvanna. Or the families who don't live near a Wal-Mart, which is the other place you can go to deposit money into an inmate's account. Most people here certainly can't afford to pay a huge surcharge to get their money. They really screw you coming and going here; if they can squeeze out a few extra dollars, then that's more important to those people than anything else. Screw the fact that if someone has to live hand to mouth in here that they will probably go right back to their earlier behaviors as soon as their feet hit the pavement outside the gate. Screw the mere Christian decency that so many of our legislators ostensibly believe in. Let's line the pockets of someone else in Richmond. It's disgusting."

"And yeah, this may be a bit selfish, but once in a *very* rare blue moon I get a random 25 bucks from someone who doesn't send me money with any regularity. Now they are going to send it on back. Since you're footing all of my bills, I'll bet that you are glad that there are friends who take the pressure off of you once in a while, that the financial black hole that is your beloved elder daughter is not solely your responsibility. It would be different if we were properly clad and fed here, but when you are walking around in the rain and snow in shoes that are little more than sieve-like plastic covered with cheap, tattered nylon, when you are eating uncooked beans for the third time in a week, that $25 makes a big difference."

I paused to take a breath, then my father diplomatically asked me what books I had been reading lately.

And now rumors are buzzing through inmate.com about more J-Pay monopolization. I first heard about this during one of my weekly rock fests with Tianne. Every Saturday, we hang out all day, snacking on commissary chips and listening to CDs for hours. It is a welcome weekly oasis of fun in what is otherwise often a grim and stressful life. We can plug our headphones into the same personal CD player, so we each haul out our respective collection of 12 CDs (the maximum allowed) and proceed to immerse ourselves in the music. I can't say that we merely listen; it is so much more than that. It's a full body experience (we imagine the guys in master control saying, "Those two crazy chicks in the Honor Wing are acting like idiots again. Let's make some popcorn and watch."). To the delight of our fellow inmates, we often play along with each song. Because Tianne actually knows how to play the instruments, she mans the air guitar and air keyboard. And since I lack any musical training, I am relegated to air drums. What I lack in talent and accuracy, I make up for with my enthusiasm and flair. You should see my drum solo in Phil Collins's classic "In the Air Tonight." Frickin' awesome.

Our likes run to the older stuff, and since our musical tastes largely overlap, we are happy to play the same songs over and over again. Most beloved are our Journey, Foreigner, and Styx CDs, but we also dive into U2, The Police, Squeeze, Pink Floyd, Dire Straits, and the aforementioned Phil Collins. What can I say?

We are children of the late 70s/early 80s. Our only homage to more contemporary music is Maroon 5's outstanding *Songs about Jane*, which we both love so much we each have our own copy of the CD.

At any rate, music is a major part of our lives. We both have our "guys" that we champion (I'm an especial fan of Steve Perry, of Journey, and Tianne will go to her grave adoring Styx's Tommy Shaw. Mutual mad props go out to Queen's Freddie Mercury. He did indeed rock us.), and we tell stories about our concert experiences, favorite songs, anecdotes about the bands. It is a wholly satisfying experience.

During one of these sessions, Tracy came strolling up, "Have you guys seen the memo about CDs?" Oh, no! What about CDs? Surely they are not taking away our beloved music. Tianne and I share a glance, then rush (the verb, not the band, whom we also like) to the bulletin board to see what Tracy is talking about.

A huge relief—CDs are not being taken away from us. They had done that to me once with my books. Losing my music might just render me catatonic. The memo said that, as of October 2013, inmates will no longer be able to buy CD players. No alternative musical device was indicated, and we joked that they were probably going to bounce us back to reconditioned 8-tracks from the 70s. According to the memo, people with CD players could still order CDs, but everyone else was out of luck. (Believe it or not, there are still women here who have battered cassette players from the 80s. There is nowhere for them to get cassette tapes anymore, but they can't afford anything else.)

The next day, rumors began to abound, enough rumors that I began to believe that there might actually be some truth to them. Because I work in the library, I am in contact with lots of inmates and thus get all of the scoops pretty quickly. This day it was Jenny, knowing that I am famous (notorious) for my obsessive love of music, who hurried up to the counter to fill me in.

"Have you heard about the MP3 players we are going to get?"

In fact, all that morning I had heard garbled descriptions of what the institution was going to replace the CD players with. Since most of my friends have been down for a considerable time, some never even having touched a DVD player or laptop computer before, I had patiently explained to them what an MP3 is, how an I-pod works, etc. Tianne, for example, insisted on calling all MP3 players "google pods." She knew it was not accurate, was just trying to be funny, but I thought that it actually captured the spirit of the whole concept, and it delighted me to adopt that term as well. I'm trying to make it a "thing."

Jenny, though, had some very authentic sounding details. And because her boyfriend (and co-defendant) was locked up in a men's prison and they were three-waying mail to each other, I was pretty certain that her 411 was accurate.

I sat up straighter. "Tell me!" I demanded.

Jenny laughed. "Girl, you won't believe this shit. They're going to be selling us MP3 players, The men have had them for a while now. Only they come from J-Pay, so they call 'em JP3 players. Your family can buy them for you."

"Well, how do you get the songs on them? What do the songs cost? How many songs does it hold?"

"They're going to put kiosks up in each wing where you can download stuff onto it. The men are paying $2.99 a song."

My squeak of outrage interrupted her. "$2.99! You can download songs from I-tunes for like $.99 a pop! That is so jacked up."

She continued without responding. Jenny had seen enough J-Pay/Keefe BS not to be surprised at further evidence of their price gouging. "The men were allowed to download all of their CDs onto the JP3 player. Plus they have photos and games on there, too."

That stopped me. "Photos? How do they get digital photos?"

"Their families email them to them," Jenny answered nonchalantly.

I was gobsmacked. "Email? The men have email?" I felt myself getting wound up. One of my main beefs is that male prisoners are treated differently from women in what they are allowed to have. Jenny saw my reaction and went into "calm down" mode.

"Chill! I heard that every inmate is going to have email soon. Your folks can send you pictures, and emails too. You can't print out your emails, and it costs money each time you send one, but if it's less than the cost of a stamp, I guess it's good."

Well. I sat back in my chair. Changes like this were too much for me to grasp immediately. If they were truly going to happen, that is. Jenny had more, though.

"We've been approved to get e-readers, too. Well," she amended, "the warden hasn't approved it yet, but all the other prisons have, and we are going to get them too, I hear."

E-books! Dare I hope that I might soon have access to hundreds of books at my fingertips? No, it's too much. Better not think about that. "How do you know all of this?" I ask.

"Well, my friend Tom goes onto the DOC website for me all of the time and sees what they have posted. It's full of information. They say that they are doing all of this so that people who are going home are up to date on the technology that is out there, to help them get jobs." Hey, whatever works. I may not be going home any time soon, but I'll be delighted to benefit from what is actually a somewhat intelligent (albeit lucrative) plan on the part of the DOC. Though I wonder if it would be embraced so enthusiastically by those in power if there weren't the added honey of all that tasty income.

This is an awful lot to absorb at one time. I pause, then revert to the original topic. "So, about these google pods." Jenny giggles. I've made a google pod convert, I can tell. "Say I get a hundred songs downloaded, all for the low, low price of $300. What happens when the damn thing inevitably bursts into a ball of flame or crumbles into dust, as does all of the Keefe crap they fob off on us? Do the men have the ability to back up the MP3s and other digital info somewhere? I'll be mighty vexed if I spend all that cash and then lose it a year later due to their faulty equipment."

"I don't know. . . . I'll sent my co-defendant a letter and ask him, OK?"

"Hey, thanks Jen," I say, then come around the counter to give her a hug. "You're the best. Keep me informed!"

Despite lack of confirmation, I immediately did my part to spread all of the "news" I had just heard. People were just as amazed as I was. When I called my mother that evening, I told her about it.

"I'm glad, honey," she said. "Actually, I'd read in the paper a while ago that Virginia is one of seven states that have approved for inmates to have tablets. I'd been wondering why you hadn't mentioned it." I did not mention the obvious question in my mind: namely, why didn't you mention it to *me*, your book fanatic daughter, if you had heard this already? Oh well. Never mind.

So it appears that J-Pay is poised to take over my world. I can imagine a postapocalyptic world wherein J-Pay is dominant. I will be wearing J-Pay underwear and lathering up with J-Pay shampoo. J-Pay brand potato chips will be crumbled up and rehydrated into my swoles, and J-Pay shoes will be the ones actively rotting to pieces on my poor, abused feet. Oh goodie. I can hardly wait.

REFERENCES

Bernstein, N. (2005). *All alone in the world: Children of the incarcerated.* New York: New Press.

Jewkes, Y. (2002). *Captive audiences: Media, masculinity and power in prisons.* Devon, UK: Willan.

Johnson, R. (2004). *Poetic justice: Reflections on the big house, the death house, and the American way of justice.* Thomaston, ME: Northwoods Press.

Johnson, R. (2007). *Burnt offerings: Poems on crime and punishment.* Washington, DC: BleakHouse Publishing.

Johnson, R. (2008). Hard time: A meditation on prisons and imprisonment. In S. Nagelsen (Ed.), *Exiled voices: Portals of discovery-Stories, poems, and drama by imprisoned writers* (pp. ix–xvii). Henniker, NH: New England College Press.

Nagelsen, S. (2008). Afterword. In S. Nagelsen (Ed.), *Exiled voices: Portals of discovery— Stories, poems, and drama by imprisoned writers* (pp. 219–228). Henniker, NH: New England College Press.

CHAPTER 7

Living with Loss

For women in prison, especially those with little or no hope of release, life and loss are two sides of the same coin. Loss can be thought of as a tangible consumer item, something women like Erin George can almost taste. Separation from family is painful and evokes complicated emotions and problems. Fond memories can sustain but also cause pain. The death of loved ones is difficult and, for the lifer, highlights the fact that someday they might have to face the prison world alone.

The barriers that separate prisoners and loved ones go beyond walls and fences, cells and bars. Prisoners often are emotionally needy in ways that civilians cannot appreciate. It is hard for those on the outside to keep in touch with loved ones in ways that fill the great need many prisoners feel. George felt that her first birthday in prison didn't produce many cards or letters and she was hurt. But on reflection, and after being reminded by her mother that things were hard on everyone in the family, George came to understand that it isn't easy to write to someone wishing them the first of an endless string of birthdays behind bars. Hallmark doesn't make cards for that; no cloying sentiment covers the loss of someone who might never breathe free again. Sometimes people in the free world fail to tell prisoners of bad news, such as the death of a loved one, on the grounds that they don't want to hurt the women when they are down. We learn in no uncertain terms from George that it hurts more not to know. To know is to be included, a prized commodity.

Erin George has family to stand by her—at least some family, at least for now— but losing family to death, abandonment, or both is a continuing concern for women in prison. This concern has grown in salience for George since the publication of the first edition of this book. Her children have grown apart from her; there are signs this may only be a hiatus in family relations, but no one can tell for sure at this point. George's father passed away from cancer since the publication of the first edition, a grievous loss (discussed in the epilogue) that also leaves Erin's mother on her own. Losing family means losing the daily interactions that are part and parcel of normal life in the world—the regular phone calls, the talk about "nothing and everything" *that make up normal life, from the latest TV show to the lives of the children. Separation from children, even if only briefly, means falling out of touch with their rapidly evolving lives. A mother might know everything about her children in the world and then in prison have to face the fact that their lives are different and that they now turn to others for comfort, not to her. One day the mother in prison might no longer be a part of her children's lives. The children will have moved on, however reluctantly or ambivalently, leaving her in their wake (Bernstein, 2005). These grim realities are awful possibilities for any mother in prison, especially a mother serving a long term (Enos, 2001; Lamb, 2007; O'Brien, 2001). Prison families, which can include roles for surrogate children, provide a limited and imperfect substitute for the real thing (Pollock, 2002; Rierden, 1997). Erin, in particular, has shown little interest in establishing relations with surrogate prisoner families.*

Visits offer the prospect of meaningful connection if they are arranged properly. Some visiting rooms, however, are poorly designed and offer little chance for interaction. This was the case for George in the local jail. It is ironic that visiting conditions in jail often are more restrictive than in prison, even though in jail most of the inmates are pretrial detainees and hence are innocent until proven guilty. Be that as it may, Fluvanna offers contact visits in a congenial setting, allowing visitors to buy snacks to share. I have visited George at Fluvanna and have had pleasant, private, and extended conversations over machine-bought snacks and drinks.

There is a wonderful program at Fluvanna called MILK (Mothers Inside Loving Kids) mentioned earlier by George as a program that meant a great deal to her during her early years of confinement, when visits from her children occurred with some regularity. In this chapter, George conveys the emotional power of those early visits with her parents and, once a year, her children, who came all the way from England for this program and spent a day with her. These visits, now reduced to sustaining memories, are emotional treasures for George. It is true that mothers inside can't do much to help their children, but they can reach out and share their love, or stand ready to reach out and share their love when the opportunity presents itself. There is no doubt that these visits, under the best of circumstances, are bittersweet for the women, but families might survive with the benefit of these visits, even perhaps only the benefit of the memory of these visits. Be that as it may, the welfare of the family is what is best for all. —Robert Johnson

Without a doubt, my great, unabating source of grief is the separation from the people I love. I yearn for the joys I shared with my family, and my memories of our times together make me long for them. I remember our annual Easter feast (complete with the coconut Easter Bunny cake with licorice whiskers that Aunt Eileen would bake each year), the fiercely competitive games of charades and 20 questions, and all of the little touches that made the McCays so special.

One of the customs I miss most is a tradition my Aunt Lynne brought into our family when she married my Uncle Michael. For as long as I can remember, Lynne had a Christmas card depicting the Three Wise Men hung over her front door for the entire year. I remember asking her when I was small why she always kept a card there, and her patient explanation was that displaying the first card you receive showing the Magi guarantees your home good luck in the upcoming year. Even though this wasn't something that my parents did at home, I would always feel safe and comforted whenever I saw the Wise Men being led across the desert by a gold-embossed Nativity star in her dim foyer. It seems such a small thing, that moment Lynne and I shared, but it created an unbreakable connection with her.

My first Christmas in Fluvanna I was able to get a Christmas card showing the Wise Men, which I sent to Mike and Lynne, describing inside how much that memory meant to me, how it in so many ways encapsulated my favorite holiday. I doubt that my Magi Christmas card was the first that they received that year, but I wept when Lynne wrote me back and told me that mine was the card that would hold that special place over the front door.

As powerful as the positive memories are, though, in many ways I feel the separation from my family more keenly when it comes to the losses. Some of them have been singularly awful, like the death of my Aunt Marianne. I hadn't been down very long when she finally succumbed to the cancer that she had been diagnosed with just after my arrest, so this was my first tragedy inside. Because there was no way for me to receive phone calls directly, my mother had to call the prison and ask the counselor on duty that weekend to tell me about Marianne's passing. I can't imagine that it is a pleasant duty to break news like that to a prisoner, and I'm sure that the counselor did try to be sympathetic, but when he kept calling me "Karen," I had to turn away.

Marianne's death, my grandmother's recent illness, the unexpected passing of my old friend Tia—as terrible as those things were, they were made worse by enduring them without my family to hold and comfort me. We had always clung to each other in times of grief, bolstering each other with shared laughter and tears. Through time I have grown to trust and love a small group of the women in here, and I know that I can rely on them for genuine compassion, but no matter how long we are down together they can never replace my real family.

The subject of family can be a painful one for lifers. Secure in the knowledge that my parents are always available to advocate on my behalf if I am being treated unjustly or need anything, I tend to forget that most of my friends aren't as lucky. Parents might be dead or, more often, permanently estranged. Other family members and friends might be locked up as well, or lost in their own whirlpool of addiction.

When I was first locked up, I didn't consider the lives at home that my friends had lost. Trust doesn't come quickly for lifers, and although they welcomed me readily as one of them, it took a long time before they began sharing aspects of their past with me, and then only in dim glimpses and shuttered allusion. I naively assumed that they all had what I did: a set of loving, involved parents and a cadre of relatives and friends on whom they could depend. I realized that this was not the case when my friend Sadie came in one afternoon after a medical appointment, face flushed and eyes red.

Before being locked up over a decade ago, Sadie had her stomach banded to lose weight, and as a result she was suffering from terrible medical problems. She couldn't digest most of the foods that the chow hall served, and because she didn't get any money from home, she couldn't buy anything to eat from commissary other than cheap but nutritionally bereft Ramen noodles. She had been steadily losing weight for months, constantly vomiting after each meal she attempted to eat, and was in constant pain. Sadie had been waiting for over a year to get the surgery necessary to have the stomach band removed, and she had at last gone to medical with the expectation that the procedure had been scheduled. Obviously it hadn't gone well.

We had been watching the wing door for her return, and as soon as her roommate, Belinda, saw her face, she knew the news wasn't good. "What happened?" Belinda asked. "Are they sending you out soon?"

Sadie, a veteran of years of wrangling with medical over her myriad health issues, laughed bitterly. "What do you think? Now they're saying that they want the doctor who originally did my surgery to do the procedure. Never mind that he was in Norfolk and I wouldn't be able to go there to get it done. Never mind that he did it 15 years ago and he may be dead for all I know. You know how medical is. If they can put off treatment, they will."

Everyone around the table except for me knew that there was really nothing that Sadie could do. Outraged on her behalf, I asked with all the complacency of the newly incarcerated, "I know that writing a grievance won't work, but can't your mom call and complain? That worked for me when medical didn't help me."

Sadie and the others looked at me as if I were well meaning but daft. I realized immediately that I had committed a faux pas but was still too new at lifer etiquette to realize exactly what I had done. Finally, Sadie said shortly, "I don't hear from my mom much." She didn't say it with obvious grief or in anger at my naiveté, just the matter-of-fact acceptance that the long abandoned assume in public.

All I could say was, "Oh, I'm so sorry."

Sadie smiled at me. "It's going to be OK." The rest of the table rapidly segued into a recital of their own harrowing experiences with medical, moving past my gaffe. All I could think about, though, was this woman whom I knew to be intelligent, compassionate, and self-deprecating. She had such wonderful qualities, but except for the small cluster of us who shared her fate, she was alone. As my friendship with Sadie deepened I began to understand that she took responsibility for the rift with her family, but nothing could erase the image of the vulnerable, amazing woman I knew. Whatever the past had been, she was no longer the person she had been outside.

Many lifers (and a fair number of short-timers as well) are virtually cut off from the outside. Their names are rarely called during mail call, and they never seem to make phone calls or receive visits. Most of the women are pretty frank about the reasons why. Because many had a history of drug use and its attendant destructive behaviors before committing the crimes that brought them to

Fluvanna, they had managed to alienate relatives and friends who would otherwise be supporting them emotionally and financially now.

Because of this schism, their families don't see the positive changes that many long-termers have effected during their bid. Sadie's ex-husband doesn't see the remorse and accountability that she demonstrates daily now, or the quiet longing for family that infuses her existence, so she remains cut off from her three children. Gina's mother stopped speaking to her when she was a teenager, so for all she knows her mother isn't even aware that she's serving a life sentence. This woman, who has been taking college courses for 3 years and who lives in the Honor Wing, is not the crack-addicted adolescent that constantly lied to and stole from her mother until running away at 16. But the letters that Gina sends out remain unanswered and, presumably, unread, and her phone calls unaccepted.

To compensate for their lack of outside connections, many inmates fabricate a new family behind bars. There are a number of women in their 50s and 60s here, and many of them are nicknamed Granny or Nanna. They act as surrogate caregivers, offering food and comfort to the abandoned, and in return are treated with the respect offered an esteemed matriarch. Other women play the role of aunt, cousin, sister, or even "wife," depending on age, proximity, and intimacy of relationship.

Unfortunately, this situation is not that unusual. All of us experience the absence of loved ones to some degree. In my case, many of my relationships have actually grown stronger because of my incarceration: my parents, my sister, my godmother, my Aunt Janet, and even people that before my arrest were barely a part of my life are now constant correspondents and supporters. But my sad reality is that I don't hear from most of my relatives very often. I might get cards at Christmas but usually hear nothing the rest of the year. At first this was exceedingly painful for me. Ours had been a family that shared hardships and joys together, and I had been raised by my father with the concept that family always comes first. This tenet had underpinned my formation as an adult and shaped the view I had of how a family should act. But the insidious effect that a life sentence has on the family dynamic is inescapable and profound. Who is emotionally prepared to cope with a loss like that?

My first birthday in prison a few months after my arrival was the hardest. Each afternoon at mail call the week before my April birthday I waited to hear my name called. I got a few cards, but wondered where the rest were. For weeks I waited, telling myself that the mailroom had screwed up again, or that the postal service had made an error. Eventually, reluctantly, I got it. But where were all of the people who had been an integral part of my life? I had never celebrated a birthday, graduation, or childbirth without an accompanying flood of love and attention from my relatives, so why now, when I felt most alone, did they ignore me?

My first reaction was anger. How could these people betray me like this? If the situations were reversed, I would never abandon them like this, I told myself. As usual, my parents bore the brunt of my emotion. "Why didn't they even send me a birthday card?" I kept asking my mom during our weekly phone calls. "It's not like I asked them for money or anything. Just a card would have been wonderful. Don't they believe in me anymore?"

Mom didn't offer explanations or excuses. "I suppose they do," she said. "I don't know, honey. Maybe it's just too hard for them right now."

Too hard for them? I was the one serving life. I was the one who had lost her family, home, and freedom. And they were struggling? But after a lengthy bout of self-pity and martyrdom, I began to think about what Mom had said. It had to be overwhelming for them, really. What would they say? Happy birthday? I thought of the typical sentiments I'd seen in commercial birthday cards, and I realized that Hallmark didn't exactly have a "Felicitations for Felons" section. I wanted them to extend concern and grace to me, but didn't I have to do the same?

After several years, I have, I think, reached a level of equilibrium. I am grateful to hear from those who write. I enjoy the letters that I frequently receive from certain people, and am pleasantly surprised when I hear from anyone else.

My parents have stuck by me, as I've said, but maintaining an honest relationship with them has not been easy from in here. I want to protect them as much as possible from my experiences inside, but I also frequently need to ask them for help. It's humiliating, being 45 years old and having to ask Daddy to send you money to buy underwear, or to call up Mom and beg her to contact the prison because I'm not getting the medical attention that I need. I'm used to running a household, managing a family, and holding down a job. Having to constantly ask for help is more demeaning to me than being strip-searched or peeing into a cup in front of a stranger. And this reliance on my parents begs the inevitable question: What will I do when they are gone?

Whenever I call home or see Mom and Dad at a visit, I want to keep things light, putting a darkly comic spin on the more outrageous occurrences, but unfortunately I'm not very good at faking it with them. I find that the most innocuous things make me cry. Who knows what random recollection will trigger a bout of tears? What petty, stupid occurrence will make me weep? It doesn't take much. But it hasn't even been 10 years yet since leaving. Maybe I'll stop being so sensitive after a decade or two. Or three. I've got nothing but time.

It's not easy from Dad and Mom's perspective, either. They are the conduit for any bad news I have to receive, and it can't be a pleasant prospect, having to serve that role to a potential emotional basket case. At least my parents don't try to "spare" me by keeping sad news from me. As hard as it is to hear, I have seen many women in here hurt even more because some well-meaning family member has tried to shield them from painful events. I first realized how terrible those concealments can be when my friend Rita received a letter from a family friend. I watched her rip open the letter, then the sudden look of shock after reading just a few paragraphs. My usual group of friends and I were hanging out in the dayroom, leafing through magazines or grumbling about only getting crappy institutional mail when Rita dropped the letter to the floor and began to cry "No, no, no. . . ."

Flora, her roommate, hurled herself from the chair and ran to Rita's side. "What happened?" she asked. "Who is it?" We all knew that only illness or death could have provoked such obvious anguish.

"It's my grandma," she answered. Sadie, Nadia, Laura, Belinda, Dizzy, and I looked at each other wordlessly. We all knew how important Rita's grandmother had been to her, certainly more of a mother than the heroin addict who had basically abandoned Rita when she was only two. Tenderly, Flora led her weeping roommate into their cell. They had been together for years, and we knew no one could take better care of Rita than Flora. All we could do as they left the table was tell Rita that we loved her and that we would pray for her. Laura, the maternal figure of our little group, offered to pass around a condolence card for everyone in the wing to sign, and the message was quietly passed that Rita had lost a loved one.

The death of a family member is not unusual among the lifers. As the years pass they become far too common. But I was surprised when Flora returned to the table an hour later, absolutely fuming. "Rita's gone to sleep, thank God, but you won't believe this crap. Her grandmother died 3 weeks ago and nobody in her family even told her! She had to hear it from her old next-door neighbor who thought Rita already knew about it. Rita's devastated. The letter that she got from her sister last week said that everything was fine. Why do they lie when they know we'll hear about stuff eventually?"

I had only been down a few years, so I didn't realize that this was a common occurrence. "Why wouldn't they tell her about her grandma dying?" I asked Flora. "I know that she's not going home, but certainly Rita would eventually notice that she stopped getting letters from her own grandmother? Why would they try to hide something like that?"

"Oh, her sister is always pulling crap like that," said Flora. "She says that she can't stand to see Rita hurt any more, blah, blah, blah, so she lets someone else handle the sucky job of passing along bad news. She's just too much of a coward to do it herself—she hates anything that makes her 'uncomfortable' or 'stressed out.' Selfish bitch! She knew how close Rita and her grandmother were. Don't these people know that we feel even more excluded from our families when they shut us out like that?"

I nodded my head. When I had been dealing with all of the stresses of my children moving to England, my mom had tended to try and gild the unpleasant truth as much as possible, but I asked her to be honest with me. We struck a deal: she would always tell me the truth and I wouldn't let myself overreact. It's a compromise that has worked well for us ever since. Although the truth can be bitter, I would rather hear it immediately and try to begin healing than to find out days, weeks, or even months later that a tragedy has occurred.

Ironically, the hardest deprivations inside are the small daily losses, the minutiae of my family's experience from which I will always be barred. So many seemingly insignificant aspects of my life are now desperately mourned. I don't really miss my pleasant house, or driving a car, or being able to wear attractive, properly fitting clothes. Everything I miss deeply revolves around the relationships I shared with my family.

Before my arrest, I would phone my mother, who was and is my best friend, almost every day. We would talk about nothing and everything: the kids, TV shows, and the political gossip that we both reveled in. Several times a month, James, the kids, and I would visit Mom and Dad's house, often showing up just for dinner but staying for the weekend. Now my parents live in another state and I am fortunate if I have a 2-hour visit from them every few months. And although Mom and Dad accept my phone calls happily, I know how expensive they are, so I try to limit the calls as much as possible.

It's even worse when it comes to my children. Jack, Francesca, and Giovanna live in England, so I have just one visit with them a year. They live with my in-laws, who do their best to keep me informed of what is going on in the kids' lives, but I am insatiable, avid to know every aspect of their existence. Before I was locked up, I was thoroughly immersed in their lives, and the shock of withdrawal from that closeness is irreparable. I once knew everything that my children did and hoped for, every person who entered their world. Now I can't even tell you what Franny's favorite animal is, what Gio watches on TV, or the name of Jack's girlfriend. I know that he has one, but, being 13, he was too shy on his last visit to tell the mom he hadn't spoken to in a year such a personal detail.

Someone else comforts them when they suffer the small defeats of childhood and shares their triumphs of acing an exam at school or winning a role in the school play. It remains an endlessly painful bafflement to me that I don't even know what my daughter's best friend looks like, or how my son's room is decorated.

When I am feeling particularly vulnerable to loneliness, I torture myself with anticipated loss: the little confidences that I won't be there to receive; the school concerts, graduations, and weddings I can't attend; all of the inexorable erosion of my influence and participation in my children's lives for which no card or letter can compensate. I also dwell on the inevitable death of my parents, the only people who are unequivocally there for me at any time. I can't permit myself to think of things like that too often, though. I have to be as strong for my family as they have been for me.

VISITATION (LIFELINES)

Thank God for visits. They are the greatest sustenance I have in here. Visitation at the jail was awful, a dim and clamorous room oppressive with the smell of Wal-Mart cologne and mildew. All conversations had to be shouted through a few tiny holes punched into the metal and plastic barrier that divided us from our visitors. At RRJ, the visitation room didn't look like it does on TV or in the movies. There wasn't even a telephone to let me speak more clearly to my parents or the friends who would wait an hour or more just to have a scant 20 minutes with me surrounded by the weeping children, pissed-off relatives, and the loudly (and often obscenely) affectionate boyfriends of my fellow inmates. Of course, there was absolutely no hugging or handholding possible with any of my visitors, so I went for almost a year without feeling my mother's touch and even longer before I was able to hold my children.

Before I was shipped to Fluvanna, I asked one of the women who had done time at the prison what the visits were like here. She told me that they were contact visits, so I would be able to hug and kiss my family when they arrived and left and that each visit would last for an hour or two. I presumed, though, that the visitation room would be just as noisy and chaotic as it had been at the jail. I was thrilled at the thought of being able to kiss my parents again and speak to them without being separated by that vile and inhumane barrier, but other than that my expectations were pretty low. Bereft of human contact as I was at the jail, the loneliness I was vulnerable to would have been almost debilitating if I had allowed myself to think about it, so I didn't dare let myself expect too much from my visits.

My first visit at FCCW happened a few weeks after I was shipped. Although visitation is now held in the gymnasium to allow for the large numbers of visitors that arrive each weekend, at the time the visitation room was about half the size of the gym, with a colorful mural on one wall of a woman in a long pink dress taking flight into the stars. The prison had commissioned a local artist to paint it when Fluvanna had first opened, and it was an incongruously cheery note in the otherwise colorless room. There were no barriers separating the guests: families sat chatting and laughing with each other, clustered around a small green plastic table piled high with snacks from the vending machines. In one corner a couple of inmate recreation aides were busy taking photographs of the women holding their grinning children close or clinging to friends and family. Each picture cost a $2 picture ticket that could be purchased from commissary.

Mom and Dad came the first weekend that I was permitted guests, and I rushed to the visitation room as soon as the C.O. called into my cell and told me that they were at the facility and being processed. Unsure as to when they would arrive, I had been ready for hours. When I got there, I was patted down for contraband (I couldn't bring anything with me to a visit), then stood nervously behind the glass window of the door separating me from the visitation room. I would only be allowed to enter when my parents appeared.

Our hugs and kisses of greeting were a blessing to me. I, like most of my family, enjoy physical displays of affection: we are touchers by nature, and even as an adult it was normal for me to hold my mother's hand as we walked down the street together. Touch is a vital bond for us, one we had all missed dreadfully. After our weepy hellos, we settled in around the flimsy little table. Although it is against the rules to have any physical contact beyond greetings and goodbyes, Dad and Mom kept surreptitiously touching my arm or my knee, as if they couldn't quite believe that we were really together again.

I can't remember much of what happened during the visit. We probably spent most of our time talking about the new rules that governed my life and how much I missed them and the children. I suppose that Dad bought me snacks, too. That's what he does every visit. If I show up to the visitation room and he has gotten there before me, he will have filled the table with my favorite treats from the vending machines. And the moment that I have finished eating, he clears away the trash, always asking me if I want anything else. Although he's never told me this, I guess he does that because it's the only thing he can physically do for me himself, the only way he can care for his daughter. It is so hard on him to be unable to rescue me, to make everything all better as he did when I was a child, so he shows his desire to protect me by buying me the candy bars and sodas that I can't get otherwise.

Although there is nothing striking that I remember about the visit itself, I vividly recall their departure. We held each other closely for as long as we could, then they watched as I went back through the glass-windowed door to leave. When I turned around to get one last wave goodbye, I saw my mother holding up two of her fingers. She was showing me the dancing olives! When I was growing up, my father had always loved to eat green olives, and Mom used to exasperate him by sucking out the pimientos and putting the emptied olives on her fingers, dancing them around as we sat around the dinner table. Shannon and I thought it was delightful, though, and the dancing olives became a slightly bizarre family game, capturing perfectly my mother's sweet and slightly daffy personality. I don't know what made her think to do that as she left me that day, but she managed to find the perfect memory to help me temper the grief I felt at their departure. Mom does it every time she leaves a visit. I'm so blessed to have the parents that I do. Their unconquerable sense of humor is one of their greatest gifts to me.

Even with the emotional and physical separation from my children that I'm now enduring, the memory of my first prison visit with them is still a sustaining joy to me. I remember it clearly. Once I was transferred to Fluvanna I lived only to hold my children again. I felt that they were doing OK, and I spoke to them often on the phone, but my sister, who had custody of the kids, wanted to give them time before they had to see their mother in a prison uniform. Of course, I was selfish—I wanted them brought in to see me immediately! However, I soon realized that Shannon and her husband were making their decisions based on what was best for Jack, Fran, and Gio. My children were suffering from the psychological aftershocks of two tremendous losses: the death of their father and my own incarceration.

Jack, the oldest, understood a little of what was going on with me. He was 7 years old when I left home and fully aware that a tragedy had occurred. Francesca, at 5, and 3-year-old Gio just knew that everyone was sad a lot of the time and that Mommy and Daddy weren't there anymore. As the months passed, Franny and Jack didn't allude to my absence very often during our phone calls. I always tried to be cheerful whenever we talked, but I was never able to keep from crying the first few times that they asked about my absence, so like many children of the incarcerated, they quickly learned to avoid the painful subject. But Gio always wanted to know when I was coming home or, even worse, if she could come and live with me where I was. It took a year before she, too, finally stopped asking when I would come back to her. My relief at not having to cry through an answer to her question was mixed with the awful certainty that she had come to accept my absence as a fact of her life. That was the first time, I think, that I knew any real hope I had of resuming our lives together was gone. Even if through some miracle I came back, there would always be a distance between my children and me.

Still, seeing them was all that I wanted to do, so I was thrilled when about a year after my arrival Shannon told me that the kids were secure enough emotionally to see me. Our first visit was a prearranged special visit. My parents, my sister and her husband, and my much-missed children were able to spend three hours in a small, empty conference room. There were no vending machines or books, but I could have cared less. I was holding my children at last, and we reconnected immediately.

I did what I could to share the safer aspects of my world with them. By that time I was in the dog program, so I had arranged for another dog handler, Nadia, to walk my dog past the narrow window of the conference room at a predetermined time so that the kids could see him. When 10:00 came around, they all clambered onto a chair so that they could see, laughing and pointing at my canine roommate. Nadia told me later that they looked like a totem pole in the window, three adorable faces cheering as she put the puppy through his tricks.

I was grateful to Shannon and Keith to find that my little ones were still basically the same children I remembered despite everything they had been through. Jack was the nurturing big brother, standing back patiently so that his sisters could have a chance to hug me first before coming up to me for a long embrace. Francesca clambered up into my lap immediately, catching up on several years' worth of embraces. Gio was still my ever-comical littlest one, giggling around the room in between her own demands for cuddles. It was hard to have to rotate my little ones so that each had equal time with me. I wanted to hold each of them forever.

We spent most of that afternoon laughing, actually, talking about "safe" things: school, TV shows, friends, and my latest assignment in the dog program, a sweet-natured Labrador mix called Nicholas. The biggest laugh of the day was when Gio, after about an hour of shy near-silence, put on my burgundy uniform coat, which I had laid on one of the chairs in the overheated room at the beginning of the visit. She pranced around the room for a few minutes in the oversize garment, then began exploring the pockets. Curious when she felt something crackling in the side pocket, she pulled out one of the unused plastic dog poop bags that I and the other dog handlers always seemed to have in our pockets.

"Mommy, what's this for?" she asked, waving the crumpled plastic bag in the air.

"That's for when I go out with the dogs," I answered, not going into details. I hoped that she wouldn't ask for more information, but being my irrepressibly curious smallest child, she did. My sister was laughing as she watched our exchange—she knew that Gio wouldn't stop without a complete answer, and she knew what the bag's intended use was.

Gio had paused at my incomplete answer, looking probingly at the ball of black plastic. "But what do you do with it?" she demanded.

I smiled. "Well, honey, it's a poop bag. When the dog goes to the bathroom we pick up the mess with one of those bags."

"Oh," she said in a small voice, and was silent for several seconds. Then strolling casually to a far corner of the room, she surreptitiously slid the bag back into my coat pocket and laid the coat exactly where she had found it. Nonchalantly, she took a seat next to me and grabbed my hand.

Pulling her into my lap, I asked, "Honey, did you think that there was poop actually inside that bag?"

We were all chortling at this point. Gio, with all the dignity a 6-year-old can muster, replied, "Of course. It's a poop bag, isn't it?" Seeing the glee on our faces she seemed on the verge of being offended, but within seconds decided that whatever the joke was, it was better to play along.

Like her brother and sister, her laughter-loving nature trumped everything else. This was the little prankster that I remembered. They were still my own Jack, Fran, and Gio. Thank God.

MOTHER'S MILK

After that first visit with the children, I was selected for a parenting program called MILK. It was and is the greatest blessing I have ever experienced here.

I first heard about Mothers Inside Loving Kids while I was at the jail. "You definitely need to try and get into MILK when you get to Fluvanna," said Stephanie, who was waiting to be shipped to FCCW for the fourth time. She was relatively blasé about going back to prison. She had lots of friends that she was looking forward to seeing again, and her girlfriend was already there on an assault charge.

Steph was a gregarious woman, always voluble with advice about my future home, but I had discerned that she was not often reliable in her information. For example, it was she who told me about the prison graveyard just beyond the fence where, she claimed, lifers were unceremoniously dumped after death, as well as darkly hinting that not all inmate corpses made it beyond the walls to that barren cemetery. A few, she implied, got no farther than the prison kitchen. Most of her other lies were not nearly as gothic as that one, though. They typically centered on the officers who were passionately enamored of her or her fabulous escape attempts and other acts of derring-do, so when she told me about this great program where I would be able to actually hold my children and play games with them for hours, I had grave doubts.

From my earliest days at the jail, I had learned that hope is usually just a source of powerful disappointment, but on the slim chance that Steph was telling the truth for once, I wrote to Fluvanna inquiring about the MILK program. Not only did it exist, I discovered, but I actually received a reply from the counselor who ran the program telling me that once I took a parenting class I would be eligible to apply! That was good news, but surely MILK wasn't as great as Steph made it out to be. I figured that it was probably just a few cheap puzzles and coloring books in a dirty, cramped room. I'm so glad that I was wrong.

My first order of business once I was housed in general population of the prison was to sign up for both of the parenting classes that Fluvanna offered. There were long waiting lists for each of them, but somehow I was lucky enough to almost immediately get into the class run by a former inmate. Once I had my certificate of completion for the 6-week class, I was ready to apply for MILK.

There are only about 45 slots available to the approximately 1,200 women at Fluvanna, and applications are solicited a few times a year. Some inmates are not eligible because they have been convicted of crimes against children, because they have restraining orders against them forbidding contact with their offspring, because they have recently received disciplinary tickets, or because they have not completed a parenting class. Beyond those restrictions, though, any inmate who has a child is welcome to apply to be in MILK, regardless of her length of sentence. The rewards for belonging are almost unbelievable for an incarcerated mother: up to 6 all-day visits a year where you play games with your children, sing songs, and do crafts. Every visit has an educational theme, and all of the activities are designed to work together to create a seamlessly enjoyable day.

MILK is co-sponsored by the Girl Scouts of America's Beyond Bars program, so we are fortunate to not only receive occasional financial grants but also to be supported by a number of dynamic, creative women affiliated with the Girl Scouts. In addition to helping make each MILK visit a success for our families, they offer workshops to the inmate moms on subjects ranging from learning styles to leadership to parenting from prison. Everything that is offered to us is geared toward making us grow as individuals and as role models to our children.

That sounds a little lofty, probably, but many of the women I've met in here have never been able to effectively parent their children while on the street, much less cope with the more difficult task of parenting from prison. They had been busy dealing with all of the problems that brought them to Fluvanna to begin with. You can't be a mom to your child when you are strung out on heroin or on the pipe, or if you are trapped within an abusive relationship. Survival is all you can hope for.

I guess I was pretty naive when I first joined MILK. I assumed that almost everybody had connected with her children in the same way that I had. I was unusual. My family life was stable prior to my incarceration. We didn't do drugs or drink too much, and James and I had been able to provide for our children both financially and emotionally. But one of the most powerful aspects of meeting this group of strong incarcerated mothers was learning that most of the stories were quite different from mine and that through this amazing program some of the participants were trying to overcome years of alienation from their families and in some cases be an engaged parent for the first time in their lives.

Divina, sometimes affectionately called Dee, was the first woman who shared her story with me. It was during one of the weekly MILK meetings where we talk about plans for upcoming visits. These meetings are also opportunities for us to share what is going on with our children and their caregivers or to ask for advice on how to deal with problems at home. I didn't know Divina well, but I could tell that she had been crying as she pulled up a chair. Paulette, one of the officers, spoke quietly to her before the meeting was called to order, and I saw that a few of the women that Divina typically hung out with walked up to her to give her a long hug, but other than that she sat silently until the call was made for personal business to be shared. Hesitantly, Dee raised her hand and spoke about her two sons, Marquise and Varden.

"Most of you guys know that Marquise has been having a real hard time in school," she said, "but I haven't spoken a lot about Varden. I was hoping that he would be able to come to one of the MILK visits so that some of you would be able to meet him and maybe talk to him a little. I know that he's tired of hearing the same stuff from me, so I thought maybe he would listen to one of y'all. But the foster care lady he's been staying with wouldn't never bring him; she said he was too upset to see me."

Divina pulled a wad of toilet paper from her pocket and continued, "I just got a letter from my grandma telling me that Varden has been getting into lots of trouble, hanging around with some of the nastiest bangers in the neighborhood, and that now he's dropped out of school." Her crying was obvious now, and most of us were unashamedly in tears ourselves. Someone had gotten a roll of toilet paper from the nearby bathroom and it was being passed from person to person around the circle. "He's only 15. Why is he getting into the exact same shit that I did when I was his age? How can I stop him from making the same mistakes that I did when I am locked up in here? I write to him every week, but that nasty woman has put a block on the phone, so I can't even call and try to talk to him. And what can I do to keep Marquise from doing the exact same thing?"

The front of her uniform was strewn with shreds of the cheap prison toilet paper when she finished speaking, and she began slowly brushing them away, continuing even after her top was a pristine burgundy again. Although she had asked for help, her feeling of hopelessness was obvious. This question had been asked too many times without a real answer. Some of the older members offered a few suggestions: write him more often, try to write his caregiver, write to his school—all the correct things that we had learned to do in our parenting classes. Divina listened, but all of us in the circle knew the truth. The greatest casualties when we were incarcerated were our children, and the reality is that if they don't have a strong network of support in place on the outside, there is very little we can do to protect them from the pressures they face.

When my kids came for their first MILK visit that August, our theme was "An International Adventure." I waited eagerly for my family to show up, and by 8:30 I was almost deranged with anticipation, surrounded by a cluster of other MILK moms, all almost as eager as I was for them to arrive. At 9:00 I knew that something had happened, a mix-up on the date, a flat tire, an airline tragedy. . . . I was certain that I was never going to see Jack, Franny, and Gio again, and, martyr-like, I was bracing myself to endure an existence utterly without them. My friends told me that they would be there soon, but I knew the bitter truth: I was doomed to a life of endless loneliness.

My flair for melodrama was effectively squelched when I heard someone yell, "Erin, I think your family is here!" Rushing to the entrance of the enormous room where we held our MILK visits, I first saw my parents and sister, then, thank you God, my children. Jack and Franny shook off my parents' hands and ran toward me. "Mum, mum!" they said as they tangled their arms around me. It sounded so odd, hearing their English accent. They had been in England for over a year by then, and of course they had absorbed the slang and diction of their new home. It was charming but also painful—a reminder of the distance between us. Gio held back, weeping softly as she clung to my sister's hand.

My immediate thought was, "She's forgetting me—I'm a stranger to her." I began to mentally gird myself for an awkward hello to my baby girl. Gio and I had had several conversations on the telephone since the children had flown in from Gatwick a few weeks earlier, but I knew that my physical presence was quite different from a distant voice on the telephone, "Mum" more of an idea than a reality. Maybe it wasn't a good idea to see them after all. Then my mom touched my shoulder.

"Erin, I know you, and I know exactly what you're thinking. Don't jump to conclusions. Gio's not crying because she's nervous about seeing you or scared about being here. She's just upset because she had picked out a pretty dress for the visit and they wouldn't let her wear it into the prison because it was sleeveless."

It has always been a little eerie to see how well Mom can sense my thoughts and concerns. I never noticed it before being locked up, but I suppose that her maternal radar has been well honed in the past years of seeing me through arrest, conviction, and sentencing. She and Dad both seem to have developed a kind of ESP regarding my welfare, physical and emotional. Even though I am almost 40 years old, it's still comforting to have that.

Whatever made Mom say it, I was grateful that she removed that anxiety from me. Taking my Gio in my arms, I felt absurdly grateful for her tears now, glad that I could be a comfort to her. I set aside for the moment the frustrating fact that my 7- and 8-year-old daughters had to wear my sister's crumpled shirts over their perfectly modest sundresses because of a draconian interpretation of prison regulations (it's a good thing Shannon had her suitcase in the car or I wouldn't have been able to see Franny or Gio at all that day). All that mattered was that they were really here.

I can't imagine a better day in prison than that August visit. The kids and I did all of the activities together, answering trivia questions about different countries to collect stamps on their "passports" so that they could win a prize. They each made me a drawing I could keep and wrote a letter to me in my MILK journal. We sang songs and danced with the other families and played the "What Would You Do?" game, where we were asked questions about how we would handle situations where we face peer pressure. These were all serious questions, but everyone was weak with laughter when Gio answered the question "What would you do if someone had been drinking and wanted you to go somewhere the car with them? Would you go too?"

Of course, all of the moms, caregivers, and older kids playing said that they would never, under any circumstances, get in the car with a drunk driver. Then it was Gio's turn. She appeared to be concentrating very deeply on the question when it was time for her to answer, then gravely turned to Sharon, who was moderating the game, and replied in her BBC accent "Well, of course I wouldn't. . . ." She paused dramatically. "Not unless I was drunk as well." Like her mother, Gio is never one to miss the opportunity to get a laugh.

Whenever I sat down that the day, I had at least one child in my lap, a luxury I wouldn't be allowed in the regular visitation room. At Fluvanna, children over 2 years old aren't allowed to sit in their mother's lap during regular visits, ostensibly because the cheap plastic chairs we use might break. That has always seemed to me to be one of the harshest rules of visitation. How do you explain to a 2-year-old that he isn't allowed to sit in his Mommy's lap? I reveled in holding them, trying to catch up on a thousand missed embraces. Even Jack wasn't too mature to sit in my lap. I hope he never grows up that much.

The thing I wanted to do most, though, was to spend some time alone in one of the small side rooms with each of my children to talk about anything they wanted in private. This was another thing that I would not have been able to do during a regular visit. Gio demanded to go first, of course. We talked about her school and her friends, and that she loved giraffes, and that her drawings were great, and that she knew a funny joke but had forgotten it, and that she wanted to be a guitar-playing ballerina when she grew up. Gio had big plans for her future, lots of social and professional success ahead. "I will be very popular when I grow up," she confided, "but still be kind to everyone." I was delighted that she had her priorities in order.

Francesca was quieter than her chatty baby sister was, but being able to hold her was profoundly satisfying. "Mum," she said as she crawled into my lap, "would you please tell me the story about Frangelica the Fish?"

"Frangelica the Fish" was a story that I began telling Francesca years ago when she was nervous about learning to swim in our backyard pool. Jack took to the water immediately, but Franny needed a little cajoling, so I created the story of a little girl named Frangelica who loved swimming so much that she refused to leave the swimming pool, even when her mother called her to dinner. She stayed in the water so long, in fact, that Frangelica turned into an enormous fish. She was only turned back into a little girl when her mother found a doctor/veterinarian in the phone book who advised the distraught mom to slather the giant fish in dirt so that she would remember what the land felt like.

"Frangelica the Fish" was no *Charlotte's Web*, but Francesca and I had both been enchanted by the brave but stubborn Frangelica. I would tell the story to her almost every night at bedtime when I was at home, so it was especially pleasurable to be able to hold her again and retell it.

My time with Jack was, in one way, the most important thing I had to do during his visit. Older than his sisters, Jack had been the most affected by the police investigation and trial, and he was beginning to ask a lot of questions about what had happened. He had suffered from the classic symptoms of a child who has endured a traumatic loss: depression, anger, sleeplessness, and developmental regression. It hadn't been easy for Shannon or, later, for Jack's caregivers in England. Perhaps now, as Jack healed, he was finally ready to talk to me about what had happened.

Like Gio and Fran, Jack headed immediately into my lap, tucking his blond head under my chin like a cat. As I held my long-legged boy, I felt his nervousness and he probably felt mine as well. He knew that we were going to have a "talk," despite my efforts to be low-key about it. We shared a few moments of silence, and then I tried, as gently as I could, to broach the subject. I had planned what I was going to generally say to him after discussing it with Shannon; I didn't want to inadvertently say anything that would undermine what she was doing in regards to the kids. Basically, my thought was to be candid and nonjudgmental with him. I hoped that would encourage him to talk to somebody, if not me.

"Hey, Jacko-man," I said to him after he had settled in. "How are you doing kiddo?"

"I'm OK."

More silence. This was going to be difficult.

"Um, your auntie told me that a lot had been going on with you, and that you have been asking some questions about my being here." Jack, who hadn't made eye contact since we had started talking, burrowed his head into my shoulder. "Sweetheart, it's OK to ask questions. If you are uncomfortable talking to me, you can talk to Aunt Shannon, Uncle Keith, Grandma, Bapa, Auntie Maxine, Uncle Christian. There are so many people who love you and want to help you. Or if you want to talk to someone you don't know as well, we can find somebody like that for you." Unconsciously I began to stroke his head as I used to do to comfort him during the excruciating ear infections he had endured as a toddler. "The important thing for you to know is that it is alright for you to be feeling sad, angry, and confused, and that anything you ask me I will do my best to answer honestly. I love you so much," I added.

I waited. I didn't want to force him, but I knew that the only way to really heal was to get everything out. Jack was like his dad in more ways than his physical resemblance—he tended to keep a stoic front over a sensitive and fragile interior and to take care of other people rather than himself.

"No, I don't have any questions about anything." His muffled response was accompanied by a tighter grip of my hand.

"Are you sure, sweetie? There's not anything that you want to talk about at all?" I felt his barely perceptible headshake. "Well, why don't you think about it? I will be able to call you a few times again before you leave for England, so we can talk about anything you want on the phone. And you can always write me letters. Just remember that I love you more than anything in the world, OK?"

"OK." He looked at me, his flushed, somber little face so like James's. "Mommy, I love you and miss you all the time, too." I hadn't been "Mommy" for a couple of years. This time I had to turn my own head aside so he wouldn't see the quick moisture in my eyes. I had been doing my best not to let any of the kids see me cry, but hearing that was too much. "I miss you too, Jacko-man. Promise me you'll never forget that."

Straightening up, I began to tickle him and changed the subject to something less emotionally volatile. "So, look, my little Brit, Grandma told me that you had tried out for the soccer, oops, I mean football team. What's going on with that?"

I managed to avoid crying for the rest of the day, but after the last wave through the glass as the kids left at 3:00, I couldn't seem to stop. Naomi, who was one of the inmates who founded the MILK chapter at Fluvanna and who probably was closer to me than anyone else there, hustled me off into an empty corner and gave me a hug. She didn't try telling me that it would be OK or, even more ridiculous, that it would get easier with time. She just let me pour out my grief. When I seemed to be slowing down, she grabbed my hand and said, "Look. I love you, so I'm not going to lie to you. This is never going to get any easier. It will always rip your heart out when your kids walk away from you at the end of a visit. This is not OK. It's a screwed-up situation, but all you can do is try to make the most of the time you can spend with them. But as long as you need someone, I'm here whenever you need me."

Among all of the women in MILK, to me Naomi epitomizes what the group is all about. She enthusiastically takes all of the seminars and classes, works hard as secretary to keep the paperwork and scheduling in order, and pitches in wherever there is a need for an extra hand. More important than that, though, she reminds us all constantly that MILK is not about making the prison look progressive, or even making our time in prison easier. Every moment and every action should be about healing our children. It's easy to dwell in selfishness when you are locked up, but Naomi never lets us forget that our children need us to be strong for them. They are, after all, the reason for everything.

REFERENCES

Bernstein, N. (2005). *All alone in the world: Children of the incarcerated.* New York: New Press.

Enos, S. (2001). *Mothering from the inside: Parenting in a women's prison.* Albany: State University of New York Press.

Lamb, W. (2007). *I'll fly away: Further testimonies from the women of York Prison.* New York: Harper Perennial.

O'Brien, P. (2001). *Making it in the "free world."* Albany: State University of New York Press.

Pollock, J. (2002). *Women, prison & crime.* Belmont, CA: Wadsworth.

Rierden, A. (1997). *The farm: Life inside a women's prison.* Amherst: University of Massachusetts Press.

CHAPTER 8

Programs, Privileges,
and Oases of Creativity

Creative work, by definition, entails the assertion of self. In prison, where the prisoner's self is suppressed as a matter of course, creative work is a valuable means to autonomy (Johnson, 2012; Nagelsen, 2008). Certainly it was for Erin George, whose creative writing flowered in prison and gave her the confidence to write original poems (see George, 2008) and, ultimately, this fine book. George entered her first prison writing class tentatively, unsure of herself, unaware of her considerable talent. Support from a gentle, accepting teacher was crucial (for an insightful examination of the role of supportive staff, see Tabriz & Hassine, 2009). We know that prisoners can deal with difficult topics in their lives when they are accepted as individuals and their reflections are "disguised as a poem" (Tannenbaum, 2000) or some other work of fiction, such as a short story (Lamb, 2007). We also know that poetry and other creative work offers a window into prisons that helps outsiders get a sense of daily life behind bars. A writer once said, in effect, "Writing is easy; just open a vein and let the words flow." Inmates sometimes refer to writing in this way. When they bleed, we learn (Johnson & Chernoff, 2002; see also Brooks & Johnson, 2010).

George's poem, "Cloistered," the frontispiece for this book, is a case in point. (Note that the poem is reprinted from a book of original poetry by George, written during her confinement.) "Cloistered" is a superb poem with a richly detailed set of images that take us into her world. Not all creative work in prison is this good, in my opinion, but creative work does take us into the world of the prisoners and connects their world with ours. And in classes like the ones described by George in this chapter, the prisoners invite each other into their personal worlds, making the prison a more meaningful community (Nagelsen, 2008).

People can be creative without a basic education, but a basic education helps enormously, providing the tools with which to express ideas. George works as a tutor, which allows her to see firsthand the hunger for learning that exists in her prison. Her fellow prisoners want to learn, sometimes with a desperate sense of urgency. Basic deficits are barriers, sometimes formidable barriers, but

George's experience as a tutor reminds us that many prisoners want to learn, and want to earn the right to say they have an education. They want to transcend the symbolic walls of ignorance, just as they no doubt would like to surmount the literal walls of prison. Our job is to provide a supportive environment in which learning can take place. As we see in this chapter in the case of Svetlana, George does her part to lobby officials to provide suitable educational opportunities for inmates with limited English skills. George knows well that moments of learning can take prisoners out of the prison and into a world of individual expression and achievement. In George's experience, praise for real accomplishments goes a long way to motivate the women, women who in many cases have had few positive experiences in school. The promise of creative work down the road is an incentive as well.

People can also bring creative talent with them and see it flower in the prison. One such case is tattooing, an art form much valued among prisoners (Kornfeld, 1997). George's engaging discussion of Abby, a respected tattoo artist, explores this largely hidden dimension of life in the women's prison. —Robert Johnson

It was a typical, boring evening. I was sitting out in the dayroom a few minutes before mass movement, doing nothing very memorable, when my friend Frog strolled up to me. Frog is a petite, exuberant woman who adds an almost child-like sense of enthusiasm to everything she takes on. "I'm just a big kid!" she'll say as she roughhouses with the kids at an MILK visit. Frog is one of the most popular MILK moms, and one of the people that my son actively looks forward to seeing each year, so if for no other reason than that, I am fond of her. But she is also impossible not to like, with her charismatic personality and cheerful attitude, and I always enjoy hanging out with her.

"Hey girl, what's up?" I said as she approached my table. Frog was a handler in the dog program with me, so I thought that she might want to talk about her latest dog, Cicely, who was turning out to be a real handful.

"Nothing much. I just wanted to find out if you wanted to go to this program with me. It's called the Voice Project," she said.

"The Voice Project?" I felt a little doubtful. I was never a big one for signing up for programs in here. "That's not one of those 'I'm OK, you're OK' touchy-feely things is it? I hate that." I had been forced to take a few programs where "group" (the catch-all prison phrase for therapy sessions involving large numbers of inmates sharing intimate details of their lives and emotions) was involved, and I wasn't eager to join another one. Group was usually just an opportunity for women to moan about how miserable they are, and how life has tormented them, and drop a few of the pop psychology terms they had picked up from the 50 other groups they had taken in the past.

"Naw, it's nothing like that. This cool chick named Amanda runs it, and we do poetry and stuff. I know you like all those big words and you read a lot," Frog shrugged. "I just thought that you might like it. We have a really good time, and there are a lot of cool people in the class."

"That sounds good, but I didn't sign up for it. Will I be allowed to go?" I asked.

"Yeah, no problem. All she has to do is call for you tonight, and she can add you to the master pass list for next week on." Frog grinned. "This is the perfect class for you!"

I was willing to give it a try. I had never read poetry before (other than class assignments in high school), much less written any, but any class that Frog liked had to be OK. Frankly, poetry had always bored me, as did all of those pretentious, arty kids in school who claimed to be deeply and utterly moved by it. What little poetry I had read when I was younger I hadn't much enjoyed. But maybe I wouldn't have to actually write anything.

Frog and I were the first people to show up when master control called for the Voice Project, and Frog excitedly dragged me up to Amanda, the volunteer who ran the class. Amanda was just the kind of person I had imagined would be teaching poetry to prisoners: a young, artistic, liberal woman motivated by the idea of bringing the light of creativity to the darkest recesses of the prison system. Despite her idealism, though, I liked her immediately. She was very smart, very compassionate, and full of joy, and I quickly learned that she was committed to the class and every writer in it. As I grew to know her, I realized that she was a great deal more than the stereotype I immediately pinned on her, but in prison you are quick to label—it's safer that way. Rarely do I get close enough to someone to learn if the label is accurate.

Amanda was emptying her book bag of tattered poetry books as we approached, each one shedding small slips of paper from marked pages as she piled them on the cheap folding table where a listing tower of photocopies sat next to the rec department boom box and an array of CDs. Amanda had brought the music with her to inspire the night's writing, which was one of her favorite exercises. Hearing Frog approach, she turned and smiled, a real one—not the "I'm extremely nervous about potentially having to talk to a murderer or child abuser but I'm gamely trying to cover it up" smile that most visitors to the prison wore.

"Amanda, this is Erin, she uses all of those big words that you like, so I thought she'd be good in the Voice Project," Frog said.

Amanda laughed, something she did a lot. "Welcome to the class," she said. "Do you like to write poetry?"

I had to be honest. "Well, I've never really written any. I'm not the 'poetry' type, I guess. I do like to read a lot, but I always stick to prose. But Frog said that this was a good group, so I thought I would try."

"I'm glad to hear it," she said as other inmates began to file into the classroom. "I think you'll enjoy it."

There were about 12 of us in the class, and since I had only been at Fluvanna for a few years, I didn't know most of them. Frog was the only one I had a friendship with, and I was a little nervous about making a fool of myself around these women, confidently discussing sestinas and synecdoche. Clearly, I was out of my league here. It's only one class, I told myself. I don't have to come again next week if it's awful.

After we all settled around the tables and chatted for a few minutes, Amanda asked if anyone had brought in something to share. Savannah, a slender inmate with a puckish grin and lovely brunette hair, raised her hand. My expectations were low: this was prison after all, and what little poetry I had read by other inmates who would come to me for help in spelling and grammar was of the type I mentally termed "Hallmark" poetry—obvious rhymes and of no more emotional depth than a greeting card.

Instead, Savannah began to read a poignant letter to a child who had died—one conceived under horrific circumstances, but cherished and mourned nonetheless. When she finished, her words still lingered like the echoed cries of her child, and I was startled by the artistic control she had over her emotional subject. I might not have known a lot about poetry, but even I realized that Savannah avoided the bathos of many novice poets. We were all crying, but these were not the cheap, pleasurable tears evoked by a Lifetime movie.

Amanda asked for comments, but there wasn't much that we could add. Savannah's poetry was too powerful to absorb immediately. Her head was on the desk as the next poet stood to speak, and she remained in that position for the next 10 minutes, her friend Stephanie occasionally reaching out to touch her shoulder.

Next up was Country, who wrote rambling prose poems about lighthouses. She haltingly read a new one to the class every week. When she was done that evening, we all made supportive comments, but her writing was empty next to the dark vibrancy of Savannah's work.

Eventually I found that none of the other poets in the group could match Savannah, the clear and deserving poet laureate of the group, although there were several other talented writers. Some of the class's output, like Country's mass-produced lighthouse poems and the clichéd love poems that Dell wrote to her girlfriend (before finally being hauled off to seg for a 209), would never be more than sentimental indulgences. But Stephanie, Pris, and Frog all wrote movingly of life before and behind bars, showing flashes of imagery that were unforgettable. I was especially amazed by Frog's poetry. She was a lifer, too, and I knew that not only had she earned her GED in prison, she had in fact learned to read while incarcerated. It grieves me to think of what she might have accomplished if she had been given the sort of family life that I had enjoyed rather than her own tragic past: profound physical and emotional abuse while a child, then raped at 14 and forced to live on the street with a newborn baby girl. There are, I'm afraid, too many women like Frog serving hard time behind Fluvanna's walls.

During the second half of class, Amanda suggested that we try free writing while she played a CD. After she popped in a recording of dreamy, impressionist music, I tried to put myself in poetry-writing mode. It wasn't easy—the only writing I had ever done was scathing liberal editorials in my college newspaper and humorous essays. I had certainly never attempted anything as personal as poetry before.

I was amazed, then, when I found myself immersed in the challenge of expressing myself through literary tropes rather than intellectual argument or camouflaging satire. I scrawled my words on the cheap prison notebook paper until Amanda called the exercise to a halt, then asked us to take turns reading what we had written. After everybody else had finished, Amanda said "What about you, Erin? Do you want to share what you've written?"

Now, I'm a pretty confident person. I usually have no trouble expressing myself verbally, but I was ashamed of my ineptitude. I didn't know anything about poetry. How dare Frog and Amanda put me in this position? The group was staring at me in a way that I'm sure was encouraging but that I perceived as being judgmental. I hastily jabbered through my scribblings, then crumpled the paper into a ball. Thank God that was over.

"Hold on," said Amanda. "Read that again, please. And more slowly. I want to hear what you have to say."

Reluctantly I smoothed out the paper and began to read, the trembling in my voice more obvious as I tried to speak slowly. I don't remember much of what I wrote—only a phrase or two, really. Something about life here being like a cushioned coffin. It wasn't very good, but Amanda said, "That's a pretty disturbing image. I like that. Why don't you try writing something about what it's like to live in prison and bring it with you next week?" I realize now that she was just trying to be supportive of a novice poet, but any sort of validation from an outsider is rare in prison, and here was someone telling me that I was capable of creating something of value. I hadn't felt that in a long time, so it inspired me to actually try to write.

The poem that I wrote that week was called "Cloistered," and it compared my new life with the closed-off existence of a cloistered nun. "Cloistered" turned out to be my first published poem, and that, too, was thanks to Amanda. When the class was finishing up for the semester, she arranged to have a group of local poets and actors read our work at a poetry reading in Charlottesville, Virginia. I was delighted that what I had written would be shared with people outside, and thrilled when my mom and dad, my niece Molly, and my grandmother all attended. My family was grateful as well for the attention and support that my writing received. Like me, they had quickly learned that inmates are usually perceived as being valueless in our progressive society, so this demonstration of worth was unexpectedly gratifying. My father was even given the opportunity to speak at the end of the reading. As always, he was an eloquent portrayer of my feelings as well as his own.

A month after the poetry reading I received a letter from a Charlottesville literary magazine, Streetlight, telling me that "Cloistered" had been selected for inclusion in an upcoming issue. An editor of the magazine had been present at the poetry reading and liked it enough to include it. This was the first time that I became aware that there were many people who looked beyond my legal status and saw my inherent worth. I have satisfying relationships via mail with other poets, writers, and editors. And I found others, staff members and volunteers within the system, who lent me enormous amounts of support.

My immersion in poetry began after my first meeting with Amanda, and I began eagerly reading any books on the subject I could find, trying to find poets that reached me most clearly. Through the Voice Project I discovered Mark Strand, Sharon Olds, Li-Young Lee, Seamus Heaney, and Billy Collins, none of whom were in the outdated poetry books that the DCE library carried.

I also signed up for another class offered through the Chaplain's office, called Poetry for the Soul. Despite its religious classification, the class offered a broad survey of traditional English and American poetry, as well as some more current poets, like Rita Dove. Poetry for the Soul was taught by an amazing man named Paul Priest. A former English professor, Mr. Priest had to be in his 70s but still managed to share his profound love for poetry with almost everyone in his class. Some didn't get him: Who was this old guy in his paint-spattered khakis and tattered plaid shirt, with a corona of Einstein hair? These women were the ones who were only there to hang out with their girlfriends, pass kites, and smuggle contraband.

A small group of us, however, became devotees of the cult of language in his class. He would have us recite poetry together, exhorting us to be more creative in our interpretations if the rendition was flat. You could see that he was a closet thespian, and he adored reciting poetry himself. Mr. Priest had a trove of poems that he had long memorized, and a random comment would be enough to bring on a snatch of Whitman or Emily Dickinson. His performances of certain pieces were legendary: it's his voice I hear, his adopted feminine movements I see whenever I reread Maya Angelou's "Phenomenal Woman." We all loved it when he recited, and those of us who had been in the class before would often shout out the titles of those poems we knew he particularly enjoyed, making suggestions as if we were listening to a garage rock band.

Mr. Priest doesn't offer Poetry for the Soul anymore. He's moved back to England, and although I miss him, he writes me often. He is just as busy there, working for human rights groups and doing his best to share his love of the world. The Voice Project is still here, but its focus has changed to drama since Amanda moved to California to work on her master's degree. I'm not very interested in the new format of the class, so I don't do that anymore either. The transience of life is a constant here.

Fortunately, a more significant constant is the gift that Amanda and Mr. Priest gave me. I now have a way to filter and share my experiences with others in an effective way. My long-standing love of language is well fed by poetry, and I have the intellectual challenge of writing and revising. Best of all, I have been lucky enough to find people who appreciate what I have written, so that Jack, Fran, and Gio all have copies of books and magazines that include their mother's poems, especially the ones that are inspired directly by them. In this way I am able to do something that my kids can be proud of. They can talk about their mother, the poet, not their mother, the prisoner. They have that much, at least.

LEARNING AND EARNING A SENSE OF WORTH

Although now I work in the library, in the past I have worked as a tutor in one of the 5 pre-GED DCE classes offered to inmates (all inmates trying to gain their GED take classes and are tested through the DCE). The educational levels of our students range from prekindergarten to 12th grade. I spent most of my day helping the students prepare for their GED or ABE tests (the precursor to the more difficult GED) and checking students' homework. It was actually an extremely gratifying job, an opportunity to do something for people who have a chance at going home and to try to help prevent them from coming back. There were two other inmate tutors in our class, but they can only be there half-day because of vocational classes they are taking.

One afternoon, as I was going over some fractions worksheets that the previous class had completed, I felt a timid tap on my shoulder. Glancing up, I saw that it was Bonnie, one of my favorite students. Bonnie comes from a little town near the Virginia–Tennessee border, and when she got to Fluvanna on a meth charge, she initially tested at a third-grade level in math and first grade in reading. I love Bonnie, who is so sweetly determined to get her GED but is hampered by her lack of formal education. She's one of the students who is there to work, not just hang out and waste time whispering gossip and staring out the window at the activity in the yard. Actually, a surprisingly large percentage of our students work on their studies with the intensity of doctoral candidates. It's only a few that seem to come to class because their treatment plan requires that they attend.

"Erin, I know I keep bugging you. I'm sorry I need to ask you a question." She glances apologetically at the papers spread out on my desk. "I can talk to you later if you're busy."

"I'm not busy at all," I answer. "This is why I get paid the big bucks."

Bonnie chuckles at the stale response I always give to her apologies and pulls up a plastic chair. "I've been trying to figure this out, but it doesn't seem to make sense." She's working on determining the difference between topic sentences and supporting statements, a subject that many of our students struggle with. Math comes more easily to them; there's a reliable concreteness to it that the ambiguities of English lack. 1 + 1 always equals 2 in arithmetic, but the main idea of a paragraph could be phrased in so many different ways that the students tend to become overwhelmed and shut down.

Bonnie puts her reading book on my desk. Like most of the textbooks we have, the many inmate hands it has passed through are immediately apparent to both eyes and nose: not only are the covers barely attached and the pages tattered, but it reeks from several years' accumulation of stale cigarette smoke, although we are now a smoke-free facility. The school's limited budget doesn't allow for new books for each student to keep. Sometimes they can't even get new replacement copies when the old ones wear out. And because books are frequently lost when an inmate goes to seg or is shipped, they are always struggling to have the appropriate books for the students.

I involuntarily push the reeking book away from me, then force myself to bring it forward again so we both can see it clearly. "Let's try talking about it and see what we come up with," I suggest to Bonnie. I read the paragraph aloud and, using the process of elimination, help her narrow down her choices to two. "So, which do you think it is?"

She looks a little panicky and makes an obvious guess. Fortunately she chooses the correct one, so I can tell her how terrifically she's doing. "Let's try the next one," I say. After going through several of the questions, Bonnie feels confident enough to try the rest on her own. She walks back to the work table grinning. This is the third time we have gone over this lesson, however. I hope that she won't be back the next day saying "I thought I understood this, but. . . ."

A few days later, Bonnie comes to class excitedly waving a piece of notebook paper in her hand. "Erin, I don't know what happened! I woke up this morning and it seemed like I finally just understood how to do those decimals I'd been messing up on. It was like I learned it a long time ago, and I just remembered or something! Please check this right away. I want to know how I did. Do you think that I will get a star on this one if I do all right?"

I take the homework from her and grab my marking pen and the answer key. Bonnie had been trying to get a star on her paper since she had gotten into class and realized that any paper that was 90% correct or above had a hand-drawn star on the corner. I knew how much she wanted one and had a lot of respect for the work she had put into achieving that goal. Only a week ago she had come close. We had been checking one of her math papers together, and each time we came to an incorrect problem, I would say, "Why don't you take another look at this one?"

Bonnie would rework the problem (without any help from me), always getting the correct answer on her second try. When we were finished, I started to put a 100% on the top, but Bonnie stopped me. "Wait a minute. Is that fair?"

I, too, really wanted Bonnie to get that star, so I tried to justify the grade. "Well, you did all of the work yourself. All I did was suggest that you take another look at some of the problems. I would do the same thing for someone else who had done all of the work herself."

But Bonnie was already shaking her head. "Naw, I want to earn my star the right way. I feel really good and I don't think it will take me long to get one on my own." Breaking the rules against inmate contact, I gave her a hug. And a week later I happily waved one of her papers in the air and called out to the teacher, "Hey! Bonnie got a 100% on her decimals! She gets a star!" Several of the other students cheered as the teacher drew an ornate star in the upper corner of the paper with a flourish. Bonnie had earned her star at last, and I don't think that even getting her GED will surpass that moment for her.

There are several students like Bonnie in each of the 4 class periods: there's Delia, a maternal 60-year-old who is close to finally earning her GED; Ramona, who proudly brings me the paperback romances that contain words she's learned in her vocabulary textbook ("Look, I know what 'palpable' means!"); and Juana, a swaggering little boy with ornate braids who will belligerently demand that you explain every incorrect answer on her homework so that she won't make the same mistake again. No matter how different they are, though, they all are tenacious in trying to achieve their goal.

I worry, however, that they might never be able to conquer the unalterable facts of their lives and pasts. If she were allowed to stay at Fluvanna, Delia would certainly pass her GED next year. Unfortunately she is a level 1, so she will probably be shipped in the next few months. Ramona, despite her hard work, isn't making what the state deems to be "sufficient progress," so she will soon be exempted from the requirement to earn her GED. Juana is going home before the next scheduled exams, and the odds aren't good that she will make the effort to finish up her GED preparation at home, despite her protestations otherwise.

Some of the obstacles the students face are more diffuse, but just as crippling. I had been working closely with Chandra, a bright young mother of three who was going home in 6 months. She had passed all of her TABE tests and each part of the GED except for the Social Studies portion, and the teacher had asked me to work on that area with her before she had her last chance to take the GED exam in 3 weeks.

"I'm just too dumb to get this part," she wailed one morning. "I don't know enough about any of this. I did good on math—can't that be enough? I don't know why you need to know this other crap anyway. It's not like I'm ever going to use it!"

I tried to tell her why learning social studies was necessary, not only to pass the GED, but also to live a more informed life, but Chandra wasn't buying it. "I've never been out of Virginia in my life, and I don't plan on going anywhere anyway. Why do I need to know what countries are in Europe or who fought in some stupid war a hundred years ago?"

It was difficult not to concede her point. Realistically, knowing how the American electoral college system works is of no use to someone who has never voted and isn't likely to in the future. "Look at this question," she said. We were studying a practice GED exam, and the question she pointed to showed a political cartoon of a hammer and sickle surrounded by fossilized dinosaur bones. "What does this even mean? I don't even know what those are!" she said, pointing to the symbol for the USSR.

I began to explain to her what the significance of the hammer and sickle was, but I knew that there was simply too much foundation knowledge that Chandra had been denied growing up, bits of information I took for granted. I could teach her what this particular cartoon meant, but there were too many other symbols and facts that the exam developer assumed she already knew. I had learned through osmosis about the Soviet Union, the Cold War, Stalin, and Marx—not to mention countless other topics that engaged my intellectually omnivorous family. There were thousands of conversations between my parents on national and international news, history, and science that I first just listened to but that later I was actively encouraged to participate in. On the whole, I spoke and wrote well because I had heard English spoken correctly all my life. I might not have been able to define exactly what an adverbial phrase was, but usually things just sounded right to me.

Most of the inmates here weren't that lucky. They have been deprived of the background that ensures the possibility of success if it is accompanied by the desire to achieve academically. And now that they are finally removed from the seduction of drugs or a survival-mode life of poverty and abuse, they realize that they do have the determination to learn, but 5 hours a week in an over-crowded classroom (if they are not locked down or called to work instead) cannot provide the infrastructure necessary to take what we try to teach them and use it to enhance their lives. Many do eventually get their GEDs, and I in no way mean to minimize that accomplishment, especially in an environment as distracting as prison. But the majority of the women here are barred from that innate love of learning, the hunger to improve the mind that leads to intellectual freedom. We have failed them from the cradle, and it is too late to begin trying to correct this when they are already locked up.

The teachers and tutors do what they can. They provide encouragement and affirmation, celebrations of achievements by women whose accomplishments on the street were ignored or ridiculed. So they take our successes where we find them. I might not have set Paulette on the path to mastering astronomy the day I crawled under the table in the classroom to show her that even though she could no longer see me, I was still there, but I did teach her that even though we can't see the sun at night, it is still there, waiting to appear and light our way again.

SVETLANA

I noticed her first because she was weeping. You see lots of people crying in prison: anguished moaning into the telephone during a phone call home, stifled sobs of pain in the medical waiting room, the angry tears of someone being hauled off to segregation. But this woman was in the middle of the library, which is not usually the site of extreme emotions. (Unseemly groping and covert pass-ing of contraband, though, yes indeed; this is the place.)

She wasn't weeping loudly—it was obvious that she wasn't just trying to get attention. I was speaking to Ms. McCarthy, the volunteer who comes into the prison every week to facilitate a book club and teach a poetry class, and Ms. McCarthy and I both swiveled our heads around as she approached. "Excuse me for a moment," I said as I rose to approach the crying woman.

"May I help you?" I asked her. Because I had never seen her before, didn't know how she might react, I had to stop myself from reaching out to touch her arm or connect with her in some other physical way . . . the raw pain that she exuded made me want to wrap her in my arms. She was, obviously, a woman lost.

She seemed to be surprised that I approached her and blinked her eyes a few times without responding to me. Her eyes were stunning in spite of the evidence of hours (or days) of crying, the clearest blue I had ever seen. She was tall, taller than my own 5'10", solid, and appeared to be about 50 years old. But despite her height, she carried herself like a smaller, frailer person. Although her pale skin was unmarked, she still appeared bruised.

"Can I do anything for you?" I asked again.

"Yes? Yes?" The woman looked perplexed for a moment more, then relaxed and smiled tentatively.

"You help me?" I realized that she had a thick Russian accent, as exotic as a leopard in rural Virginia.

"Of course I'll help you," I said. "What do you need?"

"I would need books please. Can I get books here?"

"Of course. What kinds of books are you looking for?"

"Do you have books in Russian maybe?" she asked.

I laughed a bit. It was only in the past few years that we had been allowed to have foreign language books in our library at all. All foreign language materials had been banned in the prison for years on the flimsy excuse that they didn't have anyone who could translate that Spanish-language edition of James Patterson's latest novel, and who knew what subversive information it might contain? That rule only changed after a class-action lawsuit was filed against the Virginia DOC because it was illegally curtailing the reading materials accessible to inmates. The DOC lost (for once), and as a result not only could our library stock foreign language books—if we had the same book in English—but inmates could purchase books for themselves and, even better, have books, magazines, and CDs sent to them by family and friends. I had spent several years unable to receive the kinds of books that interest me (I like books on history and the sort of fiction that our library, a bastion of pulp romance, urban drama, and fornicating vampires, didn't usually stock) and was thrilled that I could finally have access to books, wonderful books again. Of course, just because they could, the DOC imposed several annoying hoops that we have to jump through before they will let us have said books and CDs: we have to submit a list of all the book titles for approval prior to receiving them at property; only books and CDs from a vender are permitted; and, their favorite trick, they frequently "lose" books in the warehouse so that property is not officially aware of the order's existence and thus it can take months to finally get the books to the offender to whom they are addressed.

It must have really irked the administration that they have to do this, because we didn't even officially hear about the new availability of these kinds of orders until inmates transferring from other prisons began showing up at Fluvanna and asking why they could have *Fifty Shades of Gray* sent to them at Goochland Prison, but not at FCCW. But once the word was out, it was on. The prison (ooh! those damn spoiled rotten inmates who dare to want to read) was flooded with printed material and CDs. All those Nora Roberts books. All those copies of *Sports Illustrated*. Imagine the havoc.

But this lady, I guessed, didn't have a clue about any of that. And with her fractured syntax, I doubted that she was able to even write an IMS effectively, much less negotiate the Byzantine processes of personal property. I herded her to the table where the volunteer I'd been chatting with sat. "Sit down, won't you? I'm Erin, by the way. What's your name?"

"I am Svetlana Wilton, thank you," she answered. "I need help please."

Ms. McCarthy introduced herself to Svetlana. "What do you need help with?"

"Well, do you have books in Russian? Or books with simple words in English? I look at books with pictures now."

"We don't have any books in Russian, I'm afraid," I said. "I didn't realize that we even had any Russian speakers here. How long have you spoken English?"

"Oh, I teach myself some English so I talk OK. But I don't know what a lot means." She began to cry again. "I don't have no one to talk to me."

One of my particular brands of emotional unhealthiness is that I am a "fixer." Got a problem? Give me half a chance and I will swoop in and take care of that for you, no problem. No, no, you don't need to do any of the hard work yourself, I'll take care of the heavy lifting. As I said, unhealthy. But in prison I had begun to learn to channel those impulses into positive avenues: I had become a crusader. One of my main causes, my passion, really, was to start an English as a second language (ESL) program. For years Fluvanna had had Spanish-speaking inmates, many of whom could barely communicate. All I could do was imagine how I would feel, trapped in some *cárcel* in Bolivia, unable to convey my simplest needs or understand the most basic orders. I was perplexed by this situation. Wasn't the prison obligated to help these people? In my liberal mind, this was an obvious problem that could be easily fixed.

Apparently not. After months of fruitless requests to anyone I could think of, ignored proposals, and verbal demurrals from the few prison officials I could pin down on the boulevard, I came to the conclusion that this obvious need would continue to go unmet unless I persisted. So I did. I spoke to my supervisor, the prison librarian, who allowed me to tutor a student from Peru who had been referred by a GED teacher who knew of my interest in Spanish and ESL. The librarian even contacted a certified ESL teacher whom she already knew and encouraged her to take the volunteer training all civilians who donate their time to Fluvanna must undergo.

For my part, I wrote to a friend who attended a university in Michigan and explained what was happening. She gathered hundreds of dollars worth of ESL workbooks, CDs, and dictionaries and sent them at her own expense to the prison library. Armed with the necessary supplies and someone qualified to teach ESL, I rewrote my proposal and again submitted to all and sundry. And, again, I got no response. Eventually, I tracked down the principal of the DOC schools and asked him if he had gotten my proposal. Mr. Wilbur is tall, handsome, smells delicious, and, unfortunately, is prone to making promises that he can't keep in order to placate whomever (inmate or not) he is speaking with. In short, he is a politician.

"Mr. Wilber, may I speak to you a moment?"

"Yes, Ms. George. What can I do for you?"

"Well, I was wondering if you had read my proposal regarding starting an ESL program here at Fluvanna. As you know, we have many non–English speaking inmates, and I think that we should help them."

Mr. Wilbur's face was a polite blank for a moment, then he said, "I haven't had the opportunity to carefully examine your proposal, Ms. George, but it may not be viable to start such a program at this time."

I barely restrained myself from stamping my foot in frustration. "Why not? It is a huge need here. We may not have all that many such women here now, but you know that inevitably we will have more and more. Also, if there is one woman here who is unable to communicate effectively and it's within our power to help her, shouldn't we? Is it a matter of finances?"

"That's always a major consideration, Ms. George," he began to respond when I cut him off.

"If you read my proposal, you will see that the cost to the institution is minimal at best. All you will need to do is to cover the cost of paper, pens, maybe some photocopying. . . . I've had all the books and CDs already donated to the facility."

"You have?" He was clearly surprised by my initiative. "Where is it?"

"It's over there, on that shelf." I pointed to the full shelf. "It's already been cataloged into the library collection, so it's ready to go."

"Hmm. Well, who is going to teach the class? There are no staff members here who can speak Spanish and teach ESL."

"That's the thing, Mr. Wilber. First of all, you don't need to speak any foreign language to teach ESL. In fact, you should never speak anything but English in a class like that. Also, we have a trained volunteer who is an ESL teacher ready to come in. I would be happy to assist her as a volunteer for as long as the class existed."

Mr. Wilber looked decidedly more cheerful, confident that he'd caught me up. "Ah, but who will do it when you've gone home, Ms. George?" Satisfied, he grinned at me.

I sighed. "Mr. Wilber, I have 603 years with no parole. I guarantee you that I will be here as long as you need me to be. I've done all of the work. All we need from you is a room and a yes."

After a few vague promises to "look into it," Mr. Wilber ambled off. That conversation was 19 months ago, and still nothing has been done. So now here was Svetlana, barely able to ask to see a doctor or understand a call for mass movement, and with no one official willing or able to significantly help her.

"I'm so sorry, but we don't have any English classes here right now. But if you need help writing an IMS or anything, just bring it to me in the library, and I will be glad to help you."

The volunteer asked me, "Do you think that I could bring in some Russian novels for her? I think I saw some at the local library book sale." At my agreement, Ms. McCarthy went to talk to the librarian about seeing if this was permissible as I spoke more with Svetlana.

"You have a dictionary?" she asked.

"No, not for Russian," I said. "Lots of Spanish, even a couple of Italian, German, and Latin dictionaries. But we don't have a lot of demand for Russian." I paused. "Really, though, how are you doing? Is anyone helping you in the wing?"

She began to speak rapidly, losing many of her English words. "No, no, no, my dear . . . there are people who seem nice. I tell them that I don't belong here. I am innocent! No one helps me, no lawyer helps me. But I am innocent. I don't know what to do. My case. . . ."

I grabbed her arm to cut her off. "Look, it's going to be OK. Yes, things seem awful now, but we will find a way to make them better. But first, you need to be careful about what you say to people. Don't trust anyone with personal information about your case, or about your life, not unless you know them really well. Seriously, you need to keep all of that private from most people here."

She started to cry more. "But there are people who are so nice, they talk to me. . . ."

"There may be people who seem very nice, but I promise you that most of them do not have your best interests in heart. Do you understand what I am saying? They do not really want to help you." I could see that Svetlana didn't fully grasp what I was saying, despite her nods. "This is really important. Be careful who you talk to."

"I don't have anything that anyone could steal," she said.

"There are more things to take from someone than just their commissary. Please promise me that you will be careful." She nodded her head. "Do you have anyone on the outside to help you, maybe someone who speaks English well?"

"My daughter, she is a student and speaks English and French as well as Russian. She helps me." Svetlana looked proud.

"That's great," I said. "Why don't you let me write down a quick note to her, telling her some of the things that she could do to help you from out there? You can put it in your next letter to her. I'm also going to put my name and address on it so that she can write me if she has any questions."

"Here, here!" Svetlana pulled out a scrap of paper and began scribbling on it, "You write her, tell her."

"Honey, that's what I'm talking about. You don't know me. I could be some lunatic who will get out next week and rob your daughter's house or something. I mean, you're pretty safe in this case, but you've only just met me. Please be careful who you share stuff with."

"I trust you, my dear. I trust you!" she insisted. I sighed. Obviously I was not able to make her understand just how treacherous people in here could be. So I took down her daughter's address, promising to write, and gave her the names of some trustworthy people in her wing she could go to for help.

I wrote to her daughter, introducing myself and telling her how to send her mother books and magazines, whom to contact if she had concerns, and any other information I though she could use. I also asked her daughter to tell Svetlana in Russian just how dangerous it could be in here to be too open with some of her fellow inmates. I didn't get a response, but two Fridays later, an obviously buoyed Svetlana came back to the library, calling me out of the tiny cubbyhole where I do most of my work.

"My daughter, she got your letter, my dear. Thank you, thank you. Do you have any books for me?" At her last visit we had determined that the only books that she could really enjoy were the oversized "coffee table books" of paintings and books full of photographs of animals. Since I received *National Geographic* magazine, I had also stockpiled a few of those for her. She embraced me enthusiastically, and said, "Now you need books in Russian!"

As of today, our library can boast of two, count 'em two, books in Russian: *Anna Karenina* and *War and Peace*, both of them donated by Ms. McCarthy. Oh, and a Russian–English dictionary. For that I have to give Mr. Wilber credit. When he found out that there was an inmate who only spoke Russian, he purchased one for our library. I hope that this is the first step toward an ESL program, but I'm not allowing myself to get too confident. But it will happen, eventually. It has to.

BODY OF ART: TATTOOING AS AN (UNAUTHORIZED) ART FORM

Abby is a stunning girl, even by street standards (the pickings are slimmer behind bars, so the standards for beauty inside are substantially lower). Tall, with glossy chestnut hair that brushes against her shoulders in a trim bob, Abby's physical beauty is matched by a laughing, generous spirit and a wry, somewhat reckless personality. She and I have lived in the same housing unit together for several years, and she is one of my favorite people. I've never seen her on the boulevard without receiving a smile and friendly greeting.

More striking than her looks, though, are the tattoos that cover her arms and legs. A few date from the street, but she has done most of them herself while locked up. Because I am a rarity in here—an inmate who doesn't have at least one inked image on her body—I asked Abby why she decorated herself in this way. She was surprisingly candid with me.

> I have always been interested in art, even when I was a kid, so I started getting tattoos when I was about 15 years old. After my first one, I was addicted! Once I got locked up, I realized that I could draw anything that I wanted, so that and my interest in body art made me want to be an "ink slinger." Not that you need to be talented to be an "inkie" in prison-there are too many women here giving bad tattoos.

Abby, who has 3 years left on an armed robbery charge, hopes to use the tattooing expertise she gained in Fluvanna when she gets home. "When I get out I want to have my own shop, but there is a big difference between being an inkie in prison and being one out in the free world. The biggest thing is that in prison it is against the rules to tattoo yourself or anyone else. Out there you can tattoo anyone who is crazy enough to allow you to insert permanent ink into their skin!"

One of the things that Abby takes the most pride in is her reputation. Everyone knows that her tattoos are among the best, so she has a thriving cottage industry, one that she approaches with all the savvy of an MBA. She subscribes to several magazines that cover the world of body art so that she can be up on all the current trends. "On the outside, it's easy to get a good reputation," she says. "More than likely you will have set up a legal shop, have a professional tattooing license and respectable clients who can pass on the word that you're the best inkie on the South Side. You can also put advertisements in the newspaper or on TV to improve your business and reputation. It's a different story when you're incarcerated. Here, there are both pros and cons to having an established reputation as an ink slinger. On the plus side, it's good for your pride to be known as a smoking ink slinger." She laughs and pats herself on her own back. "That's what I am!"

> The con is that if you're a known tattoo artist you're more likely to be shaken down a lot, maybe even on a weekly basis. It's the risk you take when you let anyone know that you can sling. There are quite a few of us inkies here in Flu Flu. Some are good, most are terrible. There's a good friend of mine, Maryland, who is really talented. Her prices are really decent for the quality of work that you end up with. She's the one who is well known, so they shake her down almost every week.

Prices for the tattoos depend on how large they are and how much work was involved in creating them. Abby charges $3 a letter for her tattoos and has created a few that cost over $50. She is usually paid in commissary goods like stamps and picture tickets, but for a few of the larger commissions the family of her client has actually deposited money directly into her account. She prefers using items from commissary as payment, though. "That's the best way to go," Abby says. "There is less paperwork involved when you don't have a third party put money on your books. There's less chance of getting caught that way, especially if someone tells the police what's going on. Any commissary I have I could have bought myself."

Although Abby's body art is skillfully administered, most of the tats created here are roughly drawn. There are some exceptions, of course. Elliot, an inmate student of mine, once asked if I knew anything about Queen Nefertiti. I knew a bit, but I wrote my dad asking if he could print out some info and photographs of her from the Internet and mail them to me. Elliot was trying to get her GED, and I was delighted that she was showing an interest in history. She usually spent her time in class leafing through a magazine or staring out of the window. I was amazed when, a few weeks after I had given her the printouts, Elliot came into class and proudly displayed a fantastically detailed tattoo of Nefertiti that she had placed on her shin. "Thank your pops for the stuff, man," she said. "It looks good, don't it?"

I have to admit that it did. And at least her subject matter was more artistically valid than most of the ink in here. The majority of prison tattoos are clearly created by less skilled hands. One woman attempted to write her name on her hand, a letter on the first joint of each finger. Unfortunately, she ended up tattooing A-N-I-D rather than the D-I-N-A she wanted. Abby has little respect for those who dabble in body art without meeting her high standards.

"Some of these people think that they're good and they actually suck," said Abby. "Their work is spotty. They can't draw. The bad part is that you're stuck with the work unless you can find a decent inkie to do a cover up. Once it gets out in the prison population that you're no good at slinging ink you'll be totally laughed at and what little business you had will be gone."

Typical subjects for tattoos are the name of a girlfriend or child, or a simple design like a spider web or heart or other personally significant symbol. One inmate that I have seen in the chow hall has a crudely tattooed teardrop under her left eye, which is supposed to indicate that she has committed murder, usually gang-related. Maybe she has, but the lifers that I hang out with in here eschew such crassness. It's more likely that she is just grandstanding, trying to look cool or get some sort of reputation for toughness. All the people I know in here who have taken a life would never exploit that tragedy in such a way. They don't need any reminders in the mirror of what they have done; it's carried inside them every day.

The work of body artists like Abby and Maryland is far superior to that sported by most inmates. I was shocked to learn how crude the methods are for creating some of the delicate and extensive tattoos they've given their clients:

> The equipment we use is completely different from what you would get in a professional shop. The needles we use here were from the sewing kit that they used to sell on commissary. You would wrap thread around the tip of a needle several times, dip it into ink, then go to town. The purpose of wrapping the thread or string around the needle is to hold the ink. Without the string to absorb the ink, it wouldn't stay on a bare needle. They have stopped selling sewing kits, though, because of the tattooing and fear of staph infections. That meant that we just needed to find another alternative. So we have to use either lighter springs or staples now unless you have some needles hidden away.
>
> The lighter spring is just a spring that you pull from a disposable lighter. To get it out, you have to have a friend hold the spring and pull it out while you burn the middle of the spring. The point of this is to pull the spring straight. Burning it will make the spring break in half. When you get the straightened half spring, you'll wrap the thread around it like you did with the needles. Save the other half of the spring for another client. Each spring works just as good as a regular needle, if not even better. It makes a smaller, finer line, unlike the sewing kit needles.
>
> If you can't get a lighter spring, I've known people to use staples, like you would use to connect papers together. First bend the staple straight, then take it with you into the shower without being conspicuous and file the staple on the grout that fills the cracks between the shower tiles. This makes the staples very sharp. Then wrap the string around the tip, dip it in ink, and start tattooing.

The ingenuity of inmates is well known—we can make just about anything we need from the barest of materials. The business of body art is no exception.

Some of the inkies make homemade tattoo guns out of cassette players. They will break the radio open and use the motor, an empty pen casing, and a few rubber bands to make it, then attach it to a battery or electrical adaptor that you can plug into a wall socket. Stick on the needle and you have a gun. Don't forget the thread and you're all set.

I've even used an electric razor as a tattoo gun. Take the guard off of the top of the razor and pull off the black grill to show a white piece that you can stick the needle on with a rubber band. Dip the needle in ink and turn on the razor. One word of advice though: turn the razor off before you dip the needle in ink or it will splatter everywhere. I didn't do that once and got ink all over my cell. It was a real pain in the ass to clean up, but I learned my lesson!

Getting the equipment together is the easy part, according to Abby. Harder to find is decent ink. Not all ink can be used to make tattoos, and if you're spending your hard-earned commissary on a new tat, you want it to last.

A lot of people on the outside wonder where we get the ink for our tattoos. What kind of ink you use makes a big difference in how well a tattoo turns out. One thing you can do is use colored pencils. To do this, bust open the pencil with your combination lock to pull the lead out. Then take the lead, put it in an envelope, and grind it into powder with your lock. Put the powder in a container with some cigarette ashes. Some people even add a little bit of shampoo to the mixture. Then put in enough boiling water from the hot water pot to melt it all together and stir it all together. You can use that for OK ink.

If you have an inside connection, someone who works in or around one of the offices, you might be able to acquire actual liquid ink from an ink cartridge. These can come from the rec department or from one of the printers. Those are the little black boxes that you need to pry open. Wrap the cartridge in one of the state towels (why mess up one of your own?) and, making sure that the police aren't in the wing, put the cartridge between the metal door and the door jamb of your cell. Then very carefully shut your door on half of the cartridge. This squeezes the sides, which will make the cartridge dip in the middle. Use your nail clippers to pry the cartridge open where it is bent, then pour the ink into a container.

There's a catch to using the liquid ink, though. If by chance you come across some blue ink, chuck it. It doesn't stay in your skin and it burns like hell when you use it. The only liquid ink that stays is the black. I got ripped off one time over this. Someone sold me blue ink, which looked just like the black when it was out of the cartridge. I ended up having to trash it all. I was heated, let me tell you! I'm a lot more careful about who I buy my supplies from now.

If you don't have an inside hook-up you might be able to find someone who tutors one of the classes to get you a gel pen, Pilot pen, or Uniball liquid pen. All you need to do is snap the pens in half to get the ink out. Of the three, the Uniball pen ink is the best, the gel pens the worst. Any color ink from these pens should work out.

Like any professional, Abby is extremely careful about the health risks of having a business that involves direct exposure to bodily fluids. A disproportionate percentage of inmates suffer from communicable diseases, so prison tattoo artists have to be extraordinarily careful or risk exposure. This is one of the main reasons that prison officials are trying to eliminate prison tattooing completely. Abby is matter of fact when she talks about the hazards of her career. "With all the inkies there are great risks," she says.

> There's always the risk of catching a disease from your clients. You don't really know what anyone has unless you check their medical papers. It's best to wear the latex gloves they give us for cleaning whenever you tattoo. It's really the only option you have. Wear the gloves or don't tattoo.
>
> Lots of people will lie if you ask them if they have anything. I once tattooed a girl who had Hep C. When I asked her if she had anything, she claimed that she didn't. A week later I found out that she had hepatitis. There wasn't anything that I could do about it by then except go over to medical and get blood work done to see if I had contracted it. Lucky for the girl I was fine. But that's why you have to be careful. You never know in here who's lying and who's telling the truth.

Those who get tattoos in prison can't seem to get enough. No one ever seems to have just one. I asked Abby if it hurts to get a tattoo, and she looked at me as if I were crazy. "Of course it hurts. How can needles poking into your skin not hurt? But as painful as street tattoos are to get, prison tattoos are even worse. The reason for this is that tattooing by hand or using a homemade gun is not as fast as a professional's tattoo gun. The pain is less when the gun goes fast. But the pain is awful when it's slow and only uses one needle." She looks down at the pattern of ornate climbing roses that intertwine her left arm. It's beautifully rendered, a tattoo that she did herself the last time we had a weeklong lockdown. "This took forever, hours of pain. It's definitely not worth it. Go get your tattoos professionally done."

I was amazed. Here was an intelligent, thoughtful woman covered in prison body art, one who earned a nice little living at it, in fact, advising against it. Why, I wondered, did she do it then?

"I know that it doesn't make much sense," she said, "but I meant it when I said it's an addiction." She paused, obviously considering her motivations for subjecting herself to a long, painful process that she herself wouldn't recommend.

> Some clients get tattoos as a reminder of something important from home, for artistic expression, or to show that they're in love. But for me, I think a lot of it comes down to self-mutilation. You know that's really trendy to worry about now, girls "cutting" themselves in the Lifetime movies and stuff, but tattooing for me serves the same purpose. It releases stress and lets me feel that I have some control of my life. I guess that's not really mentally healthy, but at least I'm honest with myself. And I'd rather tattoo myself than cut myself with a razor. At least this way I have something other than those ugly scars to show for it. And I know that I'm not the only one who does this. I've actually used tattoos to cover up self-mutilation scars for several clients. They've just swapped one for the other.
>
> I've decided to stop doing tattoos. There's just too much hassle involved. I'm sick of getting shaken down and looked at naked by the police all of the

time. Plus, lately they're giving out tickets even for old tattoos, so I know that I'll be snitched out by someone and sure get a charge if I get a new one. I want to get shipped out of Fluvanna, so I can't let myself get any more tickets.

"What are you going to do when it gets too stressful and you want to do it again?" I asked.

I've been re-tattooing over the tattoos that I already have. I've done this one three times already. As long as it's not a new one, I guess I'll be OK. Anyway, the police are probably going to start hassling people about something else pretty soon. They'll give up on this like they do everything else they try to get rid of, and the inkies will be back in business again. That's the Fluvanna way!

REFERENCES

Brooks, A., & Johnson, R. (2010). Exposed yet unrevealed: Reflections on the poetry of women prisoners. *Gender Issues, 27*(3–4), 146–164.

George, E. (2008). *Origami heart: Poems by a woman doing life.* Washington, DC: BleakHouse Press.

Johnson, R. (2012). Art and autonomy in prison: Prison writers under siege. In L. K. Cheliotis (Ed.), *The arts of imprisonment: Control, resistance, and empowerment* (pp. 168–188). Aldershot, UK: Ashgate.

Johnson, R., & Chernoff, N. (2002). "Opening a vein": Inmate poetry and the prison experience. *The Prison Journal, 82*(2), 141–167.

Kornfeld, P. (1997). *Cellblock visions: Prison art in America.* Princeton, NJ: Princeton University Press.

Lamb, W. (2007). *I'll fly away: Further testimonies from the women of York Prison.* New York: Harper Perennial.

Nagelsen, S. (Ed.). (2008). *Exiled voices: Portals of discovery—Stories, poems, and drama by imprisoned writers.* Henniker, NH: New England College Press.

Tabriz, S., & Hassine, V. (2009). The prison librarian. In R. Johnson & S. Tabriz (Eds.), *Lethal rejection: Stories on crime and punishment* (pp. 165–170). Durham, NC: Carolina Academic Press.

Tannenbaum, J. (2000). *Disguised as a poem: My years teaching poetry at San Quentin.* Boston: Northeastern University Press.

CHAPTER 9

The Sick and the Dead

*I*t is tragic for a life to end in prison, a place that is a monument to failure and defeat. The death of a fellow prisoner is, moreover, a haunting reminder of one's own mortality, and of the grim prospect of one day dying in prison. For lifers, that prospect is very real and very disconcerting (Aday, 2003; Corley, 2008; Johnson & McGunigall-Smith, 2008).

The story of one woman's death, recounted in this chapter, speaks volumes about prison life. First, the schedule of counts is disrupted. The woman died just before a count, so her death caused a delay of the count. The delay was only one hour, a short time in our eyes but a rupture of the rigid routine that gives structure and coherence to the prison world. The count is like the prison's heartbeat, if a prison has a heart; when the prison misses a beat, people worry. As it happens, the reason was serious—the death of Pebbles, a woman not known to Erin George or her immediate circle of associates. We learn that there are several women nicknamed Pebbles, which is interesting in itself. (Pebbles is perhaps best known as the innocent child character in The Flintstones, *a waif, really, but also something of a schemer who flirts with trouble.) Her cellmate discovered Pebbles, awakening images of traumatic possibilities for each of the women, who might one day find her cellmate dead or perhaps be that dead cellmate. Pebbles had a panoply of medical problems. Although she had been treated, and indeed seemed to be getting better, prison medical treatment itself often is in need of critical care (Pollock, 2004). The practice of medicine in prison is bureaucratic and unresponsive and oriented to profit (or at least cost-cutting) rather than individual care. Pebbles's fate, the women believe, could be their fate as well.*

George catalogs her encounters with the prison's medical system as well as that of several women she comes to know well. We are given a disturbing look at how the medical process works or, more often, fails to work. An underlying issue affecting all the cases George describes, including her own, is that medical care is hard to come by because good care requires caring and trust. Caring and trust are uncommon in prison, a place where manipulation and deception are the main ingredients of interpersonal relations (see Hassine, 2011; Johnson, 2002). Many inmates, we learn from George, try to play the medical system to get a break from routine or to gain access to drugs. Medical personnel are cast as gatekeepers. They can only be so good at this difficult form of triage, and the result is that a lot of people in need of care are treated carelessly. —Robert Johnson

Pebbles died last night. We all knew something was wrong when master control didn't call for 9:30 p.m. count until well after 10:00. Count, one of the most important security features of prison life, is never called late. Of course we didn't know what had happened at the time, just that something strange was going on. And we knew that whatever it was, it wasn't good: they are not going to delay count because the governor had decided to pardon everyone at FCCW.

The next morning we all clustered in the dayroom, waiting for mass movement to be called and talking about the weird count the night before. Joanne, a yard worker whose only connection with the rest of the inmate population is her love of gossip, wandered in and several of us surrounded her. "What's going on?" we demanded.

Eager to be the one to break a juicy story, Joanne launched into the gossip on the yard. "It was someone named Pebbles. She died last night. They figured it out when her roommate tried to wake her up for count and she was dead!" We conferred. There were at least three women at Fluvanna nicknamed Pebbles, and we wanted to figure out which one she was.

"What building did she live in?"

Joanne thought for a moment. She was usually pretty sketchy about the details of a story and barely able to accurately recount the basics. There was always enough to her rumors, though, that we would go to her when something was going down to get some scoop. Joanne was a sad case, really. The only time people talked to her was when they wanted the 411 on something, so she usually sat alone in the dayroom, munching on ice and blatantly dipping in every conversation going around her. Those of us who lived with Joanne knew not to trust her with any confidence, but we all sure liked hearing what she had picked up.

"I think she lived in Building Five," Joanne guessed. After a few more questions, another, more reliable, yard worker came in and Joanne was abandoned.

"Kit, what's the story?" Lena asked.

Kit was much better informed than Joanne had been. "It was that older black lady, Pebbles. She lived in 6-C. You know, Linda is her roommate? Man, Linda is freaking out! She says she tried to wake her up a few minutes before 9:30 and Pebbles looked like she had been dead for a while." Kit shook her head. "That shit would really mess up my head," she said.

I didn't really know Pebbles. She was just one of the faces that become familiar after being locked up together for a long time. Because I never heard her name mentioned in any of the salacious stories that are always spreading about this or that inmate, I doubted that she was involved in disastrous prison relationships or other regular trouble. She was probably a lot like me—just trying to get through her time as smoothly as possible. The story was that she had suffered from several cardiac issues during her incarceration, but people who knew her well said that she'd been looking better lately—going to her job in the kitchen, even taking a few turns around the boulevard during walking rec. Her death was completely unexpected and unexplained. I never did hear a reason, not even supposition couched as fact. It's the suddenness of her death that disturbed me the most—it's almost a certainty that someday my own roommate will try to rouse me for count and find me just like Pebbles.

Medical issues are a major concern for lifers. Short-timers have the luxury of saying, "Hell, no, they're not getting their damn hands on me over at medical. I'm going to see a real doctor when I get out." Not lifers. We are stuck with Prison Healthcare Services (PHS), which provides all of the medical treatment on site and supervises any offsite procedures. I don't know that much about PHS. They are the contractor who, I suppose, gave the lowest bid for providing health care to inmates. That's how things usually work around here. I understand that they provide medical care at prisons in several states.

PHS is just like any other large medical provider on the outside, I suppose, except that they are even more overworked and undersupported than the usual HMOs and health care providers. The environment in prison is not conducive to effective medical care, and all of the blame can't be placed on PHS alone. The nurses have to weed out the women with real medical issues from the constant stream of inmate hypochondriacs and rendezvousing girlfriends who usually drop sick calls. The doctors often have to fight their superiors to get approval for appropriate medical treatments.

As on the outside, the main priority here is revenue. It's just easier to make a profit when the people being treated are inmates. Any problems are almost always initially dismissed as being the usual "inmate BS," and frequently no attention is given unless someone from the outside advocates on the inmate's behalf, if they have someone to do that for them, that is.

About 6 years before my incarceration I was diagnosed with systemic lupus erythematosus (SLE), an autoimmune disease that causes, among other symptoms, severe joint pain. I informed the intake nurse of my condition when I arrived at Fluvanna, but for some reason it was never noted on my records. Or maybe they didn't believe me. I don't know. At any rate, I then had to spend the next year trying to convince the prison doctor that I did, indeed, have SLE. This stalwart of the medical community insisted every time I saw her that I could not have SLE because I was not black. Only black women, she informed me, had lupus. Look at the malar rash on my face, I'd tell her. How could I be faking that? Test the ANA levels in my blood, I would plead. Surely that would be proof.

The doctor (I have mercifully blocked out her name, but still remember her fondly as Dr. Mengele) wouldn't do anything until the afternoon that, because of almost crippling pain, I fell in the bathroom stall and gave myself a black eye. Even then it wasn't until my irate mother phoned the warden's office that I was seen.

It was a Friday, and an impatient Dr. Mengele asked a few cursory questions, then demanded to know why I thought I was so special that I could be seen by the doctor whenever I wanted. There wasn't much I could say to that, so I kept quiet. After a few prods, the doctor abruptly left the curtained examination room. Five minutes later, the nurse came in.

"I'm afraid that we are going to admit you to the infirmary," she said.

I groaned. A weekend in the infirmary was dreadful: no books, no radio, no pencil or paper, no commissary. All I needed was to get on a course of steroids. I'd had enough flare-ups to self-diagnose. The doctor knew it, too, but this was the best revenge she could get—trapping me in the medical ward until the next Monday.

"Can I at least get some of my stuff?" I asked.

"Let me see what I can do," she answered.

They couldn't find a wheelchair for me, so I painfully dragged myself to the other end of the medical building and was locked into one of the medical wards (about 12 beds and a blaring TV chained to the wall). I will say this much: This was the first decent bed that I had been in for years. Unlike the prison mattresses, which were durable, green plastic sacks that felt like they were filled with sawdust, these beds had standard hospital mattresses. Not Sealy Posturepedics, but damn comfortable nonetheless. And in the infirmary the sheets actually reached to the bottoms of the mattress. All of the sheets they issued in GP only went down about two thirds of the way, leaving your feet sweating on the bare plastic mattress.

In the middle of the night they woke me up to give me a pillowcase full of personals and clothes. The choices made by whoever had packed my stuff were baffling: five bras, but no panties; no T-shirts; toothbrush without toothpaste; no soap; no shampoo either, but two (count 'em, two) bottles of hair conditioner and a jar of hair grease of undetermined provenance. I never did find out where they had gotten that, but it certainly wasn't mine. The officers had packed up all of my belongings when I was transferred to the infirmary, but quite a bit managed to go missing. My roommate at the time later told me tragic tales of the officers carelessly tossing around my bottles of lotion and bags of chips and popcorn. She added this delightfully vivid embellishment: "Those damn officers just threw your shit on the floor, stomped on it and laughed. I told them to stop, but you can't tell the police, nothing. You know that." According to her, they left her a dreadful mess to clean up, but knowing Penny, who would steal anything that wasn't red hot or nailed down, it was far more likely that her girlfriend was now wearing my Calgon body lotion and my "destroyed" commissary was long since digested by Penny and her cronies.

The next day the doctor showed up to examine me. As I splayed flat on my back like a frog in an anatomy class, she grabbed one leg and began rotating it roughly. When, naturally enough, I clenched in pain and began to cry, she demanded to know why I was "resisting her."

"Because it hurts! Stop it! My legs don't move like that!"

After a few minutes she stopped, then said "I'm going to order some blood work to confirm your alleged diagnosis of SLE."

That was the last I saw of her, but a few weeks later I received a notice from medical informing me that I had SLE. Glad to finally be official, I guess.

Doctor Mengele is gone now. Doctors don't stay for long at Fluvanna, but at the moment we have two decent ones. The doctor I usually see now is great—he not only has prescribed me medication to keep my lupus under control but also remembers me each time I see him, asking what books I've read lately or how my job is going. I appreciate the bedside manner, but I don't bother going to see him when I am in a flare-up. If I did, medical would just charge me $5 that I would rather spend on stamps or cheese curls, because by the time I've put in a sick call, seen a nurse, and waited for a provider appointment to be scheduled, I would be feeling better.

Most lifers avoid medical completely unless we are in absolutely unbearable pain that can't be relieved by a hot compress (an empty shampoo bottle filled with hot water), a few tablets of generic aspirin, or what I call "Civil War surgery." Civil War surgery is any medical treatment that we can perform on each other or ourselves in the wing. I've become adept at removing painful ingrown toenails, for example, using nothing more than some ice cubes for anesthesia and a pair of dull nail clippers. Ingrown toenails are a regular problem because the state gives us the cheapest shoes available, and they never fit well. I wear a size 9½, but have been issued shoes ranging from size 8 to size 12, depending on what they had on the shelves—not exactly the pathway to proper podiatric care.

Although normally I am pretty squeamish when it comes to blood, I've had to learn to remove the toenail myself; the first time I went to medical to have it done by a professional, the nurse struggled for a few minutes to remove it, then gave up because it was almost count time. She handed me a wad of cotton (contraband, by the way) and advised me to "just stick it under your toenail." Then she charged me $5.

Because most lifers have jobs with a bit of responsibility, 2 or 3 hours squandered at medical are an annoying delay, especially because the waiting room is always full of girlfriends beefing or wooing and the genuinely ill inmates who haven't quite mastered the art of covering their mouths when they sneeze and cough. And there is always the sneaky thought in the back of my mind, at least, that the hastening of death might not be so bad a thing. Why would it?

Whenever I joke about that, well-meaning short-timers say, "Oh, don't claim it. God can do what man won't," or some other platitude. I wish that they would stop. They don't know what it is like to face a life in prison, and their paltry 3 years, 5 years, or even decade behind bars is not even close to what I have to deal with. Unless you're inside with that, you can never really know the inexorable, daily decay of your hopes. The sooner this all ends, the better. And honestly, I would prefer sooner rather than later. So I accept the risks of health care with a morbid sense of equanimity.

I know that miracles can happen, that innocent people are exonerated or new trials infrequently granted. As grimly permanent as my sentence seems, there is a chance that I might luck out and get geriatric parole. But the only way that I can function, the only way that I can create a viable existence for myself in prison, is by accepting that this is it for me. I'm not going home. Ever. By embracing this, I have no choice but to adapt. The people who try to offer me hope are doing what under normal circumstances would be appropriate and supportive. Intellectually I know this. But hope is a dangerous commodity for lifers. I am almost inevitably disappointed on the small desires, so why would I ever take a risk on something big like going home again? It's hard enough to get your heart set on having chicken for dinner and then find a desiccated meatloaf patty on your dinner tray. So I keep expectations low. I don't allow myself any anticipation about seeing my children, working on the assumption that they won't be able to visit for some reason. I don't expect answers to my letters. Any rumor about a positive change at the prison is treated with skepticism until I see a memo posted. That way, if something good does happen, it is a delightful surprise.

But I do all of the right things to stay healthy: go to rec when I can, try to avoid junk food, even go to evening pill line for the prescribed daily multivitamin that is, it seems, too dangerous for me to keep in my cell. Pill line is crazy, a mad rush of the infirm racing to Building Two when their wings are called to be the first in line to receive their medications. Women who normally move shakily on walkers or crutches break into a wind sprint to the pill line window, slipping past their slower moving neighbors like stock car racers on a straightaway.

I learned quickly to recognize what my meds look like. Some of the women have a pharmacist's expertise in identifying prescription drugs. One of my cellmates, Patty, could immediately identify any pill at a glance. It's important to be informed. More than once I have pulled my little plastic cup (half-filled with water so that I wouldn't be able to pocket the medicine it contained and sell it later) back from the nurse's window, only to find two little beige pills or something else other than my lonely red vitamin. On one particularly exciting afternoon, a potpourri of medications appeared in the cup: a couple of pink and purple capsules, three tiny white pills, one inhumanely large brown pill, and what appeared to be an orange baby aspirin (that one even I recognized).

"Hey, this isn't my medicine," I protested to the nurse.

Patty leaned over my shoulder. "Hmm, that looks like Benadryl, HZTZ, and penicillin. The Benadryl is an antihistamine, the HZTZ is for high blood pressure, and the penicillin is a sulfa drug."

I was impressed. All that knowledge, and because she was a felon she wouldn't be able to legally use it on the street. Patty sure knew her pharmaceuticals. She was in for prescription drug forgery, and although she had been through Narcotics Anonymous, she still liked to dose herself with a few aspirin and a Diet Coke whenever she was stressed. "Better living through chemistry!" was her motto.

When I handed back the cup full of someone else's meds, the pharmacy nurse dumped the pills into the sink and, without even bothering to rinse it out, filled the cup with more water, and plunked in my vitamin. I guess I'm lucky that I didn't get piss-tested that week. God knows what residue was on the inside of that cup.

I always feel sorry for the pharmacy nurses, actually. They are usually pleasant, even though they have to deal with all of the inmates bitching about prescriptions that go unfilled for weeks, or asking about appointments that have never been made. I think that they are a little overwhelmed. Pill call is chaotic, even though the inmates who are waiting in line are supposed to be silent. Sometimes when I get to the window I am dismayed to see loose pills scattered on the floor and on the counters. And I've gotten the wrong person's meds often enough to worry not only about the newbies who don't know enough to check their cups for incorrect medications, but also for the poor women whose meds are dumped down the sink because they were given away to someone else. Do they get their meds at all?

Medication is a hot issue here. One of the chief complaints against medical is that prescriptions go unfilled for days, sometimes even weeks. And this is for chronic conditions. It baffles me that a medical facility will let itself run out of someone's heart medicine. How can that be? I might not be a medical professional, but I know enough about computers to know that surely there must be some sort of tracking software to alert them when supplies are getting low. This happened all of the time to Brenda. Brenda is only 26 years old, but she has the body of a 90-year-old chain smoker. She takes medications for her heart, blood pressure, thyroid, autoimmune, God-knows-what else, plus the ever popular psych meds (in her case, antidepressants). Brenda is a passive woman, but even she would get agitated when medical had again neglected to renew one of her prescriptions. "Don't you realize that I could die if I don't get this?" she would ask despairingly. She might have been exaggerating, but based on the dozen packets of self-meds that she picked up at self-med call every 2 weeks, I doubt it. No one gets that many meds in prison unless they are really sick.

FCCW is the only women's prison that has a comprehensive medical facility. We have an x-ray machine, dialysis, dental, and mental health treatment. But there are some things that can't be taken care of here, and for that we are sent to Medical College of Virginia (MCV) or the University of Virginia's hospital. Usually these medical trips are planned. It may take months (or years) for a necessary offsite procedure to be scheduled, but there always comes that sleep-destroying shout over the intercom to pack up your stuff. You are never supposed to know when you'll be transported to the hospital so that you can't arrange for any unscheduled digressions, but inmates who have been dealing with medical for a long time usually have a good idea of when they're going to go. Most of the people who work for PHS take their Hippocratic oath seriously, despite being shackled by a money-obsessed, rather than human-oriented, company and the ponderous prison bureaucracy.

My friend Sadie had been wrangling with medical for years over surgery that she needed, but eventually it reached a point where it looked as if all of the scheduling complications that PHS had been creating were resolved. We were all so happy for her when she came back from a doctor's appointment one afternoon and said, "I'm definitely going to get my surgery by the end of the month." Nothing was absolutely certain, of course. By this time I was seasoned enough to know that.

It was a great relief the next Monday when Belinda went to each of our rooms soon after 7:00 a.m. count to tell us that Sadie had packed out the night before. We knew that Sadie would have to spend at least a few days in the hospital but grew worried when almost a week passed and we hadn't heard that she was back. She was going to have to be housed in the infirmary before being allowed to move back into her room with Belinda, and each Building Two worker (where the infirmary is housed) knew to say "No, she's not back yet!" whenever they caught sight of one of us.

A week after Sadie went out, Belinda, Dizzy, and I trudged to pill line. As we stood waiting for the nurse, we heard a rapid knocking at the sally port door of the infirmary. It was Sadie! Crying and gesticulating frantically to us, but obviously our Sadie and well enough to be upright. For the next few days she sent messages to Belinda and the rest of us by anyone who had even a slim chance of being near our wing, then finally moved back home.

"God, it was awful!" she said as we grouped around her. She had lost about 10 pounds that she desperately needed, and her face was raw and splotched. "I can't believe that I was gone for 2 weeks—to the fucking day!" That phrase resonated with us. "Two weeks—to the fucking day" became our standard answer to any question with an answer that was a period of time. "Diz, how long did you have to stand in line at commissary this morning?" "Two weeks—to the fucking day!"

Sadie had an awful time. After her surgery, she had developed pneumonia and, even more devastating by an inmate's standards, a painful and disgusting mouth infection called thrush. "I couldn't eat anything," she wailed. "They kept bringing things like Jell-O and grilled cheese sandwiches, and everything I ate tasted terrible. It sucked!" One of the perks of an in-patient hospital stay is the hospital food, which is, compared to our chow, positively gourmet. A missed opportunity for a decent meal is a tragedy for almost any lifer. From what I hear, hospital stays are, in some ways, a real treat: a decent bed, much better food, cable TV, and the junkies appreciate access to the high-quality painkillers.

Staff at the hospitals always treat prisoners exceptionally well, perhaps realizing that this is a rare chance for the inmates to be coddled. And usually the two transport officers that must always be with the inmate are more relaxed than they are at the prison. The barriers of formality can hardly be perfectly maintained, I suppose, when you see an inmate struggling to recover from illness or injury.

Some officers are scrupulous in maintaining their rigid mindset, but few of the C.O.s are able to treat an inmate with utter coldness when they see her obviously suffering. It can be done, though. An inmate here named Ronnie would tell the funniest stories about her experiences while on transport. My favorite was the one about when she needed to have an MRI. The technician told the officer escorting her that all metal had to be removed from the patient before the procedure, but the obdurate C.O. insisted that Ronnie keep on her leg shackles. "It's procedure," Ronnie would say, mocking the officious C.O.'s reasoning. Needless to say, when the machine was powered up, it began to suck Ronnie inside, drawing the metal leg chains into the chamber and tearing into her legs in the process. I know it wasn't a fun experience for her, but whenever she retold the story, we were all helpless with laughter. Only to a prisoner could a story like that happen.

Not all of the stories are so amusing to the inmate involved. Jackie, a woman in our wing who is confined to a wheelchair, still talks about the time she once had to go out for eye surgery. The surgery went fine, she said, but when they were driving her home the officers forget to properly secure her wheelchair into the back of the vehicle. One sharp turn later she was tangled in her toppled wheelchair on the floor of the van, battered and terrified of ever having to go out on transport again.

In 2008, I had to overcome my reluctance to deal with medical. One area where FCCW is very attentive to inmate health needs is in the administration of mammograms. This conscientiousness did not stem from some aberrant cleaving to the Hippocratic oath. Rather, when I wondered aloud to someone about my mysterious appointment for preventive treatment, I'd been told that Fluvanna was in the midst of a lawsuit filed by the family of a woman who had died from breast cancer that had—shocker!—gone undiagnosed far too long. In an effort to close the barn door long after that particular horse had been turned into dog food, they had ponied up the cash to buy a state-of-the-art mammogram machine and had established a regular schedule of exams for inmates.

So there I sat, shivering and half-nude, in the tiny, freezing cubbyhole that held the admittedly rather impressive mammogram machine. After a few minutes, an officious nurse bustled in. "I'm Ms. Raymond," she informed me. "Come here."

I approached the machine, and Ms. Raymond eyed my naked chest, heaved an exasperated sigh, and pulled a large plastic tray from a low shelf. Without a word, she grabbed my breast and pushed it onto the tray. Then she stepped back to look, muttering, "Lift your arm. Grab this handle." I tried to contort my body as she directed, but clearly did not understand exactly what she wanted me to do. Reluctantly, Ms. Raymond moved my shoulder herself. When she was finally satisfied, she tersely told me to stay still, and then moved behind a protective barrier to take the x-rays.

I endured the process 3 more times before she had enough pictures and allowed me to get dressed. "We'll let you know what the results are," she said as she left the room.

A few weeks later I received a letter from the Breast Health Center at the University of Virginia hospital. My x-rays showed some areas that needed a closer look, and an appointment for an off-site examination would be made.

Now, I'm not by nature a hypochondriac, and I didn't take this letter as a death sentence. I am fairly rational, and I understood well enough just how minimal my concerns should be at that point. But I also had 2 aunts who had suffered from breast cancer, only one of whom had survived. So for the first time I had to consider the prospect of death as more than just a pleasant fantasy. Also a factor was the idea of what it would be like to suffer from such an illness in this environment.

The most alluring future I imagined was a diagnosis of cancer, followed by a swift death. Since suicide was never a viable option for me, this, I reasoned, was an out. I played it all out in my mind: my dignified calm as the doctor told me my prognosis; my quietly determined stance of refusing all treatment; telling my parents that there really wasn't much sense in their coming to visit me any more. This was not from any sense of melodrama. But the thought of receiving chemo or radiation treatments was abhorrent, and more important, the thought of finally being finished with everything was too appealing to resist. I wanted my parents, children, and friends to "move on," if I can use that decidedly overused phrase.

So I thought I was prepared when the C.O. removed my manacles at UVA so that the doctor could perform more tests. The doctor was genial and considerate as she moved the ultrasound scanner across my breast, describing everything she was doing, although I wasn't asking any questions. But soon she stopped talking, then moved the scanner abruptly to my underarm area. "Uh-oh," I thought. I didn't know much about breast cancer, but I realized that she was probably looking to see if there were signs of cancer there as well. It was then, despite my plans for calm acceptance, that I began to genuinely think that I might really have cancer.

The doctor stopped scanning, and began to speak. I can't remember any of the medical details. All I recall is her gently telling me that there seemed to be something there that was a type of cancerous growth she was familiar with. I was going to have to have surgery in order to confirm the diagnosis.

Forget calm. Forget acceptance. I bawled like a child. The C.O. who was in the examination room with me, who had been professionally detached during most of the exam, began to make shushing noises and looked as if she had to restrain herself from grabbing my hand. C.O. Ralston and I had had a good laugh earlier, when we were alone in the small room, because she had taken about 20 latex gloves from a box on the counter, shamefacedly telling me, "My hands are so small, I can't get examination gloves that fit me for pat downs back at Fluvanna. These are the perfect size."

As she looked for a uniform pocket large enough to secrete the wad of gloves, I, the practiced felon, suggested, "Hide them in your hat."

"Thanks," she responded, popping them briskly into her large-brimmed officer's hat.

But now the misery on her face was obvious. After I calmed down and the doctor left, she began to put the restrains on my wrists. "Don't worry," she said in almost a whisper, as if there were hidden microphones in the room that might capture her crossing of the boundary between inmate and officer. "My sister had breast cancer, and they took real good care of her here."

When we rejoined the male officer waiting for us in the checkout area, he took one look at my red, tear-stained face, and immediately went into father mode. "Let's get you home where you can relax," he said, holding my elbow as he helped me into the transportation van. "Be careful of those steps. It's easy to trip on those shackles."

After we got back to FCCW, the long wait began. I didn't know when I would go back for surgery, lest I tell a family member or friend ahead of time and plan some sort of spectacular prison break. I called my parents, though, and as soon as my father heard my voice, he said, "Let me get your mother."

Mom took down all of the details I could remember, and asked if I wanted them to come up to see me that weekend. "Call me as soon as you know anything," she demanded.

A few of my friends knew what was going on, and I told them what the doctor had said. One of them was Sadie. I knew that she was a notorious gossip, but I was stunned when, a few days later, I was called back into the housing unit at the middle of the day. That only happened under special circumstances. "Dear God, what now?" I asked myself as I trudged back.

I was seated in a tiny office. A few minutes later, the radiologist, Ms. Raymond, came in, followed by a correctional officer. "Ms. George," she said, "You need to stop talking to people about your medical condition. I want the officer here to confirm that this conversation is taking place."

At first I was confused. "What in the world was she talking about? What had I said to get this response? You need to stop telling people that you are going to have surgery. You are most definitely not going to have to have surgery."

By now, I had moved from perplexed to pissed off. I could speak to anyone I wanted about my personal issues. And how dare she talk about my condition in front of this clearly embarrassed officer? "Are you kidding me?" I demanded. "I can say whatever I want as long as it is not a profanity, a lie, or otherwise against the rules. What rule am I breaking? And I know what the doctor said to me. It sounds like you need to read my file a little more closely."

Ms. Raymond backed down a little. "Just keep your mouth shut," she muttered. As I tried to respond, she cut me off. "Go back to your housing unit now."

I stomped back to my wing. "I can't believe this shit." I said to my friends. "That woman is telling me that I'm not allowed to talk to you about my own health. Who does she think she is? And what prompted her to do this in the first place?"

Sadie, who had gotten very quiet as I explained why I was so angry, had the grace to blush. "Well, I might have something to do with that," she said.

"What do you mean? Jesus, what have you done now?"

"All I did was stop Ms. Raymond on the boulevard and ask her when your surgery was going to be and what exactly your diagnosis was. She told me that you were not having surgery and that your diagnosis wasn't confirmed yet," Sadie said.

"That bitch talked to you about my personal medical information? That's against the law! And who do you think you are to pry into my business? If I want you to know something, I'll frickin' tell you myself." I was livid. Sadie's vicarious hypochondria was one of her more annoying traits, one I had zero tolerance for.

I wrote an IMS to the medical director, complaining about Ms. Raymond's inappropriate actions, but he never responded. But to be fair, IMS inquiries to the medical director almost never get responses. All the better to CYA, my dear. And I was too worried about my health to pursue it.

Eventually I did go in for my surgery. Even during the operation itself, I wasn't left alone. Ms. Ralston was with me during my lumpectomy, and she could not have done more for me. I think she actually enjoyed seeing the operation. "The doctor pulled this lump of stuff out and just sort of squeezed it!" she told me with quiet glee as I recovered from the anesthesia. She was very decent to me as I recovered, offering me tissues, and even helping me with my bedpan, looking away discreetly as I used it. I was driven back to the prison a few hours after the surgery, so I was still pretty woozy when I returned. C.O. McCall was helpful too. He didn't say a word when I handed him the bag I had vomited into during the ride back. I was alert enough, however, to somewhat acidly say, "I'm back from my surgery," when I saw Ms. Raymond in the medical unit just after my return.

I was not given any postoperative care. The ice packs that the nurse at the hospital had given me were confiscated, and the vague promises of Tylenol at pill line never materialized. Mary, my roommate, did her best to care for me. Bowls of soup materialized so that I wouldn't have to walk to the chow hall, and she scoured the wing to find new magazines for me to read. She also begged or borrowed as much aspirin as she could to help stave off the pain from the surgery. God bless is all that I can say.

I suppose that I'm lucky that the biopsy showed that the growth was benign, but I still wonder what I would have ended up doing if it had actually been cancer. Since then, I've begun refusing my automatically scheduled mammograms. Truthfully, I hope that if I do get cancer, I find out about it when it is too far along to do anything about.

Considering my general health, I have managed to avoid most extended stays in the prison infirmary. However, 2 years ago, I found myself entombed there for a week. It was one of the most miserable weeks I have ever experienced since coming to Fluvanna.

My ordeal began Thanksgiving night; I was in the shower shaving my legs in preparation for a visit that I was going to have with my parents the next day. I'm usually pretty slack about such niceties (baggy uniforms cover a multitude of grooming sins), but I try to be as presentable as possible when I'm going to have to get naked in front of someone. (Tragically for me—and her—the only someone I ever get naked in front of is some unfortunate C.O. That is the extent of my social life).

Anyway, as I unbent from my feeble attempts at grooming, I felt a small twinge in my back. Like my father, I have the "McCay" back—he once nearly crippled himself just by making a bed—which makes me particularly alert to potential problems with my own back. I stopped a moment to take inventory, gingerly twisting my torso left and right. Everything seemed to be OK, so I didn't give it another thought.

The day after Thanksgiving, though, I was in noticeable pain. I was able to walk with the help of my cane, and I shuffled to my visit. It was an extended visit (we were allowed over 2 hours), but I ended up having to go back to my housing unit before the officer ended it; sitting in the uncomfortable plastic chair was becoming unbearable. When I made it back to the building, I crawled into my bunk and prayed for relief.

As much as I was grateful to see Mom and Dad, that visit was a big mistake. By Saturday morning, I was in agony. I managed (I'm not sure how) to drag myself to the bathroom but was unable to make it back to my room. I stood in the dayroom, literally weeping. Belinda came up to me hesitantly and asked if I needed some help. The hesitancy was because I am notorious for refusing assistance. No matter how much my lupus is affecting me, I almost never ask for help, and when people offer it, I am, admittedly, often a little abrupt in my refusals. It's never a good idea to show weakness, and my health is a major weakness for me. But this time I didn't have a choice.

"God, yes. Could you please get the nurse for me?" The Honor Wing was housed in Building Eight at that time, and because Building Eight also included seg and structured living, there was usually a nurse on site. Belinda, who knew me well, gave me one silent, stricken look (the mere fact that I was begging for help was an obvious clue that I was in trouble) and rushed to the wing door.

A few minutes later, the nurse strolled in. I was sitting on a plastic chair (yes, another of those god-awful plastic torture devices) in the middle of the dayroom, quietly crying. She asked me a few perfunctory questions, poked gingerly at my back, and said, "Well, I can't do anything for you without a doctor's permission, and I can't send you to the clinic without orders, so you're just going to have to tough it out until they can see you on Monday."

Tough it out? For days? I cried a little harder, and told the nurse that I was really in a lot of pain. Couldn't she do anything for me at all? A Motrin? Sheesh, even a kind word would have been received with gratitude. No dice, though. As the nurse left, Belinda hauled me up and staggered under my weight as she lugged me to my room.

The 2 days that followed were nightmarish. My metal bunk, padded only by a skimpy pad, was a medieval torture device—an iron inmate?—and every infinitesimal movement brought torment. I didn't have to endure it alone, though. Although I didn't have a roommate, Tianne appointed herself my caretaker and stationed herself at a table in the dayroom just outside my door. Every time I twitched, she was at my door. "Are you OK? What do you need?"

She did everything for me another human being could possibly have done, including dressing and undressing me, carrying me to the bathroom and advocating for me with the officers. She was a godsend. Although I was ignored by the nursing staff, Tianne rallied the C.O.s, who gave her permission to enter my room to help me. The C.O.s were great, not only did they check in on me every time they did a round, they called to the kitchen and had meal trays sent over for me (a big no-no).

By Monday afternoon, I had had enough. I began the intricate process of hoisting myself from my bunk, and Tianne rushed into the room. "Where are you going?" she demanded.

"I can't take this anymore. I'm going to call my parents." Having to call Mommy and Daddy for help is one of the more humiliating aspects of confinement (although I'm grateful beyond measure to have them to call), but they are the ones I ask for money to buy new underwear or a new pair of glasses, or if I would like a magazine subscription or information from the Internet. To their credit, they perform this same role for more than one of my friends, the ones who don't have anyone to do that for them. Mom is also the one I reach out to when I need a voice from the outside to speak on my behalf. Sadly, such voices are heeded far more than often than those on the inside.

"Get your ass back in that bunk," she ordered. "I'm going to get Bright." C.O. Bright was the wing officer that day, a really decent guy who had taken a particular shine to me, Tianne, and Dizzy. He loved bringing us riddles and brain teasers and clocking how long it took for us to solve them. We also shared a continuing dialogue about the state of corrections in Virginia, politics, and society. He was insightful, compassionate, and realistic—a rare combination in a correctional officer.

Thirty seconds later, Bright was at the door. "I'm on this," he said. "I don't know why medical hasn't called for you yet (it turns out that the helpful weekend nurse had never notified medical about what was happening with me), but I'm going to call them now. If nothing else, I'll call a 10-52 and they'll bring a stretcher over for you. You can pretend you can't move or something."

I squeaked out a laugh. "Pretend? Yeah, all this is a huge act for attention. You should see me doing pirouettes in the room when no one is looking." Bright flashed me a grin, and trotted out to the bubble.

Whatever he said to medical must have worked, because Tianne was at my door immediately with a wheelchair. "Let's get going," she said.

We managed to maneuver me into the chair, and she carefully took me across the compound to the medical building. Every jolt was excruciating, and the entire walk was accompanied by her apologies. When we finally got there, a nurse immediately took my blood pressure.

"Oh, dear," she muttered. "We are going to admit you to the infirmary immediately."

"Why didn't that happen on Saturday," I asked her. "I've been in misery for days."

"What do you mean?"

I explained the timeline, and as I did, her face blanched. She's been here for years and knew that I was not a malingerer or attention-grabber, and she also knew what life was like in the wings. "Oh, honey, that was a mistake. She should have sent you over here immediately. If you can't walk to the chow hall, you need to be in here."

They rolled me into J Ward, and I was assigned a bed in the noisy, messy room. A TV was mounted on the wall, blaring some soap opera, and the other patients looked at me with interest. After I was settled into the surprisingly comfortable bed—a real mattress!—the nurse appeared with a paper cup full of meds. I didn't even ask what they were, just gulped them down. Whatever she gave me must have been powerful, though, because I was asleep almost immediately. I woke up about 5 hours later, and a helpful inmate said, "Damn, you were out of it. When they came in for count, you didn't even move. The officer even shook your leg, and you didn't wake up!"

For the next 3 days, the doctor would come in once a day, speak to me briefly about my progress, and then leave me alone. The muscle relaxers and pain killers they gave me made a huge improvement, and when the doctor told me that walking would help me recover enough to get me released back to my housing unit, I started making a slow circuit on my walker around the ward. By the time I was able to ditch the walker and upgrade to my cane again, I was hot to get out of there. Although the women seemed decent to me while I was there, they were noisy and annoying. "Are you going to eat that?" they would ask when I got my dinner tray. "Can I borrow a honey bun?" they would plead. "I'll pay you back." Yeah, right. But I coughed up the honey bun with no complaints, smilingly shared my tray's meager contents and begged daily to be released.

Thursday morning, the doctor said I was released. "Great" I thought. "I'll be moving this afternoon." But when the hours passed and I wasn't told to pack up my stuff (which the officers had brought to me the day after my admission to J Ward), I began to worry. I'd heard horror stories about people being trapped in the infirmary for weeks after their release. Dear God, would this happen to me? I searched out Building Two's Unit Manager and Lieutenant in order to plead my case and, doubting the efficacy of the staff to accomplish this, began sending frantic messages to the Honor Wing: GET ME OUT OF HERE!

On Friday, I got the word that I would be moving back to my bunk, which had been saved for me. When I gratefully pushed a cart of my belongings into the wing like a tattered wanderer from the desert, I was surrounded by my friends. "It was Pippa who got you back here so fast," said Logan. Pippa worked in the administration building and is famously well connected. She has more clout than most sergeants around here, and isn't afraid to use it.

"It wasn't no big thing," said Pippa when I thanked her for her help. "We didn't want you stuck there all weekend." Later, as I unpacked my stuff, I discovered that some of my food and one of my CDs had been stolen by one of the girls in the infirmary. Never mind, I looked around gratefully at the Spartan cinderblock room and smiled contentedly. I was home.

Sometimes trips to the hospital are unplanned. I've known inmates that have been sent out for conditions ranging from a broken leg to attempted suicide.

Pregnancy is another common reason for an unplanned trip outside the walls. For a while, it seemed that Fluvanna was inundated with pregnant inmates. "It must be against the law to get knocked up," Belinda observed. They were everywhere: the chow hall, the library, the gym. And, inevitably, they all had to eventually give birth. Most were shipped before that happened here, but a few went into labor while at FCCW. Nadia told me about the time she was a reluctant observer of Fluvanna's handling of the situation.

I happened to be walking past the back windows of the wing one evening and I saw four or five officers around this woman in the infirmary, which was just across from our building. Being an inmate, I stopped to see what was going on, and I was mesmerized. I could see that the officers were around a woman who was clearly in labor. Her face was in such anguish that I could almost hear her screaming.

It tore me up. I could see some orange fabric, and I realized that they were wrestling her into one of the orange jumpsuits that we need to wear when we are on transport. They weren't being rough or anything—it was just something that they had to do. The rules, you know? Then they put the leg shackles on this poor screaming woman and it tore my heart to shreds.

When a Fluvanna inmate gives birth, she has to forget about being able to hold her new baby. She won't be able to cup her child's fragile head, or have the chance to memorize his cry, his scent. The new mother is returned to the prison immediately afterward. She has almost no time with her newborn, which is usually handed off to a relative or foster parent. Postpartum care appears to be minimal. It's a sad situation.

Fluvanna does offer dental care. Sort of. But again, it's a case of too many patients and medical care providers struggling with the burden of dispassionate, corporate control. In the 6 years that I've been locked up, I've been able to have my teeth cleaned once. I have been on the waiting list for fillings for over a year. But I have high hopes that it will be soon. And maybe I'll luck out and score a teeth cleaning as well. You never know.

When I had my first dental visit, the opening question the nurse asked was, "When are you going home?" Good question. I understand the necessity of triaging inmates by sentence. If you are going home in 6 months, it doesn't make sense to take up a valuable appointment slot. Of course, I come at that as a lifer. Good dental health is vitally important to me because I am absolutely terrified of the inevitable time that I will have to get dentures. I know that no matter how many times a day I brush, my soft teeth have doomed me. It's not the idea of dentures that bothers me so much, though. It's the year or more that I will have to walk around the prison toothless that upsets me most. It's a humiliating prospect, an excellent way to dehumanize us.

I don't think that is the primary reason that dental waits so long to give us our dentures after they have pulled out our teeth. That would be because the dentures are made by male prisoners at another Virginia facility (guaranteeing an inferior product), an inexpensive but time-consuming proposition. The pain and humiliation is just a happy side benefit. I know several women who have not been able to chew a meal properly or smile at their children in visitation for over a year because they are waiting for their dentures to finally show up. And once they have endured the year of not being able to eat 50% of what is served in the chow hall because it is too hard to gum into submission and they've mastered the art of speaking without opening their mouths, the dentures arrive. Of course they never fit properly, though, because the woman's mouth has caved in (that happens when you pull out all of her teeth and do not replace them with new ones), reshaping the topography of her mouth. Wearing them is torture, almost impossible to endure. And the new teeth don't even look good. Unless the equine look has become suddenly popular, most women wearing their new dentures look utterly ridiculous. Dental might try to refit the false teeth, but that is never really a success. So the dentures sit in a box, only pulled out for a few painful hours at visitation, and the woman continues her time at Fluvanna, toothless and humiliated.

CHICK

"Chick, what's up?" I said to the tall, pale woman who had just finished brushing her teeth at the sink next to me. In a population of women that are, for the most part, merely tolerated by the majority of the inmates and staff members, Chick is an anomaly here (and, I would imagine, outside the walls as well); she is almost universally loved and admired by those who are fortunate enough to know her today. Not that she's some paragon of pure saintliness. Chick is, for example, very often simply goofy. Always self-deprecating. Occasionally even a bit wicked in her assessments of the lunatic world we both inhabit. A good person by all reckoning, but on paper no one's idea of a good candidate for canonization. But there is a quality to her that you would expect to find in the Dalai Lama. Not a convicted felon serving 38 years for murder.

When I first met her, Chick had been down for 7 years. She was exceedingly pleasant and well mannered, a "good old country girl" as she described herself, but not remarkable in any significant way. We lived in the same wing, spent some time together, but no one would suggest that we were particularly close. We got along, though, which is more than can be said about a lot of people at Fluvanna. Then, in 2009, she was diagnosed with cancer.

Now, inmates seem to fall into two camps when it comes to coping with medical situations. The majority seem to enjoy nothing more than emoting prolonged, semi-hysterical (or fully blown hysterical if at all possible) monologues about their medical conditions. Anything, everything, needs to be gravely and weepily discussed with anyone foolish enough to sit at the same table or even make the profound error of politely asking "How are you?" (You know, that question that just about everyone asks perfunctorily about 73 times a day, expecting an answer no more profound or lengthy than "Fine.") Call me cruel, but I have little patience for these histrionics.

I'll never forget the afternoon that Cindy came dramatically into the wing. Supported by two friends, she staggered into the housing unit, weeping vigorously and clutching chest like a heart attack victim; I expected the rending of clothes and smearing of ashes to commence immediately. A woman sitting next to me as this spectacle occurred was mesmerized. Unlike me, she hadn't seen

Cindy's multiple previous similar performances, so she accepted it at face value. I, on the other hand, waited to see what life-threatening issue caused of all this. Each time something like this had happened before, she upped the medical ante. What would the diagnosis be this time?

At last she was able to form words through her grief. "They've killed me! They've killed me!" she shrieked. "Medical has finally killed me!"

(My rather uncharitable impulse—which I managed to resist, I'm proud to say—was to remind her that she had eluded death several times before, so chin up! The odds are in your favor!)

When the whole wing didn't swarm to her side in support (or even merely to enjoy the drama), Cindy looked momentarily annoyed, then ratcheted up the drama level by collapsing to the floor. This did get some attention, and she allowed herself to swim back to consciousness in order to answer the questions that people were throwing at her. What happened? What did the doctor say? Cancer. It was definitely cancer. At the very least stage 4, possibly stage 5 or 6, she wasn't sure. Is there a stage 7? More tests were needed. Extended, invasive, debilitating tests. It was everywhere, anywhere. Lungs? Yes. Liver? Sure, why not. Yes, she was being strong; she would get through this with the help of her friends. Oh, yeah, and God, too. Sure. (For the record, Cindy is very well today, ostensibly suffering from some obscure condition that only 25 people in the entire history of medical science have ever borne. And since no one has ever heard of this condition, it has the happy side effect of rendering her utterly safe from probing questions. Too many people knew too much about cancer for Cindy's comfort level.)

While this exemplar of reasoned response keened and moaned, I noticed Chick sitting quietly by herself in the back of the day room. I didn't approach her then. A few days later, word got around that Chick had been diagnosed with cancer. She was a part of the other end of the inmate spectrum: no fuss, no drama, no hysterics, so those of us who were friendly but not intimate friends with her knew little more than that.

Over the next 3 years, she and I grew closer, culminating in weekly lunches where she, her roommate, and I would spend each Saturday afternoon together laughing, talking about faith, reading poetry, and discussing our histories. I had always been wary of discussing her health, other than offering her any support I could give. It was not that I didn't care, but Chick is extraordinarily private, and I didn't want to intrude. But one afternoon, as we sat over the chicken salad sandwiches we had made, she quietly asked me for my advice.

"They're telling me that they want to do surgery on my spine," she said. "I don't know what to do. I totally rely on God to heal me, but what if getting the surgery says that I don't have faith in Him?" Chick is a devout woman. She never curses or, as far as I know, even gossips about anyone in an ugly way. Her faith is genuine, subtle, and encompassing, and we had spent many hours grappling with how to maintain the balance of one's faith while living in prison.

"I'm not sure what to advise you," I answered. "Do you mind telling me exactly what's going on with your health? What exactly happened?"

Chick paused for a long moment. I could see the pain in her face, the pain that never seemed to really go away. But still she smiled. Chick almost always smiled.

"I had been having lower back pain since 2007, and my hip seemed to keep coming out of joint. I had to miss so much work because every 3 months or so this would happen. Oh my Lord, I was in so much pain, the only way I could walk was if I pushed in on my back. But medical didn't do anything for me—no tests or anything. Then in 2009 my rib felt like it cracked! All I could think was 'did I sneeze hard enough to crack a rib?' The only way I could move was if I bound myself up. I'd tie myself with tube socks to make a pressure bandage."

I interrupted her. "How in the world did you get into work without the police finding that?" Chick worked in the tailor shop and was patted down every time she left in order to make sure that she hadn't stolen any fabric, needles, or thread.

"Oh, all I did was tuck the knot up under my breasts to hide it. Anyway, Anne and a few of my other friends wouldn't shut up about it, so I ended up going back to medical. The nurse sent in an order for an x-ray. My breathing was so labored that I didn't have to wait the normal 14 days for an appointment. I went directly from medical to the x-ray lab down the hall. You know that they normally just send you printed results, but they actually called me back to the medical building to tell me that 'Yes, you have a broken rib. But your rib broke from the inside out because you have a tumor that's growing larger than the rib itself.' I was floored. I'd been complaining to medical for 2 years about pain and been told time and again that it was nothing. And now this? There was a mass on my kidney that was so large that the x-ray of the rib on the opposite side picked it up."

I wish that I could say that. I was stunned by what she was telling me, that her story was a gross aberration in an otherwise well-functioning medical system. But there have been too many women with stories just like this. Pam had gone to the doctors complaining of stomach pain for years and was told that she needed to eat healthier food (this to a person who has almost zero access to healthy food. You can't eat a banana if the chow hall doesn't provide one to you. Commissary sells potato chips and Ramen noodles, not fresh broccoli). "Drink more water!!" they would suggest. "You're under stress. Try to relax." Not surprisingly, additional hydration and yoga was not effective in healing her stomach cancer, and when she was finally diagnosed, she died so quickly that I heard about her diagnosis and death in the same sad conversation.

Victims of medical are legion. Women still stagger around the yard clutching swollen cheeks from botched and infected dental procedures. You may have to wait weeks to see a doctor. Infection had killed at least one woman in the prison infirmary after she had otherwise successful brain surgery. Every profoundly ill person I knew had a story that was preluded by a long period of denial by the prison medical community. The assumption that we are all goldbrickers and layabouts is firmly entrenched in their minds. All of this was firmly in my mind as I listened to Chick continue her story.

"Once they finally diagnosed you, did they take good care of you?" I asked.

"They sent me to UVA (which provides the majority of off-site medical that FCCW's inmates receive) to get a CAT scan. I couldn't get an MRI because I had been shot in the head in 2004, and I still had a bullet in my brain." My eyes glanced involuntarily to the small scar at her temple. That, too, was something I had never asked her about.

"This was the first time I ever heard the word 'cancer' from one of my doctors. They seemed scared, and they gave me a bunch of tests at once. They even sent me to a kidney specialist."

Anne interrupted her. "That's when you finally announced it to everyone in the tailor shop."

Chick smiled at her roommate and best friend. "Everybody was so worried about me; I asked the C.O. if I could announce it to everyone at one time. She let me do it. I think she was a little worried about me too, 'though she couldn't tell me, of course."

Anne said, "I was so sad and confused because you don't imagine your friends as having cancer."

"Everyone's support meant so much," Chick said, "It gave me strength. I made the decision then that The Big C doesn't stand for cancer to me. It stands for Christ. I'm not going to believe the words written in black and white on a CAT scan, but the ones written in red in the New Testament. I took my stand with Christ that day, and that's what I told those girls."

She continued her story. "The kidney specialist told me that the mass had been growing for at least 2 years, in all probability 3. I'd been telling them that something was wrong, and they kept ignoring me." For the first time, she let frustration color her voice. 'When I saw the doctor, I didn't seem able to say anything. When the doctor asked me if I had any questions, I just said no. But one of the officers who had taken me to UVA was Ms. Barnard, and she stepped in like a sister. She asked all the questions that I would have wanted to ask, and even told me 'you can cry if you want to.'"

"I'm very grateful to her and C.O. Randall, who are the two officers that accompanied me on some of my medical visits. They were so kind. It was kind of hard for me to cry over my cancer that day with those two fools keeping me laughing. They were a regular Laurel and Hardy team watching me. I know God put them there especially for me."

I had to ask the biggest question. "What was your prognosis? How much time did they give you?"

Matter-of-factly she said, "The kidney specialist gave me 6 months to 2 years to live. I was told that it was already stage 4 with cancer metastasized." Laughing, she looked at an imaginary watch on her wrist. "I think that was an underestimate!"

"What was their plan of action?" I asked.

"In January 2010, they removed the kidney," she said. "They tried to do it laparoscopically, but the mass was too large, so they had to take it out the old-fashioned way. They were supposed to address the rib next, but that didn't happen."

"Good lord, why not?!" I demanded. "What the hell?"

"Well, between January and June 2010, I'd been speaking to a lawyer as a part of a lawsuit that was going to be filed against Fluvanna," she said.

I'd heard about the lawsuit which was filed in July of 2012 and was covered by the local news media. "Oh, you were a part of that?" I asked. "I didn't realize."

She looked grim. "Oh no, I wasn't a part of that when it was filed. I noticed that when I started meeting with lawyers, I stopped getting treatment for my rib. It had cracked two more times, and they were supposed to put some mesh in to hold my heart because the broken rib was supposed to be removed. It was a necessary rib to hold the heart."

"Are you serious?" I said.

"I was scared. I told them, 'please take me to get this taken care of because it keeps going somewhere else.' No cancer was found in the tubes or lining of my kidney, so I wanted to press the issue to stop further spreading. My mom called the prison, my sister called. . . ."

"So I dropped the lawsuit, and they finally sent me out again. I knew that they were retaliating against me, and I told the doctors that. The prison doctors told me that it wasn't true, that there were lots of people who needed treatment and that it was UVA's fault they weren't scheduling me. I told them that I forgave them, could we start over, and could I get treatment?"

"Did they start helping you again?" I asked.

"After the lawsuit was dropped, they finally tried to remove my rib, but by then it was too late. The cancer had moved to my spine and they had to take care of that first. The tumor in my spine was called a blood-fed tumor, and because it was moving into my stomach, they couldn't get it all out. I spent 5 days in the hospital. The C.O.s who were with me were so kind, and the nurses couldn't have been better. I think that they respected that I didn't lay down with it. I decided to stand up and keep going, not to cry over spilled milk, but clean it up and keep going. The nurses would bet that I would push the call button, but I never did. When I was leaving, a nurse told me, 'I won two Pepsis off you because you never hit that call button.'"

"That's about the time I became your roommate!" Anne said.

"I'd heard some stories about how that happened, but don't really know the truth. How'd that all go down?" I asked. It had seem mighty coincidental that Chick's best friend became her roommate, but no one seemed particularly upset about it as they might have been if it had happened to someone less well liked.

Chick answered first. "I was in my cell alone because I didn't have a roommate at the time, and the lieutenant came over my intercom and asked me if there was someone I wanted to help take care of me and not be mean to me. I said yes, my friend Anne." She stops to look affectionately at her friend. "Three days later, Anne moved in."

Anne said, "I had just wrote to my counselor to ask where I was on the list for the Honor Wing, where Chick already lived, and she told me that I was 42nd! I was devastated; I thought I'd never get there because there isn't a high turnover in that wing."

"For once the medical and security staff worked together," said Chick, "worked for the good of an 'offender,' however you want to word it. I just said 'Thank you, Lord!' They tried to take good care of me at this point. Gave me two mattresses, two pillows, an egg crate pad. It was the difference between day and night after the lawsuit was dropped. So I got some radiation afterwards, and 14 days of chemo. In June of 2010 the tumor was removed."

"Where are you now?" I asked.

"They still say they need to do some more surgeries, and I'm in a lot of pain. I hate that I can't go to work anymore. I really need my pay because I hate to ask my family for money. But I'm trying to keep positive. I'm involved in a support group here for prisoners with severe conditions like mine. We are working to permit fewer restraints when profoundly ill people are sent out for treatment. We want more wholesome food on commissary, and we were successful in pushing for vitamins to be sold to inmates. We would like to get permission for inmates to come in and read and talk with terminally ill inmates, but that's on hold right now because of the lawsuit. The medical director has left because of the lawsuit, all of the old doctors are gone, and everything seems to be at a standstill. Right now, I'm still waiting."

I wasn't able to provide Chick with any profound advice about her surgery decision, but we did spend more time talking about it. Eventually, she decided to have the surgery, and this morning she was brushing her teeth in preparation for another day at the tailor shop, another day that Chick would walk through smiling and grateful for her blessings.

Since this was written, Chick has quickly gotten sicker. Two months ago she was taking a shirt from the dryer and her arm suddenly snapped. I was in my room, and her scream was so shrill that I could hear it despite the thick metal door. When I got to the door, I saw that she was on the floor, surrounded by other inmates.

"Get to your rooms, the nurse is coming," the officer in the bubble yelled over the intercom. The women reluctantly left Chick leaning against the dryer, clutching at her arm and sobbing. It took the nurses a shamefully long time to get there—master control had to call for a medical emergency twice—and when they did, it was like a grotesque slapstick comedy: neither one could figure out how to physically lift Chick into the wheelchair, and every time they tried, they clumsily jostled her back into agony.

"Dammit, I wish they'd get the hell out of the way and just let me do it," my roommate said. Beck had been an EMT for several years when she was locked up and had hoped to be a doctor someday.

Eventually they got Chick to the infirmary, then to the hospital. It turns out that the broken arm was the least of her problems. Because she hadn't been properly evaluated, the doctors didn't realize that the cancer had pretty much spread all over her body: shoulder, skull, jaw. I was devastated by guilt because it was *my* shirt that she had been lifting when her arm snapped.

"I am so sorry, Chick! You didn't have to try and move my laundry!" I said to her the next day, when she was back with her heavy cast.

"Oh, please," she said, smiling. "The doctor told me that I could have broken my arm just by rolling over in the night, the cancer is so bad. Don't you worry one minute about that."

"So what did the doctors say?" I asked her.

"Well, they're gonna have to do some more tests, but it looks pretty bad, I guess. . . . It's all up my arm."

I started to cry, loudly and embarrassedly, in the middle of the dayroom. "I'm so sorry. I don't know why I'm getting so upset."

She gave me a look. "Don't you, honey?"

I knew what she was referring to. A week earlier, my father had been diagnosed with esophageal cancer himself, and I had been exerting an extraordinary amount of energy trying to keep from falling apart. I hadn't told many people about it, not being that keen on sharing my personal information here, but Chick was one of my dearest friends and confidants. This was too much, and I was conflating my fears for Dad with my pain over Chick's news, and it was too much to hold in. So rather than me comforting her, she grabbed me with her one good arm and held me.

As the weeks progressed, she underwent further tests, then radiation therapy. One day she came back from UVA and told us that the doctors there had officially told her that she probably had no more than 6 months to live. The prison doctor confirmed this, and he began the process for her to receive medical clemency. "The doctor says that the hard part of applying for medical clemency is getting the UVA doctors to write letters confirming the prognosis," she said. "But the UVA people have already done that. Doctor Miller is going to work with Counselor Rodman to get this thing going. I'm going home!"

Chick is still waiting to go home. Her roommate takes such tender care of her, they are more like sisters. Mouse is the most patient, loving nurse and friend imaginable. Thank God she is in Chick's life.

Chick is handling her situation with her usual humor. Yesterday when we were walking to chow, one of the officers yelled, "Hey! Get in a single-file line." This officer was a good guy, one we habitually joked with, but who may not have realized just how sick Chick is.

"Don't worry," Chick shot back with a tired grin. "The doctors tell me that you only have to put up with me for 4 months more!" The rest of us tried to laugh—we know that humor is how she copes, but it is still painful to hear—but Chick just grinned wider and said, "Look at his face! I love doing that."

That's our girl. Laughing to the end.

BILLIE

Billie, at age 71 and after 26 years in prison, finally "maxed out"—served her full sentence without being given parole. Unfortunately, Billie died a month before she reached that magic number. I had met her soon after I was sent to Fluvanna. I say met, but it was years before I actually had a conversation with her. Prior to that, she was just a woman that I saw making her way to and from the chow hall every day, one that attracted comment and ridicule wherever she met.

She was hard to miss. Even a decade ago, Billie looked far older than she actually was. Ancient, really. But she seemed to embody tenacity to me as I saw her slowly pushing her walker as she made her way around the compound. Although it was May the first time I noticed her, unseasonably warm even for Virginia, Billie was swaddled in a winter coat over a clear plastic rain poncho and wearing brown gloves. Pulled low over her face was a bright orange wool watch cap. I could see that she had an orange mesh commissary bag tied securely to her walker and wondered what it held. One day I was in the same chow hall with her and realized that it held the hemorrhoid pillow she always carried, delicately placing it on whichever stool or chair she was forced to use.

I had been living in general population for a few months when I finally asked my roommate, Lori, who she was. "Oh, that's Billie. She's been here for about a hundred years," Lori said blithely.

"Jesus, she looks like an Egyptian mummy," I replied. "Seriously, how long has she been locked up?"

"I think that she's been down for about 20 years. Her daughter, Penny, is here too. This is Penny's third bid. She must like the food here," Lori joked.

"Her daughter is here too? That's so sad. Do they live in the same wing?"

"Nah, the DOC won't let relatives live together. They even try to keep them out of the same building. They're more likely to shank each other than regular folks, I guess." Lori laughed. "They try to go to rec at the same time, and the prison lets them eat together on Mother's Day, Thanksgiving, and on Christmas, though."

"That really is so sad," I repeated. "It would break my heart to have my mom or daughter here. I'd rather never see them again than have that happen."

Because people get moved around the facility frequently, Billie and I eventually ended up living in the same wing together, and I got to know her more intimately. I'm not sure what I thought she would be like, but I sure wasn't expecting her to be the cranky old bird that I found her to be. Billie wasn't a sweet old lady (we have a few of them here—but under that candy-coated exterior they are the ones who are the first to drop an anonymous IMS snitching people out or have their children and grandchildren call to grouse about perceived injustices which are actually instances where once in a blue moon another inmate gets a lucky break and they are irked that it didn't happen for them too). She was ornery. Irascible. Downright unpleasant at times. Billie had no compunction whatsoever about dressing you down if she felt it was warranted.

We had our first spat at the sinks one morning before school. Billie worked as a housekeeper, and each morning, as soon as count cleared, you would find her grimly moving through the wing, a spray bottle of cleaner and a cane hooked on the bar of her walker and a rag clutched in her hand. She would wipe down tables, which bothered no one. She would take 2 hours to remove the 50 or so books from off the small bookshelf available to the whole wing and meticulously dust each battered paperback, which was a bit annoying, but bearable. But she also had the habit of draining the hot water pot and leaving it empty as she then moved to the 3 sinks and liberally spraying each of them with cleaning fluid and filling them with wadded up paper towels, effectively barring the entire wing from completing 2 of the most important activities of the busy, busy prework hour between cleared count and mass movement: brushing your teeth and getting that first vital cup of coffee.

Now, bear in mind that doing that once could be considered an oversight. Two or e times might be construed as the vagaries of age. But every day! Every single day there she was, keeping us from our caffeine and hygiene. It was a perfect storm of potential conflict, and flare-ups occurred regularly. Sometimes inmates were tactful, but more often real rage accompanied these confrontations. Many inmates are former addicts who have traded whatever chemical that previously ensnared them for the sweet siren song of caffeine; depriving them of their morning kick is tantamount to a slap in the face. It didn't matter if the exchanges were dripped in honey or vinegar, though; all complaints were met with the same mulish taciturnity.

My confrontation with Billie began as I staggered blearily from my cell, already brushing my teeth. Sink space is at a premium during that time of day—three sinks for 43 women is not a particularly effective ratio, especially considering that only 2 of the sinks actually have soap dispensers (at least one of which is almost always broken and/or empty) and one is a "handicap" sink with a mirror (or, rather, a scratched and murky sheet of metal) at chest level. As a result, sink time is at a premium, and morning ablutions often begin well prior to actual arrival at the wash basins.

So there I am, literally frothing at the mouth like a rabid pit bull, toothbrush clutched in hand and soap dish and washcloth tucked under one arm, trying to focus on Billie. She had managed to spread her range of activity to each of the sinks, moving between them like an exceedingly sluggish pinball. A cluster of irate inmates already stood behind her, muttering imprecations ("Damn it! She does this every morning!" "I'm gonna tell the building manager about this shit. I'm sick of this crap." "You can't tell me that she doesn't do this on purpose.") Billie feigned deafness, as was always her habit when anyone complained about her.

I, I'm afraid to say, did not handle the situation as gracefully as I should have. "Hey! Why do you pull this stunt every morning?" I demanded loudly enough for her to be unable to pretend that she can't hear me.

Her walker creaked as she slowly spun to face me. "I have to do my job," she said.

"Yeah, but you have all morning to do this. It's not like there's an inspection today. Would it be the end of the world if maybe you emptied the damn hot pot and cleaned the damn sinks at, oh, I don't know, *after* mass movement?"

"I'm going to do my job," she muttered as she painfully revolved back to the sinks. Clearly, in her mind the conversation was finished.

"Dammit!" I snatched out the wad of paper towels from the sink and violently spat out my toothpaste. Then, even though I don't even drink coffee, I marched to the hot pot and elaborately (and with much loud, unnecessary commentary) filled it up. This set the tone for the next 8 years we lived together. She and I managed to irritate one another with regularity, but we also shared the same living space and the same type of sentence, so inevitably we formed a bond, albeit a tempestuous one. The thawing really begin when it was announced that all of the housing units were going to be painted and that, because we lived in the Honor Wing, we would have the extraordinary privilege of painting our own cells, rather than having one of the inmate paint crews do it. Don't sneer; the quality of the work produced by such inmate work gangs is utterly execrable, and they were infamous for coming into a cell, slapping some paint haphazardly around, and leaving as much damage behind as they possibly could. All the other housing units had to have their cells painted for them. While all this took place, the entire population of the wing was trapped in the prison gym for hours.

There was actually a psychological reward to being allowed to paint our own living quarters in that you could plug in your radio and focus on doing the job well. Most of us had painted rooms of our own homes before being locked up, so it was easy to forget for a few hours that you were in prison. You were just painting your bedroom again, as you had probably done time and again in the past. It was a comforting and satisfying domestic task.

Billie, though, obviously couldn't paint her own room, so I volunteered to do it. The afternoon of paint day, after my roommate and I had finished our own digs, I moved over to Billie's single cell. Once I had gotten her set up in a chair outside of her door (still bundled up in her rain poncho—which acted like a greenhouse, trapping her minimal body heat against her tiny, frail body—and her coat, she alternated between snoozing in her plastic chair and nibbling on half of a Snickers for the entire 3 hours I was painting her cell), I moved out her half-empty property boxes, draped tarps over the metal desk and bunk, and began. After I had resettled Billie into her cell, she merely thanked me in a dignified way, then offered to give me some commissary for my work. I knew that Billie lived on her scant state pay and wasn't inclined to get paid for something I was willing to do for free, so I said, "Honey, you keep your food. If you need anything else, please let me know."

Over the years, Billie grew increasingly weak and was forced to rely on others more than she had in the past. She wasn't much for sharing personal information but ended up confiding to another oldhead that the doctors suspected that she had cancer but that she was absolutely refusing to seek any kind of treatment. By this time, the thought of going out on transport was anathema to her—she wouldn't be able to wear her long johns, poncho, coat, gloves, and hat, and the metal shackles would probably break her ankles if she was forced to walk in them—and, many of us suspected, she was terrified of the thought of facing cancer treatment from the prison medical unit. Considering her condition, such treatment would almost certainly entail a move from the Honor Wing, where she was surrounded by people who had known her for decades in some cases, to the prison infirmary, a horrifying, dirty place where inmates were rumored to languish unattended for hours, all the while in need of food, a bathroom, or even more significant attention.

We, in turn, became very protective of our still-cantankerous neighbor. When she could no longer carry her own tray in the chow hall, we would fetch it for her. This required special procedures, of course: Billie insisted that her water cup be rinsed out, dried with one of the paper towels she carried especially for that purpose and that it hold only 3 ice cubes (the water couldn't get *too* cold). She also managed, in her own inimitable Billie way, to annoy everyone at her table by taking the sole salt and paper shakers on the table and refusing to give them up until she had been given her tray and received her nice, clean cup of tepid water.

Even the staff seemed willing to cut her slack that no one else was afforded. As she got sicker, she needed to spend massive amounts of time in the bathroom. And because she was who she was, she developed the habit of choosing to go whenever she heard the intercom announce "5 minutes to count." Instead of rushing to her cell as everyone else would, Billie would slowly, still using her walker, make her way across the wing to the handicap bathroom, knowing full well that whatever she had to do would take far longer than 5 minutes. Being out of one's cell once count was cleared was a major charge, so because my cell was next to hers, I got in the habit of letting her know when it was 15 or 20 minutes before count time so that she could get a head start (no pun intended). "Thank you," she would say serenely, then wait until that 5-minute alert to start off.

I would stand at my cell door nervously, worried that she would get a ticket and be moved from our wing. Soon, though, I realized that all of the officers, no matter what shift or temperament, would loiter in the bubble area outside of the wing waiting for her to return to her cell before coming in and blowing the whistle for count.

Eventually her cancer was no longer deniable, and Billie was so ill that she reluctantly gave up her job and medical took charge of her health care. We did what we could to help her; she needed to use a wheelchair, and even struggled to dress herself—whenever she tried to, she would fall. One afternoon I was taking her back from chow when she asked me if I would help her change out of her uniform.

"Of course," I said. Billie, of course, had established a system for her unofficial helpers to undress her, and she walked me through the steps.

"First, take my coat and fold it on the end of the bed," she asked. "You can put my shoes under the desk, but leave the socks on please. OK, now help me pull off my jeans, but don't pull down the long johns." She sat in her wheelchair lightly, gingerly lifting each hip as I slowly pulled off the baggy state jeans. Then she collapsed back into the chair. "Fold them up . . . no, not like that. Here, let me do it myself. Now drape them over my walker. Unbutton the top 3 buttons of my shirt and pull it over my head. Fold that like I did the jeans. That can go in my box." I swaddled her into an oversize sweatshirt and lifted her from the chair to help her into the bed, putting both of my arms under hers to raise her up. She was so light, she felt like a child. As she and I awkwardly shuffled from to the bunk, she joked, "At least this way I can get a hug."

Billie never had expressed a desire for any kind of friendship or intimacy, so I was stunned for a moment, then immediately propelled 30 years into the future, to the time when I will be the cranky, stubborn old woman still trapped far from home." Oh, Billie, you can have a hug whenever you want," I said, and squeezed her as tightly as I dared.

Others did all that they could for her. Because Billie was afraid of falling in the shower, against all the rules Blythe would go into her room and give her a sponge bath every few days. Billie wasn't able to stomach most of the food in the chow hall and had no money, so people would spend 5 or 10 dollars to buy her treats from commissary or make her hot meals.

My roommate, a former EMT, took on the role of unofficial nurse. Supervising her pills, urine output, and pulse, Beck knew better than anyone just how ill Billie was. She would come back to the room shaking her head. "I'm really worried about her. I don't think she's going to last more than a few weeks."

Despite the rigid bureaucracy of the prison, accommodations were made. She was given permission to wear her coat, poncho, and other regalia whenever she was sent out on transport to UVA Hospital. C.O.s continued to look the other way as she was blatantly given fruit stolen from the chow hall (she was too dispirited to continue her ill-timed forays to the bathroom and now meekly complied with all announcements about count). Best of all, her daughter Penny was moved into the same building and sometimes (although a few of the nastier officers balked at this) was permitted to come into our wing to bathe and dress her mother as well as escort her to medical appointments and the chow hall—a major violation of prison policy.

There was only one person who complained about Billie, her extended stints in the handicap bathroom, the considerations that she received from the staff, and the kindnesses of the other inmates. This was Dru, who was a famously unpleasant spewer of profanity and hate (she often entered the dayroom for no apparent reason and yelled at the top of her lungs such charming sentiments as, "You are all bitches who deserve to be dead and buried under this prison. Fuck you all. You should all be dead."). Even she didn't gripe too loudly, though. Dru was barely tolerated as it was and knew that she could be ousted from the wing if everyone complained enough about her.

Counterpointing Billie's clear devolution was our awareness that if she could only hold on for a few more months, then just a few more weeks, she would be able to go home. There was family waiting for her there, and we all wanted that for her: a few nights in a comfortable bed, some meals of palatable food, a chance for her to finally be warm enough. We knew that she was in terrible pain, unable to take decent pain meds because of her refusal to move to the infirmary, but still we wanted her to hang on.

There is something in Virginia called medical clemency. It is intended for inmates who have 6 months or less to live. How on earth a woman who has served 26 years, is 72 years old, who has a family that will take financial responsibility for her, and who is so riddled with cancer that she can barely lift a spoon is not eligible for medical clemency still eludes me, but I figure that it is just like the other liberal fictions employed by the state to prove that they are not monsters (i.e., geriatric parole and decent medical care).

One afternoon medical came for Billie. They did leave her in the Honor Wing for as long as they could, but it was clear to everyone that she had to go. But she didn't go quietly. Feeble as she was, our last sight of Billie was of a doctor pushing her in a wheelchair past the large windows in front of the wing, clearly livid and cussing like a crackhead. We ran up to the window to wave goodbye and shout out love and goodbye, but the lieutenant banged sharply on the glass and shouted for us to "shut up and get away from that window." This lieutenant was a charming fellow who not much later was walked off the grounds because, I heard, he shoved an inmate and it was caught on camera. (It was no small pleasure to me that the inmate this paragon of compassion chose to shove was the most litigious woman on the grounds, a gifted amateur lawyer. Needless to say, she is currently suing his ass off.)

Billie spent less than a week in the infirmary before she died. Her daughter, Penny, had had to fight to be able to see her mother in the ward. The officer in charge of that instance of cruelty was good buddies with the aforementioned lieutenant. He, too, has since been fired. Rumor is he cussed out the warden. One can only hope that this is true. The nurses in the infirmary didn't want Penny to be with her mother when she died, saying that it would be too "emotional" for Penny. So Billie and Penny made a plan: when Penny knew that Billie was about to go, she wasn't going to ask for any of the nurses. Instead, she was going to just let Billie pass away quietly. At least that's what I hear happened. At any rate, Billie didn't die alone. It's a sad fact that this may be the best a lifer can hope for at Fluvanna.

REFERENCES

Aday, R. H. (2003). *Aging prisoners*. New York: Praeger.

Corley, J. (2008). Life in four parts: A memoir. In S. Nagelsen (Ed.), *Exiled voices: Portals of discovery—Stories, poems, and drama by imprisoned writers* (pp. 41–60). Henniker, NH: New England College Press.

Hassine, V. (2011). *Life without parole: Living in prison today* (5th ed.). Robert Johnson & Sonia Tabriz (Eds.). New York: Oxford University Press.

Johnson, R. (2002). *Hard time: Understanding and reforming the prison* (3rd ed.). Belmont, CA: Wadsworth.

Johnson, R., & McGunigall-Smith, S. (2008). Life without parole, America's other death penalty: Notes on life under sentence of death by incarceration. *The Prison Journal, 88*(2), 328–346.

Pollock, J. (2004). *Prisons and prison life: Costs and consequences*. New York: Oxford University Press.

CHAPTER 10

Other Voices, Other Venues:
Self-Portraits by Women in Prison

The following collection of essays offers other voices from other perspectives and often other penal settings, including other state prisons and a federal prison. Each of these women (here, as elsewhere, the names are pseudonyms) wrote an essay for George to help her convey a fuller picture of life in prison and the promises and pitfalls of incarceration. Each essay offers insights in areas touched on by George in the main text: religion and spirituality offering journeys of redemption; programs that connect women and loved ones, transcending prison walls; self-proclaimed "outsiders" in the prison world who learn and grow from their unlikely (and often unliked) neighbors, almost in spite of themselves; and finally, the remarkable promise of rehabilitation programs when treatment is given a chance to flower in the prison, promoting autonomy and self-reliance. (For the male counterpart of these entries, see Hassine, 2009; Paluch, 2004.) —Robert Johnson

SIDETRACKED, THEN SAVED: TWO JOURNEYS—
LEAUDREY AND NADIA

LeAudrey
I first noticed LeAudrey because of her smile—I never saw her without it. And it wasn't the surface smile that most of us paste on for the world. Her smile actually reached her eyes. LeAudrey worked in the intake area of my building, and we would often catch each other's eye, then grin and nod through the unit's glass windows as she was busily working in the bubble area. The unspoken rule not to acknowledge someone you don't know simply didn't seem to apply to her. We became friends when she was eventually moved into our housing unit a few months after she began working in the building.

LeAudrey is a stunning woman, gentle and generous. She used to have her own small business selling beauty products, so she is the resident expert on beauty advice. She is always there to give a haircut or help someone primp for a special visit. She came to Fluvanna 3 years ago. Like a lot of us, she came in behind a man.

He was not a very savory guy, and trying to please him, LeAudrey participated in some illegal sexual activities. She was so sickened and shamed by what she was doing that she actually turned herself in to the police in an effort to detach from her husband and force him to take responsibility for his crimes. Confession and repentance was, in her mind, the only way to achieve freedom. —Erin George

My name is LeAudrey. I am a Christian, African-American, mother, daughter, sister, aunt, friend, hairstylist, recovering addict (10 years), and inmate, and in that order. I really don't know where to start but I guess I could start with the relationship that led me here. I was in love and a very needy person, and I did anything for him including choosing him over my own children. I didn't listen to that internal buzzing that said "Run like hell." I felt it was nothing and that things would work out in the end. As things got worse, controlling, manipulating, perverted acts took place. I couldn't do it anymore. My heart was torn, my soul was empty, and my relationship with God on hold. I had left and never thought about turning back, wanted to so bad, but knew it would be a lot worse than I could imagine. This relationship left me so full of anger and hate, so lonely, sad, confused, irritated, very, very empty. I couldn't go on thinking that people were going to be OK while this man roamed around thinking this was his world and making people feel like I felt and I also had to face my responsibility for my actions and my part in this madness and I understood that it was serious and I could be locked up. I asked God to help me find a way through this and if it was the right thing to do. I got my answer and soon I was on my personal journey of life lessons with a whole lot of grace.

I was convicted on sexual crimes that my husband encouraged me to participate in and I received 22 years and they suspended all but 72 months. I started my time July 2005. I thought that I would die, but I didn't. God's grace and mercy saw me through. Jail wasn't what I thought it was, it was worse. That's when I understood that I was different from everyone else. Not better, please understand that. Just different from a lot of the ladies who either were on drugs or stole a lot of money for drugs, and I had been clean for at least 8 years at that time and there was no way I was turning back, but I didn't know that I was still an addict because I just gave up one addiction to turn to another (men). I had out-of-body experiences. I would look around at everyone and I tried to understand all they were going through and I saw it all-hurt, pain, sadness, brokenness, abandonment, anger, confusion, the same feelings I went through before I came to prison, and now I am seeing it in here and I understand, not making up any excuses for our crimes, but I understood. I finally made my journey to prison and it wasn't much different from jail, just bigger and a lot of hurt and wounded women, many on their way to healing, some not at all. I got here March 2006. I miss my kids dearly and my family and friends, but I now understand when I became saved that my relationship with God would not be the same. I have been tested and tried, not realizing that with each test that I was given from God was another life lesson. I trust myself to my creator. A couple of times I failed badly, but others I made it through.

I have been judged in here by my smile and my kindness, but I was taught that my smile could take me places. But I never thought that this prison would be one of my stops. I have friends here, I think I could call them that, though before they didn't care too much for me. I couldn't understand why at first, but when I prayed about it God revealed to me that it was something they wanted from me that was internal and they just didn't know how to go about asking how I got it. It was either despise me or compliment me and they took the despise road. It seemed to be easier for them. I found that for me if I wanted to know some things to ask and not be jealous over it and that way I could learn to do it. But here people aren't taught to ask. They were brought up pretty rough and it showed on a lot of folks, some of it was hard to see. My journey has me facing a lot. I have only 2 years to go and I am still holding on to the fact that I will be home soon. Some of the most wonderful people I have met in here won't be going home and that makes me sad. Once again, a journey in life. I came to understand that God brings us to it, but we choose how we get through it.

Nadia

Nadia and I have been through most of the ups and downs of prison together. I got to know her a week after she moved into my wing. I was strolling past a table where a friend of mine, Patrice, sat. In front of her was a bowl of cheddar snack mix, a weakness of mine. Because Patrice and I had it like that (as they say in here), I dipped in without asking and snagged a handful. 'Trice just sat there smiling until I gulped down the whole handful, then gleefully informed me that it wasn't her snack mix after all. In fact, it belonged to the new chick in the wing, Nadia.

Well, shit. All I knew about Nadia was that she was a lifer. Because I was only a few months into my bid, I still had an outsider's view of what a lifer probably was like. Sheesh, was the girl going to pound me or something?

I stood at the table, gritting on the cackling Patrice, until Nadia strolled up, smiling pleasantly. "I'm sorry," I said to her, "but I ate some of your snack mix. I thought," pausing here for a glare at Patrice, "that it was hers. I can give you some back when we get to commissary. That cool?"

Nadia smiled. "Don't worry about it," she said. "Want some more?"

That was the beginning of my longest, most treasured prison relationship. I am closer to Nadia than anyone else inside. Part of that is because she is so much like me, but a bigger part is that she is simply special. We've never had any romantic interest in each other; our friendship is far more satisfying than that ever could be. But she is the only inmate that has ever inspired me to write poetry.

Although Nadia has talked with me often about what brought her to Fluvanna, I respect her wishes not to discuss those facts with anyone else. All I can add is that, despite what happened when she was much younger, she is an inspiration to me now for the spiritual and emotional growth that she has shown during our years of friendship. No one has worked harder on rebuilding her life than she. —Erin George

I was about 17 years old when I was locked up. At that point I hadn't completed high school. I came from a typical middle-class family, so my parents and I assumed that I was going to go to college. Everybody in our family did, so not going wasn't even an option. At the time my passions were architecture and interior design. Then I got sidetracked.

After my crime, I was held in detention until I was old enough to be sent to Goochland Correctional Center for Women at age 18. I was transferred to Fluvanna when that prison opened in 1998.

After I was arrested I was totally depressed, suicidal even, which lasted a few years, until I turned 19 or 20. I was never in denial about what had happened. If anything, I tortured myself about what had happened. I had no real set goals, motives, or hope for several years. I was just adapting to my environment. I didn't have any real hope for the future until just a few years ago.

I survived in prison for about 10 years until I got involved in a really destructive relationship because of loneliness and hopelessness. This woman and I were together off and on for almost 3 years when I finally realized that there clearly was emotional dysfunction that I was trying to use this relationship to cover up. Instead, it was just bringing all my problems into focus.

The breaking point was when I physically struck out in anger at someone I cared about, a friend who I thought was interfering in my dysfunctional relationship. When that happened it became painfully clear that something was wrong with me and that I needed help, because for the first time since coming to prison I had lost control of myself. I'm in here for murder. I knew that I was never going to do that again, but there were serious behavioral issues that the prison system wasn't helping me address. Whatever had caused the violence that brought me here was still unresolved, and assaulting my friend like that forced me to acknowledge it.

After the moment that I hit her, I ran to my room, slammed the door shut, and sobbed because there was no way I could deny the reality that something was really wrong. This was the first time that I prayed to God to really fix my brokenness, not just meet my selfish needs. And He came through for me. I met a lay chaplain and enrolled in the baptism class. Everything just happened-it was totally God-orchestrated. It happened so quickly that I didn't realize that God was behind it all until I looked backward and was amazed. I'd been in many dilemmas where He'd fixed external things for me, but in answering this prayer He began to heal the core brokenness of my being and my past. I believe that all this was because it was the first time that I took responsibility for my own shortcomings and let Him in.

The first few years after I began my self-renovation were extremely painful and difficult-having to confess, examine, take responsibility for my crap. It was slow going, but with each year I gained momentum and learning skills that give me a very real hope for the future for the first time. I have a parole date, so I'm preparing for that future. I'm doing everything within my power to make that future a reality, like focusing on my education.

During my first decade in prison I had taken a few college courses because they were free, back then we still could get Pell grants. I knew that my parents would have wanted me to, but it was only done half-heartedly. I tried my best with what I had, but my emotional capacities didn't allow me to properly take advantage of the opportunity. Now I plan on having my associate's degree by the end of this year, and actually I have so many credits I am close to qualifying for a bachelor's degree. And I still belong to a group to help me with my spiritual and emotional growth, as well as continuing to meet with my lay chaplain regularly.

I don't see any specifics in my future, but I know that I can't wait to be a part of a big church family. . . . I never had that growing up. Job-wise, I know that my degree is what circumstances permitted me to get, but God will lead me where I need to go-maybe working as an administrator in a church. I've conquered the violence inside of me, but the process of recovery never ends. All of us on this journey have our sins, and it doesn't just end when you conquer one. It never ends for the rest of your life. But with the momentum of growth I look forward to each challenge, each opportunity to become better.

CONNECTIONS: KEEPING FAMILY INTACT, AGAINST ALL ODDS

Naomi

I got to know Naomi when I moved into a special housing unit Fluvanna used to have. Although it is now disbanded, there used to be a wing dedicated entirely to long-termers. Everyone in the wing had to be serving at least 15 years, and most sentences were much longer than that. There were no special privileges per se, but the indefinable perk of living amidst fellow lifers eased life considerably. Naomi is one of the women I grew closest to as we shared experiences through the MILK program. She has also become a real part of my family—I think my parents write to her as often as they do me.

Despite our closeness, I don't know many details of her crime. All she ever says is that someone lost her life and that she will never be able correct that wrong. She has exceedingly high moral standards and a strong enough personality to make her opinions known, so she has become a welcome influence on the women in MILK, encouraging them to stay committed to the high standards of that organization. She is another one of those women who seem permanently chained by the "serious nature of the crime" she committed. Nothing she does seems to ever be enough.
—Erin George

When I became incarcerated in 1987, my five children's ages ranged from 3 to 12. I saw them often at the jail, but it was 7 hours to the prison at Goochland, so after being transferred there my visits were usually when the prison held family day once a year. (*Editor's Note*: FCCW does not have a family day.)

In 1990 I became a member of a group called MILK—Mothers Inside Loving Kids. At that time we were blessed with four all-day visits a year. Thus began our time in prison. My children became young adults that I actually felt I had a hand in rearing. Our visits were times to talk and share and my means to teach the values I thought to be so important. Year after year passed by—I was very grateful for the MILK program but didn't realize the importance or impact until several years later.

The first weekend in December 1992, my mom and sister brought my kids to an MILK visit. We had a wonderful day-just enjoying being together. They usually came back for a regular visit on Sunday then drove home, but this weekend they left right after the MILK visit on Saturday. After MILK visits it always took me about a week to settle back into prison life-to put the heart longing back in the locked place and refocus on my daily life. On Tuesday I went to work at the mundane, mindless job of keying data into a machine. The man who delivered our work came in and asked if I knew anyone in the mine explosion. I didn't realize that there had been an explosion in a mine, and after a few frantic questions I went in to call home to learn that my youngest brother was trapped in a coal mine, fate unknown. Mom had called the prison the day before, but no one told me.

The story was big news. On Wednesday night they realized that all eight men had died, but because of methane gas they could not get to them. My counselor was supposed to get the paperwork ready for permission to go to the funeral whenever the arrangements were made. On Thursday he informed me he was leaving for the weekend. It wasn't until Friday that they were able to reach the bodies and bring them out for identification on Saturday morning. At the MILK visit on Saturday I spoke with the warden, who had the counselor who was running the MILK visit go to the counselor's office, retrieve the paperwork, and have everything approved pending the date of the funeral. The warden's compassion and efficiency made it possible for me to attend my brother's funeral. The two officers that took me couldn't have been better chosen. They were the epitome of kindness and allowed me to grieve. At the funeral they let me grieve with my family and friends and both C.O.s were treated as friends by the community. The distance required that we spend the night, me in the local jail, they in a motel. The trip back was time for me to cry in safety. I haven't recovered from the death of my brother. I still wait for the message that was never given and subconsciously anticipate the next message.

At 15 my oldest daughter became pregnant. She had a son and named him after my brother who had been killed. I saw him from a few weeks after birth and then every 3 months. I was "Grandma Naomi." I really enjoyed my time with him and bemoaned to myself that he really didn't know me. When he was a little over 2, we had our first visit outside in the ball field. The families walked down from the admin building and down the handicap access ramp to the field. He spotted me through the fence coming down the road and ran down the ramp yelling "Grandma Naomi, Grandma Naomi!" It made me realize that because of MILK he actually did know who I was. Eighteen years and six additional grandchildren later, MILK continues to maintain our family's quality time together.

Without MILK, I'm not sure how much of a part I would have played in their lives because of distance. Here at this prison we have six visits a year and are affiliated with the Girl Scout program. When my family isn't here I'm able to be a part of the visits with all the other kids and share what I've learned over the years. MILK helps us break the cycle with our kids and I am deeply grateful.

In 1998, after 11 years of incarceration in a place that looked more like an old college than a prison, I was transferred to Fluvanna on the whim of some staffer. My co-worker had had an incident with a staff member's false accusation of passport theft (why would you have your passport at prison?) and our employer requesting to downtown [the Department of Correction's main office] that we be held there for our job, and off we went. Everyone was required to have a physical before being shipped, which was the clue you were going. I wasn't ever called for a physical, so I knew I was safe. Not!

We were packed up at 10:30 p.m., given very small boxes for our belongings and limited lists of items allowed to be taken. Everything else I'd been allowed to have over the years had to be thrown away or mailed home. Arrival at Fluvanna was soul-crushing. An empty, echoing concrete block building; stark, dirt-covered ground with more holes than mole heaven; no birds, no butterflies, no trees, no grass, not even a weed in sight. Nothing to lift my spirits. After a month of tears, nothing to do, nothing to read, just monotonous walking around the circle of the courtyard over and over, I heard the whisper, "Look up." I began looking upward each time I stepped outside to the most beautiful skies I have ever seen. As I began being filled with the beauty that was painted for me each morning, the loss and desolation of coming here began to recede. I would again survive and thrive.

In 1995, after 8 years, I was interviewed for parole for the first time. It was also the year the new governor abolished parole and brought in "truth in sentencing." Each year I was interviewed and denied parole for the serious nature of my offense-a factor that was taken into account when I was sentenced. Under the old system I would have been paroled in 1996 because I had behaved and proven myself to be rehabilitated by all of the classes I had taken and skills I had obtained. Thirteen years and more accomplishments than most inmates later, I continue to be denied parole for a factor I can never change. I watch the same people granted parole only to return within 6 months to a year, over and over again. Many have been in and out five and six times since I began in 1987. They are deemed nonviolent and so rehabilitation is not required.

When I was sentenced, my court-appointed lawyer explained to my brother that the judge sentenced me the way he did because he wanted me to spend 12 years in prison. When I earned the good time available it brought my first parole interview back to 8 years. As I received my first turndowns I tried to explain to my brother that it was politics. He insisted that the judge just wanted me to serve 12 years and then I would be released. Each year he was adamant that I would be released after the 12 years but I tried to help him understand the reality. When I received the turndown at 12 years he just knew that the next year would

bring release. The next year I received a denial of parole along with a 3-year deferral. He was devastated. He had believed absolutely in the justice and fairness of our
system and it had failed him. He has not yet recovered from the helplessness he felt.

Helplessness and hopelessness are the emotions that try to overwhelm those
of us still under a law that doesn't exist anymore. No one measures the justice and
fairness of our system and the cracks we've fallen through are wide and deep. Yet
we continue to try to teach our children to believe in justice and fairness and
second chances, because that's what our country was built on. Wasn't it?

OUTSIDERS LOOKING IN: LEARNING BY LIVING

Diandra

*Diandra lived in the cell next to mine when I first moved into general population.
Now, years later in the Honor Wing, we are only two cells apart. Lifers seem to end
up together, no matter what the administration does to prevent it.*

*Unlike Naomi, I know all of the details of Diandra's case. I've read the newspa-
per clippings and legal papers she's shared, and I have to say that she is one of the
few people in here that I actually believe when she claims she is innocent. Having
experienced the fervor of the Virginia Commonwealth myself, I am not surprised
by what she says her experiences were. Plus, she just doesn't seem the type. In all of
the years I've lived with her, I've never seen her anything but calm and pleasant
(and not calm and pleasant in that scary "I've been medicated but boy you better
hope they don't run out of my meds" way). She goes to work every day in the print
shop. She crochets. She goes to Catholic mass, dare I say it, religiously.*

*She also has something that I've never seen with anyone else in here. There is
an active, international movement to get her released. Specialists have prepared
reports and published them online detailing why it is very likely that she did not,
in fact, poison her husband as the state avers. There are newsletters, Web pages,
and letter-writing campaigns asking for her release. Diandra receives more mail
than anyone else inside—5 to 10 letters or cards each evening. Family, friends,
church . . . no one who knew her on the street believes that she is responsible for her
husband's death. If anyone has a chance of ever getting home again, I think that
she is the one. —Erin George*

I am a 50-year-old, educated, upper-middle-class woman who has been falsely
imprisoned for 6 years now, never expecting it to take this long for the nightmare to end. So my viewpoint is that of a temporarily displaced outsider.

Author Philip Margolin summed up my prison experience pretty well in *The
Attorney*. The lead character, an attorney who became incarcerated for only a
short time, said, "Being in jail is like being back in high school, in a class filled
with bullies, liars, and lunatics." One can easily imagine these people back in
high school, even though a few never finished. They were the underachievers who
liked to pick on those of us who excelled. It comes as no surprise that the matu-
rity level hasn't increased at all.

Think of going to prison as being dropped onto another planet, with rules and standards of behavior that are totally alien. To "fit in," one must forget most of what they learned about manners. Personally, I'm grateful to be secure enough that fitting in with these people is not an aspiration of mine.

Inmates are very clean people. Even if they have lived in roach-infested crack houses, here they scrub the walls of their cells several times a week. Those of us who don't engage in elaborate cleaning rituals are labeled as "dirty." Allowing any part of your body to pass over, or even near, another person's tray in the chow hall will elicit a barrage of words that you've probably not heard all at once before. Afterward, the owner of the "contaminated" tray will demand and receive a fresh tray of food. After all, something harmful, unseen to the naked eye, may have "fallen off" into the food. That's why they usually cover their plates with a paper napkin when leaving the table to get a drink.

The public rest rooms, which of course are all of them, are never to be used to have a bowel movement. Doing so is considered to be rude and will offend others. To point this out, the obviously well-bred inmates will loudly proclaim, "Somebody lit up the bathroom!" lest they themselves be accused of the offense.

Besides learning manners here in prison, I have also gained some insight into human behavior that I wouldn't have otherwise. A lot can be told about a person by how they relate to food. Here in prison, "pleasure foods" come from canteen. Sweets appear to be a substitute for drugs. Those with addictive personalities will go "bumming" for "anything sweet" when they run out. Most here lack the ability to budget their canteen to last until the next scheduled commissary day. Instead, they eat it all and spend the rest of the days borrowing. That total lack of the ability to practice self-deprivation is likely the same behavior that brought them to prison.

On a more positive note, I have met some kind, gifted, and intelligent people here, which has been a delightful surprise. A few, like me, are here by mistake. Others are victims of circumstances. The act that put them here was a single, isolated incident and not a pattern of behavior. Here in a maximum security prison, a high percentage were convicted of murder. However, unlike men, most are not violent. I quickly learned that in a place like this, the so-called "murderers" are the safest people with whom to associate. The ones you have to watch out for are the druggies and the career criminals.

I have also learned that it is possible for people to change. I have met women here who are guilty of horrific crimes, but are clearly not the same people they were 20 years ago. It is not the prison system that rehabilitated them, though. They managed to change despite the system.

Here in Virginia, parole was abolished in 1995, but those convicted before then are technically still eligible for parole. However, the parole board now is a joke. Women who will have been incarcerated for 20-plus years, done everything that could possibly have been expected of them, have recommendations from staff members, and in no way would pose a "threat to society" are denied parole year after year. Meanwhile, the repeat offenders, who haven't changed their ways and will most likely return, are the only ones granted parole. This is a situation about which the citizens of our state need to be made aware. Tax dollars are being wasted, keeping potentially productive members of society behind bars.

On a more personal note, I have learned a lot about myself over these past 6 years. A situation like this shows you who your true friends are, and they aren't necessarily those with whom you were closest before. Even the most independent of us are forced to depend on our outside support system. It's a humbling experience. Material things mean a lot less once you learn to live without them, and it takes a lot less to make you happy.

If it seems that the prisons are full of a lot of gifted artists and craft persons, it's because being incarcerated gives you the time to hone the talents you already possess. It's amazing what undiscovered skills we all have. In the outside world, I was too busy to draw or crochet, and will likely not take the time to do so again, but I hope not.

Now that I can see the light at the end of the tunnel, I can honestly say that, aside from the time apart from my daughter, I wouldn't trade what I have gained from the past 6 years. At one time, when I saw men that had been exonerated by DNA after spending 20 years or more of their lives behind bars who claimed they had no bitterness, I thought they were lying. Finally, I am at the point where I understand what they must have figured out along the way-that God has a purpose for us in every situation. There is a lesson learned from every ordeal and every person who crosses our path, good or bad. I've learned more in the past 6 years than in the previous 45, most of which wouldn't have been possible otherwise.

Now, can I go home?

GROWTH: PROGRAMS THAT WORK

Shelly

I got to know Shelly at Rappahannock Regional Jail. She's one of the women I played cards with every day, all day. We shared a love for the Redskins and an appreciation for a good joke. I was delighted to see her each time she has come to Fluvanna. She is a great person, but one who seems to struggle when facing the challenges of sobriety on the outside. There are many women in here who share that struggle, and I really don't know what the system can do to help them. The recidivism rate for drug users is far greater than that for violent offenders, so these are the people that we usually see using the "revolving door" here at FCCW. Most of Shelly's charges are, I believe, drug-related and nonviolent.

I was fascinated to hear her stories about her Fed time. Federal prison is like El Dorado to state prisoners. We don't fantasize about going home—a really great lock-up is what we dream of. And the tales about Fed time make it sound wonderful: steaks for dinner, real baths, wearing your own clothes. It gives me a heady feeling to even imagine it. —Erin George

I wasn't really worthy of the federal penal system, a peon compared to most of the women there. I was just there for some minor trafficking and drug convictions after serving state time for similar charges, but because this time they occurred on federal property, I ended up at Alderson Federal Prison Camp, known affectionately as "Camp Cupcake." The growth that took place there is what I am most grateful for.

Coming from the Washington area, I had known diversity my whole life, so I was able to mix among many cliques. My drug and alcohol abuse brought me around the lowest and my middle-class upbringing brought me around the highest. I really learned just how alike we can be.

Most of my time incarcerated there took place in the L.I.V.E.S. program (Ladies in Vigorous Everlasting Sobriety). It is a 9-month residential cognitive therapy behavior program. Not only can you make life changes, but you can leave prison up to 18 months early, making this program very attractive to many. When it is completed, there is a 1-year follow-up aftercare program.

L.I.V.E.S. is ranked among the top five programs in the United States for lowered recidivism rates. I have never been offered a program like this at the state level, and gratefully took advantage of this tool. When you are in this program, you are placed in residential housing units. I lived in cottage housing. The cottages available were old, full of asbestos, and soon to be shut down. They consisted of three stories that included dayrooms and hair rooms, and they were equipped with microwaves, TVs, and vending machines. I was delighted to find the rumors true about bathtubs. In a huge, desert-sized room sat a large claw tub, along with a side table and window. After using the available Comet cleaner, brush, and sponge, I plopped my butt in a bubble-filled bathtub, along with a magazine and mountain view. I can't say that there weren't rare moments of true relaxation there.

Unlike at some state facilities, a job is required. There are many areas of interest. You literally hit the pavement and seek employment. After being confined in county jails and arriving in the spring, I took a landscaping job and got to mowing and mowing . . . the job paid $5.25 per month (yes, you read that right). The federal system, contrary to popular belief, doesn't pay you and you do serve 85% of your sentence, as you do in Virginia state prisons. I was able to move up, eventually, and trained and was employed as a 411 directory assistance operator. I made around $120.00 a month with room to grow.

I had mixed feelings about this job, as it served me well and I realized how it could also serve a small community. The company I worked for, Excel, is Canadian and it uses several federal prisons, both for males and females, to obtain employees. What a deal. Reliable, on-site employees working below minimum wage and no benefit package needed: "Oh, Canada. . . ." This might not benefit Alderson, but it does do its part for the community.

Alderson helps the community in many forms, the biggest being the Alderson Federal Fire Department, which includes training prisoners to be fire women and drive a fire truck. They respond to both the prison and the community when needed. It was fun to watch them train and a hoot to follow their continual reign in the local county rodeos.

The Yarn Project aids with locally needed hats and scarves distributed by the inmates, as well as lap blankets for the elderly from the Loom Project. Everyone crochets at Alderson. Yarn is available at the commissary. This was brought to national attention by Martha Stewart's famous poncho. She left on a Friday, and I came the following Wednesday. I just missed her.

Martha isn't Alderson's only interesting character. I met activists who protested with Martin Sheen, the rich and elite, judges, madams, embezzlers, tax evaders, money launderers, drug traffickers. Quite a nice bunch. I found most to be college graduates, polite and intelligent. I give credit to the federal system: With all of those brains incarcerated, they utilize the talents available. I gained much from the electives they taught, from entrepreneurship and credit repair to Women in U.S. History, to name a few. The state system makes no effort to use what they have outside of classroom tutors. They rely on teachers from the community, many of whom have questionable work ethics. Similarly, vocations are offered by both federal and state, but because the federal system gives you more electives and choices, it prepares you more for a community setting.

Alderson, West Virginia, and Troy, Virginia, are both rural and rely on locals to staff the prison, which is not always the best choice. The beauty of Alderson is undeniable: the foliage, mountain views, trees, and Green River are peaceful. A coal train runs around the perimeter, a harsh contrast and constant reminder that these areas are being stripped of their natural resources. The federal administrators, including the warden, medical services, case managers, counselors, and so on, are welcoming and attentive at a weekly "Open House." Their availability is a relief. The staff, outside of officers, at the state level are usually unseen, evasive, and, for the most part, unhelpful. Both systems do evaluate inmates yearly, but in quite different ways. Federally you are scheduled for a "sit-down" with your counselor, case manager, and unit housing manager. Your gains, strengths, and goals are discussed, as well as any infractions or behavior problems. The state sends you a form to be filled out, and it could be months until you hear what they feel is best for you.

Along with academic programs, there are many other programs available federally, including seminars, workshops, religious programs, crafts, book clubs, and so on, providing outlets for rehabilitation and self-expression, thus forming good habits and helping us learn to grow from within and utilize a community. The oppression in state prisons builds negative emotions, a feeling of uselessness and inadequateness. Without the reality of daily decision making, you become dormant in this vital life skill.

At state, camp-level work is the primary object, with little concrete therapy for cognitive skills, To establish life skills inside, a prison must utilize a form of decision making, provide outlets for education, interaction with others, chances to give back, and opportunities for self-expression to mimic life on the "outside." Developing these vital skills will provide the tools needed to become a productive citizen.

I can say being an inmate of both systems that the state must start to think outside the box if recidivism rates are going to drop. I have truly grown physically, mentally, and spiritually due to the federal prison system. Punishment is a removal of loved ones, loss of future, financial loss, future plans, basically a disrupted life. I believe the state could learn from the federal system to make incarceration pay off.

REFERENCES

Hassine, V. (2009). *Life without parole: Living in prison today* (4th ed.). New York: Oxford University Press.

Paluch, J. A., Jr. (2004). *A life for a life—Life imprisonment: America's other death penalty.* New York: Oxford University Press.

CHAPTER 11

Looking Out and Looking Back: Recidivism and Religion; Remorse and Redemption

A discouraging number of women (and men) recidivate and return to prison in relatively short order. Three years out, fully two out of every three released prisoners are arrested for a new crime (Cooper, Durose, & Snyder, 2014). The reasons are many, including defects in character, limited social circumstances, disabling addictions, and, in some states, notably California, rigid and repressive parole policies (Johnson, 2002; O'Brien, 2001; Pollock, 2004; Travis & Visher, 2006). George, normally an accepting person, is unforgiving when it comes to recidivists. They blow the one chance she'd give her life to have, and many of them act as if it is no big deal—a psychological defense, surely, but one George sees as an insult to her hopes and aspirations. Everyone is affected by prison, altered and often hardened in one way or another (Haney, 2006; Toch, 1992). As a permanent resident of prison, George has become hardened to the failings of women who get out but can't stay out. She knows this is a blind spot, but we don't send people to prison for life to open their eyes and hearts to the plight of others. We bury them alive, then watch as they struggle to keep hope alive. It might be too much to ask lifers like Erin George to show empathy for those who squander the one thing the lifer will never know—freedom from prison.

George's future is both complex and simple: complex because she has evolved during her years in confinement, simple because the end point for a prisoner serving life without parole is stark and unyielding. George has adapted to a world at first quite alien to her. She has become religious, something unthinkable before her incarceration. She has found common ground with many, if not most, of her fellow prisoners. Again, this is an outcome that would have been hard to imagine in her prior life. She has transcended media stereotypes of female prisoners as "lower-class drug users and whores" and has found common ground with others on issues large (shared faith; shared fates) and small (shared antipathy to prison food or intrusive procedures). In prison, George found a community of lifers who help her through the daily grind and are there for her when she needs emotional support. (For the male counterpart of the lifer prison community, see Hassine, 2011; Paluch, 2004.)

Prisoners who comprise the little community of long-termers, mostly lifers, who make up much of George's prison world need each other more than ever as the character of prison life in America moves in a more rigid, punitive direction (Bozelko, 2013; Johnson, 2008). Like many women's prisons these days, Fluvanna is becoming more repressive, restricting the daily liberties of inmates and even officers as well (Zaitzow, 2004). Parsons (2007, p. 232), describing the hardening of routines in Connecticut's York Prison for Women, observed, "It doesn't have to be like this. It didn't used to be." Women in Fluvanna and many other institutions now walk in lines, as if they were on military parade. Searches are more invasive, leaving some women in "dry cells" (without toilets or running water) to soil themselves or their cells while they wait in vain for an officer to let them out to relieve and wash themselves. Less dramatically, but perhaps more tellingly, basic resources for education, even simple literacy programs, are in short supply. With tight budgets, staff turnover means empty slots. Teachers work under harder conditions, as do officers. Lockdowns become more common, the prison more barren—more like a warehouse—every day.

It is telling that for the last several years, the women at Fluvanna are called "offenders" (who presumably "offend" others by their very existence), rather than "inmates" (who simply reside in prison). For George and her fellow captives, the term offender is one more dehumanizing insult freighted with moral condemnation. Did anyone in authority consider this or care to consider the meaning of a change in labels for the women? One imagines not, and it is certainly true that any such consideration was not made known to the women who must live with the new appellation. More telling, perhaps, is the fact that the women acquiesce in the larger dehumanization that is part and parcel of their confinement, seeing people from the free world as "real people" and themselves as something less, perhaps something unreal, certainly something less fully human than their counterparts in the "real world."

Prison life is sterile and stultifying, and it is not surprising that George wonders what will become of her as she ages in the coming years. Will she evolve into a disoriented, quirky character, someone maimed socially by the prison world, seen by others as odd, somehow, "not quite right"? Or as a strong, colorful character, a bossy "strong-willed grandmother" to the younger convicts who come and go as she lingers on, only to share adjoining beds in the geriatric ward with a feisty fellow lifer? One hopes that Erin George will stay who she is, a vibrant, verbal, insightful, and funny woman who has adapted to adversity with more panache than she could have ever imagined. And one hopes she will preserve hope, sustaining the belief, however improbable, that one day the keys will turn for her, opening the prison door and allowing her back into the world from which she has been banished. —Robert Johnson

I was recently at the library, scanning the shelves for some thick books to last me through the shakedown that inmate.com, the prison rumor mill, says will be going down next week, when I felt a tap on my shoulder. When I turned, there was a small, chubby woman in Smurf blue standing beside me, smiling as if she were a dear friend. She looked vaguely familiar, but I had no idea who she was. Because she was in intake scrubs but obviously knew me, I deduced that she was yet another one of the inmates who are doing the "life sentence on the install-ment plan."

"Erin! How are you?" she asked.

"OK," I answered tersely. The people who come back to prison after having the chance to go home get very little sympathy from me. It might be harsh, but as someone who would do anything to go home again, I find these people hard to stomach. Because I can't say what I want to (namely, "Why can't you people crawl out of your crack pipes long enough to see that you've been given a chance that I can never hope to have? What the hell is wrong with you?"), distant civility is the best I can hope for. They, on the other hand, are often chatty, reconnecting instantly with that knack that so many recidivists have. In many cases, they are just picking up again where they have left off 2, 3, or 4 times before, and because no relationship is of any more value to them than what they can get out of it, it's easy for them to act as if they hadn't spent the last 6 months outside, squandering their chances.

"Well, I'm not doing so great. I'm back here again, as you can see." She offered a rueful chuckle at the silliness of ending up in such a pickle. Gosh, what a scamp!

I sighed. "What're you here for?"

Another insipid giggle. "I assaulted a cop. Well, I chased him with my car, really." I stared at her. Then she got defensive. "But it wasn't my fault! I was just a little messed up when I did it. The Commonwealth Attorney made a bigger thing of it than he should have."

"How long?" I asked.

The woman looked pissed off and grief-stricken simultaneously. "The damn judge gave me 6 years. With another 60 hanging over my head if I screw up. Can you believe that shit?" Maybe she has forgotten (if she ever knew) that my own sentence is 100 times that. Not that remembering would have stopped her. For women like this, the world stops at the end of their own noses.

"Jesus Christ," I mutter and begin to walk away as she is still talking.

"It was great to see you again, Erin!" she said as I began to move to the oppo-site end of the library. "Let's try to get in a class together or something, OK? I'd love to hang out with you again...."

I didn't bother to answer and left the library without glancing once at her ID. I still have no idea what her name is.

It's hard not to get angry at the people who come back to Fluvanna again and again, with no more compunction than if they were returning to summer camp. Three women from my own jail have come back to FCCW just this week. One of them was sitting across from me and my friend Dizzy in the chow hall the other day. After effusive, unreturned greetings to me, the woman turned to the woman sitting next her and began bitching about the food. This was actually a pretty decent meal by prison standards, a vegetable soup that was more than just water, cabbage, and potatoes, and Dizzy and I were genuinely enjoying it. But listening to this woman go on and on about how dreadful it looked, smelled, and tasted, I lost my appetite. Diz and I glanced at each other and simultaneously stood up. Enough was enough. As Dizzy shoved her tray through the dish window, she said "If she doesn't like the food, why the hell does she keep coming to the same damn restaurant?"

That's a question that I will never have the answer to. Really, I don't care enough about these women to invest the effort to understand. I don't have the emotional resources to explore the psyches of people who aren't introspective enough to realize that they are destroying their own lives, and probably the lives of their families as well. They are an affront to me and to anyone else who will never have the opportunity to go home again, no matter how well they behave in prison. I don't have access to the statistics, but I have seen enough to realize that the people who keep on coming back are the only ones who get parole. It's frustrating to see them walking past our wing from intake every Tuesday and Thursday, peering in through the glass entrance for a familiar face and waving frantically when they find one. We don't wave back. Instead, we sit at our table and watch them as one of us (usually Sadie or Dizzy) will say "crack, crack, OxyContin, meth, crack, meth, meth," attaching the probable crime that brought each bedraggled, deloused newcomer to prison. Sadie and Dizzy have been down long enough to have an uncannily accurate skill in this. Just one look and they can usually peg someone's crime immediately.

"Frequent fliers" (as we call the women who keep coming back again and again) also have the happy talent for saying just the right things to irritate lifers.

A perpetual favorite is the greeting of most new returnees: "Wow! When did you get back?" Because it would be impolite to say, "You waste of oxygen, I've never left," the best response to an idiotic remark like this is silence. It's especially delightful when the same returnee uses that same opener on their multiple consecutive sojourns at Fluvanna. They really never learn. Maybe when some provoked lifer wallops them they will get the hint.

Even more insulting are the ones who try to lay the groundwork for a scam as soon as they see you. "Hi, Erin! It is so great to see you!" she might effuse, softening me up for the pitch. "Man, did you get my letters? You know how screwed up the mailroom is here. They're useless. . . ." she'll trail off to silence as I stare at her. Then she'll try another tack. "I meant to write, at least. It just got real busy out there. I wanted to send you money, too, but I never had the chance." Under no circumstances will I respond verbally, and at this point even eye contact is risky. I won't do anything to encourage the impending request for food, stamps, picture tickets, personals that is inevitable.

I once even had a letter three-wayed to me from RRJ, written by a woman I had done time with there. Annie wrote to tell me that she had been on the run from the police for over a year, but that they had finally caught up with her and she was on her way back to Fluvanna. It was several pages of nothing, then a closing hope that she and I would be able to "hook up when she got back to Ol' Fluflu" and maybe I could help her out a little because her old man was going to be locked up, too. I admired her audacity, but mostly I was angry that she had put me at risk by sending me something from the jail. I threw her letter out as soon as I got it and never bothered to write back, but if the mailroom monitors had read that particular letter I would probably have spent a very uncomfortable afternoon in the investigator's office.

I do try to muster up compassion sometimes for the ones who come back. Intellectually, I know that drug addiction is a disease. And I want to be a loving person. But my own situation taints any sympathy that I might feel. I am distressingly human, and I'm afraid that seeing so many former inmates reject such a rarity as a second chance has left me a poor advocate for compassion. Maybe someday I'll get there, but I doubt it.

RELIGION

Many people on the outside speak mockingly of those who "find religion" in prison. There is the prevailing opinion that faith among the incarcerated is only a pose by those working a scam, crafty cons faking it for a parole board. I'm sure that happened a lot in the past. It probably still does for some of those who are eligible for parole. But for many of us serving life without the hope of going home, our faith is a sustaining, vital aspect of our being, a roadmap to forgiveness and calm that everyone deserves and needs. Chaos and violence are as prevalent as oxygen in prison, and lifers must make the choice to embrace that lifestyle or deliberately step away.

Most lifers eventually come to the conclusion that messing up requires more energy than one can easily muster up in prison. Man, it's sure hard work to "delay and hinder" long enough to be able to holler at your boo across the yard when she goes to her Cosmo appointment or to steal a uniform so that you can sneak into your baby's building for a tryst. I would rather lie in the bed, eat cheese curls, and read a decent book.

I remember that when I was still in the jail, trying desperately to cope with the baffling fact of my being behind bars, I would jokingly assure my parents that I wasn't going to "find God" in lockup. Humor had been the tool I had always used to survive, and I clung to it desperately in those initial rocky months. After I was first convicted, I didn't consider religion an option. What good would some myth of an omnipotent deity do for me? My desperate prayers during my trial certainly hadn't helped. I say "prayers," but in retrospect I realize that I was bargaining with God, and as a backup plan at that. I had been assured by my lawyer that based on the flimsiness of my case I would never be convicted, but just to be on the safe side, I figured that a little insurance would be in order. So here was the deal: if God let the truth come out (and wasn't this whole "Christian" thing about truth? I vaguely thought so) and I went home, I would start going to church. There was no humility in my prayers, no real sincerity (other than my patently sincere desire to be acquitted), but words were what I was best at. I didn't think that there had to be any substance behind them. Not surprisingly, my prayers were not answered in the way I would have hoped.

But after coming to Fluvanna I was forced to deal with the realities of my situation. Humor wasn't doing it for me. So many things were missing from my life, I didn't know how to begin constructing a new one. I had made the choice at the jail to maintain an existence I could be proud of, but beyond that vague goal I was flailing around, trying desperately to maintain while trapped in an ethical quagmire. Religion was not a natural refuge for me. I had been raised in a decidedly nonspiritual household. The closest we came to a religious life was a Christmas tree in December and a basket full of candy in the spring. Religion, I thought, was for people who were being suckered by preachers and money-grubbing televangelists or who were right-wing manipulators using the faith of the gullible to promote their own political agenda. I relied on my mind and will to direct my life. Sure, the basics of the Bible were morally correct—who wouldn't agree that stealing and murder were wrong? But the rest of the story was not something I was willing to accept.

In the weeks after moving into Fluvanna's general population, my sense of aimlessness grew. There was a path that I needed to follow, but I couldn't seem to find it. As I grew accustomed to the furor of the dayroom and the volatile personalities of its inhabitants, I noticed a woman named Carmen who always seemed to be an oasis of calm in all of the clamor. She would sit quietly at one of the tables, crocheting rapidly although her hands were malformed from what I later learned was rheumatoid arthritis. I was strongly attracted to her air of peace, and after a month or so, I got up the nerve to start talking to her (I had quickly learned that broaching conversations in prison is risky. Someone can be docile one moment, then vilely obscene at the most innocuous comment). We had said hello a few times in passing, but never anything beyond that.

"Hi there. I'm Erin. That's a beautiful blanket that you're making," I said, admiring the heather gray afghan that covered the table. Carmen smiled back. "Thanks. I'm going to send it to my son," she said. "Do you crochet?"

"No, I never had the chance to learn," I answered. "Look, can I ask you something?"

"Sure."

"I heard that you will make things for people sometimes. I'll pay you if you would be willing to make an afghan for my parents. I want to send them a present."

"I'll make you a deal," she said. "Rather than do it for you, how about I teach you to crochet so you can do it yourself? It would probably mean a lot more to them that way." After a pause she added, "You don't have to pay me for it. I'd be happy to do it."

I was surprised by her offer. Kind gestures were rare in my prison experience. I had assumed that I would have to pay for anything I got. I gladly accepted her offer, and Carmen quickly taught me the basic stitches, as well as the special stitches for the afghan pattern I had selected for Mom and Dad. She spent hours each day patiently sitting with me as I ripped out row after imperfectly stitched row, until I had a gorgeous cream-colored blanket to send home.

We never talked about religion as we worked, but after spending so much time with her, I had to ask how she stayed so steady in here, why she always seemed content amidst the constantly complaining women around her.

"Why, honey, what do I have to worry about? Things are taken care of for me," she answered. "I know what I need to do with my life. Sugar, just read your Bible. There's a lot of good wisdom in there."

"Oh, I don't believe in that stuff," I said.

"Well, if you ever want to talk about this some more, I am always here," she said.

I was shocked. Where was the hard sell? Why wasn't she asking if I were "saved" or if I had "accepted the Lord Jesus into my life"? These were the tactics of the jailhouse preachers I had encountered, scattering exhortations to "come to the Lord" between arguments with their girlfriends and sassing the officers. Carmen wasn't anything like that. She seemed actually genuine.

Carmen and I began to have conversations about faith and God, I arguing for the atheistic point of view, she mildly but firmly expressing her own beliefs.

Through our talks I grew interested enough to join the In-depth Bible Study class. I wasn't sure what I believed, but certainly discussing the issues would be helpful. And I would rather do it in an intellectual environment—I wasn't interested in going to church, a major meeting place for the girlfriends. I might not have been religious, but I had enough respect to know that you shouldn't make out with your girlfriend during a sermon.

Through the class I met T.J., a fiercely intelligent, tenacious teacher. T.J. would seek me out in the library or on the boulevard to talk. Not to pound me with his religion, but to give me the answer to a question he had researched for me or just to ask how I was. This was, I realized, what Christianity uncorrupted by man should be: loving, nonjudgmental, unwavering. I was only able to spend about a year with the benefit of T.J.'s company. He was hit by a car and killed not long after I began to get close to him. The entire compound grieved when he died. Murderers wept at the news of his passing, and not a parole board member in sight. The anguish was palpable.

Eventually I got to know the chaplain at FCCW. The chaplain, I discovered, is a liberal, compassionate woman who seems to know the name of every inmate at the prison. As we became friends, she fundamentally changed my ideas of what a Christian could be. The chaplain tries to offer classes and resources to all faiths, from Jewish to Muslim to Wiccan. She is not homophobic, unlike most of the religious teachers at the jail. (They were real gems, those holier-than-thou visitors to RRJ. I used to have lively debates with them about the historical accuracy of their lectures. It was very satisfying to show those smug women that I had a better understanding of the history of the church than they did.) But the chaplain at the prison was different from anyone I had met before. She was even a Democrat!

I had struggled with reconciling my growing faith with the entrenched belief I had that Christians had to be intolerant and unforgiving, adamant in forcing their beliefs on the country. How wonderful it was to learn that you could be

Christian and not be a right-wing fanatic. Once I took the time to read the Bible, absent the slant that different sects put on it, I found a powerful compass. Compassion, generosity, and love—now that was something I could believe in.

The more I read and spent time with other women who had strong faith, the clearer my choices became. Not easier: being a Christian, especially surrounded by the corruption of prison, is a challenge. Living a moral life inside makes you stand out, and drawing attention is not exactly desirable inside, especially when you are already labeled as a snotty white bitch. As I have found friends who share the same views, it has become less difficult. It's still a challenge, but one that encourages and inspires me.

Openness about my faith continues to be hard for me at times. I was baptized in the prison gym on Christmas Eve a few years ago but was afraid to tell my parents about it. Although the jokes about not finding God had long disappeared from our conversations, I had been reluctant to share my theological explorations with them, especially as I found myself more and more drawn to Christianity. I was afraid that they would think that I was weak-minded or judge me for my belief in something that is not tangible or provable. As I had often done in the past, I underestimated them. Mom and Dad were completely supportive when I did eventually confide in them, although a bit perplexed as well. But to be completely honest, my parents have been more puzzled by the inexplicable obsession with NASCAR I have also developed. When their eyes glaze over during our visits after a mere 15 minutes of my traditional homage to Jimmie Johnson and his canny crew chief, I only shrug and say, "Hey, prison changes a person."

I understand why people on the outside are so willing to assume that religion is a sham in here. It can be. And it is probably easier for the public to believe that there are no truly religious people behind bars. Genuine repentance and change are not concepts that are eagerly embraced by a society that is enamored of a punitive rather than rehabilitative system (despite the progressive whitewashing that the United States, as an ostensibly humane society, must reluctantly apply). But just as often, religion is a façade for people who claim it on the outside as well. False fronts are not the sole domain of the incarcerated. At least in prison the opportunities to act out the teachings of the Christian doctrine are more heartfelt and immediate. If outsiders could see the woman who has one pack of noodles in her box but who gives it smilingly to someone even hungrier than herself, they could not deny the verity of her belief. The real acts of love in here are often small. We are constrained by the rules that bind our every action. But they are true offerings, hidden from any authority that could report their piety to a parole board. These women give for no other reason than that it is the right and pleasing thing to do. A pair of used socks that are not yet in tatters is a blessing during a cold prison night, and a candy bar given to an otherwise forgotten sister on her birthday takes on enormous worth.

My faith gives me order in chaos, and purpose in aimlessness. It would be simple for me to rail against my incarceration, to dwell on all that I have lost. But because of my beliefs, I am sure that there is a reason for my being here. Most of the time I'm not sure what it is, but knowing that there is actually a purpose for my incarceration makes my time here bearable. And when I am feeling the most vulnerable to despair, I am inevitably reassured that I do serve some good here. Recently, one of the students I tutor, knowing that I love books, asked if I would be willing to find an Easter poem to send to her children. Rather than searching out an existing poem, I spent an hour with her, talking about her three little boys. I asked her what they enjoyed, what their smiles looked like, what memories about them she cherished. I didn't tell her why I was so interested in her family. I just promised to find her something to send to Micah, Dwayne, and Tyrell. The next day I gave her a poem I had written about the love her boys had for her and each other, including the details she had shared the day before. It wasn't a great poem—some of the rhymes were a stretch and it didn't scan very well. But Laurinda didn't care. Here was the perfect poem to reconnect with her family.

I am grateful for the opportunity to share the gifts I have been given. When I meet women who struggle to survive in here, I realize that I am truly blessed. Like Carmen, I have everything I need, plus a little bit more. Many people who are technically free aren't nearly as fortunate as I am.

FUTURE

A lot has changed in the years since my journey through the Virginia countryside to the Fluvanna Correctional Center for Women. Some of the more welcome changes have been within me. Before I was arrested, I had never known anyone who had spent time in lock-up. No one who would admit it, at least. I led a safe life, surrounded by people who loved me. My home was in a gated community on a golf course, my three children were polite and attractive, I drove the mandatory suburban SUV, and my family's debt was no greater than that of any of our neighbors. There were no hidden toxins in my world, either. James didn't beat me, and neither of us did drugs. We didn't even drink alcohol beyond a few social occasions every few months. It wasn't perfect, of course, but it also certainly wasn't the kind of lifestyle that normally would end up shattered in the way it has.

Because of this, when I began my sentence I considered myself an outsider, different from the women who usually end up behind bars. I had always been liberal, both politically and philosophically, and was a strong supporter of human rights. But the insidious stereotype of all inmates as lower-class drug users and brawlers had been inculcated within me by the media, so despite the enlightened teachings of my parents, a part of me assumed that the people I would find myself living among would be very different from those I had known on the street. I didn't think that I was superior to them, just that our experiences were so disparate that we would never be able to connect in any meaningful way.

And at first, the shallow stereotypes were all I saw—the junkies, the thieves, the thugs, the shoplifters. I was in survival mode, scrambling to make a niche for myself in an alien world. Gradually, though, I realized that the world wasn't so alien. Many of the women could just as easily have been standing behind me in line at Wal-Mart. Rose's daughter had gone to the same ballet class as my Francesca, I discovered, and Brianna volunteered at our local library. Most were worried about all the same things that I was. As I began to focus on our similarities rather than our differences, I was able to see them as individuals, not just the subjects of the liberal mouthings of the activists and politicians who have never experienced the worst our society has to offer. As I grew more accustomed to incarceration, I found that there almost always was something I had in common with the women I now lived with. If nothing else, we all hated the lousy jail chow. Connections as tenuous as these were often sufficient to establish detente between potential enemies, if not an even more friendly relationship. It didn't work with everyone. Some were too broken to let anyone in, especially a woman like me, who hadn't been through the hardships that they had. To them, I would always be "that stuck-up bitch."

It was a little different when I got to prison. In my jail, very few people had charges like mine. At RRJ, most of the women were serving brief sentences, in many cases not even hitting state ground at one of the DOC facilities. When I got to Fluvanna, though, I found a community of women doing time like mine. There is a certain level of refuge in that. No matter how much we annoy each other (and we irritate each other with great frequency), we also rely on each other for emotional support, intellectual stimulation, and the occasional hug (out of camera range, of course). These women were inordinately kind to me as I acclimated myself to spending the rest of my life here. They were not the hardened cons that, before my arrest, I would have expected to find in a maximum security prison. These were women who explained the nuances of prison etiquette to me when I first arrived and endured my frequent gaffes with grace and good humor. They also helped me avoid tickets and confrontations. "I'm telling you some good shit," Dizzy (or Sadie or Belinda) would say, then relate a certain perverted officer's tendency to time his rounds for when he sees you coming out of the shower, or they would clue me in on the shifts where it is OK to stand in a friend's doorway to chat.

Now that I've learned how not to make a fool or a target of myself, I rely on them to comfort me when I grieve and share my few, small triumphs. We gossip, bicker, and laugh like any large family, and although a common refrain during our conversations is, "I'm so sick of all these backstabbing women, if I never see another female again it'll be too soon," the rest of us hear this complaint with the comforting knowledge that our circle is exempt from the disparagement. No matter how our circumstances might change, our lives would be irrevocably empty if one of us were to leave.

We need each other more than ever now. As the public's fears of the incarcerated rise, the length of sentences is increasing. Parole is an ever-dimming possibility for the few lifers who are eligible and nothing more than a hazardous fantasy for those, like me, who aren't. Geriatric parole, in our experience as mythical as the unicorn, is not a genuine source of comfort or hope. And it doesn't look like that is going to change any time soon, despite the overcrowding in Virginia prisons. The prison business is too lucrative for Virginia and the businesses that feed off the penal system. As inmates, we aren't privy to all of the financial dealings of the DOC and its vendors. All we know is that we pay substantially more for products than the prices we see quoted in catalogs and that our families pay the highest collect call charges legally allowable (on top of a hefty connection charge). I can't begin to guess how far the gouging of us and our families goes, but I would imagine that it's a pretty sweet deal for everyone involved. Except, of course, the inmates.

I've experienced many changes in how Fluvanna operates during my time. Most aren't profoundly life-altering. We aren't allowed to buy the pink, turquoise, or yellow T-shirts that we used to be able to get from JCPenney—now, all T-shirts are gray and must be purchased through the prison. The women who work for the yard crew weeding and planting the flower beds aren't allowed to kneel or sit on the ground to do their work anymore; they must instead bend over to do their work. They have even eliminated walking rec. Fresh air isn't that important, I suppose. These all might seem like little things to outsiders, but they greatly reduce our quality of life.

There is always the looming unknown to contend with. Some blows hit harder than others. For example, I was particularly devastated when Bertha, an inmate intake worker, came to my door. Intake workers are always the first to hear about changes coming down and are typically quite reliable. When I saw Bertha's face, I thought someone had died. "Girl, I have some bad news."

"Oh my God! What is it?"

"Honey. I know how much you like books, so I wanted you to hear it from a friend. You can't buy books anymore." I must have staggered a little because Bertha reached out and grabbed my arm. No more books? I couldn't process the thought. I began to cry and considered all of those years ahead of me without the comfort of my books. It was one of the cruelest things that they could have done to us. I guess they'd rather we spend our time gambling and bulldagging instead of improving our minds.

After several long years, the institution was sued for preventing inmates from accessing information, and because the prison lost, we are now once again allowed to buy books. Of course we have to jump through a dozen flaming hoops to do so, but I'm still grateful. Even better, they are now forced to let our friends and family send us books as well. Saved from a degenerate life of loose women and card playing!

We've not been the only target of new regulations and policies. One day during 11:00 a.m. count my roommate glanced out the window and began laughing. The two wooden gazebos that had graced Fluvanna's yard for years were being hauled out of the gates by tractors. A C.O. later told me that the officers, who were the only people who were allowed near the wooden structures, had been told that they were not permitted to sit in them anymore but they had ignored the order. A week later, it was bye-bye gazebos!

Officers are also affected by the general tone of the facility. A hardass warden or major with a lot of picky rules can always come up with some doozies for her subordinates as well. C.O.s were really irate when they were told that they couldn't bring in their own lunches anymore and instead would have to either eat the same crap for meals that we did or pay big bucks for the overpriced, unhealthy food in the vending machines. They get bitched at about the length of their fingernails and their hair, just like we do. We inmates just hope that their bad days won't become our bad days as well.

More disturbing was what happened during the recent lockdown the prison endured. We had been isolated in our cells for 2 days when my roommate said, "There goes the seventh person to seg today. They must be really shaking them down somewhere." Our cell's window faces the boulevard, so we can see whenever anyone is locked up. "They must have found cigarettes or something," I answered. I didn't give it much thought; lately seg has been seeing a lot of action.

When we finally were let out, we learned why all of those women were locked up. Only the Honor Wing, segregation, and the SLU have wet cells (cells that have a toilet and sink). The other buildings all have dry cells, so the women housed there have to press the intercom button to be popped out of their rooms to use the bathroom. Unfortunately, the bubble officers weren't letting the inmates out to use the restroom, so some of the women had been reduced to urinating on the floor near their cell doors like puppies. It was so bad, one kitchen worker said, that a few actually defecated in the dinner trays. Not a pleasant surprise, I would imagine, for the person who had to pull off the trays' lids when it came time to clean them. It made me grateful for the first time to have a toilet in my cell. And we have a sink, so going without a shower for several days was bearable. Unlike the rest of population, we, at least, could take a "whore's bath," squatting over the toilet and washing ourselves the best we could with the tepid sink water. Not as thorough as I would have liked, but better than nothing.

The state is doing its part to make things harder as well. Although Virginia demands that the DCE teachers achieve a certain level of literacy education with their students, because of budget cuts the DCE teachers can't buy the new textbooks and supplies that they desperately need to accomplish this. In an effort to train inmates for "the real world," when I was a DCE tutor we had to allot each student a certain amount of time for computer-based training. The computer software that they insist we use, however, is poorly designed and riddled with incorrect information. "Erin, will you please come over here?" a student would say. "I know that this is the right answer, but this stupid computer keeps telling me it's wrong. What the hell?" Annabelle and I would both look up, exasperated. How could we encourage the students to develop a love of learning and confidence in their education if they are frustrated by the teaching tools Virginia forces them to use?

Each time this happened, I would go over, confirm that the computer was, indeed, answering incorrectly again, then do my best to reassure the student that the problem was the software, not her. And these were the problems that the students catch. The errors were obvious to anyone with a layman's knowledge of history, science, and grammar. I was scandalized to see the social studies portion of the software refer to the "Monguls" of east-central Asia. The program is rife with errors like these, errors that the woman will accept as correct and proceed to use.

Schoolbooks are scarce and in terrible condition, and our supply regularly diminished as the books were thrown away by C.O.s during shakedowns or taken (intentionally or not) to other facilities by transferred inmates. Pencils were handed out one at a time; to get a new pencil, you needed to turn in the stub of your old one. If we had enough of it, the poorly printed paper churned out by the prison print shop was doled out three sheets per student each day. There is still a hiring freeze, so no new staff can be brought on. If a teacher leaves, that position will be eliminated. I hear that this hiring freeze affects the security staff as well. If enough C.O.s quit, the institution might have to go on lockdown because they won't have sufficient workforce to staff the prison safely.

A major upheaval in the daily life of the Fluvanna community was the prison's recent decision to make FCCW a nonsmoking facility. I have never smoked, so that's not a hardship for me, but the effects on the prison as the smoke-free deadline passed have been terrible. Cigarette-deprived inmates, yearning for nicotine, were fighting more often and more violently. One of the women, Tracy, told us about a fight that her roommate had been in the night before.

"This girl who had just got out of structured living went up to my roommate and starting screaming at her about being a baby killer. Next thing I know she's grabbing her by the head and banging it against the wall outside our room. When I swept up the hair on the floor afterwards it looked like someone had left her weave laying on the floor outside my door." But with the equanimity of a seasoned inmate, she added, "I'm glad she got beat, though. I couldn't stand her. I slept real good last night after she left!"

Because the prison tried to wean the women off of cigarettes by gradually limiting the amount of tobacco products they could buy, by the time the ban was in place, the product was scarce and demand was insanely high. Prison commerce is thriving. Shorts (cigarette stubs filched from the officer's ashtrays) were selling for $10 until they removed the outdoor ashtrays from outside each building. Bonita traded three Newport cigarettes from her stash for a sterling silver necklace. There are still cigarettes hidden all over the compound, I hear. Handrolls are going for $5 apiece, real cigarettes for even more. Women were going broke paying back their cigarette debts—Breeze spent $75 on commissary, but almost $65 of it went for payback for cigarettes.

The girls who can't get tobacco were smoking anything they can find. Ground tea from tea bags was the usual choice. Some tried to use dried potatoes stolen from the kitchen. The grounds crew even had to uproot a eucalyptus bush that had been growing out in the yard since the prison opened because the women were breaking off pieces and smoking it. The C.O.s had to remove feminine hygiene products from each wing, doling them out on an "as-needed" basis. The women, it seems, were using them to make cigarette filters and for rolling papers. "That's a waste of time, though," offered Belinda. "They're just going to start using pages from their Bibles."

In their desperation, some inmates will try anything. A student approached the teacher I worked for, asking about the potted plant that she had on her desk. "Is that a clove plant?" Tricia asked.

Looking confused, my supervisor said, "No, it's a shamrock."

After the student walked away dejectedly, I said to the teacher, "Don't you know why she was asking that?"

"No, why?"

"She thought that your plant could be made into clove cigarettes. She wanted to smoke it!"

"Good grief," she said, then moved the plant to a bookcase safely out of the students' reach.

I tried to talk to my counselor once about the ever-stricter path that Fluvanna's administration seems to be on. "Well, Ms. George, all I can tell you is that the mindset here seems to work like a pendulum, and eventually it should swing back in the other direction." Well, it's been swinging like this since I showed up here, so I can only hope that its return arc is imminent.

Instead, it keeps on moving to the right. I found out recently that I am no longer an "inmate." Instead, I am to be referred to in all official documentation as an "offender." Frankly, I find that a little, well, offensive. It just seems to be a more pejorative term than "inmate," another little jab from the powers that be to make us feel even less human. This is one of the more overt tactics in the state's subliminal campaign to dehumanize us, a campaign that is extraordinarily effective.

We inmates even buy into it ourselves. People who are not a part of our prison world, those inspectors or gawkers who sometimes spend a few hours behind Fluvanna's fences, are referred to as "real people." It happens so casually, most of us aren't even offended by it. If you ask an inmate if she had seen a particular woman at VCE yesterday, for example, the inmate will usually first ask, "Was she an inmate or a real person?"

This harsher trend has resulted in some absurd rules. A recent memo informed us that we will no longer be able to receive photos of our children if the pictures are in any way inappropriate. You might wonder what sort of depraved poses the children are in, what salacious situations are being documented to mandate such a restriction. Are we talking about the standard "naked baby in the bathtub" photos that every camera-happy new parent produces? Or worse, an insidious ring of kiddie porn purveyors? No. I am not allowed to have the perfectly decent photos of Jack, Fran, and Gio's trips to the pool because they are wearing (gasp!) bathing suits. Giovanna in her Lion King one-piece is too risqué for the prison population. The moral arbiter who developed that standard is probably the same person who decided that women doing time in a maximum security prison can't handle R-rated movies. PG-13 is as racy as it gets here in Fluvanna.

This ban on approved media goes to a troubling extent. We were told that we would not be allowed to get Prison Legal News (PLN) anymore. The aim of PLN is to keep inmates aware of all the current legal cases against prison systems and jails and to highlight cases of mistreatment and neglect. PLN doesn't contain profanity, obscenity, or anything else detrimental to the moral and mental health of inmates. But it does make us aware of the pandemic of prison abuse currently debasing our penal system. And knowledge like that in the hands of prisoners could cause major problems for Fluvanna. After all, inmates who are aware of the myriad lawsuits against PHS are probably more likely to initiate their own legal actions in the future. Better to keep us isolated and ignorant. The same lawsuit that gave me back my books, however, barred Fluvanna from blocking PLN.

So, what does my future hold here? Barring the opening of an even stricter prison for level 3 and higher offenders, I will be at Fluvanna until I am eligible for being shipped—in 15 or 20 years–to a lower-security-level prison. Because geriatric parole is a not real option for me, there are a few types of lifers I could probably evolve into. One is to be an inmate like Thelma, a woman here who arouses in me mingled pity and, too often, fear for my own future. Thelma is always slightly out of sync with the new generations moving through FCCW. She rarely sits with the rest of us during movies or wing bingo games—her chair is usually pulled a few feet away from the group. I've seen her struggle to adapt socially, to find that balance between falsely cheerful intrusions into private conversations and her frequent, brutal rebuffs of those who try to initiate conversations with her. She is like a poorly prepared actress, struggling to deliver lines from a script that she has just been handed. Something's not right, but she can't seem to get a bead on what it is, much less how to fix it. Thelma has a release date but is clearly not prepared to exist outside the insulated safety of the prison. I don't think she'll last long out there.

Tianne is another, more hopeful story, although the odds of my emulating her are remote. Her stay here has been rocky at times (she's spent a lot of time in segregation, discussed earlier), but the salient and redeeming fact is that Tianne is an "old law" lifer and hence is technically eligible for parole. I've been with lifers like Tianne as they reluctantly started hoping for that miracle, parole, then experience the inevitable crash of the refusal that follows. Most people in the prison never realize when a lifer is up for parole—she holds her emotions in check, doing little more than quietly asking a few close friends to mention her in their prayers. Mostly, their hopes and subsequent disappointments are concealed behind the "I'm functioning" façade lifers wear when they face the world. Parole creates genuinely intense emotions that aren't fodder to the typical prison gossips. It's too uncomfortable and real beside the steady stream of cheap drama they enjoy.

I don't normally ask people about their personal information (prison etiquette frowns on that), but over the years Tianne and I had become close enough that I felt comfortable in asking her what exactly the parole process entailed. She allowed me to interview her at some length, during which she gave me a glimpse into her experiences with the Parole Board and the feelings that it dredged up:

> My first time up [for parole], I got a 3-year deferral. I knew that I wouldn't get parole. I didn't really have any hopes-I was more afraid of the deferral. That's the worst-waiting 3 years more. . . . I'd rather have the stress of going up every

year for the chance. It's like the ultimate slam, like they're saying you're never going to make parole. My first parole hearing was 2½ hours long. I think that's some kind of record. Most are more like 15 minutes. We never see the Parole Board. Instead, we talk to the Parole Examiner, who is not even a member of the Parole Board. That's who interviews us. It was during my first Parole Board hearing that I was told, "You're probably going to get a series of deferrals, but you are never going home."

The entire time I was talking to this guy during the interview, he was very pleasant and friendly. He wanted to hear about my writing. When I told him that I wanted to be the female Stephen King, he seemed really interested. I told him that I wanted to be as prolific as King, and the Parole Examiner looked stunned that I even knew the word "prolific," much less be able to use it properly.

For some reason, we transitioned from King to baseball . . . I don't know how, but that's how friendly this guy was to me. When he found out that I liked the Yankees, he ragged me because Stephen King was a Red Sox fan. So, being the Yankees fan that I am, I started spewing venom about Manny Ramirez and the BoSox. He let me rant for a few minutes, but I had no idea that I was digging myself into a hole. When I was done, we sat there for a few moments in silence, both of us smiling. Then he gave a little sigh, leaned back in his chair, and quietly informed me that he, too, was a lifelong Boston fan. I threw up my hands and said, "Well, there goes my parole!"

Tianne has a gift for seeing the darkly ironic aspects of her situation. As with me, humor is one of her most powerful tools for survival. She recognizes the absurdity of what the system forces her to do, but complies as cheerfully as she can. She clearly recognizes the silliness of her first parole hearing.

"We never really talked about my classes, my crime, my goals," she said, "but he was busy typing something through most of the interview."

"After the kind of conversation we'd been having, then him telling me that I would probably never go home, I felt like I'd been hit in the face by a brick." Tianne shook her head slowly:

I recoiled when he said that. He eventually said, "Are you OK to leave?" I nodded and left the room. I was hysterical by the time I got to the metal detector, but the two C.O.s who were standing at the building door were very kind and encouraging to me. For the next few weeks, I worked on deleting from my mind his prediction about my going home. The interview was in December, right before my birthday and Christmas, and I got my answer in January. It was dated a month before I actually got it. I was devastated, but it didn't stop me. I cried for 10 minutes and then carried on with my life.

I didn't really deal with it until I went to seg a few months later and all the anger came out. I was angry at the Parole Board, the system, the C.O.s, my [co-defendant] Ben, and myself. Because of it I started smoking after 7 years and buried myself in schoolwork and my job.

My next hearing was 3 years later, but I was denied for the same reason as before-the serious nature of my crime. That's what they always tell lifers. I don't even know if there is another reason. . . . I've never heard of one. I can't imagine what another reason might be. It sucks that the reason they keep denying us parole is something we can never, ever change. Makes good behavior seem pretty pointless, doesn't it?

I understood her frustration. Daunting odds are nothing new to lifers, but because none of us has a time machine, the immutable facts behind our incarcerations are an inescapable burden. In many ways, my new law sentence of life without parole is better. At least I don't have to torment myself with a parole decision that is guaranteed not to go my way.

So this time I was refused again, but at least I didn't get a deferral. The funny thing about it was that I had spent time with a lay chaplain trying to get my head screwed on. What that meant in my head was that I wanted to be able to handle a deferral without doing stupid shit like smoking or falling apart. I wasn't concerned about getting in trouble. That's not my style, and I'd worked too hard for the quality of my life to just throw it away over something I had no control over. I'd gotten really pissed at myself for smoking before. Physically hurting myself was just stupid. I had a little bit of "I don't give a fuck" that had manifested by smoking. Just dumb.

For this parole interview, I hadn't prayed for anything other than peace over what the final result was. I spent a lot of time with my chaplain preparing. I wanted to be able to go gracefully through a turndown, or enter freedom without too much baggage. So when I got the turndown I was fine. I didn't get that deferral that I feared. Later, I had a little laugh because I had prayed for peace, and that was exactly what I got. What if I had prayed for something else?

This time a woman interviewed me for my parole hearing, and I was in and out in 15 minutes. She was very professional, kind-but not too friendly. She put me at ease. She asked me questions about me, not Ben, and was interested in the fact that my father said I could move in with him. I remember almost hollering for one question, "That's such a fair question!" When she smiled at me it was such a nice, friendly smile. Then, on January 11, I got a turndown, minus the deferral.

Tianne is preparing for her third parole hearing, which is scheduled for next month. She wants to be ready spiritually, emotionally, and practically for both the interview itself, and the possibility that she'll be able to go home.

So now its 9½ months later, and needless to say, I've been praying for a "Yes." It's amazing to me that it is happening again so quickly, much sooner than I expected it. I'm not hanging onto false hopes, but hope gets me out of the bed in the morning. I'm anxious, but it's a good anxious. This time my hearing is 2½ months early, but I don't know if that means anything. To get ready for a job, I've spent more time in the [optical] lab [where Tianne has been trained as a technician], getting hands-on experience, then tutoring the students. I want to be ready to work. I've been "collecting" businesses to send my resume to. I've spent a year trying to be more specific with my prayers and not succumbing to the negativities of everyday life here. People here are constantly negative: "No one ever makes parole" and "Lifers can't make parole" they keep telling me. I hear it from C.O.s, counselors, other lifers.... I get really worn down. This year I've refused to engage in those kinds of conversations. It keeps me buoyed, functioning, enjoying the quality of my life. That faith is also what will carry me through the absolutely worst scenario. When I hear that negativity, I answer, "Well, somebody has to be the first." I just pray for a miracle.

I try to keep religion out of the hearing on the advice of my previous counselor. I guess it could be a turn-off to some people, but it's not like I'm going to go into the room and say, "Howdy, do you know Jesus?" But my faith is important to me, it's part of who I am now.

This year, for the first time, my counselor gave me an eight-question questionnaire about what I've done to improve myself, my involvement in my crime (which was all after the fact-I drove the car after the murders and lied my ass off to the police to protect Ben, but I wasn't even there when it happened. The police said that I planned it, though), my family ties, my plans if they release me. The questionnaire was just for my counselor, so he could write a report on me for the Board. I wrote my poor counselor a dissertation!

I gave the completed questionnaire to my counselor. Two weeks later, he stopped me during mass movement and I asked him if he had read my dissertation. At first he hung his head, and I had another one of those "heart falling out the bottom of my pants" moments. I started to walk away, but he called me back to him and said that it was the best he had ever gotten. I didn't realize that I was holding my breath until the air flew out of me. He said that he wanted me to send it to the Parole Board just as it was. He added that he had never made a recommendation for someone to make parole, but that he was going to do it for me. That meant so much because no staff member had ever clearly made a stand for me. Everyone else was just stapled to the fence. I don't know if they're afraid of losing their jobs or what.

So, I've collected letters from my supervisors here, friends and family outside, even from a few inmates. I've updated a kick-ass resume and have my list of possible employers ready. I am going to mail the whole thing to the Parole Board and to the Examiner as well.

Emotionally, I'm swinging back and forth between fired-up and ready to go—I know that I would be successful, I have a great support system—and thinking that I don't deserve parole. People are dead, and it doesn't matter that I didn't pull the trigger. That will never go away. I know that it will never happen again, but how do you convince a stranger of that? As I said in my questionnaire, I don't want to keep explaining or defending the person I was 22 years ago. The person I am now is the one who can be paroled. That's where my focus is-that's what I want to get across. You're going to release me, not her. I've spent 22 years taking groups, getting therapy, proving myself to be a responsible person. I've done the self-inventory, even the worst stuff. I've spent the last 22 years digging myself out of the pit I spent the first 21 years of my life creating.

It's easy to believe all of the negative crap in your life, to roll around in your disgust. It's all lies, though. I'm not a bad person, but I was involved in a bad thing. If I can't believe that, no one else will, either.

And I'm excited. This is the first time I've let myself think beyond prison-to plan, consider how I'll handle that hard question at the interview, even down to mentally listing who I'm giving what to when I go home and who I'm going to keep in touch with. For the first time, I'm daring myself to say, "Why don't I deserve another chance?" I still can't approach that head-on sometimes because of my own self-loathing, but I can sidestep my ass up to it on most days. And on the real good days, I can ask myself, "Why shouldn't I deserve a chance, too?"

People think we're all stupid or evil. They lump us together and only get to hear about the really bad inmates, the bad incidents, and the repeaters. But there are a lot of women in here so very worthy of that second chance, and I'm finally able to include myself in that.

When we were finished talking, Tianne looked at the scattered pile of my scrawled notes and laughed. "I guess I had a lot to say, didn't I?" she grinned. I smiled back, but couldn't help thinking what a loss it would be to the world if Tianne weren't allowed to rejoin it.

When I look around for lifers who give me a reasonably realistic idea of what the future might hold for me, I find that I hope to end up more like a woman named Laura, who has been down for over 20 years but who treats her friends with the loving bossiness of a strong-willed grandmother. Laura has a full-time job as well as learning Braille in the evenings. Her mind is as keen as mine, and her sense of morality even greater. I have never heard her say an unkind thing, and when the rest of us are busy gossiping or complaining, she never participates except to suggest that perhaps there are lots of blessings in our lives that we're forgetting. Laura has built a fulfilling life for herself here, one that probably is very similar to the life she would have if she were home: caring for others, crocheting, cooking, working, and praying.

Belinda and I joke that we will end up in adjacent beds in the geriatric wing (if they ever get a geriatric wing—that is something that lifers have been trying to establish for years) because we are almost exactly the same age. And, of course, because Belinda doesn't have parole either. So we vow that we will be "Miss Erin" and "Miss Belinda," the two most ornery, demanding geriatric inmates the state has ever seen. (Prison etiquette demands that anyone who is elderly or infirm—either physically or mentally—be addressed as "Miss" whoever. I get really irritated when people call me "Miss Erin" now, but it will probably be more acceptable when I am 70.) When we finally get old, there will be payback for years of meekly abiding by the rules! As selfish as it sounds, a part of me is glad that she has time like mine. At least there will be someone I like and trust around me when the end comes.

One thing I try never to do is contemplate going home. That's too overwhelming a concept. But sometimes I can't help but think about a prison superstition someone first told me about shortly after I arrived at FCCW. They say that when someone drops a set of keys, it means a prisoner is going home. Now, I'm not a superstitious woman. Intellectually I realize how foolish it is to believe in such a thing. I know that it's ridiculous, but each time a bunch of keys clatters against the dirty tile floor, always that damn, unreasonable, unquenchable hope insists that maybe it might be true. In the few seconds it takes for rationality to regain control, my mind spins elaborate fantasies of pardons, newfound evidence, and life-restoring lawyers. And despite myself, each time it happens I hope desperately that this time the keys are for me.

REFERENCES

Bozelko, C. (2013). *Up the river: An anthology.* Washington, DC: BleakHouse Publishing.

Cooper, A. D., Durose, M. R., & Snyder, H. N. (2014). *Recidivism of prisoners released in 30 States in 2005: Patterns from 2005 to 2010.* Washington, DC: Bureau of Justice Statistics.

Haney, C. (2006). *Reforming punishment: Psychological limits to the pains of imprisonment.* Washington, DC: American Psychological Association.

Hassine, V. (2010). *Life without parole: Living and dying in prison today* (5th ed.). Robert Johnson & Sonia Tabriz (Eds.). New York: Oxford University Press.

Johnson, R. (2002). *Hard time: Understanding and reforming the prison* (3rd ed.). Belmont, CA: Wadsworth.

Johnson, R. (2008). Hard time: A meditation on prisons and imprisonment. In S. Nagelsen (Ed.), *Exiled voices: Portals of discovery—Stories, poems, and drama by imprisoned writers* (pp. ix–xviii). Henniker, NH: New England College Press.

O'Brien, P. (2001). *Making it in the "free world."* Albany: State University of New York Press.

Paluch, J. A., Jr. (2004). *A Life for a life-Life imprisonment: America's other death penalty.* New York: Oxford University Press.

Parsons, B. (2007). Reawakening through nature: A prison reflection. In W. Lamb (Ed.), *I'll fly away: Further testimonies from the women of York Prison* (pp. 215–240). New York: Harper Perennial.

Pollock, J. (2004). *Prisons and prison life: Costs and consequences.* New York: Oxford University Press.

Toch, H. (1992). *Living in prison: The ecology of survival.* Washington, DC: American Psychological Association.

Travis, J., & Visher, C. (Eds.). (2006). *Prisoner reentry and crime in America.* New York: Cambridge University Press.

Zaitzow, B. H. (2004). Pastel fascism: Reflections of social control techniques used with women in prison. *Women's Studies Quarterly, 32*(3&4), 33–48.

Origami Heart

I can see how carefully
you always fold your letters,
intricate layers of notebook paper,
compact,
like a note you might slip
to a friend in class,
hidden in cupped palms
or push through the vents
of some boy's locker,
too shy for anything more overt.
When I pick them up at mail call
I feel them slide back and forth
in the flimsy blue and red striped
airmail envelopes,
a core of your words
and so much emptiness enclosed.
Sometimes I let myself imagine
that the empty space
still contains your air,
the envelope a lung
breathing out the same
uncomplicated, milky sweetness
I remember from before,
when I could hold you.
You would reach up
and stroke my earlobe
with your thumb
to lull yourself to sleep.
As I inhaled you,
your fingers were as soft
as felt
as soft as the creases
in your letters
after my manifold readings-soft, threatening severance,
but still holding.

Erin George
_Reprinted with permission from Origami Heart: Poems by a Woman Doing Life (2008, p. 1),
by Erin George. Washington, DC: BleakHouse Publishing._

EPILOGUE

A few weeks after the revision process for the second edition of *AWDL* was completed, my life fell apart. On Christmas Day, 2013, I called my parents. My dad had been suffering from a resurgence of the throat cancer he'd battled through a decade before, but, I thought, he was responding to his treatment. He'd had to have a tracheotomy tube put in, but his last letter had mentioned that he was looking forward to getting it removed. But after I told my mom "Merry Christmas!" she said, "Honey, I have to tell you something. They've decided to stop treating Dad's cancer."

I couldn't speak for a moment, then managed to choke out, "Is he in pain? What is his prognosis? How long will we have him?"

"Dad's OK," she answered. "He's still able to get around, work on his computer. Some hospice people came in and set up a bedroom for him downstairs, in a room with big windows so he can sit outside. He really is OK," she assured me.

I was trying not to cry too much; the unspoken part of our deal to tell each other necessary, unpleasant news was that I wouldn't fall apart. "I'm sorry I'm getting so upset," I said. I felt myself moving into that hyper-reasonable mode where that weeping inmate was someone detached from me, someone across the room. I was just describing to Mom. "I'm really fine. Of course I'm upset, but you don't need to worry about me."

Halfway through our 20-minute phone call, I knew my rational façade was crumbling. "Mom, I'd better go," I said. "Tell Dad I love him." Because of his trach, I thought Dad couldn't speak. "No, wait!" she said. "Dad wants to talk to you."

After a few moments, Dad picked up. His voice rasped, but still, it was *him*. "Hey, baby," he said.

"Hi, Daddy," I managed to say. "Are you all right?"

"Oh, I'm fine. Don't worry about me."

"Dad, I love you so much. I know it's hard for you to talk, but I'm so glad to hear your voice. I love you, Daddy."

"I love you too, Fritz. I'll talk to you again soon."

Calling me "Fritz," his childhood nickname for me, was too much, and I hung up the phone, weeping. That was the last conversation Dad and I had.

For the next month, he seemed to be maintaining. Mom and I spoke often, and one day she mentioned that Dad had given his pocket watch to my niece's new husband. I knew that I would never be allowed to have a keepsake like that, but I did ask for an old baseball card I'd given him years ago. It showed his favorite player, Wally Moon, and he had displayed it on his dresser for almost two decades. Surely that, I thought, would be allowed by our rigorous mailroom. A week later I opened a letter at mail call and there it was. It's now propped up on my desk.

It was during this time that Mom told me that Dad was determined to visit me. Since I had assumed that I'd never see him again, I hadn't bothered to tell Mom about the oner-ous, new visitor registration process just instituted for Virginia prisons. It required mul-tiple visits to a poorly designed Web site to figure out, followed by a one-month (or two, or more) wait for approval. But if Dad wanted to make the long trip to FCCW, then I would have to act fast.

After giving Mom the Web address, I wrote a long, question-filled IMS to Ms. Dee, my counselor, explaining my situation. Ms. Dee was awesome; she answered all my ques-tions about wheelchair access, special visits, and, most urgently, Mom and Dad's approval status. Ms. Dee even contacted the Treatment Program Supervisor (a fairly high-level administrator), who confirmed their approved status and promised that they would be allowed in when they visited.

While all this was happening, my life was unraveling in other ways. A recent trip to medical had turned up another growth in my breast. I was sure it was benign (as it turned out to be), but it would entail several stressful trips to the hospital. Then I was suddenly fired from my job at the library. I had worked there for years and taken pride in my work. Not only did I love my job and excel at it, but it was a great solace to me as I coped with my father's dying.

My supervisor, Mrs. Kendle, knew this, so I shrugged it off when the institutional in-vestigator came into the library and closed the librarian's office door behind her. Of course all of the library workers knew something was up, but when I was called back there 10 min-utes later, I was genuinely shocked; I was always so scrupulous about following the rules, what could I possibly have done to rate a face-to-face with the institutional investigator?

"Close the door," said Ms. Jillian. "Can you explain this?" She handed me a small bundle of papers, and I realized that it held a photocopied article from an academic jour-nal and six or seven handwritten editorial notes for the latest edition of this book.

"Those are just some papers of mine that I guess I forgot to throw away. Why?"

Ms. Jillian peered at the handwritten sheets. "What's this about?" she asked.

It took me a few seconds to decode my scrawl. "That's a note on how kind everyone here was to Teresa Lewis before she was executed."

"How about that?" She pointed to another page.

"That's about my friend Chick's struggle with cancer."

After a few more explanations, Ms. Jillian dropped the papers back onto the desk. "Am I getting a ticket?" I asked. I'm ashamed to admit that I was crying.

Ms. Jillian looked at me sympathetically and said, "No, this isn't contraband. Just be fair when you write about the prison." Despite my own jangled emotions, I'd noticed that she had never acted unpleasant or aggressive throughout the interview. In fact, her ques-tions were almost perfunctory. She knew me and knew I didn't get into trouble. I pre-sumed she was there at the instigation of the librarian, who hadn't said much during this process. Now, though, she chimed in.

"But it's personal property, which you can't keep in the library."

I stared at her in disbelief. This surely couldn't be happening. For two and a half years I had been the only inmate to support her unconditionally. I never stole, never lied, and she was hemming me up over a few sheets of paper that weren't even contraband? "Ms. Kendle, you know I would never deliberately break the rules or disrespect you. You know this was an accident."

She allowed as to how this was probably true, but I was gone nevertheless. And, per policy, not allowed to get another job for at least 3 months.

In late February, Mom told me that Dad had deteriorated to the point where he needed to be moved to a hospice care facility. My longed-for visit with Dad wouldn't happen. Mom and I had already agreed that a deathbed visit, which the prison allows, would be too painful and too expensive.

Mom had spoken with Ms. Dee as Dad's situation worsened, and the counselor had gotten into the habit of seeking me out daily to see how I was doing. On February 26, Ms. Dee was waiting for me when I entered the wing after lunch chow. "Ms. George, you need to speak to your mom."

I stopped abruptly. "Oh, no. So soon?"

She gave me a compassionate look. "Your mom wants to tell you." Ushering me into her office, she shut the door and dialed Mom's number, putting the phone on speaker. Then Ms. Dee turned to her desk, busying herself with paperwork and given me the illusion of privacy. When Mom and I were done, she turned to face me. "How are you really?"

I slapped on my best "I'm coping" expression through my tears and said politely, "I'm fine, thank you. I'm very grateful for everything you've done." As I started to get up, she said, "Ms. George, you've just suffered a huge loss." Then she did something wonderful. In a place where I was totally isolated from anyone who knew the astounding man that was my father, she gave me a great gift just by saying, "Tell me about your dad."

I did. For 20 minutes, I cried and told her stories about this intelligent, funny, loyal man who had consoled and supported me during my trial and imprisonment. At that moment, in that place, nothing could have given me greater comfort.

Now, 2 months later, I've been given a new job. I've been selected to be part of a pilot program called "peer-to-peer teaching" where inmates teach 2nd- to 4th-grade–level students so they can earn a GED. What makes this program so innovative (at least by Virginia standards) is that inmates rather than civilian teachers create lesson plans, assess test scores, set learning goals, and teach, all without supervision of staff or C.O.s. Twenty-four inmates alone in a room is a radical thing here. For me, it's a challenge, but also an opportunity to be of real value, and I'm eager to begin.

I still think about my dad every day, but more often with smiles rather than tears. Tianne has been a true friend, crying with me and providing all of the wisdom and compassion I could ask for. Ms. Dee continues to check in with me often. But since there was no funeral I could attend, I came up with my own ceremony to say goodbye.

During the time he was so ill, I had been enrolled in a public speaking class as a requirement for a scholarship I'd been awarded. One of my assignments was to write an elegy, and I chose my father as the topic.

This gave me an idea. I called Mary, my former roommate, and asked if she would help me. She agreed. And so I sent her a copy of my elegy to Dad. Then, on a gorgeous spring day, Mary took her phone outside into her garden and, as I listened, she burned the pages, letting the ashes release to the wind while she said a prayer.

During this terrible time, I experienced the worst and best of a lifer's decades behind bars. The inevitable loss of loved ones is possibly the hardest thing to be endured here. But occasionally, and more often than you might think, you find extraordinary kindnesses here that make the unbearable bearable. That they come from such unexpected sources as prison staffers makes it all the more remarkable. The prison system is capable of fulfilling its goals of protecting society and rehabilitating offenders while treating inmates humanely. Counselor Dee is proof of that.

AFTERWORD

Joycelyn Pollock and Alison B. Martin

Erin George has offered us a revealing glimpse into the world of incarcerated women, a world that has grown to enormous proportions. As recently as 1990, there were only 44,065 women incarcerated in state and federal prisons (Sourcebook of Criminal Justice Statistics, 2008). By 2012, there were approximately 108,772 women incarcerated, a more than twofold increase from 1990. Women represent approximately 7 percent of the total prisoner (state and federal) population (Carson & Sabol, 2012, p. 2). The number of women in prison varies from large populations, such as 12,209 (Texas) and 8,052 (California), to less than 200 in states such as Maine, Vermont, and North Dakota (Carson & Sabol, 2012, p. 25). The national rate (per 100,000) of incarceration for women has increased from 52 per 100,000 in 1997 to 65 per 100,000 in 2011 (Carson & Sabol, 2012, p. 23; Gilliard & Beck, 1998, p. 4).

This book is almost an ethnography in its scope and detail of observation. Unlike most academic ethnography, however, the author opens up her own heart and soul. She exposes her slide into depression, bullying, and lack of empathy (for those who squander their opportunities of freedom). But the work is neither self-involved nor narcissistic; she also paints a picture of her fellow inmates—some greedy, some altruistic, some pathetic. Her balanced portrayal of prison is not a stark black-and-white picture of evil guards and purely victimized women. Rather, she has developed her snapshot of prison life in sepia tones: many guards exhibit qualities of fairness, even kindness, and many inmates exhibit quite the opposite characteristics. There are good and bad people in both types of uniforms, and most personalities showed shades of gray. This is real life as played out in a prison for women.

DEMOGRAPHICS OF WOMEN IN PRISON

George mentions in passing the major demographic realities of women in prison. Female prisoners are typically low-income, undereducated, and unskilled women with sporadic employment histories. Like male inmates, female inmates are disproportionately African American, although, according to recent federal statistics, black women were incarcerated at a rate six times that of white women in 2000, but by 2011, that ratio had declined to 2.5 times higher (129 vs. 51; Carson & Sabol, 2012, p. 8). Female prisoners are much less likely than men to have committed violent offenses. Women were responsible for only about 10% of all convictions for violent crimes in 2004, 26% of all property convictions, and 18% of all drug offenses (Bureau of Justice Statistics, 2008). Because violent offenders receive longer sentences, they comprise about 37% of the total female prisoner population, compared to 29% property offenders and about 25% drug offenders (Carson & Sabol, 2012, p. 28).

Erin George describes vividly the plight of drug-addicted women in jail who go through withdrawal with very little medical assistance. She notes the importance of drugs in many women's lives, even if the only drug they can obtain is a cigarette. Researchers have documented widespread drug and alcohol abuse among female offenders and prisoners. In fact, according to some research, female offenders might be *more* likely than male offenders to be drug abusers (Brewer-Smyth, 2004; Jordan, Schlenger, Fairbank, & Caddell, 1996). Drug use has consistently been associated with high-risk behaviors, such as sex work and other high-risk sexual practices (Mullings, Marquart, & Brewer, 2000; Mullings, Marquart, & Hartley, 2003). Childhood sexual victimization seems to be correlated with a constellation of dysfunctional behaviors, including excessive drug use and high-risk sexual behaviors that expose women to HIV/AIDS and abusive partners.

George echoes academic research by mentioning the sad fact that many female prisoners have experienced sexual and physical abuse, as children and adults. This affects their relationships and their reaction to strip searches and pat-downs by male guards. Studies report that between 40% and 88% of incarcerated women have been the victims of domestic violence and sexual or physical abuse prior to incarceration. This compares to lifetime prevalence rates of nonincarcerated women of about 18% for rape and 52% for physical assault (Batchelor, 2005; Bloom, Owen, & Covington, 2003; Carlson, 2005, p. 120; Human Rights Watch, 1996; Tjaden & Thoennes, 2006, pp. 7, 25).

Female prisoners seem to be much more likely to have experienced both sexual and physical abuse than male prisoners (McClellan, Farabee, & Crouch, 1997). The most comprehensive national study was conducted by the Bureau of Justice Statistics researchers, and Harlow (1999), reporting on this study, reported that 47% of women in state prisons reported physical abuse and 39% reported sexual abuse at some point in their lives; 25% and 26% reported experiencing physical abuse and sexual abuse, respectively, before age 18.

Childhood sexual victimization has been linked to a wide range of physical and psychological consequences, including personality disorders, depression, suicidal and self-destructive behaviors, eating disorders, anxiety, feelings of isolation and stigma, poor self-esteem, poor social and interpersonal functioning, trust issues, substance abuse, sexual problems, and high-risk sexual behavior (Breitenbecher, 2001; Easteal, 2001; Islam-Zwart & Vik, 2004; Ketring & Feinaur, 1999; Tripodi & Pettus-David, 2013). Johnson and Lynch (2013) found that such victimization is connected to maladaptive coping in incarcerated women, as displayed through dissociation and coping through disengagement and denial. Childhood sexual victimization is also associated with revictimization and violent actions by the woman (Mullings, Marquart, & Brewer, 2000; Mullings, Marquart, & Hartley, 2003; Mullings, Pollock, & Crouch, 2002; Pollock, Mullings, & Crouch, 2006; Tripodi & Pettus-David, 2013).

No doubt partly due to their childhood victimization, many women in prison are in need of mental health services. Estimates suggest that 25% to over 60% of the female prison population require mental health services (for a review of research, see Pollock,

2002). Teplin, Abram, and McClelland (1996) reported a 33% lifetime prevalence of post-traumatic stress disorder (PTSD) for incarcerated women. Others have also reported that about a third of incarcerated women have experienced violent trauma and exhibit signs of PTSD and that women who have experienced abuse are about twice as likely to exhibit signs of mental illness (Jordan, Schlenge, Fairbank, & Caddell, 1996; Powell, 1999). A Bureau of Justice Statistics survey found that almost 21% of female inmates reported high levels of serious psychological distress, compared to about 4% of nonincarcerated women (Beck, Berzofsky, Caspar, & Krebs, 2013). Researchers who survey jail inmates report similar findings (Fedock, Fries, & Kubiak, 2013; Haywood, Kravitz, Goldman, & Freeman, 2000; Veysey, 1998). For instance, Green, Miranda, Daroowala, and Siddique (2005) found in their jail sample that 98% of women had experienced trauma exposure, 36% reported some current mental disorder, and 74% had some type of drug or alcohol problem.

Without the benefit of this research, George describes how the symptoms of PTSD can be identified in some of the behaviors of women in prison. For some women, pat-downs and strip searches by authoritative figures are experienced as re-creations of child-hood sexual abuse, especially when the authority figure abuses his or her position (Maeve, 2000). Even women's violence in prison relationships can be understood by recognition of PTSD symptoms; for instance, for some women, erupting in violence reduces anxiety and a partner is a likely target of abuse (Maeve, 2000). Maeve (2000) argues that female prisoners' violence, dissociation, depression, and self-mutilating behaviors could be predicted based on their prior histories. In one of the most interesting discussions related by George in the book, a tattoo artist muses about whether her addiction to tattoos might be understood as a more artistic alternative to self-mutilation. Such compulsions are better understood by considering the context of these women's lives before prison.

Maeve (2000) also describes another woman who had been sexually abused, since before the age of 7, by her father and other male relatives. She engaged in a sequence of relationships in prison that were always violent. She felt extremely possessive of the partner and explained how "flipping" meant always expecting betrayal, finding evidence of it, and then reacting in a swift and violent manner. She also "went to that place" (of violent reaction) whenever male officers would threaten her physically. A couple lines of a poem she wrote explain her violent prison relationships: "If no one fights me or fucks me, then they don't love me . . ." (Maeve, 2000, p. 493).

George offers a glimpse into the difficulties women encounter while navigating the prison health care system. Many women did not receive proper health care before entering prison due to factors such as lack of health insurance, homelessness, mental illness, and substance abuse (Nijhawan, Salloway, Nunn, Poshkus, & Clarke, 2010). Compared to those outside of prison, incarcerated women are at an increased risk of having sexually transmitted diseases such as HIV, drug and alcohol disorders, and mental illnesses, often stemming from prior sexual abuse and drug use, which require extensive medical treatment (Baillergeon, Binswanger, Penn, Williams, & Murray, 2009; Hammett, Harmon, & Rhodes, 1997; Peters, Greenbaum, Edens, Carter, & Ortiz, 1998).

A Bureau of Justice Statistics survey found that female state and federal inmates reported having more current medical problems than did male inmates, with hypertension, asthma, arthritis, and hepatitis being the most frequently reported ailments (Maruschak, 2008). These conditions, left untreated, will continue to plague women after they return to the community. In one California study, female inmates identified inconsistent or unavailable preventive care, lack of continuity of care, and time limits on health care visits as barriers to seeking and receiving effective health care (Enders, Paterniti, & Meyers, 2005). Although George's prison is actively administering mammograms, other prisons lack such policies, and most reforms are only the result of litigation and court-mandated changes.

An increase in the number of female inmates and the greying of the prison population reveals challenges regarding the delivery of health care for chronic and lifethreatening diseases and end-of-life care (Enders, Paterniti, & Meyers, 2005). The stresses of prison life age inmates more quickly than they would on the outside—in many states, a 50-year-old inmate is considered elderly and is the equivalent of a 60-year-old outside of prison in terms of the physical problems they experience (Aday & Krabill, 2011). George describes how painful it is for inmates to face their last days in prison, with little hope for medical clemency, geriatric parole, or even a reliably comfortable existence. Policies that prohibit contact among inmates and discourage providing aid to others contribute to the harsh environment that ailing inmates endure (Johnson & Brooks, 2011).

PRISON VIOLENCE

George mentioned violent prison relationships only in passing. She describes the prison for women as relatively nonviolent except for a few aggressive bullies who sought out victims who would succumb to threats and the jealously triggered violence that took place within prison relationships. Academic research generally supports this perspective. Men's prison culture has been described as a "jungle" where the strong prey on the weak and both expressive and instrumental violence is not uncommon (see Johnson, 2002; Pollock, 2004). The subculture in women's prisons has been described as very different from that found in prisons for men (Owen, 1998; Pollock, 2002). Unlike men's institutions, women's prisons have been described in academic research as having remarkably low levels of racial tension and violence (Kruttschnitt, 1983; Pollock, 2002). All researchers note that some violence does occur, but it has been perceived as relatively rare. Organized conflict related to gangs and ethnic strife is extremely rare in women's prisons (Harer & Langan, 2001, p. 522; Owen, 1998). Edgar and Martin (2003) found, in their study of prison violence, that female prisoners used weapons much less often than men and, in the few occasions when weapons were used, were more likely to use a "weapon at hand" rather than one fabricated in advance.

On the other hand, some researchers suggest that the culture is changing, and economic coercion, sexual coercion, and victimization does occur quite often in some women's prisons (Alarid, 2000; Greer, 2000; Pogrebin & Dodge, 2001). Wolff, Blitz, Shi, Siegel, and Bachman (2007), in a comparative study of violence in men's and women's prisons, found that 20% of women and 25% of men reported being physically assaulted by another inmate during their current sentence.

One type of violence noted is economic coercion, where aggressive women attempt to coerce fearful women to give up their commissary purchases. Commissary plays an extremely important role in the prison world and women's attempts to make their life more tolerable. As a middle-class woman with no history of criminal justice system involvement, George was a likely target. However, she stood up to the bullies who tried to extort commissary goods through the threat of violence. By aggressively taking a stance and, at the same time, allowing the woman to keep her self-respect, she was able to avoid any physical confrontations.

Another type of violence erupts when a woman feels "disrespected." Prison researchers have noted this personal value of "respect," long associated with young male prisoners and brought in from the street, as an element to some prisoner altercations. The concept of respect now seems to be a more salient issue with young female prisoners as well (Batchelor, 2005; Belknap, Holsinger, & Dunn, 1997; Kruttschnitt & Carbone-Lopez, 2006; Sommers & Baskin, 1993).

Generally, academic research has revealed that women's sexual relationships are usually consensual rather than coercive. As George mentioned, women, unlike men, sometimes engage in pseudo-families. These affiliations mimic familial relationships in society, with mothers, fathers, siblings, and children acting in general accordance with their role (Girshick, 1999; Owen, 1998; Pollock, 2002). As George and academics have described, prisoners form these familial relationships and friendships to soften the loneliness of the prison world, but, by far, the more obvious type of relationship is the romantic partnerships that emerge.

George describes the central place these relationships have within the prison community and their role in creating strife and violence. She described one serious fight (which was made worse by two inmates assaulting a lone victim) and mentioned other violence that occurred within the context of these prison sexual relationships. Although many women, like George, do not participate in sexual relationships with other prisoners, many others do participate. The love affairs and breakups, jealous suspicions, and blatant disloyalties that characterize prison sexual relationships lead, sometimes, to serious violence. Such relationships can be better understood in the context of women's past victimizations, their codependency, and their lack of healthy relationship models, but such understanding is unlikely to occur with the dearth of self-awareness exhibited by female prisoners and the lack of programs available to help them understand themselves.

George seems to dispute the existence of any sexual coercion. Academic research illustrates that the problem might be rare, but it exists. Hensley, Castle, and Tewksbury (2003) administered surveys to all female inmates in one facility, and 4.5% of the 245 respondents reported being victimized by some form of sexual coercion by other inmates. Other researchers found that 7.7% of women reported being "pressured" or "forced" into sexual contact (Struckman-Johnson, Struckman-Johnson, Rucker, Bumby, & Donaldson, 1996, p. 74). A later study by these same researchers found that, in three prisons for women, the prevalence rates for rape ranged from 0 to 5% and "sexual assault" ranged from 6% to 19% (this included unwanted touching and grabbing of breasts and groin areas and forced kissing, as well as other types of unwanted sexual contact). The reports of sexual coercion in the various institutions ranged from 11% to 21% (Struckman-Johnson & Struckman-Johnson, 2006).

Wolff and colleagues have also published a number of articles on their survey of sexual assault in prison, with a sample of 6,964 men and 564 women. Prevalence rates over the course of a prison sentence for inmate-on-inmate sexual assault were two times higher for inmates in facilities for women than in facilities for men (39/1,000 vs. 16/1,000; Wolff, Blitz, Shi, Bachman, & Siegel, 2006, p. 840; also see Wolff, Shi, Blitz, & Siegel, 2007). In large part, the increased number of reports by women was accounted for by abusive sexual contacts, not sexual acts.

In a recent Bureau of Justice Statistics national survey of sexual victimization in prison, 2.4% of female inmates reported victimization by a staff member, and 7.2% reported victimization by another inmate (Beck, Berzofsky, Caspar, & Krebs, 2013). The national survey defined sexual victimization as all types of sexual activity, including sexual activity, touching, and consensual or nonconsensual sexual activity in the past 12 months or since admission to the facility, if less than 12 months. Nonconsensual sexual acts were defined as unwanted oral sex, anal sex, vaginal sex, "hand-jobs," or other sexual acts with a staff or inmate. Abusive sexual contacts were defined as touching of the inmate's butt, thighs, penis, breasts, or vagina in a sexual way (Beck, Berzofsky, Caspar, & Krebs, 2013).

As more studies have been completed, it has become apparent that researchers must separate sexual assault (a forced sexual interaction involving genital contact or genital–mouth or hand contact) from sexual misconduct, which involves unwanted touching and verbal sexual harassment. Furthermore, Hensley and Tewksbury (2002) have argued that sexual *coercion* rather than sexual *assault* in prisons for women is by far the most neglected topic of prison researchers. Emerging research indicates that distinguishing consensual from coerced sexual relationships in women's prisons might be more difficult than earlier researchers assumed. Greer (2000) found that, although the majority of female inmate respondents in her study did not wish to become involved in an intimate relationship with other female inmates, such relationships were extremely prevalent. The motivations for such relationships included economic manipulation, sincere attachment, loneliness, curiosity, sexual identity, peer pressure, sexual release, and diversion from boredom. Alarid (2000) suggests that some passive female inmates submit to verbal sexual coercion by becoming involved in a sexual relationship. Because most women capitulated to sexual coercion, force was unnecessary. Women entered into relationships because they wanted to "belong" to somebody or some group to combat loneliness. Another reason, however, was that they were intimidated by threats of violence, or being "set up" (i.e., with contraband).

George described her prison's efforts—flawed, in many inmates' opinion—to comply with the 2003 Prison Rape Elimination Act (PREA). PREA mandated regular data-gathering efforts by the Bureau of Justice Statistics to measure the prevalence of sexual victimization and directed the Department of Justice to implement national standards that must be adopted by all federal and state correctional and detention facilities as well as local jails, police lockups, and juvenile facilities. Statistics gathered during the first three waves of data collection indicate that changes in the rate of sexual victimization among state and federal inmates are not significant (Beck, 2013). Over the course of the next few years, we can begin to evaluate the lasting effects that PREA may have on sexual victimization.

CORRECTIONAL OFFICERS

One of the most refreshing elements of this book is the nuanced view of correctional officers. Very often, prisoner-authors can't help themselves from portraying officers as an undifferentiated mass of *lumpenproletariat*, most often dumb and mean. Erin George describes people, not uniforms. Her stories of the petty tyrants who wear the correctional officer uniform can be understood and sympathized with by anyone who has argued with any bureaucrat over rules. One can start to see what it must like to be a prisoner faced with the omnipotent "it's against the rules." Other times, she describes those officers who try to remain professional in the midst of bureaucratic inanities. More interesting are her descriptions of those officers who are known to be jerks, but who step out of character to do something nice.

George mentions that, as a new prisoner, she feared sexual victimization by officers, but then explained that prison was nothing like the "sex in the cells" movies. Interestingly, she did mention one captain who was indicted for sexual relationships with inmates, but, according to George, the relations were consensual, not coercive. Others might dispute that view, arguing that women in prison are not in a position to be able to freely consent, given the power differential between officers and inmates. Apparent consent is also complicated by the women's histories of childhood sexual victimization, especially as incest victims, as they might have never experienced appropriate sexual boundaries with authority figures.

In studies of prison sexual victimization, sizable percentages are perpetrated by officers or staff (Struckman-Johnson & Struckman-Johnson, 2000, 2002, 2006). Reports of staff victimization in female prisons ranged from 0% to 10.7% in the Bureau of Justice Statistics study mentioned earlier (Beck, Berzofsky, Caspar, & Krebs, 2013). From the early 1900s to the late 1970s, female officers guarded most female prisoners in this country. Since the late 1970s, most states have allowed male officers to work in prisons for women. Today in many states, over 50% of correctional officers in prisons for women are men (Pollock, 2002). As mentioned earlier, standard policies and procedures in correctional settings (e.g., searches, restraints, and isolation) can have profound effects on women with histories of trauma and abuse, and they often act as triggers to retraumatize women who have PTSD.

Unfortunately, a few male officers, and even some female officers, have used their positions to perpetrate sexual abuse and exploitation of women in prison. The problem of correctional staff sexual misconduct in women's correctional facilities has been identified by the media, the public, and human rights organizations. Almost every state has had a "sex scandal" involving officers and female inmates. In fact, the United States has been criticized in several international reports on the use of male guards to supervise female inmates and the documented incidents of sexual assault and coercion that have resulted (Amnesty International, 1999; Human Rights Watch, 1996). The policy of utilizing male officers to supervise, pat down, and even strip search female inmates puts the United States in conflict with international treaties and the United Nations Standards for the Treatment of Prisoners (Flesher, 2007).

Misconduct can take many forms, including inappropriate language, verbal degradation, intrusive searches, unwarranted visual supervision, using goods and privileges to coerce cooperation in sexual activities, the use or threat of force, and physical rape (Baro, 1997; Dumond, 2000; GAO, 1999; Human Rights Watch, 1996; Siegal, 2001). Disrespectful, unduly familiar, or threatening sexual comments are the most common forms of abuse, but women have also been forcibly raped.

No doubt, some inmates do fall in love with correctional officers, some actively exploit male or female officers who fall in love with them, and some willingly participate in sexual banter. One female inmate describes a male officer's daily experience in the women's prison as characterized by "wolf whistles" and women "licking their lips," or "offering open mouths and tongues" while "flirting shamelessly with him." This officer was later indicted and convicted for sexual misconduct (Petersen, 2000). According to some authors, and Erin George, most sexual contact between female inmates and staff members was consensual. If it is true that female inmates actively seek out and consent to such relationships, one might explain women's behavior as the tactics of the oppressed, as a result of their sexualization through childhood abuse, or as a result of gender socialization and negative self-image. Beyond these personal factors, the contextual pressures are considerable. We as a society have left these women marooned in prison, lonely, and sometimes afraid. It is perhaps understandable that they might try to make the best of the limited relationships open to them behind the walls of their involuntary homes.

RELEASE

For Erin George, there likely will be no release from prison. But for tens of thousands of others, the time in prison represents a short pause in their lives on the outside. According to the picture she paints, very few incarcerated women attempt to develop the insight and skills that will help them stay out. Thus, prison becomes a very expensive "time-out" in their lives. We can conclude that prison is, for these women, mind-numbingly boring, lacking in even the basic elements of healthy living such as decent food and exercise, hurtful, and, ultimately, wasteful—of their time and our tax dollars. If women like Erin George do find some measure of grace, it is to their credit, not ours.

REFERENCES

Aday, R. H., & Krabill, J. J. (2011). *Women aging in prison*. Boulder, CO: Lynne Reinner Publishers.

Alarid, L. F. (2000). Sexual assault and coercion among incarcerated women prisoners: Excerpts from prison letters. *The Prison Journal, 80*(4), 391–406.

Amnesty International. (1999). *"Not part of my sentence": Violations of the human rights of women in custody*. New York: Author.

Baillargeon, J., Binswanger, I. A., Penn, J. V., Williams, B. A., & Murray, O. J. (2009). Psychiatric disorders and repeat incarcerations: The revolving prison door. *The American Journal of Psychiatry, 166*, 103–109.

Baro, A. L. (1997). Spheres of consent: An analysis of the sexual abuse and sexual exploitation of women incarcerated in the state of Hawaii. *Women and Criminal Justice, 8*(3), 61–84.

Batchelor, S. (2005). "Prove me the bam!": Victimization and agency in the lives of young women who commit violent offenses. *The Journal of Community and Criminal Justice, 52*(4), 358–375.

Beck, A. (2013). *PREA data collection activities*. Washington, DC: Bureau of Justice Statistics, U.S. Department of Justice.

Beck, A., Berzofsky, M., Caspar, R., & Krebs, C. (2013). *Sexual victimization in prisons and jails reported by inmates, 2011–12*. Washington, DC: Bureau of Justice Statistics, U.S. Department of Justice.

Beck, A., & Harrison, P. (2008). *Sexual victimization in state and federal prisons, reported by inmates, 2007*. Washington, DC: Bureau of Justice Statistics, U.S. Department of Justice.

Belknap, J., Holsinger, K., & Dunn, M. (1997). Understanding incarcerated girls: The results of a focus group study. *The Prison Journal, 77*(4), 381–404.

Bloom, B., Owen, B., & Covington, S. (2003). *Gender-responsive strategies: Research, practice, and guiding principles for women offenders*. Washington, DC: National Institute of Corrections.

Breitenbecher, K. (2001). Sexual revictimization among women: A review of the literature focusing on empirical investigations. *Aggression and Violent Behavior, 6*, 415–432.

Brewer-Smyth, K. (2004). Women behind bars: Could neurobiological correlates of past physical and sexual abuse contribute to criminal behavior? *Health Care for Women International, 25*, 835–852.

Browne, A., & Finkelhor, D. (1986). Impact of child sexual abuse: A review of the research. *Psychological Bulletin, 99*, 66–77.

Bureau of Justice Statistics. 2008. *State court sentencing of convicted felons, 2004* (Table 2.1: Demographic characteristics of persons convicted of felonies in state courts, by offense, 2004). Washington, DC: Bureau of Justice Statistics, U.S. Department of Justice.

Carlson, B. (2005). The most important things learned about violence and trauma in the past 20 years. *Journal of Interpersonal Violence, 20*(1), 119–126.

Carson, E. A., & Sabol, W. J. (2012). *Prisoners in 2011*. Washington, DC: Bureau of Justice Statistics, U.S. Department of Justice.

Dumond, R. W. (2000). Inmate sexual assault: The plague that persists. *The Prison Journal, 80*(4), 407–414.

Easteal, P. (2001). Women in Australian prisons: The cycle of abuse and dysfunctional environments. *The Prison Journal, 81*(1), 87–112.

Edgar, K., & Martin, C. (2003). *Conflicts & violence in prison, 1998–2000* [computer file]. Colchester, UK: UK Data Archive.

Enders, S. R., Paterniti, D. A., & Meyers, F. J. (2005). An approach to develop effective health care decision making for women in prison. *Journal of Palliative Medicine, 8*(2), 432–439.

Fedock, G., Fries, L., & Kubiak, S. P. (2013). Service needs for incarcerated adults: Exploring gender differences. *Journal of Offender Rehabilitation, 52*(7), 493–508.

Flesher, F. (2007). Cross gender supervision in prisons and the constitutional right of prisoners to remain free from rape. *William and Mary Journal of Women and the Law, 13*, 841–867.

General Accounting Office. (1999). *Women in prison: Sexual misconduct by correctional staff*. Washington, DC: Author.

Gilliard, D., & Beck, A. (1998). *Prisoners in 1997* (Bureau of Justice Statistics Bulletin). Washington, DC: Bureau of Justice Statistics, U.S. Department of Justice.

Girshick, L. B. (1999). *No safe haven: Stories of women in prison*. Boston: Northeastern University Press.

Green, B. L., Miranda, J., Daroowala, A., & Siddique, J. (2005). Trauma exposure, mental health functioning, and program needs of women in jail. *Crime & Delinquency, 51*(1), 133–151.

Greer, K. R. (2000). The changing nature of interpersonal relationships in a women's prison. *The Prison Journal, 80*(4), 442–468.

Hammett, T. M., Harmon, M. P., & Rhodes, W. (2002). The burden of infectious disease among inmates of and releasees from U.S. correctional facilities, 1997. *American Journal of Public Health, 92*, 1789–1794.

Harer, M. D., & Langan, N. P. (2001). Gender differences in predictors of prison violence: Assessing the predictive validity of a risk classification system. *Crime & Delinquency, 47*(4), 513–536.

Harlow, C. (1999). *Prior abuse reported by inmates and probationers*. Washington, DC: Bureau of Justice Statistics, National Institute of Justice.

Harrison, P., & Beck, A. (2006). *Prisoners in 2005*. Washington, DC: Bureau of Justice Statistics, U.S. Department of Justice.

Haywood, T., Kravitz, H., Goldman, L., & Freeman, L. (2000). Characteristics of women in jail and treatment orientations. *Behavior Modification, 24*, 307–324.

Hensley, C., Castle, T., & Tewksbury, R. (2003). Inmate-to-inmate sexual coercion in a prison for women. *Journal of Offender Rehabilitation, 37*(2), 77–87.

Hensley, C., & Tewksbury, R. (2002). Inmate-to-inmate prison sexuality: A review of empirical studies. *Trauma, Violence, & Abuse, 3*(3), 226–243.

Human Rights Watch. (1996). *All too familiar: Sexual abuse of women in U.S. state prisons*. New York: Human Rights Watch.

Islam-Zwart, K. A., & Vik, P. W. (2004). Female adjustment to incarceration as influenced by sexual assault history. *Criminal Justice and Behavior, 31*(5), 521–541.

Johnson, R. (2002). *Hard time: Understanding and reforming the prison*. Belmont, CA: Wadsworth.

Johnson, R., & Brooks, A. (2011). Cold comfort: Women aging in prison. *The Gerontologist, 51*(6), 884–887.

Johnson, K., & Lynch, S. (2013). Predictors of maladaptive coping in incarcerated women who are survivors of childhood sexual abuse. *Journal of Family Violence, 28*, 43–52.

Jordan, B., Schlenger, W., Fairbank, J., & Caddell, J. (1996). Prevalence of psychiatric disorders among incarcerated women: Convicted felons entering prison. *Archives of General Psychiatry, 53*, 513–519.

Ketring, S., & Feinaur, L. (1999). Perpetrator-victim relationship: Long-term effects of sexual abuse for men and women. *American Journal of Family Therapy, 27*(2), 109–120.

Kruttschnitt, C. (1983). Race relations and the female inmate. *Crime & Delinquency, 29*, 577–592.

Kruttschnitt, C., & Carbone-Lopez, K. (2006). Moving beyond stereotypes: Women's subjective accounts of their violent crime. *Criminology, 44*(2), 321–351.

Maeve, M. K. (2000). Speaking unavoidable truths: Understanding early childhood sexual and physical violence among women in prison. *Issues in Mental Health Nursing, 21*, 473–498.

Maruschak, L. M. (2008). Medical problems of prisoners. Washington, DC: Bureau of Justice Statistics, U.S. Department of Justice.

McClellan, D., Farabee, D., & Crouch, B. (1997). Early victimization, drug use, and criminality; A comparison of male and female prisoners. *Criminal Justice and Behavior, 24*(4), 455–476.

Mullings, J., Marquart, J., & Brewer, V. (2000). Assessing the relationship between child sexual abuse and marginal living conditions on HIV/AIDS-related risk behavior among women prisoners. *Child Abuse and Neglect, 24*(5), 677–688.

Mullings, J., Marquart, J., & Hartley, D. (2003). Exploring the effects of childhood sexual abuse and its impact on HIV/AIDS risk-taking behavior among women prisoners. *The Prison Journal, 83*(4), 442–463.

Mullings, J., Pollock, J., & Crouch, B. (2002). Drugs and criminality: Results from the Texas women inmates study. *Women & Criminal Justice, 13*(4), 69–97.

Nijhawan, A. E., Salloway, R., Nunn, A. S., Poshkus, M., & Clarke, J. G. (2010). Preventive healthcare for underserved women: Results of a prison survey. *Journal of Women's Health, 19*(1),17–22.

Owen, B. (1998). *In the mix: Struggles and survival in a women's prison.* Albany: State University of New York Press.

Peters, R. H., Greenbaum, P. E., Edens, J. F., Carter, C. R., & Ortiz, M. M. (1998). Prevalence of DSM-IV substance abuse and dependence disorders among prison inmates. *The American Journal of Drug and Alcohol Abuse, 24,* 573–587.

Petersen, D. (2000). Sex behind bars. Reprinted in Balkin, K. (2004). *Opposing viewpoints: Current controversies series.* San Diego, CA: Greenhaven Press.

Pogrebin, M., & Dodge, M. (2001). Women's accounts of their prison experiences: A retrospective view of their subjective realities. *Journal of Criminal Justice, 29*(6), 531–541.

Pollock, J. (2002). *Women, prison & crime.* Belmont, CA: Wadsworth.

Pollock, J. (2004). *Prisons and prison life: Costs and consequences.* Los Angeles: Roxbury.

Pollock, J., Mullings, J., & Crouch, B. (2006). Women who are violent: Findings from the Texas Women Inmate Study. *Journal of Interpersonal Violence, 21*(4), 485–502.

Powell, T. (1999, August). Women inmates in Vermont. Paper presented at the meeting of the American Psychological Association, Boston, MA.

Sabol, W., & Couture, H. (2008). *Prison inmates at midyear 2007.* Washington, DC: Bureau of Justice Statistics, U.S. Department of Justice.

Siegal, N. (2001). Sexual abuse of women inmates is widespread. In M. Wagner, *How should prisons treat inmates? Opposing viewpoints.* San Diego, CA: Greenhaven Press.

Sommers, I., & Baskin, D. (1993). The situational context of violent female offending. *Journal of Research in Crime & Delinquency, 30*(2), 136–162.

Sourcebook of Criminal Justice Statistics. (2008). Table 6.41. Number and Rate (per 100,000 resident female population) of female prisoners. Retrieved July 8, 2008, from http:// www.albany.edu/sourcebook.pdf/t6412006.pdf.

Struckman-Johnson, C., & Struckman-Johnson, D. (2000). Sexual coercion rates in seven midwestern prison facilities for men. *The Prison Journal, 80*(4), 379–390.

Struckman-Johnson, C., & Struckman-Johnson, D. (2002). Sexual coercion reported by women in three midwestern prisons. *The Journal of Sex Research, 39*(3), 217–227.

Struckman-Johnson, C., & Struckman-Johnson, D. (2006). A comparison of sexual coercion experiences reported by men and women in prison. *Journal of Interpersonal Violence, 21*(12), 1591–1615.

Struckman-Johnson, C., Struckman-Johnson, D., Rucker, L., Bumby, K., & Donaldson, S. (1996). Sexual coercion reported by men and women in prison. *The Journal of Sex Research, 33*(1), 67–76.

Teplin, L., Abram, K., & McClelland, G. (1996). Prevalence of psychiatric disorders among incarcerated women: Pretrial jail detainees. *Archives of General Psychiatry, 53*(6), 505–512.

Tjaden, P., & Thoennes, N. (2006). *Extent, nature, and consequences of rape victimization: Findings from the National Violence Against Women Survey.* Washington, DC: National Institute of Justice, U.S. Department of Justice.

Tripodi, S. J., & Pettus-David, C. (2013). Histories of childhood victimization and subsequent mental health problems, substance use, and sexual victimization for a sample of incarcerated women in the US. *International Journal of Law and Psychiatry, 36,* 30–40.

Veysey, B. (1998). Specific needs of women diagnosed with mental illnesses in US jails. In B. L. Levin, A. K. Blanch, & A. Jennings (Eds.), *Women's mental health services* (pp. 368–389). London: Sage.

Wolff, N., Blitz, D. L., Shi, J., Bachman, R., & Siegel, J. (2006). Sexual violence inside prisons: Rates of victimization. *Journal of Urban Health: Bulletin of the New York Academy of Medicine, 83*(5), 835–848.

Wolff, N., Blitz, D. L., Shi, J., Siegel, J., & Bachman, R. (2007). Physical violence inside prisons: Rates of victimization. *Criminal Justice and Behavior, 34*, 588–599.

Wolff, N., Shi, J., Blitz, D. L., & Siegel, J. (2007). Understanding sexual victimization inside prisons: Factors that predict risk. *Criminology & Public Policy, 6*(3), 535–564.

Terms of Entanglement: A Prison Glossary

Like any world apart, prisons for women have their own language. What follows is a glossary prepared by Erin George, offering a map in words and phrases of the prison world she has reluctantly made her home.

10-4: To act as lookout for someone (or a couple of someones) engaged in an illegal act.

10-52: Code for a medical emergency, announced over the intercom.

209: A ticket for sexual contact between inmates. Depending on the interpretation, sexual interaction can range from a brief hug to oral intercourse. Sadie and Nadia once received a 209 together because they gave each other an "air kiss" (no physical contact was made) as they passed each other on the stairs. Apparently the officer was having a bad day.

90: The officer who runs the yard. This officer decides when to call a mass movement, decides when middle perimeter gates are opened and closed, closes the yard when an inmate is being taken into segregation, and determines which buildings have rec.

Acute: Area of the medical building where inmates who have profound mental health issues are housed.

Beef: Either a noun or a verb. You can have a beef with someone (be pissed off at her) or "be beefing," which means actively engaging in quarrelling. Beefs are usually low-level, but often are long-lasting.

Big hat: An officer who is a sergeant or above. Lowest-level C.O.s wear baseball-style caps. Upper level officers wear larger, broad-brimmed, military-style hats.

Blanket party: When an inmate is covered by a blanket and then pummeled by unknown assailants. This is usually followed by being robbed of everything in her property.

Boo: Girlfriend.

Boulevard: The oval sidewalk that all inmates use when they are traveling from building to building or when a building's population is out for walking recreation (called "rec"). Four complete circuits around the boulevard equal one mile.

Boy: A masculine inmate.

Bubble: Each housing building has a central control area called the bubble. The bubble is a high-walled, circular station that has large windows allowing the officer in the bubble to see clearly into each wing. The bubble area contains video monitors of the wings as well. The bubble officer controls all movement in and out of a building, the wings, and each individual cell. Each cell has an intercom that allows the bubble officer and inmate to speak to each other. Some bubble officers are notorious for listening into roommate conversations through this intercom without the inmates realizing it.

Bulldagger: An inmate who constantly bends or breaks the rules to see her girlfriend.

C.O.: Correctional officer, the lowest rank of prison security personnel. I was once reprimanded for calling a C.O. a "guard." So because they're C.O.s, I want to be referred to as "liberationally challenged," which is to prisoner what correctional officer is to guard.

Cell restriction: Punishment for minor infractions. This is when an inmate is only allowed to leave her cell for meals and church. When on cell restriction, the inmate will suddenly become devoutly religious. This type of punishment is a huge pain for the inmate's cellmate because she will have to have her door popped open every time she wants to enter or leave her room. Likewise, officers hate popping the same door a million times.

Cock block: To prevent someone from contacting her girlfriend.

Code blue: Code for a medical emergency when the inmate has suffered a lack of oxygen, announced over the intercom.

Code red: Code for a medical emergency involving spilled blood, announced over the intercom.

Commissary: Also known as canteen. Each building visits commissary three times a month to purchase food, personals, stationery, and an extremely limited variety of over-the-counter medical supplies (such as cough drops or two-packs of generic aspirin). We also purchase all electronics, sweatpants and sweatshirts, T-shirts, jeans, and shoes from commissary. The DOC has a contract with a company called Keefe, which supplies all commissary items to prisons in the state of Virginia (as well as jails and penal institutions in other states). This company is like the great and powerful Oz, offering shoddy, inferior products at great cost and, it seems, at their whim. It is not uncommon to have your inmate account debited $45 for a pair of jeans (which retail for about $25.00 to the rest of the world), then wait 3 or 4 months (or longer) to receive them. If you ever do. I still haven't seen mine.

Compliance, to be in: An inmate is in compliance when she is abiding by all of the DOP and IOP regulations.

Contact visits: Visits where you are actually allowed to touch, embrace, and kiss your visitors. Heaven.

Contraband: Anything you are not allowed to have, or have too much of, is contraband. This is a delightfully fluid term, open to interpretation from officer to officer depending on mood or personality. We have lively discussions sometimes trying to decide if something is contraband. Is the paper clip that held the papers my counselor gave me contraband? Is the plastic bag that the chaplain's package comes in contraband? Never being quite sure gives life a zesty edge.

Cosmo: One of the vocational classes offered through VCE, through which women are given the opportunity to earn a cosmetology license. Inmates can sign up every month or so to go in and have their hair cut, permed, or relaxed. You are also permitted to dye your hair no more than two shades lighter or darker than your natural hair color.

Counselor: Each inmate is assigned a counselor, who is ostensibly required to meet with each of his or her assigned inmates each month, manage the inmate's annual review, and create the upcoming year's treatment plan. Your counselor is also the person you are supposed to go to when you need papers notarized, photocopies made (at 25 cents a page), a job application, an answer to any question about policy, and (although this does not apply to me) preparation of an inmate's home plan (information about where and how a released inmate is planning to live). Pray you get a good counselor. I know more than one person who has not been able to go home when her time is up because her counselor screwed up her home plan.

Count (standing count): There are four standing counts each day: 7:00 a.m., 11:30 a.m., 3:30 p.m., and 9:30 p.m. During count time there is no inmate movement between buildings and all inmates must be standing in their cells, facing forward so that they can be seen through the door. The only inmates who are excluded from this are those who are not in the wing (*see* Out count). Inmates must lock down at least 5 minutes before count time. They are not allowed to watch TV, listen to the radio, or speak during the count, which is announced by the officer's whistle. Normal movement resumes when the count clears. Emergency count can be called any time an inmate is "misplaced."

Creep: *See* Delay and hinder.

Creep door: The door between the upper tier and the utility stairwell. Officers use this door to catch inmates getting into trouble because it makes less noise when opening than the usual wing door.

Day room: A large area in each general population wing intended for socializing by the inmates. It contains five small round tables, several plastic chairs, a hot water pot, and an unmanned officer's desk. The day room hours in general population are between 9:00 a.m. and 9:15 p.m. on weekdays and 8:00 a.m. to 11:00 a.m. on Friday and Saturday night.

DCE: The building that houses all academic classes for those trying to earn their general equivalency diplomas (GED) or high school equivalent degrees, as well as the DCE library (a general-purpose library), the chaplain's library (which contains religious materials), and the gymnasium.

Delay and hinder: A tactic used by bulldaggers to move slowly or stealthily so as meet up with their girlfriends who live in other buildings. Bulldaggers have fixated on the rule that they "must be in forward motion at all times" and interpreted that to mean such a glacially slow pace that they can stretch a 2-minute walk to 15 minutes or more, especially if they can find an officer or staff member to chat with until the girlfriend appears.

Diet loaf: A combination of all of a prison meal's nutrients combined into one, unappetizing lump. Ingredients might include oatmeal, ground meat, potatoes, carrots, and egg. This meal is served to inmates in segregation who throw their food at officers, smear it onto the walls, flush it down the toilet, or otherwise abuse and misuse the contents of the regular trays.

Dip: To eavesdrop on another inmate's conversation. Usually used in the context "I didn't mean to dip, but I think. . . ." Dipping is very poor prison etiquette, but it happens all of the time.

Dirt coffee: The fabulously high-quality coffee served in the chow hall (on the few occasions that they actually serve us coffee).

DOC: Department of Corrections.

DOP: Divisional Operating Procedures. The DOP is a broad set of regulations created by the DOC and is applied to all DOC inmate facilities in Virginia.

Double-bank: When two or more people assault one inmate. Not cool.

Dry cell: A cell that does not contain a toilet or sink. All cells in general population are dry cells.

Dry snitch: To tell on another inmate without actually coming out and saying "Q-Tip stole some hair relaxer from Cosmo and gave it to her girlfriend Chi-chi." Instead, dry snitches (who are even more devious and dangerous than out-and-out snitches because it takes much longer to figure out who they are) use subtle allusions and supposedly innocent questions to the police to direct them to their targets. An example would be "Why, I thought that we were allowed to have 112 packs of cigarettes at a time because that's how many Darva has."

Ear hustle: To surreptitiously listen to a C.O.'s radio to get an idea of what is going on. This is especially helpful when you are trying to find out why the yard is closed, why things are suddenly locked down, or if waiting for a class to be called.

Fakedown: When an announcement is made that a shakedown is about to occur, but inmates are given an opportunity to discard their contraband. Inmates are then locked in their cells for a few minutes, then released to normal activities.

Fall out: Whenever an inmate collapses, you say that she is falling out. Usually falling out is presumed to be a ploy for attention or lobbying for a trip to the infirmary on a stretcher or in a wheelchair. Because of the likelihood of faking, the response time from medical when someone falls out is not a speedy one.

Fluvanna shuffle: That barely perceptible forward movement employed by bulldaggers when they are delaying and hindering.

"For real, for real": Assertion for absolute sincerity, as in "I wasn't talking to that girl at chow, for real, for real." You never hear just one "for real."

General population (GP): Where most inmates are housed, sometimes shortened to GP. There are no special requirements to live in general population. Non-GP housing units included acute (for inmates with profound mental health issues), segregation, structured living, and the Honor Wing.

Geriatric parole: This is the only parole that I am eligible for. I can try for geriatric parole when I am 60 years old (I think). As far as I know, no woman has ever been granted geriatric parole. (*See also* New law)

Gold badge: Term used at RRJ for an upper level security officer. Basic C.O.s wear silver badges.

Good time: For every day served, nonlifers earn a certain amount of good time, which is time taken off of their sentences. Good time can be taken away if an inmate receives a ticket (*see* Ticket). Every so often the rumor goes around that the state legislature is enacting a "65% law," which means that inmates would only serve that portion of their sentence. This rumor is always false. I had a friend, Donna, who found great pleasure in starting rumors like that, telling some gullible short-timer, "I know it's true, I saw it on CNN." Then she would clock how long it took the rumor to get back to her. I think the record was 3 hours.

Grievance: If an inmate feels that she is being treated unjustly, she is permitted to file a grievance. Before she can do that, however, she has to follow institutional protocol, which is as follows (as best as I can figure out-it's complex): Say that, oh, I don't know, you haven't gotten the jeans that you ordered 5 months ago. Here is how you would handle it:

   1. Ask the ladies at commissary during every commissary visit when your jeans will be given to you and listen patiently as they explain that your name is "on a list" somewhere and that this is not the real world and that you just have to be patient.

Never mind that you paid a month's salary for the jeans (subtext: be damn grateful you're not wearing rags and a chain with a big iron ball attached to it).

2. Send an IMS (a form for internal communications; *see* IMS) to commissary asking why you haven't gotten the jeans you ordered.
3. Wait fruitlessly for 15 business days to hear a response.
4. Send another, also ignored IMS.
5. Write an informal grievance.
6. Wait for the informal grievance to be returned for any one of several reasons: You did not notify the institution within 10 days of the issue occurring (well, duh-I was waiting for the jeans to eventually come) or you did not attach the IMS with which you began the grievance process (you know, the one that never came back to you).
7. Weep silently at the morass in which you are mired.
8. Start the process all over again.

Grievance, emergency: Emergency grievances are designed to deal with issues that cannot survive the lengthy process entailed by using a regular grievance (danger of imminent death or hazard to health is the usual reason for an emergency grievance). You would use it in a situation like this: Because Fluvanna is notorious for failing to have an inmate's prescription filled, an inmate will often go without her medicine until she files an emergency grievance. These grievances must be responded to within 24 hours. Emergency grievances are routinely denied because the grievance coordinator determines that there is no imminent danger to the inmate. Funnily enough, though, prescriptions miraculously appear immediately after these grievances are filed.

Grit, to: To grit on someone is to stare at her in a menacing manner. You usually hear this word used in this way: "What the hell are you grittin' on me for?" or "You should have seen her grittin' on Shaniqua in the chow hall this morning."

Head hunter: An inmate who manipulates other women into performing oral sex on her, but never wants to return the favor.

Holding cell: A small cell that is used when an inmate needs to cool down for a few hours.

Honor Wing: A housing unit that has special requirements for the inmates who live there. Inmates in the Honor Wing must be employed and ticket-free for at least 1 year. The benefits of living in this unit are being called first for chow (normally 90 rotates the buildings' order of going to eat; *see* 90), a microwave oven, a television in the dayroom, being able to do their own laundry, and having the dayroom open later than general population.

IMS: The form that inmates must use to officially contact anyone in the institution. Per policy, the staff member you are writing must respond to your IMS within 10 working days. Although a few departments, such as Property, are very good about responding to an IMS well before that 10-day deadline, the majority are not. Frequently, it depends on the content; an IMS complaining about the moldy bread and rotten potatoes served at dinner is never seen again, but praise for something new and semitasty being served is replied to immediately. (*See* Grievance)

Informal resolution: A penalty offer that is given when a ticket is served. If you take the informal resolution, then you do not need to go through a hearing and possibly receive a much harsher punishment.

Inkie: A prison tattoo artist.

Inmate advisor: An inmate whose job is to advise other inmates who have received tickets. Inmate advisors are the lawyers of the institutional punishment system. They help fill out paperwork, organize witness statements and what little evidence we are allowed access to (as we can't use such evidence as the wing videotapes to exonerate ourselves-only the prison has access to those), and generally assist the ticketed inmate.

Inmate forum: Once a month an inmate from each building is randomly chosen to be present at the inmate forum This is ostensibly an opportunity to raise issues to the various upper level staff members who attend, such as the warden, the assistant warden, and the major. Inmates come prepared with questions, which are taken up as the inmates arrive. These representatives are given 5 minutes to ask their questions. The institution decides which questions will be answered, if any. No one takes minutes during these meetings, so the "minutes" that are posted in the wings are later re-creations of what the prison says occurred. Obviously this is not an effective vehicle to convey inmate concerns. The typical response to questions is that they "will be looked into."

Institutionalized: To become so used to life in prison (with its rigid schedules and ponderous routine) that you simply cannot function when things occur that are out of the ordinary or when you have to make a decision for yourself. Inmates who are institutionalized might be overwhelmed by feelings of dread when count is called 10 minutes late or be excessively angry when their building is called to chow out of the regular rotation.

IOP: Internal Operating Procedures. The IOP is specific to Fluvanna Correctional Center for Women (FCCW). It is tailored to fit the needs of a specific facility rather than the more general DOP.

Jaunk: A general-purpose noun that can be used as a term of approbation or dismissal (i.e., "That jaunk is pathetic," or "Damn, that jaunk is the bomb!"). Probably a variation of the word *junk*.

Kirk out: To go crazy with anger.

Kite: A note that is passed between inmates.

Mass movement: Mass movement is called five times a day: twice in the morning (so inmates can go to and from work before 11:00 a.m. count), twice in the afternoon (so inmates can go back and forth from work again between lunch and 3:30 p.m. count), and finally at 6:30 p.m. (for all evening classes, which are released at different times). During mass movement, all inmates are told to move in a single file line, traveling briskly clockwise around the boulevard. The purpose of this is to keep the girlfriends from different buildings from meeting up on the boulevard to pass notes or fight. Instead, it just encourages delaying and hindering, which only slows up those of us who are actually trying to get to work on time.

Master pass list: The list of every job and program at FCCW that inmates are allowed to attend. If you are at a program and are not on the master pass list for that program, you are in an unauthorized area. The master pass list is updated weekly.

Medical clemency: Medical clemency can be granted when an inmate is so ill that there is no chance of recovery. Although I know no one who has been granted medical clemency, I have had several friends who have died in the prison infirmary from long, painful, patently terminal illnesses. I wonder what they are saving medical clemency for.

Medical profile: This is issued by a DOC doctor certifying that an inmate has certain needs that the state must accommodate. A common example is a bottom-bunk medical profile, for those inmates who are supposedly unable to climb the metal ladder to the top bunk. But because bottom bunks are usually the most desirable bunks in a room, many inmates manipulate this system to get a bottom bunk or move out of a room when the other occupant already has a medical profile mandating a bottom bunk. This is another way that inmates try to "work their shot" to have some control over housing assignments.

Middle perimeter: The area between the inner and outer fences. Inmates who work this area must have a lower security level than most lifers have.

MILK: Mothers Inside Loving Kids. A parenting program that allows extended and intense interaction between an inmate mom and her children. Sponsored by the Girl Scouts of America.

New law: I was convicted under "new law," which means I am not eligible to be considered for parole (except geriatric parole). I also don't receive good time. Lifers who were convicted under "old law" (before the late 1990s) are technically eligible for parole at some point, and thus must endure the farce that is a parole board hearing before the inevitable refusal of parole. One of the first questions inmates ask each other when discussing their sentences is, "Are you old law or new law?"

Off the chain: When a wing is utterly chaotic: noisy, violent, unbearable. Whenever a wing gets to be off the chain, the police try to break it up by moving out the troublemakers. But that just makes different wings off the chain. When I first got to Fluvanna, Building Three was a "good" building. Now, it is off the chain.

Oldhead: An inmate who has been down (doing time) a long time.

On the sneak: When an officer comes into the wing through the upper-tier service door (which does not make the loud opening noise that the main wing door does). They do that so that can bypass the 10-4 and catch inmates who are in the middle of some illicit act.

Out count: Inmates are out-counted when they are prevented from returning to their housing units for some reason. This might include being at visitation, being held at medical, or being at a job (like the kitchen) that is permitted to keep its inmate workers during count time.

Override: When the bubble officer unexpectedly opens both of the sally port doors so that inmates can leave the building without having to let the sally port fill up with inmates in between opening the doors. It is always exciting when this happens because it is a break from normal routine and we all feel a bit friskier for acting so daringly. Inmates will gleefully shout "Override! Override!" along the line of women dawdling behind them so that any laggers won't be left behind.

Pee test: Also called a *piss test.* A urine test for illegal drugs. Failure to provide a urine sample within 2 hours of one being requested results in an automatic stay in seg (*see* Segregation), suspension of contact visits for 6 months, and an interminable stretch of "random" pee tests until you go home again.

Pill line: The call for inmates to receive their medication. Inmates are allowed to have very few meds in their possession (I can't even have my prescribed multivitamin as a KOP, or keep on person, med), so every day there is a parade of Fluvanna infirm wheeling and staggering to pill line. Those on walkers, wheelchairs, and canes accompany people getting antibiotics, fiber pills, or psych meds, so it is a good idea to check that the meds you receive are your own: Often they aren't. The pill line is called for building by building at 4:30 a.m., noon, and 3:00 p.m. I would rather die of whatever disease I had than get up at 4:30 a.m. for pill line.

Pod: Term used at RRJ, and many other penal institutions, for a housing unit.

Police: Specifically, any member of the security staff, but can be used more generally to refer to any noninmate who works for the DOC, DCE, or VCE. This word is always pronounced "poh-lease," with the first syllable heavily accented.

PPR (Personal Property Request) Form: Any property that an inmate has must be accompanied by the appropriate PPR form. To purchase and receive an item from an outside vendor, you must complete a PPR form (with attached stamped/addressed envelope and filled-out catalog order form) stating exactly what you wish to purchase from the approved vendor, get this form signed by a sergeant or higher, then submit it to the business office for withdrawal of funds from your account. Property verifies that you are buying an item (or items) that you are allowed to have. The business office mails out your order and the money order. You are given a carbon copy of the approved form after it is processed by the business office. You will not be allowed to receive your purchase unless you have a copy of your approved PPR. This prevents anyone from the outside ordering you anything. Nothing other than letters, photographs, and money orders can be sent to an inmate.

Property: There are two kinds of property: state property (which is any uniform clothing that has been issued to you, Velcro-closing shoes, two skimpy towels, a washcloth, two sheets, two blankets, a pillowcase, two white mesh laundry bags, and a large orange mesh commissary bag) and personal property (anything else you are allowed to have). By policy, all personal and state property must be able to fit into our two moderately sized plastic boxes and a bag.

Property Department (also referred to simply as "Property"): This area of the facility oversees the issuing of all state and personal property. Not only do they give you all of your uniforms, but Property is also the place where inmate packages are opened. It's a wonderful day when at 6:45 a.m. you are awakened from sleep to hear "George, go to Property when count clears." All of your packages and large envelopes are opened in your presence. If you have a yellow copy of your PPR saying you can have the item, you're in luck. If not, it has to be mailed back or thrown away.

Rec: An hour of recreation time for inmates, which is called three or four times a week. The options available to inmates are walking rec (walking in circles around the boulevard), ball field rec (walking in circles around the ball field), or gym rec (waiting in line to walk on one of the two treadmills).

Sally port: The small area (about 7 feet long) between the outer building entrance and the inner building entrance. Everyone entering one of the residential buildings must pass through the sally port before they can reach the central area of the building called the vestibule, where the bubble (*see* Bubble) is located. Normally, the bubble officer opens one of the sally port doors when you are entering or leaving, only opening the next door when the first is securely closed. (*See* Over-ride)

Seg: Segregation or isolation. Area where inmates who have been found guilty of extreme tickets are housed. You can also be housed in segregation if you are "under investigation," which does not require that any tickets against you have been issued.

Self meds: Medicine you can have in your room.

Shakedown: A search of an inmate's room. These range from cursory to violently invasive.

SLU: *See* Structured Living Unit.

Smack, to talk: Talking smack is a fine art of nuanced insults that is almost exclusively employed during competitive card games. Elaborate, degrading insults are tailored to target an inmate's individual weakness. Smack talk is only really safe when used between longtime friends.

Smurf: An inmate who is unclassified. Called "Smurf" because of the baby-blue uniform she wears.

Snitch: Someone who gives information to the police. Avoid at all costs.

Squat and cough: Strip search. This process is called "squat and cough" because, among the other indignities, the inmate is required to squat down and cough to demonstrate that she is not holding contraband in her vagina.

Step down: *See* Structured Living Unit.

Store: A commercial enterprise run by an inmate. Someone running a store will lend out commissary at a rate of two-for-one (*see* Two-for-one). Eventually she will have so much commissary that she will not have to buy anything for herself. That only lasts until she is snitched out and the police compare the bounty of candy, chips, and cigarettes in a store operator's boxes with the fact that she hasn't been to commissary in 6 months.

Street charge: Some infractions committed by an inmate are so serious that they can result in a street charge-legal charges brought against her that will be addressed in an actual court of law. Of course, street charges will also be accompanied by a significant amount of segregation time as well.

Stretch: The period of time between the last commissary visit of the month and the first visit of the next month. The usual length of a stretch is about 2 weeks, and by the end of that 2 weeks inmates are begging and borrowing food from anyone they have even the most cursory relationship with. When you are on day 16 of a stretch and there is nothing in your box but three sugar packets and a half a sleeve of crackers, you get pretty desperate.

Strip cell: A cell where inmates who are a suicide risk are housed. An inmate in this cell is not allowed any property, sheets, blankets . . . nothing that she can use to harm herself.

Structured Living Unit: Special housing wing for inmates who have been released from seg but are still deemed unready to be moved into general population. Inmates are housed two to a cell, but remain locked down for the majority of each day. Unlike the women in segregation, they are allowed to buy anything they would like from commissary and outside vendors, and they can have regular visitation. They also seem to have rec almost every day, much to the annoyance of the rest of the inmate population, who not only have far less rec time, but who are also stuck in their buildings whenever the SLU girls are creeping their way to and from the gym (because the yard has to be closed when SLU is out).

Swole: A tasty dish that is a perennial prison favorite—the quintessential prison cuisine (see Appendix B). Combined crushed Ramen noodles, crushed cheese curls, a few packets of mayonnaise, a cut-up Slim Jim, and just enough hot water to make one glutinous mass and let it swell (thus the name) in the cheese curl bag. Pull apart the bag to reveal an appetizing orange rectangle that you then smear with cheese or onion dip and serve on saltines.

Three-way mail: To use an intermediary (usually your mother or other close female relative) to write letters to someone (usually a man) in another correctional facility. It works like this: Susie in Fluvanna is writing to her roommate's brother Mike, who is locked up in prison in Tennessee. Because all outgoing prison mail is stamped by the institution, Susie has to get her mother to send her letters in an unmarked envelope if she wants Mike to receive it. Mike does the same with the letters he sends to Susie. This will continue until someone snitches them out.

Three-way phone call: To call an approved telephone number, then have the person you are phoning connect your call to another number. This is done either to save money (by calling someone fairly close by and forwarding the call to someone much farther away) or to reach someone at an unapproved phone number.

Ticket: An institutional charge. Tickets are either 100 series (the really bad ones that can get you seg time or a street charge) or 200 series charges (not so serious stuff).

Transportation, to be on: When an inmate is off the grounds. When we are on transportation, it is usually for medical procedures that cannot be performed by the staff onsite. Inmates on transportation wear leg shackles, handcuffs, and an orange jumpsuit.

Treatment plan: A list of criteria that the inmate must meet, ostensibly determined by her charge(s) and length of sentence. Each inmate has an annual review with her counselor, who will go over her record for the last year and decide what programs, and so on, she needs to take during the upcoming year. Typically, treatment plans include directives to stay ticket-free, maintain steady employment, and take a class like Alcoholics Anonymous or Narcotics Anonymous. Lifers have usually taken all of the available classes already and any rehabilitative programs are pointless (because they are probably never going home, even if they are eligible for parole). Because I have never had problems with drug use, alcohol, anger management, or theft of property, my treatment plan each year says to keep a job and take "one program for personal enrichment."

Two-for-one: When an inmate runs a store, she usually will charge two-for-one. That means if you borrow one Hershey bar from her, you need to pay her back two when your building next goes to commissary (and she will know when your building goes). If you are unable to pay it back, your debt increases exponentially. This can be a vicious cycle that only ends when the debtor offers up something really significant in value (like jewelry) or with violence. (*See* Store)

Unauthorized area: Any area an inmate is not allowed to be in, especially any cell not her own. This is one of the most common charges at FCCW.

VCE: The building that houses all vocational classes offered at Fluvanna. These classes include cosmo, printing and graphic design, CAD (computer-aided drafting), plumbing and electrical, business software, optical, and HVAC.

Work your shot: To manipulate the system, usually to be moved into the same wing or same room as a friend or girlfriend.

APPENDIX B

A Prison Cookbook

Food is a central preoccupation, not to say obsession, of prison inmates. George tried to capture the importance of food to prisoners in a poem entitled "Reflections from a Prison Yard."

Reflections from a Prison Yard
One would imagine
as we stand
in the treeless autumn
of the prison yard,
our eyes snared
by the basso profundo declarations
from the skein of geese overhead
that we envy them
their utter freedom,
their strong-breasted flights
with unclipped wings.
Really, though,
we all just wish
we were having roast goose
for dinner.

Reprinted with permission from *Origami Heart:*
Poems by a Woman Doing Life,
by Erin George (2008, p. 31). Washington,
DC: BleakHouse Publishing.

Food is one of the few licit comforts available to an inmate. Not chow hall food, of course. Heaven forefend! No, I'm talking about the dishes produced in the wing (our living quarters, called tiers or pods in some prisons) using little more than the meager, over-priced snacks from commissary. Although the Honor Wing where I live (at this writing) has the luxury of a microwave oven, every other wing has to use hot water, blow dryers, or flat irons to heat their meals. There are a few basic recipes that allow for myriad variations according to taste, but every now and then someone comes up with something spectacular, the kind of dish where you say, "Man, I would even eat that on the street!"—the ultimate praise.

Here, then, are a few of the recipes that are most popular in Fluvanna, as well as suggestions for presentation and accompanying beverages. For authenticity, all meals must be prepared using nothing but trash bags, original food packaging, institutional-grade paper towels, small plastic bowls, and 8-ounce plastic tumblers and eaten only with plastic sporks.

THE SWOLE

The swole is a classic prison dish—a cheap foundation meal that can be made more elaborate as the budget allows. It is so leaden that I can only bring myself to eat one once every 4 months, at a minimum. Its name, I surmise, comes from a prison mangling of the verb "swell."

- 1 bag Ramen noodles, chicken, spicy beef, or chili flavor, crushed well
- 1 bag of cheese curls, crushed into powder
- 1 packet of mayonnaise

Add the Ramen noodles to the bag containing the crushed cheese curls. Carefully add hot water to the bag, combining the ingredients thoroughly. Don't add too much water, use just enough to make a paste-like consistency. Flatten the bag so that the wad of noodles and cheese curls is formed into a thin slab. Let sit for 5 minutes. Tear open the seam of the bag to expose the swollen and gelatinized noodles, then smear the top with mayonnaise. Serve on saltines. An added benefit of this meal is that there are no bowls to wash afterward; the swole is served directly from the bag.

Serves 1

Some variations on the basic swole:

The Tuna Swole: In addition to chicken noodles and cheese curls, use I package of tuna before adding the hot water and preparing as above. If you are feeling particularly swanky, you can use onion dip rather than mayo on top. For a beverage, the artificial lemon taste of off-brand instant iced tea delightfully complements the flavor of the substandard tuna available to us.

The Mexicali Swole: Combine chili noodles, cheese curls, and diced pickle, then prepare as described above. Top with spicy cheese dip and serve with nacho cheese tortilla chips. Serve with a Coke.

The Super Swole: Don't hold anything back when compiling the ingredient list for the most lavish incarnation of this favorite. I say the more ingredients the better when it comes to a meal that will force you to lie in your bunk for 2 days, slowly digesting like a boa constrictor that just ate a slow goat. Possible additions to the basic recipe include onion dip, summer sausage, pickle, tuna, spicy cheese squeeze, chicken, Mexican beef, and/or pepperoni. Toppings can range from simple mayonnaise, to onion dip, to a honey mustard sauce (made by combining 4 mayo packets, 1 mustard packet, and 1 packet of artificial sweetener, then thinned with a little hot water).

THE BAKED POTATO

The baked potato is another prison basic, and like the swole is both cooked in and served from a bag. It also is a recipe that can be easily adapted.

- 1 bag sour cream potato chips, crushed well
- ½ bag of cheese curls, crushed into powder (optional)
- 1 summer sausage, diced
- Onion dip (optional)

Combine the potato chips and, if desired, the crushed cheese curls in the potato chip bag. Carefully add hot water to the bag, combining the ingredients thoroughly. Don't add too much water, use just enough to let the potato chips thicken and swell. Flatten the bag so that the potato is formed into a rectangle. Let sit for 5 minutes. Tear open the seam of the bag to expose the potato. Top with onion dip for some extra zing. This recipe can be made heartier by adding tuna.

Serves 1 (but this recipe can be easily doubled, tripled, or quadrupled).

PASTA SALAD

Pasta salad is an especially popular dish at prison get-togethers because you can cheaply feed a large number of people. It also lends itself well to variation and experimentation. The recipe below serves 4. For each additional person, add another bag of noodles, ½ a flavor packet, and 4 more mayonnaises. Additional ingredients can be increased as budget permits.

- 4 bags Ramen noodles (chicken or chili flavor), crushed well. You can also use a combination of both types of noodles.
- 16 packets of mayonnaise, 5 packets of mustard, 1 package of tuna, 1 pepperoni, diced, 1 dill pickle, diced, 1 pack of salted peanuts
- 3–4 packets of artificial sweetener, if desired (most of the southern girls here, I've discovered, prefer their salads a little sweeter)
- Saltines and snack crackers

Put the crushed noodles, minus the flavor packets (save those for later), into a large trash bag. Add enough hot water to the noodles to cook them thoroughly in the bag. When the noodles are soft, drain carefully (and caution is necessary here-it is a difficult thing to wrangle a garbage bag full of hot water without burning yourself and/or losing half the noodles down the sink).

Once all the water has been drained off, add 3 of the saved flavor packets and all remaining ingredients except the crackers to the garbage bag. Mix all of the ingredients thoroughly with your hands. It might be necessary to wrap a clean T-shirt around the bag to protect your hands—the ingredients are very hot. Serve the pasta salad directly from the garbage bag onto crackers or scooped into bowls.

Serves 4

A variation on pasta salad:

Lockdown Pasta: Many meals require some form of heating, but when you are on lockdown, you don't even have access to hot water. If you are unable to leave your room, you can make a cold-water pasta that is almost as tasty as the original. Crush a bag of chicken Ramen noodles and put them into a bowl. Set aside the flavor packet. Fill the bowl almost to the rim with room temperature tap water and cover. Let the noodles soak for at least 45 minutes until they are al dente. Drain the noodles, add mayonnaise, mustard, pickle, and tuna. Stir well. To add a pleasing variety to the texture, top with crushed sour cream potato chips. A word of warning: Don't prepare this meal until you are sure that you will be let out in the next day or two. A bowl of mayo and tuna residue is pretty unsavory after it has been sitting on your desk for the entire duration of a 5-day lockdown.

BEEF AND RICE TORTILLAS

Beef and rice tortillas are tasty and complexly flavored. This is an expensive meal, so it is reserved for special occasions.

Tortillas

- 1 bag precooked brown rice
- 1 bag cooked beef in gravy
- 1 onion dip
- 1 six-pack of tortillas

Sauce

- 2 packages of instant macaroni and cheese (powdered cheese must be in separate packet from the noodles)
- 1 pack of peanuts, crushed thoroughly (this is accomplished by smashing them with a lock)
- ½ container onion dip

Cook the brown rice. When that is done, add the brown rice to the beef and onion dip in a large, well-cleaned cereal bag. Mix well. Put several spoonfuls of the beef and rice mixture in a tortilla and roll. Heat well in microwave, if available. If you do not have access to a microwave, heat the beef package in hot water or using a flat iron while the rice cooks. Combine the ingredients as directed above.

While one person makes the tortillas, someone else should be making the sauce. In a 6-ounce tumbler, combine 1 of the packages of cheese powder (the noodles can be saved for a later meal), half the peanuts, and half of the onion dip. Stir very well. Two tumblers of sauce are necessary for this meal.

When the tortillas are ready, divide them into 4 bowls (1½ tortilla in each). Cover all the tortillas well with the cheese sauce. Eat one bowl, then save the second bowl for several hours later—it improves with standing. Adding more rice and additional tortillas can stretch this recipe, albeit a tad skimpily. It's still pretty good, though.

Serves 2

CURRIED RICE

This meal can be enhanced by adding chicken, but really is fine without it.

- 1 bag health mix (nuts, raisins, banana chips, dried pineapple, sunflower seeds)
- 1 bag instant brown rice
- 10 packets of hot sauce

- 4 sugars
- 1 packet chili soup seasoning
- 1 pack chicken (optional)

In a bowl, combine the health mix, hot sauces, 3 sugars, $^1/_3$ of the chili seasoning packet, and enough hot water to cover the health mix by an inch. Stir well. Taste, and add additional hot sauce and sugar if necessary. Let soak for at least an hour.

Divide the brown rice into two bowls and prepare as directed on packaging. When the rice is cooked, divide the health mix mixture between the two bowls and stir.

Serves 2

HIGH-CLASS CHICKEN PINWHEELS

A pricey but popular snack.

- 1 package of tortillas
- 1 package of cooked chicken
- 1 onion dip
- Chili seasoning packet (from Ramen noodles)

Combine chicken and onion dip. Spread thinly on tortillas. Roll each tortilla tightly, then slice them into pinwheels. Shake chili seasoning lightly over the pinwheels for a festive look.

Serves 4 as an appetizer

PIEROGIES

This prison variation on a classic Polish dish is economical, but surprisingly a favorite. The chicken enhances both the flavor and the price tag of this snack.

- 2 packages of tortillas
- 6 bags sour cream potato chips, crushed well
- 1 bag crushed cheese curls (optional)
- 2 packages of cooked chicken (optional)
- 2 onion dips or 1 onion dip and 1 hot cheese dip

Combine the potato chips, 1 onion dip, cheese curls, and chicken (if desired) in a large, sturdy bag. Add hot water and mix well until the potato mixture forms a paste.

Spread each tortilla thinly with onion dip or hot cheese dip. Tear each tortilla into quarters. Put a spoonful of potato mixture into the center of each tortilla quarter, then fold the tortilla over so that the filling is enclosed. Heat the pierogies in the microwave until steaming hot.

Onion dip or cheese squeezers can be thinned out as a dipping sauce for this appetizer.

Serves 12 as an appetizer

LAURA'S POTATO SOUP

This soup will cure what ails you. It saved my life once. Really.

Soup

- 1 small bag of sour cream potato chips, crushed very fine
- ¼ bag crushed cheese curls
- ⅛ cup powdered milk

Garnish

- 1 chili or beef seasoning packet
- 1 bagel

Before you make the soup, toast croutons for a garnish. Take one bagel and cut into small cubes. If you are feeling lazy, you can also tear the bagel into crouton-sized chunks. Spread the bagel cubes on a paper towel and lightly sprinkle with beef or chili seasoning. Microwave, turning frequently, until they are crispy. Croutons can be made a day in advance and stored in a sealable cereal bag.

To prepare the soup, cover the potato chips with warm water and let soak for at least 3 hours. In a plastic tumbler, combine the cheese curls, powdered milk, 1 tablespoon of onion dip, and 3 or 4 ounces of hot water, then stir vigorously, making sure that the mixture is smooth. Add the mixture to the soaked potato chips, then microwave until the soup is bubbling. Watch it carefully so that it does not overflow in the microwave. Sprinkle with the croutons and serve hot.

Serves 1

FROSTED HONEYBUNS

Fast and easy.

- 1 monster honeybun
- 1 melted Hershey bar

Spread the honeybun with melted chocolate. Garnish with crushed M&M's if desired.
Serves 1

CHRISTI'S CHOCOLATE SUICIDE

The amount of chocolate in this recipe is enough to confirm its tastiness. It is a great "assembly-line" dessert, with different people crushing the cookies, breaking up the chocolate, and assembling the entire concoction. You can vary the taste of this dish by substituting different types of candy for the center layer.

- 10 chocolate chip cookies, crushed
- 6 Hershey bars, melted
- 6 swiss rolls
- 2 candy bars of choice, broken up (Snickers, 3 Musketeers, Reese's Cups, or crushed peppermint Lifesavers)
- 16-pack of Oreo cookies, crushed

Combine the chocolate cookies with 4 of the Hershey bars. You can melt each Hershey bar in its unopened wrapper by dipping it in hot water, then squeezing out the melted chocolate. Press this mixture into the bowl to make a crust. If time allows, let the crust set and harden for several hours. If you are starving, immediately proceed with the rest of the recipe.

Crumble up the swiss rolls and slowly add hot water, stirring well, until it has a creamy, mousse-like consistency. Spread the swiss rolls onto the crust.

Put a layer of candy bar (or Lifesaver) over the swiss rolls. You can use a combination of candy bars if you like; Nana's favorite mixture has one half of the suicide covered with Reese's Cups, one half with Snickers.

Top the dessert with the crushed Oreo cookies, then drizzle the remaining melted chocolate on top in a festive design.

Serves 1 hungry inmate for 2 days

CHOCOLATE POPCORN

- 1 bag microwave popcorn
- 2 Hershey bars
- 2 Snickers bars

First, melt the candy bars in a bowl. Next, pop the microwave popcorn. Tear open the bag and pour melted chocolate on top. Toss together gently.

Serves 2

ERIN'S STUFFED CUPCAKE SURPRISES

This is my personal recipe whenever I need to provide a dessert. What makes it so special is the fact that it is chilled—a nice change in a place where most foods are served at room temperature regardless of how they are intended to be served. It requires a lot of prep time, but is worth the wait.

- 12-pack of chocolate cupcakes
- 8 orange-pineapple filled cookies
- 1 Snickers bar, chopped
- 2 Hershey bars, melted
- 1 individual packet of orange drink mix

Keep the cupcakes in the plastic packaging they come in the entire time you make this recipe. Peel the frosting off of the cupcakes and discard it or give it away (I've never had a problem finding someone who wanted it). Gently scoop out the white, creamy filling and put in a small bowl. Add the creamy middles of the orange-pineapple cookies (you can save the cookies themselves for a later snack or give them away) and the chopped Snickers bar to the cupcake's filling. Stir well. You might want to add a bit of hot water to make it blend well. Pack this mixture into the centers of the cupcakes.

In a separate bowl melt the Hershey bars. Add about half of the orange drink mix to the melted chocolate. Stir. Pour the chocolate over the stuffed cupcakes.

When the cupcakes are prepared, surreptitiously take about 4 tumblers full of ice to your room and place the cupcakes on a bed of ice in your sink. Let the cupcakes chill for at least 2 hours, adding more ice as necessary. Inmates get insanely controlling of ice sometimes, closely documenting just how much someone takes and vigorously complaining if it is, in the observer's opinion, more than deserved. Sometimes it is easier just to ask a few friends to get you a cup of ice apiece.

Serves 1

DIZZY'S RASPBERRY LEMONADE

- 1 blue raspberry Jolly Rancher
- 1 individual pack of instant lemonade

In a plastic tumbler, dissolve the Jolly Rancher in a small amount of hot water, stirring frequently
to hasten melting. Once the candy is dissolved, add the lemonade and stir. Fill the tumbler almost to the top of the cup with ice, then fill with water to the brim. Stir and enjoy.

Serves 1

Cell Buddy

A Short Story by Robert Johnson
Art by Rachel Ternes

R obert Johnson's passion for detailing the prison experience is no surprise. I "met"
Rob, so to speak, after he read some of my poems in an anthology of incarcerated
authors for which he had written the introduction. He very kindly wrote me, telling
me how much he had enjoyed my poetry. From that letter sprang a genuine and
enduring friendship and, eventually, professional partnership. His compassion for
the imprisoned is undeniable; what "Cell Buddy" also proves is that his understanding of an inmate's experience and psyche is incisive. There is no shadowy corner of
a prison cell into which he has not delved.

I won't spoil the impact of his fine work by offering too many hints about the story itself. Suffice it to say that it is as surprising as it is profoundly true. Despite knowing Rob to be an intelligent, empathetic man who has spent countless hours pondering the experience of the incarcerated, I was stunned by the accuracy of his insights and the contextual detail he evokes.

If I didn't know better, I would think that he had endured his own stretch behind bars. Though, upon consideration, in a way perhaps he has. He has certainly been gracious enough to share my sentence with me, listening to all of my stories, both triumphant and despairing, without judgment. In his nonfiction and fiction, Robert Johnson is a chronicler of the American prison experience's every arcane detail. "Cell Buddy" exemplifies his gift and makes a wonderful contribution to my book.—Erin George

Amanda looked about anxiously, shifting her weight from one foot to the other as she stood in the commissary line. She'd noticed the big red box the day before but had hesitated. She didn't know a single convict who had one but she knew it was just what she needed. She was desperate. Anger was eating at her, her moods were turning sour, and her loneliness was taking on a life of its own. So here she was, placing her order.

"One Cell Buddy, please." She spoke in what she hoped was a calm, measured tone.

"Which model?" asked the inmate behind the counter, barely looking up.

"Which model?" Amanda asked, in a higher voice than she liked, sounding a bit girly. Amanda was thrown off balance for a moment. She didn't know Cell Buddies came in models and she didn't want to sound like a girl, though of course she was a girl, and in fact a girl once much sought after in the cell blocks. She paused. A small line was forming behind her.

"What do ya' mean, which model?" Amanda said, in a deeper voice, the one she cultivated for public exchanges in prison. "I want—I don't know, the standard goddam model."

"OK, OK" said the inmate, raising her hands, palms up. "Just doing my job."

Amanda nodded.

"Black or white," the inmate continued. "We're out of the mixed-race model."

Amanda paused, then frowned. Speaking carefully, "They make mixed-race Cell Buddies?"

"Brown. That's your standard Brown Cell Buddy. We do all the races. This is equal opportunity stuff."

After a pause, the counter woman said, snapping her fingers—and moving her hips—rhythmically, "You know, supply and demand, even in the can."

Amanda by now had begun to sweat. Evidently there were others in the House with Cell Buddies. There'd been a run on Brown Buddies, she thought. And what was the deal with this bitch behind the counter? She'd wanted this to be a hit-and-run thing but it was becoming a full-on conversation.

"White, for christsakes, white." Amanda was white, and she figured anybody in prison who crossed the color line on inflatable cell mates was looking for trouble.

"Papers?" The inmate now had her hands resting easily on the counter.

Amanda just stared at her, keeping herself under control.

"Adoption papers, hon." The inmate spoke as if adoption papers were an obvious consideration for a convict in the market for a Cell Buddy.

"They come with adoption papers," she continued, as if Amanda were a child. "You can fill in the name," snapping her fingers again, "and pop it in a frame."

"Frame?" A hint of nervousness had crept back into Amanda's voice. She considered turning on her heels and simply running back to her cell but was too embarrassed to move.

"We've got frames, all kinda frames. You're supposed to frame the papers. It's like a respect thing."

The woman behind the counter retrieved a big red box marked CB-White and handed it across to Amanda, together with a frame and adoption papers. Amanda gathered her haul, marked her signature on the commissary account line, then walked straight back the way she'd come. She was careful to keep the brightly colored package close to her body, hoping to avoid anyone she knew as she worked her way up the steps to her third-tier cell. When she got to the cell she looked both ways, then entered quickly, as if she were returning from a regular day at the prison canteen, eager to get her goodies put securely away, out of the view of thieves—women who moved in packs, grabbing sweets and treats and sometimes even TV sets and selling them on the black market.

But this was different, Amanda knew, really different. Snacks from the commissary were one thing; an inflatable Cell Buddy was decidedly another.

The woman at the commissary had been cool about it, like it was an order at a restaurant—but the give and take at the counter had put Amanda on edge. The whole business seemed sketchy. What did the girls in the line think about all this? Papers? Frames? Keeping one eye on the cell door, Amanda opened the box and pulled out the folded plastic figure, gently removing the sealed packaging, complete with a two-part pump system she assembled after a few minutes of difficulty. (Amanda was pretty handy but sometimes struggled with instructions.)

Now with her back to the tier, hiding the plastic figure from view, Amanda slowly pumped up her Cell Buddy until it was fully inflated. She then stood back, admiring her new friend.

Amanda couldn't help but think that her Cell Buddy cut a striking figure. A two-and-a-half foot torso, the Cell Buddy came standard with movable arms and a swivel head. The Cell Buddy was the brainchild of a psychiatrist who believed that convicts needed emotional support to help them get through their prison days. "Even convicts need love," she'd said, "prison is a lonely place, especially for women." The arms were a special feature. "They are expressly made long," the psychiatrist had said, "long enough to wrap around the prisoner's body in a secure embrace."

Wardens and administrators affiliated with the prison system thought the Cell Buddy was a joke. They assumed all convicts crave sex, not love; that a plastic figure with no orifices or appendages (Cell Buddies are smooth all over) would be a loser in the prison market. Amanda read this in a newsletter while she was waiting for her annual physical. "Easy for them to laugh," she'd thought, but the shrink was serious and for damn sure Amanda was serious. As far as Amanda was concerned, the psychiatrist was right on the money. Amanda was lonely, and she was frightened, and at times she was just plain mad at the world. There was no way to handle those emotions in prison without help.

That's where her Cell Buddy would come in, Amanda thought. Someone to listen; someone to make her cell a home.

Amanda knew that some of the worst things that can happen to a woman in prison typically happened in her cell, at the hands of a cell mate she once loved, or thought she'd loved. Domestic abuse was a hidden epidemic in prison, Amanda knew from the echoes of grief reverberating up and down the tiers. "Who'd believe it?" she once told a visitor, early in her prison term, before she had any inkling of what lay ahead for her. "We don't have men here but we still got wife-beating!" The visitor looked at her like she was talking in riddles. Amanda dropped the subject.

Amanda had joked about getting a Cell Buddy for years, years she spent with her last convict cell mate, Danielle, aka Dan the Man or simply Dan. The butch girls often took male variants of their given names, to go with their big tattoos and bigger muscles, not to mention the cold stares they cultivated for their sojourns in the prison yard, where they'd shamelessly flaunt their male bona fides, walking slow and threatening, glaring out at the world, daring women to make their day. At first, Amanda loved Dan like a sister loves a tough, protective older brother. Nothing sexual; just sheer admiration. Dan made Amanda feel secure. Safety is an illusion in life, and especially in prison, but the fact is, Dan made Amanda feel safe. In prison, that is no small thing.

Back in the early days of their relationship, Dan often said, "Amanda, when I'm gone, get yourself a Cell Buddy. Don't leave the cell without it. Why be lonely when you can have a rubber homey." Dan was a bit of a homegrown poet, if you could be generous with your notion of poetry.

Dan was also, as it turned out, a bit of a predator. He was, in the words of the women on the cell blocks, a smooth operator—patient, willing to wait out his prey. Dan knew that Amanda needed him, knew she couldn't live on her own, knew she would be easy pickings for the other tough butch cons. Dan carefully cultivated Amanda's trust, then made his move. Dan the Man seduced Amanda with the classic prison line—it's either me, or everybody.

Amanda didn't see it coming, and in fairness to her, the process was subtle. You've got to give Dan credit; he knew what he was about. First there were requests for small favors (tidying Dan's part of the cell), then tentative requests for shows of support and affection, like a back rub after a hard day. "Hey, baby, that feels good, just like that, right." Then, gradually, Dan began giving orders—first for little things, maybe with an apologetic smile, things Amanda would have done anyway, like warming up his coffee. Soon Dan demanded anything and everything he desired. Like a kind of perverted biblical patriarch, Dan the Man wanted dominion over Amanda in all things. He wanted sex (and on his terms), but even more he wanted her reduced to abject servitude. Dan wanted his bed made, he wanted his laundry done, he wanted his food served warm while he lay naked, looking at Amanda like she was a piece of meat. He wanted to use Amada as a punching bag on bad days, and there are a lot bad days in the Big House. When you come right down to it, Dan wanted Amanda to be his slave, his chattel to have and to hold and to abuse at will.

And Amanda was Dan's slave, meek and docile, pretty much right up until she killed him.

There were warning signs, but this time it was Dan who didn't see it coming. He didn't see Amanda's grief or her anguish or her rage, masked by an increasingly plastic, fixed smile. "Sure Dan, right away. Whatever you say." Always with the big smile, the too-big smile you might have found on an American slave plantation back in the day. Dan was no historian, and besides he thought of Amanda as a slave, so he took Amanda's behavior in stride, as if it were his due. Dan definitely didn't notice the small rebellions or the furtive looks as Amanda prepared his bed for him at lights out. Amanda's lips would be pursed, her eyes ever so slightly narrowed in distaste, the bed never perfectly made, the coffee a tad bitter. Dan didn't catch any of this. And he didn't see the shank coming, the one Amanda plunged deep into his back while he slept.

Shank. Dan had been insistent about calling a homemade prison knife a shank. "It's a shank, Amanda, not a shiv. A shiv is gay." He'd walk the yard with Amanda and say, "See that bitch, the skank with the shank? Watch out for her." Shank, shiv, knife—whatever it was, it took residence in Dan's body, and Amanda was on her own, alone in the abusive home she'd shared with Dan, in the prison he'd made her personal hell.

* * *

The prison at night is a scary place. It's as if the cell blocks have a life of their own, populated by the haunted spirits of prisoners past. Amanda sensed these presences, thought she heard low, murmuring voices in the night, felt cool breezes brush against her skin. Somehow, beneath the cries and the rage and the ruin, Amanda sensed a deeper hurt, the hurt of pure loss, the hurt that tells you the one thing you never want to hear— that the world is hard and cold and you are alone, completely alone. There is you, and there is suffering, and there is loss.

At these moments, wrestling with a sense of dread, Amanda would clutch her Buddy close, glad for his companionship. Buddy, that's what she called him. Short and sweet, like the little man himself. Amanda needed to hold Buddy, needed the touch. The words of a poem she'd read kept running through her head. "O'er the cell a mark still lingers," it started, "Of where a convict's bloodied fingers. . . ." As Amanda drifted off to sleep, the poem unfurled in her mind like a sail on a breezy spring day:

> "Could make stone speak of life's hard ends
> "With words that shine like darkling gems
> "I was here
> "I am a woman
> "I bleed, therefore I am. . . ."

Am what? For a moment, Amanda wasn't sure. Then it came to her: Alive.

> *"Alive, in a manner of speaking*
> *"It's raw, sweet freedom I'm desperately seeking*
> *"A prison cell's a coffin reeking*
> *"Of dreams gone sour*
> *"Of life died by the hour*
> *"Of death by decree*
> *"Until you're set free*
> *"In this life or the next."*

Amanda pulled Buddy closer, seeking warmth in his plastic embrace, hoping to shed the notion that her cell was in fact a tomb and that one day it wouldn't open and she'd be trapped there for eternity. "A prison cell's a coffin reeking. . . ."

Trapped with Buddy. Well, that was something.

* * *

Amanda hated to let the air out of Buddy each morning but she couldn't take him outside the cell in his fully expanded condition. Prison has its strange byways—hell, she'd even read about a prison called Strangeways—but there are limits. Some of the cons looked and dressed like men, even attractive men, for heaven's sake, but toting a Cell Buddy crossed the line. People didn't seem to notice that Amanda had this folded plastic friend with her wherever she went, tucked under her arm. At least, no one said anything. Amanda wasn't sure, but she thought that perhaps the rest of the tier figured she'd lost it and might be dangerous. "Mess with Buddy," she'd said under her breath, as much a plea as a threat, "and you'll come up bloody." Some of Dan's poetry had evidently rubbed off on Amanda.

Still, Amanda thought she heard the sniggers and she imagined the insults. Boy Toy, that sort of thing. The other girls just didn't get it, Amanda figured, or didn't want to get it. A bunch of them had their own Cell Buddies, she knew, or else the commissary wouldn't carry them at all, let alone have different Buddies for each race. But these women evidently kept their plastic companions under wraps, afraid of what others might think. Now that she thought about it, she'd seen women with full, puffed out shirts now and again in the mess hall. Amanda had assumed they'd wrapped magazines and newspapers around their torsos, the prison's version of a shank-proof vest. Now she marveled at their ingenuity. Carrying their Buddies around in public, hidden in plain sight!

Amanda was less discrete because she didn't care. Prison was death; Buddy was life. You had to live, if you could. You didn't have to live well, but you had to live. That's just the way it is. Some people have to go to prison to learn that. Whatever else Amanda learned in prison, she learned she needed Buddy to live. So she carried Buddy out in the open, deflated but right out there for anyone who cared to look.

At night, back in the cell, Amanda would prop Buddy up with a book in his hands, tilt Buddy's swivel head down slightly so Buddy could read, and carefully position Buddy in the middle of the bed, where he would be stable. Buddy had once taken a fall from the side of the bed, picking up a pretty bad scratch in the process when he hit the rough concrete floor. Amanda wasn't going to let that happen again.

"Feel alright, Buddy?" she'd ask solicitously.

Buddy would nod, or so it seemed to Amanda.

"Been a rough day, Bud?" Amanda would ask without much feeling. She was tired at the end of her prison day, if for no other reason than that she was protective of Buddy and worried that if some bad-ass bitch assaulted them, Buddy would be history. And if Buddy was history, Amanda would be history, too.

Buddy seemed oblivious.

Amanda, comforted by Buddy's silence, which she interpreted as his agreeable invitation for her to chat, would sometimes review the events of their day. "What'd you think of that Aryan 'ho, Bud? Me, I thought she'd lose it when you brushed up against her."

Buddy's head appeared to nod, however slightly.

"I mean, it's not like you're black or white. You're pure, Bud, almost translucent. You're your own race, know what I mean?"

Buddy shined in the glow of the overhead light, which had just then been turned on as the sun set outside the prison.

"I ain't no racist," Amanda continued, perhaps a bit defensively, "but I'm more comfortable with my own. That's just normal."

Amanda moved Buddy to the far side of the cell, just below the framed adoption papers, shielded from the view of passing convicts.

* * *

There were days that Amanda was alright and figured she was going to make it. Other days, she had her doubts. Some days, though, it seemed like she'd lost it for good. On the bad days, her temper had a life of its own. She thought her occasional explosions were normal, at least as normal as putting people in cages and leaving them to fend for themselves for years on end, sometimes with nothing more than a Cell Buddy for companionship.

Amanda had discovered a deep well of anger inside her after she'd killed Dan. She didn't even remember killing him, exactly, all she remembered was watching someone who looked a lot like her plunging the shank into Dan's back, over and over again, eyes wide, teeth bared. Like an animal.

And she had been an animal to Dan, a beast of burden. Dan was gone but the burden was still there, the burden of hurt and barely suppressed fury. Dan's abuse lived on, right inside her. The rank injustice of this made her blood boil.

At first, having Buddy cooled her hate, this toxic gift from Dan, but nothing good lasts for long in prison. Prison is like an inferno, Amanda thought, burning up everything good in a painful orgy of self-inflicted punishment. One night, the inferno raged out of control.

Amanda could make excuses for her episodes. Had Dan called his explosions episodes? Had she learned this from Dan?

He had a laundry list of excuses, when he bothered to make excuses, and now she did, too. She hadn't gotten a letter in ages. An old woman had stumbled and knocked the deflated Buddy from her arms, getting Buddy smeared in grease from the mess hall. That night, the cell lamp had burned out, so Amanda couldn't read and talk to Buddy on the schedule to which they'd become accustomed.

And somehow, Amanda couldn't really explain it, the smell of grease and the soft light of the cell at twilight, rays of a rising moon streaming through the bars of the cell window, had made Amanda amorous. She snuggled close to Buddy, drinking in his scent, redolent of fried food but appealing nonetheless, flushing and growing excited almost against her will.

"Buddy, Buddy," Amanda moaned, slowly letting go and liking it, moving easily to an inner rhythm as old as life itself but long denied to Amanda during her many years in confinement. Dan had raped her; that was violence, not sex. But this, she thought, this was something different, something good. Almost instinctively, Amanda rolled Buddy onto his back, looking at the little half-man through heavy-lidded eyes suffused with passion. "Buddy. . ."

Then Buddy seemed to mock her.

It was crazy, Amanda knew, looking back, but Buddy seemed to look at her with a vacant, rejecting stare, as if to say, "Can't you do anything right? I'm a friend, just a friend. Clean me up and let me get some rest."

Amanda rubbed Buddy's back and shoulders, hoping to relax the taut figure. No response, just mute, rejecting silence.

"Go fuck yourself," Amanda had yelled, unable to control herself.

Buddy seemed to sneer. *To sneer!*

Admittedly, Buddy came with a manufacturing defect that gave the lines forming his mouth a slightly irregular downward cast, which looked like a frown or a sneer. A bit like Elvis's famous sneer, actually. Buddy's sneer, if it was a sneer, was accentuated by the dusky light in the cell that fateful night. It spelled rejection in letters too big for Amanda to ignore.

And so Amanda wondered, not for the first time, was she a loser, even in this ersatz love on which she'd hoped to live out her prison days? When you came right down to it, could Buddy be interested, really interested, in a lonely, pathetic convict like her? Even her name, Amanda, seemed girly and a little pathetic, more fitting for a cheerleader than a self-respecting felon.

And where did one go when a relationship with a Cell Buddy went south? I mean, how embarrassing is that? It's not like you can drag your little friend to counseling and expect to hold your head up on the tier or in the prison yard. "Hi, my name is Amanda. Buddy and I are in counseling. We hope to work things out." Not happening, not in this woman's prison.

That sneer, if it was a sneer, set Amanda off. She tore the cell apart, she ranted and screamed, she banged her fists on the steel cell door, she cried tears of impotent rage. And then she slammed Buddy into the wall, tearing his plastic skin, letting the air escape and leaving Buddy a broken figure, crumpled in the corner of a cell that looked like a war zone.

"I hate you," Amanda had screamed. "You stupid plastic faggot, you can go to hell for all I care!"

Later, shocked at what she had done, Amanda sought forgiveness. "It'll never happen again, Bud, I swear. Trust me." Even as she spoke, she heard Dan's words in her head. "It'll never happen again, Babe, I swear. Trust me."

Wiping tears from her eyes, Amanda tried to pump Buddy back up. The little body would expand a bit but then the air would escape with a whoosh. Same with the head, which had a separate air chamber that had been damaged. Amanda vowed to fix Buddy and start their relationship fresh. They'd be friends, dear friends, she said to herself, and see where things went from there. "We'll give it a go, Bud. We can make it work."

"We can make it work," Dan would say, until he decided that it worked for him and that was all that mattered.

Amanda knew it would be hard to find the supplies needed to make Buddy right. And Amanda couldn't help but wonder, deep in her heart, whether Buddy would ever trust her. And whether she, Amanda, could ever be there for Buddy, when the chips were down and the desolation of a prison night held them both in its grasp.

"It'll be alright, Bud," Amanda said, as she snuggled up against the now rumpled plastic form that was her Cell Buddy, speaking in a soft, breathy tone, the one she used when she hoped she really meant what she said. "We're in this together."

Together.

Buddy shuddered at the word, or perhaps it was just the way Amanda gripped him tight as she drifted off into a fitful sleep.

Robert Johnson (author) is a professor of justice, law, and criminology at American University and editor and publisher of BleakHouse Publishing. He is a widely published author of fiction and nonfiction dealing with crime and punishment. His short story, "The Practice of Killing," won the Wild Violet Fiction Contest. Johnson's best known work of social science, *Death Work: A Study of the Modern Execution Process*, won the Outstanding Book Award of the Academy of Criminal Justice Sciences.

Rachel Ternes (artist) is an American University honors student majoring in psychology and a consulting editor for BleakHouse Publishing. Her paintings were published in AU's literary magazine, *AmLit*, in the fall (2011) and spring (2012) issues, being awarded an Honorable Mention in the magazine's fall competition and Best in Show in the spring. Three of her illustrations were published in the 2012 issue of *BleakHouse Review*, one of which earned her a Tacenda Literary Award for Best Artwork.

Cell Buddy is reprinted from JMWW, fall 2007; http://www.jmww.150m.com/Fall07con .html. Adapted for the stage by Ellen W. Kaplan, Chair of Theatre, Smith College (*Tacenda Literary Magazine*, 2011) and read at American University. Cell Buddy also was adapted for the stage by Jordyn Cahill, Gadsden Correctional Facility, in collaboration with Ellen W. Kaplan, and presented under the direction of Ellen W. Kaplan as part of the Kennedy Center's Page to Stage Program, offered under the auspices of the Safe Streets Foundation Prison to Stage Program.